Investment Banking and Brokerage

John F. Marshall

M. E. Ellis

Kolb Publishing Company
6395 Gunpark Dr., Suite N, Boulder, CO 80301
(303) 530-7778   FAX (303) 530-7773

To my many friends on the Street.
Thank you for the education.
J.F.M.

To Brenda, Neal, Karen, and Terry.
Thank you.
M.E.E.

Printed in the United States of America.

Library of Congress Catalog Card Number 94–76280

ISBN: 1–878975–38–2

KOLB Kolb Publishing Company
6395 Gunpark Dr., Suite N, Boulder, CO 80301
(303) 530-7778   FAX (303) 530-7773

Foreword

I have spent most of my professional career in investment banking. When I started, the business was primarily concerned with corporate securities underwriting and distribution, and secondary market making and trading of those same securities. Virtually all training took the form of apprenticeship. Those who rose to the top of the business often started in junior clerical positions. The business was fairly simple, straightforward, largely domestic, and principally retail. It was also well defined and regulated. Relationships with clients helped to ensure profitability.

With the passage of the years, however, I have witnessed a profound transformation of the industry and the firms, including my own, that constitute it. The business has become more quantitative and theoretical. Traders have become increasingly dependent on theory, mathematics, statistics, and technology. I have seen the birth of new markets and all variety of ways to use them. I have seen the development of the mortgage-backed securities market, the advent of zero coupon bonds, the emergence of the repo market as a financing and money management tool, and the birth of an over-the-counter derivatives market. The institutional investor has come to dominate the buy side, and the markets have become truly global. Client relationships, while still important, are now less so as the business has become more transaction driven. This has been aided, indeed fostered, by technological advances, including developments in computers, telecommunications, and data processing.

There are times I look back and hardly recognize the business. It is so different from the one I entered as a young man in 1968. Yet the principal purpose of the business—the efficient allocation of financial capital—remains the same. In this activity, my firm now competes not only with other investment banks but also with commercial banks, insurance companies, and an assortment of other "financial services" firms.

As complex and important as this business is, there are actually very few books that have described it well. Most, for example, have focused on the traditional view that limits investment banking to those activities associated with securities issuance. These books fail to recognize that investment banking is now much more than that. Today, it is hard to say just exactly what investment banking is. With this in mind, and cognizant that investment banking will surely be as different 10 years from now as it is today from 10 years ago, I can embrace the authors' broader definition that "investment banking is what investment bankers do." While simple, this definition is also fluid—providing room for changes we cannot now even begin to contemplate.

While it is impossible for a single volume to capture all the nitty-gritty details of a complex profession, the authors have done an excellent job of providing a broad overview of modern investment banking. The authors are well known to the "street" as thorough researchers and careful checkers of fact. In preparing to write this book, they interviewed many investment bankers and had each chapter of their final product proofed by still others. I was one of the investment bankers who participated in this process at several stages, but I also had the privilege of being one of the few to see the final work in its totality.

The reader will find that Professors Marshall and Ellis have captured the dynamism of investment banking. The book is clearly written and does not assume any particular background on the part of the reader. Terms are explained as they are introduced, and numerous examples and cases are provided to illustrate key points and computations.

In working through this book, the reader will get some sense of the history of the business, its current structure, its many revenue-generating products, and its support activities. The reader will also see how the various revenue functions and support activities are intertwined and mutually dependent. The book is a good starting point for the student considering a career in investment banking, for the investment banker in need of a broader overview of the business, and for both issuers and investors who are clients of investment banks. Professor Marshall's earlier books on swaps, futures, options, and financial engineering are now required reading on the Street. This book is destined to be as well.

Frederick B. Casey
Senior Managing Director
Bear, Stearns & Co., Inc.

Preface

Few industries have changed as much over the past two decades as has investment banking. Many factors have contributed to this transformation, but certain ones stand out. These include significant advances in financial theory, a more competitive business environment brought on by a globalization of enterprises, increased analytical sophistication on Wall Street, a more volatile price environment, enormous advances in technology—including telecommunications, computers, and data processing—and a general reshaping of American business.

Investment banking was at one time a single, fairly clearly defined business. Today, it is a collection of several dozen businesses. Some investment banks try to operate in all of them, becoming financial supermarkets; others have carved out very narrow niches, preferring to operate as specialized boutiques. Thus investment banks can be, and often are, as different from one another as firms within any one industry can be. Despite their differences, investment banks are and should be important to all of us. They are a critical component in the mechanism that allocates financial resources in most market economies.

Like most businesses, investment banking is cyclical. It goes through periods of both expansion and contraction. Over the past few years, the industry experienced a period of contraction and downsizing that followed one of the most expansionary periods in its history. Now, in 1993, the business is again in an expansionary mode. The work is hard, but it is also challenging and rewarding.

We undertook to write this book for two reasons. First, there are relatively few books on investment banking that are not either edited collections of disconnected material, or focused on some narrow functional area within investment banking. As a consequence, it is difficult to find a single source that can provide a good overview of the business. We wanted to rectify that problem. Second, the importance of investment banking in reshaping the face of modern business has never been as clear as it is today. We have spent years analyzing components of the business and working with professionals in the business and felt that we were in an excellent position to frame the big picture.

This book is organized in four sections. The first provides a general overview and history of the industry. The second, which is by far the longest, examines the many revenue-generating activities in which modern investment banks engage. These include the traditional roles of primary and secondary market making, as well as trading, corporate restructuring, financial engineering, investment management, consulting, and merchant banking. The third section considers support activities, such as clearing and related activities, research, funding and risk management, and information services. The final section takes a brief look forward.

We have incorporated two techniques to make this book reader-friendly. First, we boldface new terms as they are introduced; and second, we conclude each chapter with an extensive listing of references and suggested reading. This material is included to facilitate more in-depth study of particular topics.

In preparing to write this book, we conducted both formal and informal interviews with many investment bankers. As we developed the individual chapters, we circulated them to others in the industry for feedback. This project would not have been possible without this substantial level of industry involvement, and we owe a sizeable debt to all those who helped us. Specifically, we would like to thank:

John C. Braddock (PaineWebber Inc.)
Michael Burbank (Kidder Peabody, Inc.)
Frederick B. Casey (Bear, Sterns & Co., Inc.)
Joanne M. Hill (Goldman Sachs & Co.)
Laurie Goodman (PaineWebber Inc.)
David Johnson (Merrill Lynch Co., Inc.)
Ira Kawaller (Chicago Mercantile Exchange)
Benjamin D. Kraus (American Stock Exchange)
Marcia Myerbert (Bear, Stearns & Co., Inc.)
J. Michael Payte (Bear, Stearns & Co., Inc.)
Bidyut C. Sen (Morgan Stanley & Co., Inc.)
Eric H. Sorensen (Salomon Brothers)
Thomas Sullivan (National Association of Securities Dealers)

We would also like to thank Probus Publishing for its financial support and Bear, Sterns & Company, Inc., Kidder Peabody, *The Institutional Investor*, and *Coda Energy, Inc.* for sharing materials with us.

We would be most interested in your thoughts, comments, and suggestions on how we may improve future editions of this book.

Comments should be addressed to the authors in care of:

John F. Marshall, Ph.D.
Graduate School of Business
St. John's University
Jamaica, NY 11439
(516) 689-2768 (voice)
(516) 689-3527 (fax)

M.E. Ellis, Ph.D.
Graduate School of Business
St. John's University
Jamaica, NY 11439
(718) 990-6161 ext. 7322 (voice)
(718) 380-3803 (fax)

About the Authors

John F. Marshall is Professor of Finance in the Graduate School of Business at St. John's University, New York, where he lectures on investment finance, corporate finance, and derivative products. He holds M.B.A., M.A., and Ph.D. degrees. Dr. Marshall is also Senior Partner with Marshall & Associates, a consulting firm that provides trust services, training, and financial engineering expertise to a number of leading Wall Street firms, and Executive Director of the International Association of Financial Engineers. He has written extensively on futures, options, and swaps as risk management tools, and on financial engineering more generally.

M. E. Ellis is Associate Professor of Finance in the Graduate School of Business at St. John's University, New York, where she lectures on corporate finance and investments. She earned B.S., M.B.A., and Ph.D. degrees from the University of South Carolina and is a Chartered Financial Analyst (CFA). Dr. Ellis is an Associate with Marshall & Associates and has written extensively on the information content of seasoned equity issues, derivative products, and the impact of deregulation on the airline industry.

Contents

I

Section One

Introduction and Overview

Introduction

This book embarks on an interesting journey—a journey into the complex and exciting world of the modern investment banker, a place where financial theory and financial practice merge as nowhere else. It is a world that is often mysterious, sometimes even to those who have made it to the top of the industry.

A glimpse into the world of investment banking can be rigorous and structured, or a carefree voyage into personalities, politics, and games. In his book *Liar's Poker*, Michael Lewis has done an interesting job of the latter. Our job here, however, is to be scientific and analytical. We will examine the *what*, the *why*, and the *how* of this dynamic industry. Although reading Marshall and Ellis may not be as much sheer fun as reading Lewis, we hope that it will be at least as enlightening.

This book is a product of extensive study of the industry—both from the perspective of academicians and from the perspective of experienced practitioners. As academicians, we have contributed to the body of literature that helps explain and motivate investment banking. As practitioners, we have worked as consultants to both large and small investment banks. In addition, many of the industry's leading figures have shared their insights and experiences with us. This personal, firsthand knowledge was augmented by an extensive series of interviews we conducted while preparing to write this book and from industry feedback on various drafts of the manuscript.

Let's start by describing the function of investment banking in the simplest, most macroscopic terms. At the macroscopic level, investment banking is concerned with the allocation of financial resources. That is, it is concerned with how and why money is moved from those who have it (**investors**) to those who need it (**issuers**). Thus, the role of investment banking—at least in the traditional sense—is one of **intermediation** in **resource allocation**. If the allocation is efficient, then resources are allocated to their best use. If the allocation is inefficient, then the use of resources is not optimized. Since the efficiency of resource allocation affects all of us, investment banking is important to more than just investment bankers and those who use the services of investment bankers.

This macroscopic view of investment banking is, of course, too general to be of more than theoretical interest. To make investment banking concrete, we need to give our definition flesh and bone: that is, we need to make it real. In this way, we give investment banking substance that can be scrutinized and studied. This, then, is our first goal: to define investment banking.

What Is Investment Banking?

The **Glass–Steagall Act** was intended as remedial legislation to separate commercial banking activities from investment banking activities. The securities legislation of the 1930s was motivated, in part, by a stated desire to protect bank depositors from risks inherent in securities transactions. This was considered essential to restore confidence in the financial system, which had suffered cataclysmic damage in the wake of the 1929 stock market crash and the banking crisis and depression that followed. The act restricted commercial banks from engaging in securities underwriting, from taking positions for their own accounts in certain types of securities, and from acting as agents for others in securities transactions. These activities were to be the domain of the investment banks and related securities firms. On the other hand, investment banks were barred from deposit taking and corporate lending. These activities were to be the domain of commercial banks.

Ever since the passage of the Glass–Steagall Act, investment banking has been narrowly defined as those financial services associated with the issuance, called **flotation**, of new (principally corporate) securities. Such securities are issued for the purpose of providing financing for the issuing institution. This is another way of saying that investment banking is the act of making the **primary market** for securities. The primary market for securities is the market in which the securities are first issued. At an only slightly broader level, investment banking is also understood to include **secondary market** making by brokers and dealers in securities—particularly if the secondary market making is done in direct support of primary market making. The secondary market is the market in which previously issued securities are traded by investors.

Many people, including many in the securities industry, still cling to these traditional definitions. But the truth is that investment banking has been radically transformed over the past several decades. For many investment banks, primary and secondary market making no longer constitute their principal revenue sources. Indeed, many important revenue–generating activities of today did not even exist as recently as 10 years ago. As part of this transformation, the industry has become much more transaction driven—a concept we will explain shortly.

What, then, is investment banking? The most inclusive, and we feel the best, answer is that investment banking is what investment banks do. Unlike the macroscopic description, which is abstract, and the traditional definition, which tries to pack investment banking into a neat little cubbyhole that has become too small, this latter definition is both pragmatic and fluid—in the sense that it continuously adapts to a changing environment. We shall employ this definition throughout this book.

Our definition will also serve as a useful device for organizing our examination of investment banking by focusing on investment banking's functional areas. As Figure 1.1 demonstrates, "functional areas" include both revenue–generating and support activities. The revenue–generating areas include primary market making, secondary market making, trading, corporate restructuring, financial engineering, advisory services, merchant banking, investment management, and consulting. The support areas include clearing services, research, internal finance, and information services. Each of these functional areas can be subdivided further. For example, primary market making includes corporate finance, municipal finance, and Treasury and agency finance. And these subdivisions can themselves be further divided. For example, corporate finance includes public offerings, syndications, private placements, commercial paper dealing, and structured financings.

Figure 1.1
Investment Banking Activities

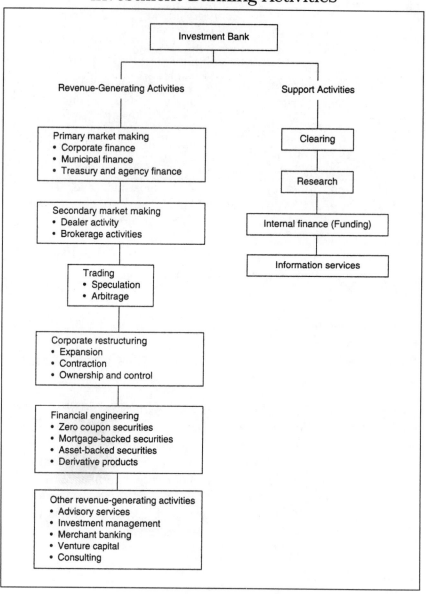

The Investment Banking Industry

The investment banking industry is perhaps best described as an **oligopoly**. That is, a relatively few firms dominate the industry. Of these, the largest firms are often called the **bulge bracket**—a term which derives from the tendency of these firms' names to be printed larger and bolder on public offering announcements (called **tombstones**) and on the front pages of prospectuses than the names of other firms making up underwriting and distribution syndicates. The bulge bracket, also known as the **special bracket**, consists of about 10 firms. The actual number is somewhat arbitrary and depends on where one chooses to draw the line. After the bulge bracket firms is the second tier of middle–sized firms, known as the **major bracket**, and then the third tier of small firms, called the **submajors** and **regionals**. Although oligopolistic in structure, the industry is nevertheless intensely competitive.

Investment banks range from full–service shops to boutiques. The **full–service shops** provide the full range of investment banking services. Boutiques, on the other hand, specialize in just a few services. **Boutiques** are also sometimes called **specialty shops**.

It is important to appreciate that even full–service investment banks vary tremendously in their strengths and are anything but clones of one another. For example, some, such as Morgan Stanley and Goldman Sachs, are largely issuer driven; others, such as Bear, Stearns, are largely investor driven; still others, such as Salomon Brothers, are essentially trading organizations; and still others, such as PaineWebber, Merrill Lynch, and Smith Barney, are primarily wirehouses. The **wirehouses** are, largely, retail brokerage firms; that is, their investor base consists largely of individuals. This is in contrast to such investment banks as First Boston, whose brokerage clientele consists principally of institutions.

Boutiques, which make no pretense of being full service, must maintain relationships with the larger firms to be effective. For example, despite its size and prowess as a trading firm, Solomon Brothers lacks a good distribution network for the securities that it underwrites. By employing boutiques which have effective distribution systems and strong investor contacts, Salomon Brothers can reach investors. In a sense, through these special relationships, major firms often "rent the rolodex" of the specialized boutique.

Investment Banking versus Commercial Banking

Just as the scope of investment banking has expanded dramatically over the past two decades, so too has the scope of commercial banking. The expansion of commercial banking is important in the study of investment banking because it is becoming increasingly difficult to distinguish between these two formerly distinct types of businesses. There are a number of reasons for this. First, by the late 1970s, risk management theory and practice had advanced to such a degree that it was becoming increasingly apparent that, at least for skilled institutions, the concerns leading to the passage of the securities legislation of the 1930s (the Glass–Steagall Act, in particular) might not be justified any longer. Recognizing this new environment, the prohibitions on securities underwriting by commercial banks were partially relaxed. At first, commercial banks, acting through limited securities subsidiaries, were permitted to underwrite municipal general obligation bonds. Later the exemption was extended to industrial development bonds and, still later, to some corporate issues. These measured relaxations of the law are widely viewed as the first steps in the phased reintroduction of commercial banks into the securities business.

Second, as new financial markets emerged, none of which were specifically addressed in earlier legislation, both investment banks and commercial banks became players. As such, they also became competitors. Without doubt, the clearest example of the emergence of a major new market is the introduction of over–the–counter derivative instruments—principally **swaps** and other **notional contracts**. Today, the dominant players in the $5 trillion notional contract market count both investment banks and commercial banks among their number.

Services also represent a new area of competition for investment and commercial banks. Advice on asset/liability management, risk management, and liquidity management are just three such areas. Indeed, it is quite routine for financial institutions to formulate strategies involving both advice and instruments, called **structured solutions**, to solve financial problems for both corporate and noncorporate clients.

Third, each subset of the financial services industry, both the investment and commercial banking communities, have discovered ways to undermine each other's areas of advantage. For example, for decades the commercial banking community had sole access to overnight sources of financing through the Fed funds market. The **Fed funds market** allows a bank to borrow another bank's excess reserves, held within the Federal Reserve System, on an overnight basis. The Fed funds market provides commercial banks with the ability to meet short–term liquidity needs easily and at very low cost. The investment banking community, on the other hand, had no access to this market and no counterpart of its own—so it created one. This took the form of a market in **repurchase agreements**. Now, investment banks have access to a very liquid **repo market** and can use it for short–term financing at very low cost. The repo market can also be used to obtain securities for short sales. The development of real estate operations and mortgage products by investment banks and the development of commodity and equity swap operations by commercial banks or their securities subsidiaries are other ways that Glass–Steagall has been gradually eroded.

Another force undermining the traditional distinctions between commercial and investment banking has been the emergence of banking on a global scale. Foreign competition for deposits, securities business, underwriting, loan making, and other "banking" services has increased sharply. Furthermore, many foreign governments do not place the constraints on their financial institutions that U.S. law places on American institutions. Consequently, both commercial banks and investment banks have been forced to focus on ways to become more full–service oriented in order to compete effectively.

The point of this review, which is not meant to be complete by any means, is to highlight the gradual erosion of the wall between commercial banking and investment banking. Thus, if investment banking is "what investment banks do," then the right way to study investment banking (and brokerage) is to examine the things that investment bankers do—i.e., the markets they make and the services they provide. But we cannot forget that commercial banks do many of the same things. Thus, though they are not called investment banks, and though they are not classified as investment banks, by the definition of investment banking employed in this book, some commercial banks may, at least in part, be investment banks.

Investment Banking and Financial Engineering

During the 1970s and 1980s, a number of forces converged to transform the face of finance. Among these were advances in financial theory, the development of a great number of new financial instruments, a more accommodative regulatory environment, the emergence of global competition, advances in technology, and a more volatile price environment. These developments, together with an increasing appreciation of mathematical and statistical tools, transformed finance from a descriptive discipline to an analytical one and, later, to an engineering science.

Financial engineering can be defined, broadly, as *the development and the creative application of financial technology to solve financial problems, exploit financial opportunities, and to otherwise add value.*[1] In keeping with the traditional meaning of engineering, the work of modern investment bankers is often described as "structuring solutions" or "structured finance." Without doubt, financial engineering is the lifeblood of financial innovation and a cornerstone of modern investment banking. This explains the many references to financial engineering that appear in this text.

Transactional Finance

Technology and competition have caused a phenomenal decrease in both transaction costs and the cost of information. The cost of transacting for institution traders, who transact on a wholesale level, has dropped to 1/20th or less of levels prevailing 20 years ago. For retail traders, the drop has not been as great, but it has still been remarkable. What's more, an incredible array of new financial products—particularly futures, options, and swaps—has made it possible to replicate or synthesize positions at such negligible cost that, in many cases, transaction costs can be reduced to less than 1/100th of the levels of 20 years ago.

---

[1] This definition is similar to that used by the International Association of Financial Engineers, and to that used by John Finnerty (1988) when he first defined the term financial engineering.

The cost of information, which drives transaction decisions, has been reduced by even greater proportions. Advances in microchip technology, data processing, telecommunications, and programming have made it possible to acquire information from markets throughout the world, process that information in a few thousandths of a second, and trade on the outcome of that analysis in literally the blink of an eye.

Trading can be motivated by (1) a perception that absolute values (i.e., market prices) will soon change and speculative profits can be earned by correctly positioning on the right side of the market; (2) a perception that relative values are out of line (arbitrage); and/or (3) a desire to hedge risks. The cost of information and the cost of transacting together constitute a cost hurdle to such would–be market exploitation. Thus, the reduction in information and transaction costs has dramatically reduced the cost hurdle to profitable trading and contributed to the increasing transactional nature of investment banking. Also contributing has been an explosion in new financial products, variously described as structured securities, hybrid instruments, and derivative products. Investment banks participate in the new product markets by playing the roles of product innovator, issuer or underwriter, dealer, broker, and trader.

The Investment Banker as an Individual

Investment banking is an extraordinarily entrepreneurial activity. Indeed, no other industry is as pointedly entrepreneurial as investment banking. The entrepreneurial character of investment banks also explains the reward structure within the industry. Throughout an investment bank, financial reward is a function of performance—not in the sense of pay raises, as in other industries, but in the sense of performance bonuses paid at the close of each fiscal year. The industry is so heavily focused on performance that bonuses often exceed salaries many times over.

It is hard to say precisely what personality traits make for a successful investment banker, but certain common characteristics seem to stand out: a keen mind, a need to be challenged, a willingness to work long hours, a love of learning, a natural—some might say learned—aggressiveness, and a strong desire to succeed. Not surprisingly, these same traits tend to characterize most successful entrepreneurs.

Competition within the industry is intense. Investment bankers compete for issuers, for investors, for clients, for a share of the dealer market, for transactional profits, for arbitrage profits, and for everything else. As financial theory has come to play an ever–greater role in investment banking, formal theories and mathematical and statistical techniques have become prized skills. Also, product knowledge has become an increasingly intense focus area as financial products and variants of financial products have proliferated. Indeed, the world of meat and potatoes (stocks and bonds) that once characterized investment banking has given way to a veritable plethora of global menus. Hundreds, if not thousands, of products exist, and many serve the same functions.

The competitive spirit among investment bankers extends to the firms themselves, known in the vernacular of the trade as **shops** or **houses**. This competitive spirit can be seen in many ways. For example, the investment banking community eagerly awaits the quarterly and semiannual reports of standings within the industry. Firms are ranked by their share of domestic equity underwriting, corporate bond underwriting, municipal bond underwriting, global bond and equity underwriting, notional derivative contracts, and so on. The periodic rankings by these activities are published in such industry publications as *Institutional Investor* and *The Wall Street Journal*. The rankings are known within the industry as the **league tables**.

To compete effectively, investment bankers must educate and re–educate themselves and their staffs regularly.[2] To this end, training programs for investment bankers and brokers have proliferated. Some programs are provided to the industry by outside vendors and others are operated from within. Typical of the outside vendors are firms such as the New York Institute of Finance, the Institute for International Research, and Euromoney.[3] These firms offer specialized, very focused courses designed to meet very specific needs. All large shops today also have their own internal training programs. Such in–house training programs

---

[2] The importance of education in investment banking cannot be over–emphasized. Most, but not all, investment banking firms require an MBA as the minimum educational requirement for their investment bankers.

[3] Many small consulting firms, including our own, provide narrowly focused training for the securities industry as well.

were once very informal, little more than apprenticeships. But over the past 10 years, many of these programs have become very formal "professional development" departments. Also, specialized books dealing with many of the functional and product areas of investment banking have been published.[4] And, increasingly, universities are developing more narrowly focused courses to serve the industry.

The compensation structure in investment banking inspires aggressive and very competitive effort. It also sometimes results in the cutting of corners—legal and otherwise. Examples include the 1992 Salomon Brothers Treasury auction scandal, the stock parking and junk bond scandals involving Michael Milken and Drexel, and the unauthorized trading and the "hiding" of losses that are occasionally uncovered.

The nature of investment banking is such that investment bankers often possess inside information about the companies for which they work or the clients they serve. At other times, the ability to create a monopoly position in a security can enable a shop to reap monopoly profits. When serving a client, an investment banker has a **fiduciary obligation** to that client. This obligation is paramount, both legally and from a business perspective. Legally, the securities laws, whether promulgated by Congress or the regulatory agencies, are specifically designed to prevent abuses of this relationship and to ensure that securities transactions are fair to the trading public. From a business perspective, each shop must ensure that it is perceived by its clients as always placing their interests first. This means taking steps to avoid even the appearance of any impropriety.

To achieve this, the industry educates its employees in the law, as it pertains to them, and often places restrictions on its employees even beyond what the law requires. For example, most shops maintain a **restricted list** of securities. These are securities in which employees may not trade for their personal accounts. Any corporation or other securities issuer for whom the shop is currently contracted to perform a service is placed on the restricted list. Only when the obligations of the shop are fulfilled may its employees again trade the securities of that client for their personal accounts. At other times, a shop is negotiating for the

---

[4] The references and suggested reading section at the end of this chapter provides examples of these specialized publications.

business of a potential client. While the shop does not yet have a fiduciary obligation, certain of its employees may nevertheless have access to privileged information. Whether or not such information is held by the employees of the investment bank, the securities of the potential client are placed on the shop's **watch list**. Any employee who is involved or potentially involved in the contract negotiations or subsequent contract fulfillment cannot trade the security if it is on the watch list. Other employees may.

Restricted lists and watch lists are just some of the ways in which the industry seeks to monitor its employees and ensure the integrity of its business. The potential consequences from a failure to be vigilant can easily be seen in the Salomon Brothers Treasury auction scandal, a case we will examine in some detail in Chapter 4.

A Brief History of the Industry

The history of investment banking has been shaped by many forces. The two most significant of these have been legislation and economics. To understand investment banking as it exists today, it is necessary to have some sense of this legislative and economic history. For this reason, we feel it is important to provide a historical perspective at the outset. This will make it easier to understand the constraints on the industry when we examine the functional areas that constitute the business.

Early History

The role and function of investment banking has changed with the changing American economy. In the period before the Civil War, most investment banking activities were conducted by private bankers whose purpose was to raise funds for governments and railroad companies. The needs of the American government to raise large sums grew dramatically during the war, causing the role and function of investment banking to grow with it.

Following the war, investment banking continued to expand. Initially, investment bankers served mainly the interests of the rapidly expanding railroad industry. As other industrial companies were formed and grew, however, so did their demand for investment banking services. At that time, these services were essentially limited to underwriting securities issuances and mergers and acquisitions (M&A) related activities. During this period of expansion, the investment banking industry saw an increase in both its prestige and its influence.

In the pre–1929 period, the investment banking industry was generally unregulated. The potential for abuse in this free market, unregulated, high–growth industry was great, and some investment bankers took advantage of this potential. Consequently, when the crash of 1929 came, the industry was perceived as manipulative and corrupt, and the public demanded regulation to curb the abuses. As a result, by 1935, investment banking had become one of the most heavily regulated industries in the United States.

Following the crash of the stock market in 1929, several investigations were conducted to assess blame, causes, and potential remedies. From these investigations, it was concluded that there was a significant conflict of interest between commercial banking functions and investment banking functions. In particular, in the years before 1929, large banks had underwritten weak securities, financed by customer deposits, then sold the securities to the public through subsidiaries. Even after the banks knew the securities were worthless, the subsidiaries would continue to sell them.

Post–Crash Legislative Intervention

The abuses and perceived abuses of the period leading up to the crash of 1929 resulted in a string of successive pieces of legislation. Collectively, this legislation, as later amended, has done much to shape the industry. A brief review of the major components of this legislation follows.

The Banking Act of 1933 (Glass–Steagall Act).   This legislation separates the commercial banking function from the investment banking function; establishes the Federal Deposit Insurance Corporation (FDIC); forbids commercial banks from paying interest on demand deposits (Section 11); and permits the Federal Reserve to regulate interest on time deposits (Regulation Q).

Securities Act of 1933 (Truth–in–Securities Law).   This law requires full disclosure of relevant information about new issues of securities through a prospectus; requires registration of new securities with the federal government; requires financial statements to be audited by an independent accountant; and forbids fraudulent and deceptive practices when a new issue is sold. If an investor is able to prove that there was incomplete and/or inaccurate disclosure of material information in the prospectus or registration statement, the law permits the investor to take recourse against the issuing firm and/or the investment banks involved in the offering.

Securities Exchange Act of 1934 (SEA).

This act establishes the Securities and Exchange Commission (SEC); extends disclosure requirements to include secondary markets; generally supports exchanges' self–regulation but permits the SEC to regulate the business conduct of broker/dealer members of exchanges; permits the Federal Reserve Board to establish margin requirements; restricts the use of securities as collateral for bank loans; and prohibits fraud and price manipulation in the secondary market.

Maloney Act of 1938.

This legislation, named for Senator Francis Maloney of Connecticut, extends the SEC's jurisdiction to include the over–the–counter (OTC) market and encourages that market to establish private trade associations for self–regulation. Since its enactment, only one organization—the National Association of Securities Dealers (NASD)—has emerged to regulate the OTC market.

Investment Company Act of 1940, as Amended in 1970.

This legislation (the "40 Act") requires open–end and closed–end investment companies, which are also called mutual funds, to register with the SEC; requires investment companies to provide prospectuses to potential investors; and requires outside directors on investment companies' boards of directors.

Investment Advisers Act of 1940.

Under this legislation, the SEC was granted regulatory and supervisory responsibilities over investment advisers. Included in the legislation are provisions that: require investment advisers who sell advice to 15 or more interstate clients to register with the SEC; set standards for behavior and advertising of investment advisers; and monitor advisers' compliance with the law.

Employee Retirement Income Security Act (ERISA) of 1974.
ERISA regulates company pension funds. The regulations require employers with pension plans to set aside funds for pension payment liabilities, to meet promised defined–benefit pension plans, and to provide vesting rights; limit the amount a pension fund may invest in the firm's own securities; and establish the Pension Benefit Guarantee Corporation to insure pension plans.

These various pieces of legislation, and in particular Glass–Steagall, were effective at regulating the securities industry from the early 1930s to the 1970s. During this period, the dollar was strong, inflation was low, and interest rates were stable. Consequently, investment bankers were able to meet the needs of the business community without taking much risk, and the investment banking industry changed very little. Also during this period, regulation was perceived by many within the industry as beneficial. It limited competition and came close to guaranteeing profitability.

Recent Developments

The stability of the economy was shattered during the 1970s. Exchange rates were allowed to float, the 1973 Arab oil embargo shocked economies throughout the world, inflation reared its ugly head, interest rates became volatile, the institutional investor came to dominate the investment arena, and both the industrial and financial services sectors began a long march on the road to globalization.

As a consequence of these changes, the commercial banking and investment banking industries became increasingly constrained by the very regulations that once worked to their advantage. Financial institutions began to call for deregulation so that they could compete in a free market environment. The call was partially met. Additionally, many firms began to push the limits in not so subtle challenges to the law. These challenges encouraged the deregulation process. Highlights of this deregulation follow.

Development of Negotiated Order of Withdrawal (NOW). In July of 1970, Consumer Savings Bank of Worcester, Massachusetts, created the first NOW accounts. These accounts allowed a depositor to write a withdrawal slip on a time deposit account payable to a third party. These withdrawal slips looked and worked like checks, yet they were technically time deposits that paid interest. Essentially, Consumer Savings had "synthesized" interest–bearing checking accounts, and an encounter with the law was inevitable. On May 2, 1972, these accounts were approved by the Supreme Judicial Court of Massachusetts. In 1973, Congress passed legislation permitting New Hampshire and Massachusetts thrifts and commercial banks to offer NOW accounts. This right was extended to all New England banks and thrifts in 1976 and to the rest of the United States in 1980.

Securities Acts Amendments of 1975. This legislation required the SEC to develop a National Market System (NMS) and a national system for the clearance and settlement of securities transactions; increased competition within and across exchanges; and increased the availability of quotations, transactions, and other exchange information. One of the most important consequences of this legislation was the abandonment of fixed–rate commissions. Consequently, on May 1, 1975, commissions on equity transactions became negotiable. This date is remembered in the industry as "May Day."

Depository Institutions Deregulation and Monetary Control Act (DIDMCA) of 1980. This was the major commercial banking deregulation legislation. The act phased out all interest rate ceilings between 1980 and 1986, and permitted all thrifts and commercial banks to offer NOW accounts as of January 1, 1981.

Garn–St. Germain Act of 1982. This legislation deregulated the savings and loan (S&L) industry by permitting S&L money market deposit accounts to compete with money market mutual funds; expanded the types of assets thrifts could invest in to include commercial paper, corporate bonds, commercial loans, junk bonds, etc.; and allowed bank holding companies to acquire problem S&Ls across state lines.

Investment Banks as Holding Companies. An investment bank holding company may now own subsidiaries that underwrite securities and are regulated by the SEC (traditional investment banking activities) as well as other subsidiaries that are not regulated. The un–regulated subsidiaries engage in merchant banking (the firm uses its own funds to make investments such as bridge loans, commodities trading, insurance, venture capital investments, and so forth).

Shelf Registration (Rule 415). On March 16, 1982, the SEC adopted rule 415, more popularly known as shelf registration, which allows a corporation to file a registration for a securities issuance and then take up to two years to sell the securities. The rule was initially adopted on a trial basis and scheduled to expire on December 10, 1982. The trial was subsequently extended until December 31, 1983. In November 1983, the SEC adopted the rule on a permanent basis (with some limitations). Shelf registration is important because it increases competition in underwriting, reduces issuing costs, and permits firms more financing flexibility.[5]

Section 20 Subsidiaries. Commercial bank holding companies were permitted to underwrite and trade securities through Section 20 subsidiaries. Under the Section 20 rules, no more than 10 percent of the holding company's revenues may come from these subsidiaries. In September 1990, J.P. Morgan was the first bank to receive permission to operate a Section 20 subsidiary. Since then, other banks, notably Bankers Trust Company and The Chase Manhattan Bank, have created Section 20 companies and are now involved in securities underwriting. These Section 20 subsidiaries are now in direct competition with traditional investment banks for underwriting business.

The Development of the Eurobond Market. Glass–Steagall does not apply to operations of foreign subsidiaries of U.S. banks. Consequently, commercial banks have been underwriting notes and bonds in the Eurobond market for many years. By 1984, 52 percent of Eurobonds were underwritten by U.S. banks, but this share decreased to 25 percent

---

[5] For further discussion concerning the impact of shelf registration, see Kidwell, Marr, and Thompson (1984); Bhagat, Marr, and Thompson (1985); Rogowski and Sorensen (1985); and Moore, Peterson, and Peterson (1986).

by 1987. Over the same time period, the Eurobonds underwritten by Japanese firms increased from 9 percent to 31 percent.[6]

During this period of deregulation, the investment banking industry expanded into new services propelled, in part, by the economic growth of the 1980s. These new services included currencies, real estate, financial futures, bridge loans, mortgage–backed securities, and a great deal more. Many investment bankers believed that they could gain an advantage over their competitors if they could become more full–service so as to meet all the needs of their customers. However, with the crash of the stock market in 1987, the mini–crash of 1989, and the downturn in the economy in the late 1980s, the demand for these services decreased. As a result, profits decreased and the industry began to contract. This contraction resulted in (1) heavy layoffs in the industry—employment decreased from 260,000 in 1987 to an estimated 200,000 in 1991,[7] (2) an increase in concentration within the industry, and (3) some return to specialization by investment banking firms.

The recession within the investment banking industry caused firms to curtail some of their activities. No longer did they feel a need to be "all things to all customers." Unprofitable activities and departments were discontinued, and firms found niches in whatever they did best. For example, Merrill Lynch closed its Boston and Philadelphia municipal bond operations, Shearson liquidated E.F. Hutton's institutional investor businesses, and Dillon Read discontinued its mortgage–backed securities operations. By 1993, however, expansion of services was back in vogue at many shops.

One important area in which U.S. investment banks expanded in the 1980s only to pull back in the early 1990s was in their globalization efforts. While the industry has undoubtedly become more international, the expense of operating full–scale offices in several countries proved to be more than some firms had anticipated. As a result, several firms that had expanded internationally subsequently curtailed some of their international operations. For example, Shearson Lehman and Merrill Lynch both scaled down their London operations.

---

[6] For discussion of the impact of U.S. and Japanese banks on the Eurobond market, see Marr, Rogowski, and Trimble (1989).

[7] See, "Cold Winds on Wall Street," *The Economist*, October 13, 1990, p. 20.

Despite some retrenching, globalization of the industry is here to stay. However, firms are finding more economical paths to achieve the expanded reach. With improved telecommunications and computer software and hardware systems, many international operations can be performed without leaving home. For example, GLOBEX is an automated trading system in futures that permits traders almost anywhere in the world to access the system, and INSTINET, an electronic order–matching system, provides trades in stocks of some 10,000 companies in the United States and Europe.

The improvement in telecommunications and computer technology may be the most important change in the investment banking industry. Computer technology has given customers the same access to news, prices, quotes, and other market data as the investment banker. As a result, for some large established issuers, an investment banker is now no longer required to perform the traditional investment banking activities of underwriting and M&A. Many issuers have even gone so far as to create their own in–house investment banking departments. Examples of such firms include Du Pont, Eastman Kodak, IBM, Philip Morris, General Motors Acceptance, Interpublic, and Toys "R" Us.

Even though "plain vanilla" trades and underwritings are increasingly handled by issuers' in–house operations, broker/dealer networks are still needed for difficult trades, and investment bankers are needed to help place complex issues. The real value of investment bankers has always been the expertise that they possess. Now, that expertise is, to some degree, changing from underwriting and M&A to innovation of new products and sophisticated techniques for structuring deals and managing risks. (These are just some of the areas encompassed by financial engineering, which has become increasingly important to the future of investment banking.) In addition to the ongoing need to develop corporate relationships, competitive pressures are forcing the investment banks to focus on cost control and providing good service at a good price.

The Plan of This Book

There are many ways that a book on investment banking could be organized. Each has its strong points and its weak points. In keeping with our working definition that "investment banking is what investment banks do," it seems to make sense to organize this book along functional lines.

This requires us to divide investment banking activities into broad functional areas and to include in each a loose amalgamation of conceptually related topics. The process of dividing up the business in this way is somewhat arbitrary, and some topics included in one functional area could just as logically be included in another. Indeed, there is considerable overlap among investment banking activities.

It is not possible for any single book on investment banking to represent an exhaustive study of the industry. To the contrary, each chapter of this book could easily be expanded into a text the length of, or longer than, this book. Our goals must be more modest. This book should be viewed as a starting point for those interested in investment banking. The reader should come away with a general overall knowledge of the industry. For those who desire a deeper knowledge of some specific aspect of the industry, we have cited readings that we feel are appropriate in a section at the end of each chapter called "References and Suggested Reading." Some of the references cited are of a scholarly nature, while others are much more operationally oriented.

Part One of this book consists of two chapters, of which this introductory chapter is the first. The next chapter examines the sources of investment banking profits and contrasts the importance of those sources for several firms. Part Two focuses on those functional areas that are revenue generating. Specifically, Chapter 3 examines corporate finance, Chapter 4 considers public finance, Chapter 5 looks at bro-ker/dealer activity, Chapter 6 focuses on trading, Chapter 7 considers the investment banker's role in corporate restructurings, Chapters 8 and 9 explore the financial engineering activities of investment bankers with specific examples of each, and Chapter 10 examines advisory services, investment management, and merchant banking. Part Three considers support activities. Specifically, Chapter 11 discusses clearing operations, Chapter 12 examines the role of research, Chapter 13 explores internal finance, and Chapter 14 considers information services and related support operations. Chapter 15 concludes the book with a brief look forward.

Summary

In this chapter, we have provided an overview of investment banking beginning with definitions. Those several definitions range from the abstract macroeconomic focus on resource allocation to the very pragmatic "investment banking is what investment banks do"—which forms the basis for the organization of this text. We considered the structure of the industry, contrasted investment banks with commercial banks, considered the relationship between financial engineering and investment banking, looked briefly at the forces that have made investment banking an increasingly transaction–driven business, and contemplated the entrepreneurial nature of the individuals who drive the industry. We also ran through a short history of the industry from the period of the Civil War through the crash of 1929. We then considered the remedial legislation that regulated the industry following the crash and the deregulation of the industry that occurred over the past decade, and which seems to be ongoing. We closed with a look at the plan of this book and its motivation.

References and Suggested Reading

Balk, M. F., "What Will the Nation's Biggest Banks Do with Their New Powers?" *Price Waterhouse Review,* 35:1, 1991, pp. 19–24.

Bhagat, S., M. W. Marr, and G. R. Thompson, "The Rule 415 Experiment: Equity Markets," *Journal of Finance,* 40:5, December 1985, pp. 1385–1401.

Bruck, C., *The Predator's Ball,* New York: Simon and Schuster, 1988.

Bush, V., "Automation Opens the Repo Market to Small Investors," *Savings Institutions,* 109:4, April 1988, pp. 68–69.

Carosso, V., *Investment Banking in America: A History,* Cambridge, MA: Harvard University Press, 1970.

Carter, R. B. and F. H. Dark, "An Empirical Examination of Investment Banking Reputation Measures," *Financial Review,* 27:3, August 1992, pp. 355–374.

"Cold Winds on the Street," *The Economist,* October 13, 1990, pp. 19–20, 22.

Cook, T. Q. and B. J. Summers (eds.), *Instruments of the Money Markets,* Richmond, VA: Federal Reserve Bank of Richmond, 1981.

Duett, E. H., *Advanced Instruments in the Secondary Mortgage Market: An Introduction to CMOs, REMICs, IOs & POs and Other Derivative Instruments,* New York: Harper & Row, 1990.

Eccles, R. G. and D. B. Crane, "Managing Through Networks in Investment Banking," *California Management Review,* Fall 1987, pp. 176–195.

Fabozzi, F. J., T. D. Fabozzi, and I. M. Pollock (eds.), *The Handbook of Fixed Income Securities,* 3e, Burr Ridge, IL: Business One Irwin, 1991.

Finnerty, J. D., "Financial Engineering in Corporate Finance: An Overview," *Financial Management,* 17:4, Winter, 1988, pp. 14–33.

Follain, J. R., "The U.S. Secondary Mortgage Market Born in a Regulated Environment but Flourishing in a Competitive One," *Illinois Business Review,* 44:5, October 1987, pp. 2–5.

Francis, J. C., *Investment: Analysis and Management,* 5e, New York: McGraw–Hill, Chapter 4, "Securities Law," pp. 112–138.

Happ, S., "The Behavior of Rates on Federal Funds and Repurchase Agreements," *American Economist,* 30:2, Fall 1986, pp. 22–32.

Kapner, K. R. and J. F. Marshall, *The Swaps Handbook: Swaps and Related Risk Management Instruments,* New York: New York Institute of Finance, 1990.

Karmel, R. S., *Regulation by Prosecution: The SEC versus Corporate America,* New York: Simon & Schuster, 1982.

Kaufman, G. G. and L. R. Mota, "Glass–Steagall: Repeal by Regulatory and Judicial Reinterpretation," *Banking Law Journal,* 107:5, September/October 1990, pp. 388–421.

Kawaller, I. G., *Financial Futures and Options: Managing Risk in the Interest Rate, Currency, and Equity Markets,* Chicago: Probus, 1992.

Kidwell, D. S., M. W. Marr, and G. R. Thompson, "SEC Rule 415: The Ultimate Competitive Bid," *Journal of Financial and Quantitative Analysis,* 19:2, June 1984, pp. 183–195.

Kuhn, R. L., *Investment Banking: The Art and Science of High–Stakes Dealmaking,* New York: Harper & Row, 1990.

Lipson, P. C., "Securities Lending, Part 2: Regulation, Pricing, and Risks Borne by Participants," *Journal of Commercial Banking,* 72:7, March 1990, pp. 18–31.

Maloney, P., "Investment Banking Lures the Regionals," *United States Banker*, 98:7, July 1989. pp. 16–18.

Maloney, P., "Slow Going for Section 20 Units," *United States Banker*, 100:10, October 1990, pp. 63–72.

Marr, M. W., R. W. Rogowski, and J. L. Trimble, "The Competitive Effects of U.S. and Japanese Commercial Bank Participation in Eurobond Underwritings," *Financial Management*, 18:4, Winter 1989, pp. 47–54.

Marshall, J. F., *Futures and Option Contracting: Theory and Practice*, Cincinnati: South–Western, 1989.

Marshall, J. F. and V. K. Bansal, *Financial Engineering: A Complete Guide to Financial Innovation*, New York: New York Institute of Finance, 1992.

Marshall, J. F. and V. K. Bansal, *Financial Engineering*, 2e, Miami: Kolb Publishing, 1993.

Moore, N. H., D. R. Peterson, and P. P. Peterson, "Shelf Registration and Shareholder Wealth: A Comparison of Shelf and Traditional Equity Offerings," *Journal of Finance*, 41:2, June 1986, pp. 451–463.

Nathans, L., "From the Many, Perhaps Just a Few," *Business Month*, February 1988, pp. 69–70.

Rogowski, R. J. and E. H. Sorensen, "Deregulation in Investment Banking: Shelf Registration, Structure and Performance," *Financial Management*, 14:1, Spring 1985, pp. 5–15.

Ziegler, D., "Stormy Past, Stormy Future," *The Economist*, July 21, 1990, pp. S1–S28.

2

Industry Structure

Overview

The investment banking industry is a very cyclical industry. During periods of economic growth, the demands for investment banking services and products increase, causing a tendency for the industry to overexpand. However, during periods of recession and downturns, the demands for investment banking services and products decrease, and the industry tends to contract and consolidate. Since the crash of 1987, this tendency to consolidate has taken its toll. More than 1,300 security firms (20 percent) mostly smaller firms, have gone out of business or merged; the number of employees in the industry declined from 260,000 to 213,800 by 1991; and almost every major investment banking firm has undergone major reorganization, reshuffling, merger, and/or bankruptcy. As a result, the industry has become more concentrated into fewer hands, and the players have become more specialized.

The 1990s have seen the fruits of this contraction. Beginning in 1991, the number of new hires exceeded the number of layoffs, and both 1991 and 1992 were record–setting years for the industry, with more deals, more securities being issued, and more funds being raised than ever before. Furthermore, 1993 also appears to be on a record–setting pace. However, the sources of revenues and the types of deals and products have changed. The 1980s were the age of mega–mergers, with mergers and acquisitions being the major source of revenues for investment banks, but the 1990s are the age of restructuring, product development, and financial engineering, with more traditional investment banking activities producing an increasing share of the revenues.

This chapter will examine the structure of the investment banking industry. We will first examine who the major players are and how they stack up within the industry. We will then examine the sources of revenues and expenses for the investment banking industry by comparing the financial statements of three major publicly traded investment banking firms. Finally, we will examine the organizational structure of investment banking firms. This overview will help us better understand the makeup of the investment banking industry.

Investment Banking Firms

The success of an investment bank depends very much on its perceived prestige within the investment banking community.[1] One of the ways this prestige is measured is by the firm's ranking in the industry league tables. These tables rank investment banking firms in terms of the amount of business they performed for a given category over a given period. We will review the league tables, published in the February 1992 issue of Institutional Investor, which rank investment banks in three major areas: corporate underwriting, international underwriting, and municipal underwriting.

Corporate Underwriting

Domestic investment banks are ranked according to aggregate underwriting (which is the sum of the debt and equity underwriting activity), total debt, total equity, mortgage–backed securities, asset–backed securities, preferred stock, and yankee bond underwriting as of 1991. Merrill Lynch was the only investment bank that ranked in the top five across all seven underwriting categories, and it was ranked first in four of the categories: total underwriting, debt, equity, and yankee bonds. The other investment banks to rank in the top 10 across all seven categories include Goldman Sachs, Lehman Brothers, First Boston, and Salomon Brothers. These firms are part of the "bulge bracket," a term that refers to the top so–called investment banking firms. Also often included among the bulge bracket firms is Morgan Stanley, which ranks in the top 10 in six of the seven categories. (Morgan Stanley ranks 12th in asset–backed securities.)

---

[1] See Ellis and Dunkelberg (1992); Bowers and Miller (1990); Carter and Dark (1990); Carter and Manaster (1990); Johnson and Miller (1988); and Tinic (1988) for academic studies on the role of the prestige of the investment banker.

Whereas the bulge bracket firms rank high across most or all of the categories, other investment banks concentrate on one market or niche. For example, Alex Brown's niche is in equity underwriting, where it is ranked fourth, giving it an overall underwriting ranking of 13th.

Of interest also is the importance of commercial banks in some of the rankings. Citicorp ranks 17th in overall underwriting, and three of the top 10 asset–backed securities underwriters are affiliated with commercial banks: Chase Securities (#5), Union Bank of Switzerland (#7), and J.P. Morgan Securities (#8). These rankings demonstrate the increasing overlap of the investment banking and commercial banking areas.

International Underwriting

International firms are ranked based on international bonds, Eurobonds, international loans and note–issuance facilities, and international equities. These rankings demonstrate the importance of international banking to the international investment banking markets. Most of the categories are dominated by European international banks. Credit Suisse/CSFB (First Boston) is a dominant player, but that may be more of a function of the Swiss ownership of CSFB. Even though Goldman Sachs, Merrill Lynch, and Morgan Stanley are strong players in the international market, they do not dominate the international markets as much as they dominate the domestic markets.

The one area where U.S. firms do appear to dominate is in international loans and note–issuance facilities, where eight of the top 10 positions in 1991 were held by U.S. commercial banks.

Municipal Underwriting

Finally, municipal underwriters are ranked based on total underwriting, long–term negotiated issues, long–term competitive issues, taxable municipal issues, long–term general obligation issues, and the following negotiated issues: education, housing, electric and power, health care, transportation, and water, sewer, and gas. Goldman Sachs and Merrill Lynch dominate this market.[2]

Revenues and Expenses

To help you better understand the makeup of the investment banking industry, we will examine the 1992 income statements and balance sheets for three publicly traded investment banking firms: Merrill Lynch, Paine–Webber, and Bear, Stearns. The purpose of this analysis is not so much a comparison between firms as an analysis of their similarities to provide insight into the investment banking industry.

Table 2.23 in the Appendix to this chapter presents the income statements as a percent of the total revenues. These statements indicate the different activities investment banks are currently involved with. The major revenue accounts include:

Commissions:	brokerage accounts, mutual fund sales, etc.
Interest and Dividends:	margin lending, effects of interest rate spreads, net carrying costs and accrued interest from trading positions, etc.
Principal Transaction:	trading activity (equity, fixed income, foreign exchange, etc.), hedging strategies, revenues from mortgage–backed securities, swaps, and derivative securities, etc.
Investment Banking:	underwriting, private placements, management fees, mergers and acquisitions, restructuring, refinancing, advisory services, etc.
Other Revenues:	merchant banking activities, some consulting activities, some arbitrage activities, etc.

---

[2] Salomon Brothers had about a 9.5 percent share of the municipal bond market when they voluntarily abandoned it in 1987. In early 1993, Salomon tried to re–enter this market by being named to a team of seven lead underwriters to sell $4 billion of New York City Bonds, but this effort was not successful (*The Wall Street Journal*, March 18, 1993, C1).

These three investment banks are considered to be full–service firms, and they are involved in all of the described activities to some extent. However, many investment banks are niche or boutique firms and concentrate on just one or two activities. For example, when Primerica purchased Shearson from American Express in 1993, the purpose was to create a large sales force by joining Shearson with Primerica's Smith Barney, Harris Upham. Primerica's goal is to have a large sales force to, in part, service the distribution needs of the underwriting investment banks. As part of this plan, Primerica has a two–year agreement with Lehman Brothers, American Express's investment banking unit, which Primerica did not purchase, to continue to service Lehman's underwriting distribution needs.

Given the specialization within the boutique investment banks, these institutions are dependent on the larger investment banks and other boutiques to provide services to compliment the boutiques' activities. For example, Bear, Stearns has one of the largest clearing operations, with over 1,200 clearing accounts, including brokers/dealers, specialists, market makers, money managers, arbitrageurs, etc. Bear, Stearns benefits from this arrangement by earning a profit on its clearing operations (which has a large fixed–cost component), and the boutiques and other accounts benefit by having a readily available clearing service. As a result of the boutiques' specialization, it is not unusual for them to maintain a close relationship with one or more full–service investment banks and/or other boutiques.

In terms of expenses, the major expense for all three firms, and for the industry, is Compensation and Benefits. Senior managers at investment banks consider their most valuable assets to be the individuals who work for the investment bank. The investment banking industry is very labor–intensive, and the working environment is very sensitive to economic conditions.

Table 2.24 in the Appendix examines the balance sheets of Merrill Lynch, PaineWebber, and Bear, Stearns as a percentage of total assets. The asset mix reflects the components of the investment banking business. In order to be able to service the firm's trading and broker-age/dealer activities, a high level of securities inventory is required. Also, the Resale Agreements and Receivables help finance the financial intermediary component of the business.

The Liabilities and Stockholders' Equity side of the balance sheet indicates the highly liquid and highly leveraged nature of the investment banking industry. Long–term borrowing and Stockholders' Equity account for 14 percent or less of the financing of these three firms. Also, the major source of financing for all three firms is Repurchase Agreements, which are generally used to finance the firm's securities inventory. This is a very liquid and well–collateralized source of funds. The major secondary source of short–term funds varies across firms, but all firms have many alternative sources of funds: commercial paper, bank lines of credit, secured loans, etc.

The analysis of these three financial statements indicates that the investment banking industry is involved in many diverse activities, including brokerage/dealer, underwriting, swaps and derivative products, customer services, etc. Furthermore, the industry is shown to be labor–intensive, highly liquid, and highly leveraged.

Organizational Structure of Investment Banks

The organizational structure of investment banks differs widely across firms within the industry. There is not any one "typical" organization, and what works for one firm may not work for another. Much of the organizational structure often is related to the internal politics and alliances within the firm. Sometimes the politics takes on a life of its own. For example, it is not unusual for an individual to be a very successful investment banker with one firm, and to be much less successful after moving to a competing firm. The lack of success may not be due to the individual per se, but to the environment at the first bank, which may have leveraged the individual's talents more than the environment at the competing bank. Also, it is not unusual that when a major banker moves to a competing firm, her entire team, or at least most of them, moves as well. It is difficult for a firm to replace a "star," and it is difficult for a star to be a star without her team.

At one time, the investment banking industry was a close–knit group of mostly privately owned partnerships. Now, of the major investment banking firms, only one partnership, Goldman Sachs, remains, and the other partnerships have either been purchased by conglomerates or "gone public." We will examine these three forms of organizations in the investment banking industry: the partnership, the conglomerate unit, and the public firm.

The Partnership

A partnership is a firm owned by two or more persons who share in the profits of the firm. A partner is a part owner of the firm. All partnerships have at least one general partner who is responsible for the daily operations and functions of the business, and who is liable for the firm's operations. However, many partnerships also have limited partners whose commitment is limited to the financial side, who are not involved in the daily operations of the business, and who enjoy limited liability.

Goldman Sachs is the only major investment bank that remains a partnership. At the end of 1992, Goldman had 162 partners and about 60 limited partners. Goldman uses an 11–member management committee to oversee the operations of the 6,000–employee firm. Most of the midlevel employees receive most of their compensation in the form of salary, with year–end bonuses averaging about 23 percent of their salary levels. But partners receive most of their compensation in the form of partnership profits, and most of the profits remain reinvested with Goldman until the partner retires. This means that a partner may have a very large retirement income. For example, at the end of 1992, Robert Rubin retired as one of Goldman's two co–chairmen to enter national politics as the president's assistant for economic affairs. Rubin's 1991 income was estimated at more than $15 million on a base salary of $210,000. But, his investment in Goldman was estimated at between $50 million and $100 million.[3]

Most of Goldman's limited partners are former partners who elect to "go limited."[4] However, on three occasions Goldman has sold a limited partnership to raise external funds. In 1986, Sumitomo Bank (Japan) invested $500 million; in 1989, a syndicate of seven insurance companies invested $225 million; and in 1991, another syndicate of insurance

---

[3] Siconolfi, Michael, "With Rubin Going, Friedman at Solo at Goldman," *The Wall Street Journal*, December 11, 1992, p. C1.

[4] Of interest, the average age of a partner to "go limited" is about 50 (*The Wall Street Journal*, November 27, 1991).

companies invested around $275 million.[5] The limited partners receive a share of Goldman's partnership profits, but they do not participate in Goldman's management.

The Conglomerate Unit

It is fairly unusual for a large investment bank to go into bankruptcy. The exception, of course, is Drexel Burnham Lambert. However, Drexel, a partnership, was involved in a securities trading scandal that badly damaged its reputation and ultimately destroyed the firm. Also, the fines imposed by the SEC on individuals at Drexel and the firm itself were debilitating. Certain individuals, including Michael Milken, the head of "junk" bonds [finance and] trading, were convicted of felonies and therefore barred from the securities business for life.[6]

Whereas bankruptcy of a large investment bank is unusual, however, acquisitions, mergers, and selling of investment banking/brokerage firms as part of a conglomerate or a multidivisional firm are not unusual, especially in the last 15 or so years. During this period, many investment banking firms were acquired or sold by other investment banking or financial institution firms. For example, Phibro Corporation acquired Salomon Brothers and Prudential Insurance acquired Bache Group in 1981; Equitable acquired Donaldson Lufkin & Jenrette in 1984; American Express absorbed Shearson Loeb Rhodes in 1981 and Lehman Brothers Kuhn Loeb in 1984, creating Shearson Lehman, which purchased E.F. Hutton in 1987. Primerica acquired Smith Barney, Harris Upham in 1987 and then purchased Shearson (the brokerage unit) from American Express in 1993.[7]

---

[5] *The Wall Street Journal*, November 12, 1991, p. C16.

[6] See Bruck, Connie, *The Predator's Ball*, New York: Simon and Schuster, 1988, for a review of the Michael Milken and Drexel Case.

[7] The new unit formed by Primerica is called Smith Barney Shearson and will be the second largest brokerage house in the United States with initially 11,000 brokers and 495 branch offices. The largest brokerage house, Merrill Lynch, has 11,500 brokers and 458 branches (*The Wall Street Journal*, March 15, 1993, p. A1).

Most of these acquisitions were to complement or support the main activities of the parent company. However, one of the changes in the industry over the last 15 years is that nonfinancial firms also absorbed investment banks/brokerage firms—e.g., Sears acquired Dean Witter Reynolds in 1981 and General Electric took over Kidder Peabody in 1986. The goal of these acquisitions was to enhance the profitability of the parent company or diversify the business, as opposed to supporting or complimenting other activities.

Generally, the acquisitions of investment banks by nonfinancial conglomerates has not been totally successful. Sears purchased Dean Witter as part of a plan for a "financial supermarket" that included insurance, real estate, and brokerage services, all at "one–stop shopping." However, the plan was not as successful as anticipated for Sears, and in 1992 Sears sold 20 percent of Dean Witter, renamed Dean Witter Discover, to the public. Also, there have been rumors of a potential sale of Kidder for years. General Electric had purchased Kidder the year before the crash of 1987.

The acquisitions, mergers, and selling of investment banks by financial and nonfinancial firms indicated a major change in the industry. It has moved from being a close–knit group of partnerships to the firms themselves being targets for takeovers and acquisitions. Consequently, the industry is now under additional stress. Profits have become more important, since a lack of profits must now be justified to other publicly owned parent companies; expenses are more closely watched and controlled; and the industry has become more streamlined, with many of the private partnership perquisites eliminated or reduced.

The Public Firm

In the conglomerate, the management of the investment bank is answerable to the parent firm, but in a public firm, the investment bank management is answerable to the owners—the shareholders. The transformation of investment banks to publicly owned firms is one of the biggest changes in the investment banking industry. Many of the major investment banking firms have gone public, including Merrill Lynch (1971), Bear, Stearns (1985), and Morgan Stanley (1986). As a result, we now know more about the operations and the workings of the investment banking industry.

A **public firm** sells ownership of the firm to the public in the form of common stock. Profits from the firm are either paid to the owners in the form of dividends or reinvested in the firm in the form of retained earnings. Additional funds may be obtained through the creation of liabilities (i.e., bank notes, accrued accounts, debt, etc.) or preferred stock, or issuing additional shares of common stock. If additional shares of stock are sold, then the ownership interest of the existing shareholders is diluted.

Shareholders in a public firm elect the members of the board of directors, who are responsible for the general strategy and policy of the firm. The daily operations of the firm are managed by a team consisting of the president, chief executive officer (CEO), and other officers of the firm. Even though it is not uncommon for members of the top management team, especially the president and the CEO, to sit on the board of directors as well, the boards of public firms also have some outside directors. The number and influence of the outside directors vary widely across firms.

The role of the board of directors in the public firm organization should not be minimized. The board has a fiduciary duty to protect the interest of the shareholders. This duty is divided into three areas:

- The duty of loyalty, or the duty to act in good faith in the best interest of the corporation.
- The duty of candor, or the duty to fully and fairly disclose all pertinent information concerning an issue on which shareholders vote.
- The duty of care, or the duty to ensure that the board has been informed of all material information reasonably available before a decision is made.

As a result of this fiduciary duty, board members are held legally liable for recommendations and decisions not made in the best interest of the firm. This is particularly true in cases involving reorganizations, mergers, divestures, or other major changes in the structure of the firm.[8]

---

[8] See Foye, Patrick J. and Samuel D. Scruggs, "Investment Banker Liability in Mergers and Acquisitions" in Rupert, Raymond, (ed.), *The New Era of Investment Banking*, Chicago: Probus Publishing, 1993.

The advantage of ownership in a public firm includes: (1) limited financial liability—the owner may lose only his investment in the firm; the owner's personal wealth may not be attached to satisfy the firm's liabilities; (2) divisibility of ownership—ownership may be divided into smaller parts (shares of stock) to aid in the selling and transfer of ownership; and (3) easy transfer of ownership—ownership may be transferred by buying or selling the stock.

The advantage of a public firm, especially a large public firm, is the ability to efficiently obtain additional funds through the capital markets; however, this benefit also has a price. Public companies are required to have more public disclosure of their financial statements and activities than private partnerships—i.e., annual reports, K-10 reports, quarterly statements, annual stockholders' meetings, etc. Consequently, as a result of investment banks' going public, the investment banking industry has became a more open and public industry, with profits, salaries, and bonuses now public information. For example, the profits and bonuses at Goldman are estimated, but the profits and bonuses at Merrill Lynch are publicly announced. As a result, the public firm organizational structure has encouraged the streamlining of the investment banking industry, with additional focus on profitability and controlling expenses.

Summary

This chapter examined the structure of the investment banking industry by examining who the players are, comparing financial statements for three publicly traded firms, and reviewing the three organizational structures used in the industry.

The dominant player is Merrill Lynch, but Merrill Lynch has competition in almost every area of investment banking from other full–service banks such as Goldman Sachs, Morgan Stanley, Salomon Brothers, Lehman Brothers, and First Boston, as well as competition from niche firms. In particular, the newly formed Smith Barney Shearson will provide major competition in the brokerage area.

From the financial statements of Merrill Lynch, PaineWebber, and Bear, Stearns, we found that the major sources of revenue in the investment banking industry include commissions, interest and dividends, principal transactions, and investment banking activities. The major expense in this labor–intensive industry is compensations and benefits. Also, we found the industry to be highly liquid and highly leveraged.

Finally, we examined the three forms of organizational structure employed in the industry: the partnership used by Goldman Sachs, a conglomerate unit as in Salomon Brothers or Kidder Peabody, and public firms such as Merrill Lynch, PaineWebber, and Bear, Stearns. Goldman Sachs is the last remaining partnership in an industry that was dominated by partnerships in the 1960s. The move from partnerships to public firms or conglomerate units has changed the industry from a private cottage industry to a more public one.

References and Suggested Reading

Bear, Stearns 1992 Annual Report.

Block, E., *Inside Investment Banking*, Burr Ridge, IL: Dow Jones–Irwin, 1989.

Bowers, H. M. and R. E. Miller, "Choice of Investment Banker and Shareholders' Wealth of Firms Involved in Acquisitions," *Financial Management*, 19:4, Winter 1990, pp. 34-44.

Bruck, C., *The Predator's Ball*, New York: Simon and Schuster, 1988.

Carter, R. and S. Manaster, "Initial Public Offerings and Underwriter Reputation," *Journal of Finance*, 45:4, September 1990, pp. 1045-1067.

Carter, R. B. and F. H. Dark, "The Use of the Over–Allotment Option in Initial Public Offerings of Equity: Risks and Underwriter Prestige," *Financial Management*, 19:3, Autumn 1990, pp. 55-64.

"Cold Winds on Wall Street," *The Economist*, October 13, 1990, pp. 19-20, 22.

Eccles, R. G. and D. B. Crane, "Managing Through Networks in Investment Banking," *California Management Review*, Fall 1987, pp. 176-195.

Ellis, M. E. and J. Dunkelberg, "The Effect of the Prestige of the Investment Banker on Positive Versus Negative Seasoned Equity Issue Announcements," presented at the Financial Management Association Meetings in San Francisco, CA, October 1992.

Foye, P. J. and S. D. Scruggs, "Investment Banker Liability in Mergers and Acquisitions," in Raymond H. Rupert, (ed.), *The New Era of Investment Banking*, Chicago: Probus Publishing, 1993.

Johnson, J. J. and R. E. Miller, "Investment Banker Prestige and the Underpricing of Initial Public Offerings," *Financial Management*, 17:2, Summer 1988, pp. 19-29.

Kuhn, R. L., "New–Age Investment Banking," *Journal of Business Strategy*, November/December 1990a, pp. 54-59.

Kuhn, R. L., *Investment Banking: The Art and Science of High–Stakes Dealmaking*, New York: Harper & Row, 1990b.

Lewis, M., *Liar's Poker: Rising Through the Wreckage on Wall Street*, New York: W. W. Norton & Company, 1989.

Merrill Lynch 1992 Annual Report.

"The 1992 Corporate Sweepstakes," *Institutional Investor*, 26:2, February 1992, pp. 73-88.

PaineWebber 1992 Annual Report.

Regal, D. T., *The Merrill Lynch Story*, New York: Newcomen Society in North America, 1981.

"The Six–Month Corporate Underwriting Sweeps," *Institutional Investor*, 26:10, September 1992, pp. 75-94.

Slovin, M. B., M. E. Sushka, and C. D. Hudson, "External Monitoring and Its Effect on Seasoned Common Stock Issues," *Journal of Accounting & Economics*, 12:4, March 1990, pp. 397-417.

Sobel, R., *Salomon Brothers, 1910-1985: Advancing to Leadership*, New York: Salomon Brothers, 1986.

Tinic, S. M., "Anatomy of Initial Public Offerings of Common Stock," *Journal of Finance*, 43:4, September 1988, pp. 789-822.

Appendix

Table 2.1
The Corporate Underwriting Leaders

TOTAL SECURITIES

A summary of the top firms according to full credit to lead manager.

1990	1991		$ Volume (millions)	No. of Issues
1	1	Merrill Lynch	$100,504.3	561
2	2	Goldman Sachs	69,641.5	442
8	3	Lehman Brothers	68,641.2	490
3	4	First Boston	57,984.1	310
6	5	Kidder Peabody	50,824.8	199
5	6	Morgan Stanley	48,232.9	278
4	7	Salomon Brothers	46,447.9	199
7	8	Bear, Stearns	33,844.7	98
9	9	Prudential Securities	17,054.9	68
10	10	Donaldson, Lufkin & Jenrette	11,479.7	67
11	11	PaineWebber	10,407.3	70
13	12	J.P. Morgan Securities	9,697.2	73
17	13	Alex, Brown & Sons	7,305.8	63
15	14	Smith Barney, Harris Upham	5,837.1	64
12	15	Dean Witter	5,595.3	37
16	16	Nomura Securities	5,306.3	15
14	17	Citicorp	5,028.3	24
20	18	Greenwich Capital Markets	4,955.4	15
47	19	Daiwa Securities	4,767.9	13
23	20	Chase Securities	3,297.7	5
18	21	Union Bank of Switzerland	2,507.2	7
22	22	Dillon Read	1,645.4	20
24	23	Piper, Jaffray & Hopwood	1,047.3	15
25	24	Montgomery Securities	850.1	30
26	25	First Tenessee Bank	725.0	3
		Total market volume	$583,339.7	3,536

Source: *Institutional Investor*, February 1992. This copyrighted material is reprinted with permission from Institutional Investor, Inc., 488 Madison Ave., New York, NY 10022.

Table 2.2
Total Debt

1990	1991		$ Volume (millions)	No. of Issues
1	1	Merrill Lynch	$87,280.4	453
8	2	Lehman Brothers	63,398.8	416
2	3	Goldman Sachs	57,530.9	371
3	4	First Boston	53,296.3	262
6	5	Kidder Peabody	49,358.9	165
4	6	Salomon Brothers	42,240.6	160
5	7	Morgan Stanley	37,810.4	219
7	8	Bear, Stearns	33,018.2	84
9	9	Prudential Securities	15,505.1	52
10	10	Donaldson, Lufkin & Jenrette	10,068.9	48
12	11	J.P. Morgan Securities	9,697.2	73
11	12	PaineWebber	8,788.6	29
15	13	Nomura Securities	5,306.3	15
13	14	Citicorp	5,028.3	24
19	15	Greenwich Capital Markets	4,955.4	15
—	16	Daiwa Securities	4,767.9	13
14	17	Dean Witter	4,446.4	17
17	18	Smith Barney, Harris Upham	3,809.7	19
21	19	Chase Securities	3,297.7	5
16	20	Union Bank of Switzerland	2,507.2	7
22	21	Dillon Read	1,003.6	9
24	22	First Tenessee Bank	725.0	3
20	23	BT Securities	598.6	4
—	24	Nikko Securities	551.1	2
—	25	Lazard Freres	373.8	2
		Total market volume	$507,329.7	2,517

Source: *Institutional Investor*, February 1992. This copyrighted material is reprinted with permission from Institutional Investor, Inc., 488 Madison Ave., New York, NY 10022.

Table 2.3
Total Equity

1990	1991		$ Volume (millions)	No. of Issues
1	1	Merrill Lynch	$13,223.9	108
2	2	Goldman Sachs	12,110.7	71
8	3	Morgan Stanley	10,422.5	59
3	4	Alex, Brown & Sons	7,305.8	63
4	5	Lehman Brothers	5,242.4	74
9	6	First Boston	4,687.8	48
5	7	Salomon Brothers	4,207.3	39
6	8	Smith Barney, Harris Upham	2,027.4	45
7	9	PaineWebber	1,618.7	41
12	10	Prudential Securities	1,549.8	16
11	11	Kidder Peabody	1,466.0	34
25	12	Donaldson, Lufkin & Jenrette	1,410.7	19
10	13	Dean Witter	1,148.9	20
14	14	Piper, Jaffray & Hopwood	1,027.6	14
13	15	Montgomery Securities	850.1	30
16	16	Bear, Stearns	826.5	14
—	17	S.G. Warburg	714.7	1
19	18	Hambrecht & Quist	686.7	21
17	19	Robertson Stephens	678.6	23
23	20	Dillon Read	641.8	11
22	21	Allen & Co.	440.8	8
15	22	Oppenheimer & Co.	365.9	10
—	23	Lazard Freres	302.8	5
24	24	William Blair	257.3	10
36	25	Inter–Regional Finance Group	256.4	13
		Total market volume	$76,010.0	1,019

Source: *Institutional Investor*, February 1992. This copyrighted material is reprinted with permission from Institutional Investor, Inc., 488 Madison Ave., New York, NY 10022.

Table 2.4
Mortgage–Backed Securities

1990	1991		$ Volume (millions)	No. of Issues
1	1	Kidder Peabody	$43,364.9	85
7	2	Lehman Brothers	31,701.1	82
2	3	Bear, Stearns	30,020.6	69
8	4	Merrill Lynch	20,966.3	70
4	5	First Boston	19,170.1	64
3	6	Goldman Sachs	17,729.2	57
5	7	Salomon Brothers	17,538.4	53
6	8	Prudential Securities	14,501.1	43
10	9	Morgan Stanley	11,661.0	37
9	10	Donaldson, Lufkin & Jenrette	8,099.7	34
11	11	PaineWebber	6,872.9	20
13	12	Nomura Securities	5,306.3	15
17	13	Greenwich Capital Markets	4,955.4	15
—	14	Daiwa Securities	4,663.1	12
15	15	Citicorp	4,421.1	15
		Total market volume	$249,155.1	722

Source: *Institutional Investor*, February 1992. This copyrighted material is reprinted with permission from Institutional Investor, Inc., 488 Madison Ave., New York, NY 10022.

Table 2.5
Asset–Backed Securities

1990	1991		$ Volume (millions)	No. of Issues
2	1	First Boston	$13,986.1	28
1	2	Merrill Lynch	11,771.8	43
4	3	Salomon Brothers	8,326.8	15
5	4	Dean Witter	4,346.5	15
11	5	Chase Securities	3,297.7	5
3	6	Goldman Sachs	1,751.6	5
—	7	Union Bank of Switzerland	1,397.2	2
9	8	J.P. Morgan Securities	1,248.9	2
10	9	Lehman Brothers	1,189.6	2
13	10	Bear, Stearns	899.0	2
14	11	Donaldson, Lufkin & Jenrette	722.4	4
6	12	Morgan Stanley	608.3	4
12	13	Prudential Securities	459.3	5
7	14	Chemical Bank	179.2	2
—	15	Daiwa Securities	104.8	1
		Total market volume	$50,289.2	135

Source: *Institutional Investor*, February 1992. This copyrighted material is reprinted with permission from Institutional Investor, Inc., 488 Madison Ave., New York, NY 10022.

Table 2.6
Preferred Stock

1990	1991		$ Volume (millions)	No. of Issues
7	1	Morgan Stanley	$6,359.9	24
1	2	Merrill Lynch	5,940.9	47
4	3	Goldman Sachs	2,725.0	13
2	4	Lehman Brothers	1,348.8	17
6	5	Salomon Brothers	921.3	7
3	6	Smith Barney, Harris Upham	755.0	14
8	7	Dean Witter	480.0	4
9	8	First Boston	427.0	6
5	9	Kidder Peabody	245.0	2
—	10	Dillon Read	200.0	2
—	11	Bear, Stearns	150.0	1
—	12	Lazard Freres	130.0	2
—	13	Prudential Securities	100.0	2
13	14	Inter–Regional Finance Group	55.0	1
10		Kemper Securites	55.0	1
		Total market volume	$19,981.8	154

Source: *Institutional Investor*, February 1992. This copyrighted material is reprinted with permission from Institutional Investor, Inc., 488 Madison Ave., New York, NY 10022.

Table 2.7
Yankee Bonds

1990	1991		$ Volume (millions)	No. of Issues
1	1	Merrill Lynch	$4,079.1	14
2	2	Morgan Stanley	3,618.4	13
3	3	Salomon Brothers	3,200.1	11
5	4	Goldman Sachs	2,947.3	16
4	5	First Boston	1,072.7	4
—	6	J.P. Morgan Securities	430.0	5
7	7	Lehman Brothers	415.8	13
—	8	Bear, Stearns	403.9	3
—	9	Donaldson, Lufkin & Jenrette	25.0	1
7	10	Kidder Peabody	20.0	2
		Total market volume	$16,212.3	82

Source: *Institutional Investor*, February 1992. This copyrighted material is reprinted with permission from Institutional Investor, Inc., 488 Madison Ave., New York, NY 10022.

Table 2.8
International Bonds

This table marks international bond underwriters in the broadest sense. It includes all Euromarket deals, as well as "foreign" bonds syndicated in domestic markets outside an issuer's home country.

1990	1991		$ Volume (millions)	No. of Issues
1	1	Nomura Int'l. Group	$25,905.8	166
2	2	Credit Suisse/CSFB Groupe	21,950.4	124
5	3	Daiwa Securities	19,000.0	130
4	4	Deutsche Bank	15,603.3	91
13	5	Goldman Sachs	14,472.9	84
11	6	Paribas	12,437.6	61
12	7	Merrill Lynch	12,323.4	51
13	8	Union Bank of Switzerland	12,206.2	86
20	9	Morgan Stanley	12,188.9	29
7	10	Swiss Bank Corp.	12,140.3	89
10	11	Yamaichi Securities	11,578.4	96
9	12	Nikko Securities	10,589.9	93
8	13	Salomon Brothers	7,956.7	26
6	14	J.P. Morgan	7,644.8	39
16	15	S.G. Warburg Group	7,302.1	34
19	16	Credit Lyonnais	6,774.8	33
14	17	Industrial Bank of Japan	5,562.5	27
15	18	Credit Commercial de France	5,373.8	21
31	19	Dresdner Bank	5,144.5	33
22	20	Hambros Bank	4,440.4	52
46	21	Scotio McLeod	3,133.2	13
—	22	Wood Gundy	3,115.5	23
33	23	Barclays Bank	3,005.2	18
23	24	Baring Brothers	2,980.7	19
37	25	Banque Nationale de Paris	2,739.8	15
		Total market volume	$299,809.0	2,184

Table 2.9
International Equities

1990	1991		$ Volume (millions)	No. of Tranches
1	1	Goldman Sachs	$4,868.6	51
8	2	S.G. Warburg Group	2,636.3	13
2	3	Credit Suisse/CSFB Groupe	2,009.7	37
9	4	Salomon Brothers	1,403.4	27
4	5	Merrill Lynch	1,137.1	17
16	6	Salomon Brothers	995.6	12
5	7	Morgan Stanley	976.2	16
3	8	Nomura Int'l. Group	541.1	3
12	9	Paribas	401.2	5
20	10	Daiwa Securities	353.8	3
—	11	Barclays de Zoete Wedd	259.4	3
7	12	Skandinaviska Enskilda Group	243.9	1
—	13	Deutsche Bank	204.8	3
10	14	PaineWebber	192.1	21
19	15	Wood Gundy	182.9	2
—	16	Donaldson, Lufkin & Jenrette	179.0	5
17	17	Baring Brothers	172.6	3
—	18	National Westminster	167.1	3
22	19	Dresdner Bank	154.8	2
—	20	Schwartauer Werke	143.4	1
—	21	Kidder Peabody	139.6	8
—	22	Westdeutsche Landesbank	95.9	1
—	23	Hoare Govett	91.7	1
—	24	Credit Lyonnais	89.8	3
—	25	RBC Dominion	87.3	2
		Total market volume	$18,881.3	282

Source: *Institutional Investor*, February 1992. This copyrighted material is reprinted with permission from Institutional Investor, Inc., 488 Madison Ave., New York, NY 10022.

Table 2.10
Eurobonds

This is the largest sector of the international bond market. The ranking is based on deals done by international syndicates with significant portions sold in two or more countries other than the country of the currency in which the issue is denominated. Global bond issues have not been included in this table.

1990	1991		$ Volume (millions)	No. of Issues
1	1	Nomura Int'l. Group	$21,327.8	121
4	2	Daiwa Securities	16,093.4	99
2	3	Credit Suisse/CSFB Groupe	14,708.6	60
3	4	Deutsche Bank	14,313.9	78
9	5	Paribas	10,994.5	28
8	6	Yamaichi Securities	10,168.1	74
6	7	Nikko Securities	9,756.9	73
15	8	Goldman Sachs	9,724.3	51
23	9	Morgan Stanley	9,272.9	17
20	10	Swiss Bank Corp.	7,942.7	36
7	11	Union Bank of Switzerland	6,954.8	33
10	12	Merrill Lynch	6,765.4	34
14	13	S.G. Warburg Group	6,633.5	28
5	14	J.P. Morgan	6,553.2	35
18	15	Credit Lyonnais	6,083.4	24
11	16	Credit Commercial de France	5,373.8	21
12	17	Industrial Bank of Japan	5,167.4	23
29	18	Dresdner Bank	5,050.9	31
21	19	Hambros Bank	5,123.6	51
42	20	Wood Gundy	2,840.9	22
41	21	ABN–Amro Bank	2,761.2	14
13	22	Salomon Brothers	2,675.7	14
30	23	Barclays Bank	2,638.2	16
22	24	Baring Brothers	2,588.9	16
35	25	Societe Generale	2,495.2	18
		Total market volume	$230,790.5	1,322

Source: *Institutional Investor*, February 1992. This copyrighted material is reprinted with permission from Institutional Investor, Inc., 488 Madison Ave., New York, NY 10022.

Table 2.11
International Loans and Note–Issuance Facilities

1990	1991		$ Volume (millions)	No. of Issues
1	1	Citicorp	$70,093.6	91
5	2	J.P. Morgan	47,157.3	72
10	3	Chemical Banking Corp.	35,490.0	32
6	4	Barclays Bank	33,032.4	57
2	5	First Chicago	33,001.3	85
4	6	Bank of America	28,733.2	74
7	7	Manufacturers Hanover	28,351.5	80
18	8	Credit Suisse/CSFB Groupe	25,393.6	41
3	9	National Westminster	24,711.9	39
—	10	Fuji Bank	23,565.5	32
9	11	Chase Manhattan	22,291.8	79
48	12	ABN–Amro Bank	21,957.0	37
12	13	Bankers Trust	21,195.4	63
—	14	Credit Lyonnais	20,623.2	28
20	15	Union Bank of Switzerland	18,972.1	32
23	16	Sanwa Bank	15,305.4	41
14	17	Sumitomo Bank	14,931.7	29
11	18	Swiss Bank Corp.	14,779.4	53
36	19	Bank of Nova Scotia	14,506.0	16
45	20	NCNB Corp.	12,490.0	8
35	21	Deutsche Bank	12,476.1	20
8	22	Toronto Dominion Bank	12,052.0	13
13	23	Midland Bank	11,570.8	16
22	24	CIBC	10,182.0	24
16	25	Continental Bank	9,374.7	16
		Total market volume	$320,509.3	1,391

Source: *Institutional Investor*, February 1992. This copyrighted material is reprinted with permission from Institutional Investor, Inc., 488 Madison Ave., New York, NY 10022.

Table 2.12
The Municipal Underwriting Leaders

A summary of the top firms according to full credit to lead manager for publicly offered long–term new issues of $5 million or more.

1990	1991		$ Volume (millions)	No. of Issues
2	1	Goldman Sachs	$21,039.0	257
1	2	Merrill Lynch	16,209.4	281
5	3	Lehman Brothers	10,688.1	211
3	4	First Boston	10,409.8	117
4	5	Smith Barney, Harris Upham	10,091.4	194
7	6	Bear, Stearns	7,279.2	83
6	7	PaineWebber	6,295.0	146
8	8	Prudential Securities	5,363.2	178
9	9	Morgan Stanley	4,935.5	72
13	10	J.P. Morgan Securities	3,650.4	39
10	11	Bank of America	3,354.3	49
12	12	Dean Witter Reynolds	3,229.4	83
16	13	Kidder Peabody	3,128.6	87
15	14	Dillon Read	2,825.0	33
14	15	Donaldson, Lufkin & Jenrette	2,254.9	56
17	16	Kemper Securites	1,844.1	86
21	17	First Chicago Capital Markets	1,812.2	46
25	18	A. G. Edwards & Sons	1,661.0	100
18	19	George K. Baum	1,646.6	70
36	20	Alex, Brown & Sons	1,565.3	38
19	21	BT Securities	1,555.0	17
33	22	Rauscher Pierce Refsnes	1,475.2	76
22	23	Stone & Youngberg	1,259.5	59
20	24	John Nuveen	1,220.0	49
23	25	Chemical Securities	1,202.2	27
		Total market volume	$158,384.5	4,450

Source: *Institutional Investor*, February 1992. This copyrighted material is reprinted with permission from Institutional Investor, Inc., 488 Madison Ave., New York, NY 10022.

Table 2.13
Long–Term Negotiated Issues

1990	1991		$ Volume (millions)	No. of Issues
1	1	Goldman Sachs	$17,011.1	220
2	2	Merrill Lynch	12,810.6	170
4	3	Smith Barney, Harris Upham	9,266.1	161
6	4	Lehman Brothers	8,215.7	138
3	5	First Boston	8,040.1	94
7	6	Bear, Stearns	5,957.1	63
5	7	PaineWebber	5,877.6	134
8	8	Morgan Stanley	3,816.6	59
9	9	Prudential Securities	3,069.5	83
14	10	Dean Witter Reynolds	2,499.8	40
11	11	J.P. Morgan Securities	2,498.1	19
10	12	Donaldson, Lufkin & Jenrette	2,215.2	55
12	13	Kidder Peabody	2,183.9	60
13	14	Dillon Read	1,964.5	25
20	15	A. G. Edwards & Sons	1,566.4	91
15	16	George K. Baum	1,562.1	62
30	17	Alex, Brown & Sons	1,513.5	34
19	18	First Chicago Capital Markets	1,427.2	35
22	19	Kemper Securites	1,264.3	52
17	20	Stone & Youngberg	1,208.4	55
16	21	John Nuveen	1,206.2	47
31	22	Rauscher Pierce Refsnes	1,091.7	55
49	23	RRZ Public Markets	1,072.3	26
21	24	Piper Jaffray & Hopwood	1,017.1	48
28	25	Wheat First Butcher & Singer	996.1	56
		Total market volume	$122,573.1	3,161

Source: *Institutional Investor*, February 1992. This copyrighted material is reprinted with permission from Institutional Investor, Inc., 488 Madison Ave., New York, NY 10022.

Table 2.14
Long–Term Competitive Issues

1990	1991		$ Volume (millions)	No. of Issues
6	1	Goldman Sachs	$4,027.8	37
2	2	Merrill Lynch	3,398.8	111
1	3	Bank of America	3,085.5	40
4	4	Lehman Brothers	2,472.3	73
7	5	First Boston	2,369.7	23
3	6	Prudential Securities	2,293.7	95
15	7	Bear, Stearns	1,322.1	20
17	8	J.P. Morgan Securities	1,152.3	20
19	9	Morgan Stanley	1,118.9	13
8	10	BT Securities	1,031.7	9
42	11	Kidder Peabody	944.7	27
33	12	Dillon Read	860.5	8
11	13	Smith Barney, Harris Upham	815.3	33
12	14	Chemical Securities	752.1	16
10	15	Dean Witter Reynolds	729.7	43
9	16	Kemper Securites	579.8	34
24	17	Roosevelt & Cross	544.3	60
14	18	Clayton Brown	521.8	40
18	19	Wachovia	515.3	34
5	20	Chase Securities	458.4	6
16	21	PaineWebber	417.4	12
21	22	First Chicago Capital Markets	385.0	11
26	23	Rauscher Pierce Refsnes	383.5	21
20	24	Harris Trust & Savings	310.8	30
22	25	Griffin, Kubik, Stephens & Thompson	297.2	28
		Total market volume	$35,811.4	1,289

Table 2.15
Taxable Municipal Issues

1990	1991		$ Volume (millions)	No. of Issues
9	1	Goldman Sachs	$1,381.5	8
30	2	Lehman Brothers	334.9	7
2	3	PaineWebber	322.1	3
4	4	Merrill Lynch	214.9	5
7	5	George K. Baum	134.4	4
22	6	Newman & Associates	125.1	6
8	7	Morgan Keegan	119.2	4
10	8	Smith Barney, Harris Upham	95.1	2
—	9	Prager, McCarthy & Lewis	95.0	2
3	10	Bear, Stearns	91.2	4
6	11	First Interstate Bank, Denver	85.3	2
—	12	William R. Hough	58.6	2
—	13	Grisby Brandford Powell	54.4	1
—	14	WR Lazard	52.1	1
—	15	BancOne Capital	47.0	6
		Total market volume	$3,592.0	93

Source: *Institutional Investor*, February 1992. This copyrighted material is reprinted with permission from Institutional Investor, Inc., 488 Madison Ave., New York, NY 10022.

Table 2.16
Long–Term General Obligation Issues

1990	1991		$ Volume (millions)	No. of Issues
2	1	Goldman Sachs	$4,453.4	31
1	2	Merrill Lynch	4,416.6	102
4	3	First Boston	3,602.0	27
5	4	Lehman Brothers	3,400.4	66
9	5	Bear, Stearns	3,044.9	21
3	6	Bank of America	2,457.3	22
35	7	J.P. Morgan Securities	2,322.0	17
8	8	Smith Barney, Harris Upham	2,303.5	41
6	9	Prudential Securities	1,748.3	80
18	10	BT Securities	1,131.7	10
11	11	First Chicago Capital Markets	1,131.4	15
10	12	Kemper Securites	1,073.4	55
33	13	Rauscher Pierce Refsnes	993.8	47
27	14	Morgan Stanley	803.8	11
22	15	A.G. Edwards & Sons	788.5	43
51	16	Alex, Brown & Sons	754.0	10
24	17	Dillon Read	702.6	4
101	18	Kidder Peabody	686.3	26
12	19	Chemical Securities	673.5	20
15	20	Dean Witter Reynolds	663.8	39
14	21	PaineWebber	647.2	20
17	22	Wachovia	568.4	35
31	23	Roosevelt & Cross	555.6	60
19	24	Clayton Brown	476.6	39
172	25	BancOne Capital	468.6	16
		Total market volume	$51,707.3	1,751

Source: *Institutional Investor*, February 1992. This copyrighted material is reprinted with permission from Institutional Investor, Inc., 488 Madison Ave., New York, NY 10022.

Table 2.17
Negotiated Issues: Education

1990	1991		$ Volume (millions)	No. of Issues
4	1	J.P. Morgan Securities	$784.8	7
26	2	Goldman Sachs	730.2	8
1	3	Morgan Stanley	626.3	7
7	4	Prudential Securities	576.9	16
6	5	Merrill Lynch	570.1	11
28	6	Rauscher Pierce Refsnes	546.5	25
5	7	Piper, Jaffray & Hopwood	500.7	21
13	8	Kemper Securites	486.1	17
16	9	Lehman Brothers	475.2	20
11	10	A.G. Edwards & Sons	453.7	27
24	11	First Boston	411.5	5
18	12	Hopper Soliday	365.4	29
—	13	BT Securities	360.1	4
15	14	Dain Bosworth	331.1	19
12	15	Smith Barney, Harris Upham	319.1	15
		Total market volume	$13,430.3	628

Source: *Institutional Investor*, February 1992. This copyrighted material is reprinted with permission from Institutional Investor, Inc., 488 Madison Ave., New York, NY 10022.

Table 2.18
Negotiated Issues: Holding

1990	1991		$ Volume (millions)	No. of Issues
1	1	Goldman Sachs	$1,984.7	69
2	2	Merrill Lynch	1,827.0	43
5	3	Lehman Brothers	1,259.7	23
3	4	PaineWebber	1,162.1	32
4	5	Bear, Stearns	1,074.1	27
11	6	George K. Baum	664.9	20
6	7	First Boston	566.0	8
10	8	Dean Witter Reynolds	474.2	6
7	9	Donaldson, Lufkin & Jenrette	372.7	13
18	10	Newman & Associates	262.2	18
8	11	Smith Barney, Harris Upham	243.2	10
17	12	Morgan Keegan	231.2	9
22	13	William R. Hough	230.7	10
9	14	First Interstate Bank, Denver	197.9	5
19	15	Stifel Nicolaus	187.0	3
		Total market volume	$12,776.7	419

Source: *Institutional Investor*, February 1992. This copyrighted material is reprinted with permission from Institutional Investor, Inc., 488 Madison Ave., New York, NY 10022.

Table 2.19
Negotiated Issues: Electric & Public Power

1990	1991		$ Volume (millions)	No. of Issues
1	1	Goldman Sachs	$2,366.3	19
3	2	Smith Barney, Harris Upham	1,301.7	9
2	3	First Boston	991.0	5
5	4	Merrill Lynch	755.7	6
7	5	PaineWebber	623.8	4
4	6	Lehman Brothers	487.6	5
—	7	Donaldson, Lufkin & Jenrette	410.2	7
8	8	Morgan Stanley	394.4	4
—	9	Bear, Stearns	200.0	1
—	10	Dean Witter Reynolds	103.9	2
—	11	Frazer Lanier	65.8	1
—	12	George K. Baum	54.9	2
6	13	John Nuveen	36.8	2
—	14	Southeastern Capital	22.1	1
—	15	D.A. Davidson	21.7	1
		Total market volume	$7,946.4	75

Source: *Institutional Investor*, February 1992. This copyrighted material is reprinted with permission from Institutional Investor, Inc., 488 Madison Ave., New York, NY 10022.

Table 2.20
Negotiated Issues: Health Care

1990	1991		$ Volume (millions)	No. of Issues
1	1	Merrill Lynch	$1,704.5	39
3	2	Goldman Sachs	1,562.5	32
2	3	First Boston	1,451.5	33
6	4	Lehman Brothers	1,207.2	33
9	5	Kidder Peabody	813.6	17
4	6	PaineWebber	801.6	18
7	7	Ziegler Securities	769.0	31
8	8	John Nuveen	735.5	21
16	9	Dillon Read	493.8	10
14	10	Morgan Stanley	493.4	11
13	11	Smith Barney, Harris Upham	487.9	10
25	12	Donaldson, Lufkin & Jenrette	379.4	11
15	13	Cain Brothers Shattuck	310.1	8
20	14	Alex, Brown & Sons	288.1	7
5	15	J.P. Morgan Securities	287.8	4
		Total market volume	$15,789.2	447

Source: *Institutional Investor*, February 1992. This copyrighted material is reprinted with permission from Institutional Investor, Inc., 488 Madison Ave., New York, NY 10022.

Table 2.21
Negotiated Issues: Transportation

1990	1991		$ Volume (millions)	No. of Issues
1	1	Merrill Lynch	$2,544.4	5
4	2	Goldman Sachs	1,659.5	12
3	3	Dillon Read	1,033.1	6
8	4	First Boston	1,024.3	7
2	5	Bear, Stearns	862.7	5
—	6	Dean Witter Reynolds	543.2	2
—	7	RRZ Public Markets	540.9	2
19	8	Prudential Securities	356.2	2
9	9	Donaldson, Lufkin & Jenrette	331.7	2
7	10	PaineWebber	320.1	5
6	11	Smith Barney, Harris Upham	307.5	6
30	12	William R. Hough	86.3	2
—	13	Alex, Brown & Sons	78.7	4
10	14	Lehman Brothers	65.9	1
—	15	Prager, McCarthy & Lewis	56.0	1
		Total market volume	$10,191.7	95

Source: *Institutional Investor*, February 1992. This copyrighted material is reprinted with permission from Institutional Investor, Inc., 488 Madison Ave., New York, NY 10022.

Table 2.22
Negotiated Issues: Water, Sewer & Gas

1990	1991		$ Volume (millions)	No. of Issues
1	1	Smith Barney, Harris Upham	$1,857.9	19
9	2	First Boston	1,462.7	17
3	3	Goldman Sachs	904.9	6
8	4	PaineWebber	841.9	17
2	5	Merrill Lynch	614.9	9
—	6	Alex, Brown & Sons	544.9	7
53	7	Bear, Stearns	525.0	2
4	8	Kidder Peabody	516.2	11
11	9	Prudential Securities	512.2	13
—	10	Morgan Stanley	467.3	4
18	11	A.G. Edwards & Sons	263.2	12
46	12	Dean Witter Reynolds	252.4	5
20	13	Wheat First Butcher & Singer	249.7	8
7	14	Stone & Youngberg	224.0	8
63	15	First Chicago Capital Markets	200.0	1
		Total market volume	$11,852.6	293

Source: *Institutional Investor*, February 1992. This copyrighted material is reprinted with permission from Institutional Investor, Inc., 488 Madison Ave., New York, NY 10022.

Table 2.23
Income Statements as Percent of Total Revenues

	Merrill Lynch 12/31/92	Paine– Webber 12/31/92	Bear, Stearns 6/30/92
Revenues:			
Commissions	18%	24%	14%
Interest and Dividends	43	33	37
Principal Transactions	16	22	36
Investment Banking	11	11	12
Other	12	10	1
Total Revenues:	100%	100%	100%
Interest Expense	36	26	31
Net Revenues:	64%	74%	69%
Non–Interest Expenses:			
Compensation and Benefits	33%	43%	34%
Occupancy and Equipment Rental	6	9	6
Brokerage, Clearing, and Exchange Fees	2	10	2
Other	11	10	7
Total Non–Interest Expenses	52%	64%	50%
Earnings Before Income Taxes	12%	10%	19%
Income Taxes	5%	4%	8%
Net Earnings	7%	6%	11%

Raw data from annual reports.
Merrill Lynch earnings exclude adjustment for changes in accounting principles.

Table 2.24
Balance Sheets as a Percentage of Total Assets

	Merrill Lynch 12/31/92	Paine–Webber 12/31/92	Bear, Stearns 6/30/92
Assets:			
Cash and Equivalences	1%	1%	0%
Cash Segregated Under Regulation	3	2	5
Securities Inventories	30	34	27
Resale Agreements	23	24	36
Receivables:			
Customers, Net	10	11	8
Brokers and Dealers	3	25	1
Interest and Other	2	1	0
Other Investments	25	0	21
Fixed Assets, Net	1	1	0
Other Assets	2	1	2
Total Assets	100%	100%	100%
Liabilities and Stockholders' Equity:			
Short–Term Borrowing	18%	5%	8%
Payable to Brokers and Dealers	1	8	4
Payable to Clients	10	9	21
Securities Sold but Not Yet Purchased	14	18	13
Repurchase Agreements	30	48	43
Other Liabilities	13	4	6
Long–Term Borrowing	10	4	2
Stockholders' Equity	4	4	3
Total	100%	100%	100%

Raw data from annual reports.

II

Section Two

3

Corporate Finance: Underwriting and Syndication

Overview

Primary market making is the quintessential function of investment banking. As the primary market maker, the investment bank acts as an intermediary between a business or government enterprise that requires financing and persons or institutions that have funds to invest. The entity in need of financing will issue securities and, consequently, is called the issuer. The parties with funds to invest are called investors. The investment bank serves three distinct but related functions in this process: origination, underwriting, and distribution. Origination involves the development and registration of the securities offering. Underwriting involves the purchase of the securities from the issuer by the underwriting syndicate for subsequent sale to the public. Distribution involves the final sale of the securities to the public.

The precise role of the investment bank in origination, underwriting, and distribution depends on a number of factors. The first is the type of issuer involved. The issuer could be a corporation, the U.S. Treasury, a government agency, or a municipality. In addition, the issue could involve some form of beneficial or ownership trust. Such trusts are sometimes used to repackage securities in order to alter their investment characteristics. Second, the securities may be issued in the United States in the traditional domestic markets and may or may not employ a shelf registration; may be issued offshore and qualify for exemption from registration requirements; or may be issued within the United States but make use of an exemptive rule for registration. Third, the securities might have a maturity short enough to be exempt from registration requirements, as does most commercial paper.

In this chapter and the next, we look at the role of investment banks in making primary markets. This chapter focuses on the role of investment banks in financing the corporate sector; the next chapter focuses on the public sector. It is important to note that commercial banks, through securities subsidiaries, also participate in certain of these financings, and their involvement is expanding. We make no distinction between investment banks and commercial banks in this regard. We assume throughout this book that the reader possesses a reasonable product knowledge from a study of investments and/or portfolio analysis. Nevertheless, we do provide a brief description of many products, particularly those that are less well understood.

Corporate Finance

Corporations issue two fundamentally different types of securities in an effort to achieve the financing that they require to fund their operations: equity and debt. Forms of equity include common and preferred stock. Forms of debt include mortgage bonds, debentures or notes, and commercial paper. There are an amazing number of variants on both of these basic forms, but that is not the subject of this chapter.

Common stock represents an ownership interest in a corporation. The owners of common stock are called **stockholders**, or **shareholders**; these terms are used interchangeably. Common stock represents a residual claim on the assets of a corporation—that is, the rights of all other claimants supersede those of the shareholders. For example, when a firm's management enters into a debtor/creditor relationship, it does so on behalf of the firm's owners. Thus, the shareholders are committed to repay all creditors in full *with interest* before the shareholders are entitled to anything. This places the common shareholders last on the list of those who hold a claim against the assets of the corporation.

In exchange for their prior claim on the assets of the firm, **debtholders** accept a stated (or formula–determined) return, called interest, on their investment and do not participate in the performance of the firm beyond this contractually agreed–upon amount. Under U.S. law, the interest paid to debtholders is deductible from corporate income before the computation of corporate income taxes. Only the profits remaining after taxes, if any, belong to the equity holders.

Preferred stock is something of an oddity. It occupies a niche somewhere between bond–type debt and common stock. Like debt, preferred stock periodically pays a fixed, or formula–determined, amount, called a preferred stock dividend, and preferred stockholders do not generally participate in the profits of the firm beyond this stated amount. Like common stock, the sums paid to preferred shareholders are paid out of after–tax profits. Reinforcing the idea of preferred stock as occupying a niche between debt and equity, preferred stock usually has a perpetual life, like common stock, but is often callable, like bonds. Also, the claims of the preferred shareholders, in the event of a liquidation of the firm, come before those of the common shareholders but after those of the debtholders.

Because of tax asymmetries between the treatments of debt and equity financing and the increased need for equity capital in the 1990s, preferred stock has become a fertile ground for financial engineers. Indeed, the number of variants of preferred stock that have emerged in recent years is mind–boggling. The issuances of these equity/debt hybrids are very often undertaken to exploit special situations, and they often involve a negotiation between the issuer and a small group of investors. Our goal in this chapter is neither to explore tax arbitrage strategies employing preferred stock nor to examine the role of the financial engineer in designing special–purpose securities. Nevertheless, it is important to know that investment banks are heavily involved in both of these activities. We take this issue up again in our discussions of product innovation and financial engineering in Chapters 8 and 9. For now, we concentrate on the role of the investment banker in intermediating between issuers and investors.

Public Offerings versus Private Placements

There are two fundamental ways for an investment bank to intermediate between issuers and investors. These are a **public offering** and a **private placement**. In a public offering, securities that are issued are offered for sale to the public investor. In a private placement, the securities are placed, via negotiations, in the hands of a small group of sophisticated, usually institutional, investors.

Public offerings of securities issued by corporations within the United States for sale to American investors must be registered with the **Securities and Exchange Commission** (SEC), and the offering procedure must satisfy a number of well–defined criteria. Foreign securities issued in the United States for sale to American investors must also be registered with the SEC. Exceptions to the registration requirement include securities having a maturity of 270 days or less, securities with a small number of holders, certain railroad securities, and so on. The SEC is the principal, but not the only, regulating agency of the securities industry. For example, securities issued in the United States must, in general, be registered with each state in which the securities will be offered for sale. These state registration requirements are called **blue–sky laws**.

The public offering route, with its tedious registration and offering criteria, is a complex and time–consuming undertaking and can, if not done properly, expose the corporate officers and directors to financial and even criminal liability. For these reasons, it is routine for such issuers to employ the services of an experienced investment bank to perform due diligence and to help the company and its lawyers understand what information investors want and need to make a reasonable investment decision. This is the **origination** phase. Following acceptance of the securities by the SEC, the investment banker participates once again, this time in the capacities of **underwriter** and **distributor**. The downside, for the issuer, is that the expertise and services of investment bankers do not come cheap. Thus, the net proceeds to the issuer are decreased (i.e., the cost of financing is increased) by the amount of the fees charged by the investment bank and associated costs. From the issuer's perspective, these costs are called **flotation costs**.

When a firm with no public financial history or experience in the public capital markets wants to offer securities to the public for the first time, the offering is called an **initial public offering** or **IPO**. When a firm with existing publicly traded securities brings out additional securities, the issuance constitutes a **public offering**.[1] IPOs present a far greater challenge to an investment bank than do public offerings, and this

---

[1] If the issuance involves securities identical to existing securities (such as new common stock that is identical to existing common stock), the offering is sometimes called a **seasoned public offering**.

will generally be reflected in the cost to the issuer. We will return to this point in a later section of this chapter.

Private placements are a much simpler affair and can work to the advantage of both the issuer and the investor. Large sophisticated investors do not need the government protection that the securities laws are intended to provide for investors. The thinking is, essentially, that these sophisticated investors have the prerequisite skills and access to sufficient information so that the registration of the securities is superfluous. Thus, registration is not required for privately placed issues.

The Public Offering Process

The public offering process is complex. We will describe it in the context of an IPO. The same basic steps are involved in a public offering, but the pricing and investigative aspects are somewhat less onerous.

As a first step, the investment bank negotiates a mandate to "do the deal" and prepares the issuance to the satisfaction of the SEC.[2] As noted earlier, this part of the process is called origination. (Within the investment bank, this function would be handled by the corporate finance group working within the capital markets division.) The process involves an investigation of the issuer, preparation and filing of required documents, and the organization of an underwriting syndicate.

The next phase is underwriting proper. In the underwriting phase, the investment banker negotiates, on behalf of an underwriting syndicate, with the issuer for (1) an **offering price** range for the securities and (2) the size of the issuance. They must also negotiate the **underwriting spread**—i.e., the difference between the offering price to the public and the proceeds to the issuer. This is also known as the **gross spread** or **underwriting discount**. At this stage, neither the offering price nor underwriting spread is binding. These terms are not set until the actual pricing of the securities.

The final phase is the distribution. Here, an underwriting syndicate and an affiliated selling group distribute the securities to the investing

---

[2] We are using the term "investment banker" to include any employee of an investment bank, including lawyers, analysts, researchers, underwriters, consultants, and so on.

public. Together, the underwriting syndicate and the selling group constitute the **distribution syndicate**. Their goal is to distribute—i.e., sell—the securities as quickly as possible. We will examine each of these investment banking functions in turn.

Origination

Investment banking, particularly in the area of primary market making, has long been a very relationship–oriented business.[3] Corporations establish a relationship with an investment bank and, barring an unsatisfactory outcome, will tend to use the same investment bank each time they have a new securities issue to develop. It is also typical that, as part of this relationship, the preparation of the issuance, the actual underwriting, and distribution are handled by the same investment bank.

This has changed somewhat in recent years—in part due to the advent of shelf registration, which will be discussed later. Today, the preparation of securities for issuance and the subsequent underwriting and distribution of those securities may not be as strongly linked. For example, in debt markets, it is now quite common for one investment bank to be employed to prepare the issuance, and, after acceptance of the securities by the SEC, for the issuer to put the underwriting up for competitive bidding by underwriting syndicates. The best bid would usually be awarded the underwriting. The separation of issuance preparation from underwriting and distribution allows the issuer to pit one underwriting syndicate against another and, not surprisingly, to significantly reduce its flotation costs. Indeed, since the advent of shelf registration, flotation costs have declined considerably.

Preparation of the issuance is still a very relationship–driven business that requires the investment banker to have detailed knowledge of the firm and its management. This kind of knowledge takes time and considerable energy to develop. Once it has been developed and an appropriate rapport has been established, it is unlikely that management would want to start the process over if it is not necessary to do so. Thus, relationship banking remains strong in the preparation phase of an

---

[3] The ability of investment banks to exploit client relationships has declined considerably over the last 10 years, but the importance of client relationships should not be underestimated.

issuance. Of course, each investment bank must still cultivate new clients on an ongoing basis, and for this purpose investment banks have new–business development groups within each investment banking area. These groups frequently put feelers out to other shops' clients in an effort to attract the business of those corporations.

There are a number of reasons that corporations come to investment bankers for assistance in issuing securities. The most obvious reason is to obtain capital—usually to finance growth. But there can be a variety of other reasons, and any mix of these is possible as well. For example, it may be that a privately held firm has grown up, and its founders have decided that they want to cash out, in whole or in part. Going public is one way to do that. Once the firm's stock is publicly traded, the original owners' stock becomes, in essence, a currency—to be sold as required to finance other activities. Another reason to tap the capital market is to acquire capital to effect a transition of ownership and control—as is typical in the case of the sale of junk bonds to finance a leveraged buyout. Still another reason is simply to alter the **capital structure**—i.e., the debt/equity capital ratio. For example, it is sometimes considered advantageous to **leverage up** the firm. This means increasing the ratio of debt to equity within the capital structure. Leveraging up is often considered desirable when earnings growth looks very strong and earnings projections seem reliable. At other times—such as after a leveraged buyout, when the debt load is often very heavy—the goal is to **leverage down**. Leveraging down means reducing the firm's debt/equity ratio.

There are 1,000 different ways for a relationship between an investment banker and a firm to develop. One possible scenario, particularly for a smaller firm whose financial managers often lack experience in capital structure theory and/or practice, is for the corporation and the investment bank to review the history of the firm, the firm's financial performance, and the status of ownership and control. Management then addresses its plans for the firm's future—earnings projections, production and sales targets, control of the firm, and so on. Where ownership and control are concentrated in the hands of a few people, there is often a strong desire on the part of the owners to retain control—a goal that is often unrealistic. In any case, after a preliminary assessment of the situation and general agreement on management's objectives, the investment bankers formulate a **preliminary financing**

plan. This will typically involve a number of financing alternatives, with associated scenarios and the accompanying pros and cons of each. Also, the corporation might be presented with a number of different scenarios that accomplish the same end result. For example, the bankers might suggest the sale of five–year fixed–rate notes; but the same five–year fixed–rate debt financing might be achieved by the sale of five–year floating–rate notes converted to five–year fixed–rate debt with the aid of a five–year fixed–for–floating interest rate swap. A similar result might be achieved with the sale of six–month commercial paper, with rollovers every six months for five years, again coupled with a five–year fixed–for–floating interest rate swap.

For reasons that are peculiar to the individual corporation, the investment bankers may suggest any of a wide assortment of financing strategies using instruments, or variants of instruments, that did not even exist a few years ago. For example, they might suggest some form of adjustable–rate preferred stock, or floating–rate debt with an **interest rate cap** (i.e., an upper limit on the payout), or floating–rate debt with a **trailing floor** (i.e., a changing lower limit on the payout), or debt with a commodity, equity, or exchange rate component, and so on. Our purpose in this chapter is not to explore these new strategies or their purposes, but rather to note that the **corporate finance desk** (which routinely handles corporate issuances) must work closely with the **derivative instruments** group, which makes markets in such things as interest rate swaps and interest rate caps and floors. And it must work closely with the **structured products** or **structured finance** group, which designs new financial instruments and variants for special purposes. All of this, by our early definition, is captured under the title "financial engineering."

In addition to structuring a solution to management's stated needs, the investment banks must also consider the investor appeal of the securities that will be issued. After all, if investors find the securities unattractive, the offering will fail. Thus, the investment banker must consider both the issuer's needs and the investors' requirements. Sometimes, as part of the financial engineering process, the investment banker will structure a financing which has one set of characteristics for the issuer and a different set of characteristics for the investors. This is made possible by placing an intermediary between the issuer and the investor. This intermediary adds features to the instrument. For now, however, we shall simply accept that the investment bankers offer a menu of financing alternatives, and the firm's management and the investment bank negotiate a final selection. The formal process of preparing the issuance then begins.

Preparation of the issuance involves a number of steps. First, the investment banker must perform a very thorough investigation of the issuer. This is called a **due diligence** investigation. Second, a **preliminary filing** with the SEC may be required (we will assume that it is). Third, after addressing the concerns of the SEC, a **preliminary prospectus** is prepared. Then, a second and (one hopes) **final filing** with the SEC is made. At this point, the origination phase is complete. The most important component of origination is the due diligence investigation. Given its importance, it is worth our effort to focus some specific attention on this activity.

The Due Diligence Investigation

The Securities Act of 1933 was enlightened legislation in the sense that it sought to *regulate by information*. That is, rather than promulgate absurd rules that would dictate which firms could offer their securities to the public and which could not, Congress chose to leave that decision to the public investor. However, so that the investor can make an informed decision, the Act requires that a firm offering its securities to the public make a reasonable effort to disclose to potential investors all material information or be held liable for its absence. The responsibility for the due diligence investigation, together with financial liability, extends to the underwriters as well.

Primary responsibility for the due diligence investigation generally falls on the investment bank that will subsequently manage the underwriting syndicate. This firm is referred to as the **lead underwriter**, the **lead manager**, or the **book-running manager**. Often, one or more additional investment bank will share some deal management responsibilities. In these cases, they are referred to as **co-managers**. We will return to the structure of an underwriting syndicate later.

The potential liability associated with the due diligence investigation provides a powerful motivation for investment bankers to dig deep and ferret out all material information. Accountants and lawyers review in minute detail the financial statements and practices of the firm going back at least five years. The audited statements, together with the accountants' opinion letters, constitute an integral part of the process. If appropriate or warranted, the investment bank also does a thorough background check on all members of senior management. There may also be one or more lengthy management interviews by the underwriter's counsel, and anything suspect is researched and verified.

The disclosure of information required in the issuing of securities often results in a conflict between the investment bankers and the issuer's management, who are often the original owners—particularly in the case of an IPO. The managers, who built the business and never before had to account to anyone but themselves (except perhaps the Internal Revenue Service), suddenly find that they are required to disclose a great deal of information—information that they consider confidential and competitively sensitive. Contributing to this adversarial relationship is a powerful desire on the part of corporate management to project the most positive image and the most promising future possible for the corporation. Indeed, the prospectus, which will disclose all relevant information, is in large part a promotional document. The investment banker, always conscious of his responsibilities to present all material information in a fashion that is never misleading, is inclined to downplay the rosy projections and the positive image. If anything, there is a tendency to prepare documents that sound less than enthusiastic. This helps ensure that no investor can later bring a charge of misrepresentation. Supporting this position is the law, which prohibits revenue, sales, and profit projections in the prospectus of a public offering.

The role of the investment banker in this process is paradoxical. On the one hand, the investment banker represents the firm and is being paid by the firm, and needs to present the firm in the most favorable light possible to preserve the investment bank's relationship with the firm. On the other hand, the bank is ever conscious of its legal responsibilities and the potential liabilities for both the bank and the firm from misstatements of fact, misrepresentation, and absence of material information.

Technically, the law requires that the investment bank perform a "reasonable investigation" of the issuer or be held responsible for the lack thereof. The exact meaning of this provision is not entirely clear. In the early days, the wording was enforced quite literally, and the investment bank was held liable for any misrepresentations, misstatements, and absences of material information irrespective of how the errors occurred. But in recent years the courts have taken a somewhat more lenient position. Now, the investment bank is held harmless if it can show that it conducted a thorough investigation, and as a consequence of this investigation, it had reason to believe that the registration statements were accurate and complete. For example, the argument that management made false representations to the underwriter's counsel, and there were no reasons to suspect that such representations were false, could relieve the investment bank of liability. The line between what is "reasonably believed to be true" and what is simply a shoddy due diligence investigation is often cloudy, and undoubtedly this will continue to be a source of some friction between underwriters and shareholders.

SEC Filing Process

The next step in the process is to file the appropriate documents with the SEC to begin the registration process. In most cases, SEC Form S–1 is used; however, special registration forms apply to certain types of businesses.

The form consists of two parts. The first part represents the preliminary prospectus, called, in market slang, a **red herring**. It is the principal document used by investors in evaluating the offering and is the only marketing document used by the underwriters. The red herring is often printed and circulated before the firm has received final approval from the SEC. The second part of the form includes various exhibits, such as legal documents and a draft of the underwriting agreement. This part is deposited with the SEC and made available for public scrutiny at SEC offices.

The SEC will generally comment on the adequacy of the preliminary filings within 20 business days, and may express reservations that must be addressed before the registration statement is accepted. The issuing firm and its counsel then prepare a second draft of the registration statement. The second draft includes certain information not required for the preliminary filing and addresses any concerns that the SEC has expressed. The revised registration statement is then filed. This process is repeated until all reservations on the part of the SEC have been satisfied, and the document is accepted and the offering can go forward.

There are several important things worth noting at this point. Acceptance of the registration by the SEC does not constitute an endorsement of the securities or represent an approval of the merits of the offering. It is merely an affirmation by the SEC that the filings appear to contain the required material information and the offering is structured in accordance with the law.

While the registration process is progressing, (1) an underwriting syndicate is formed by the lead underwriter; (2) arrangements are made to print the preliminary prospectus, the red herring, in large quantities for distribution; (3) filings with the states to satisfy the blue–sky laws are taking place; (4) certificates (stock or bond) are printed; and (5) the investment banking community and the issuer's managers tout the company to the investing public in what is called the **roadshow**. The roadshow is particularly important in IPOs, where it may represent the first opportunity the investing public has to examine the company and its management. In the roadshow, the investment bankers and issuer's managers travel from city to city to present the firm to the public. They also make themselves available to answer questions.

The Underwriting

The final decision to offer a security depends on completion of the SEC process and the marketing of the issue. These two events should be timed to be completed contemporaneously. As soon as the registration is accepted by the SEC, a number of things happen very quickly. First, negotiations take place between the underwriting syndicate (with a leadership role taken by the lead underwriter) and the issuer with respect to the price of the offering to the public, the quantity to be sold, and the amount to be paid to the issuer. Alternatively, the issuer can put these matters up for competitive bid. (The latter is more common when a shelf registration is employed, as opposed to the traditional registration process described here. However, certain issuers, most notably public utility holding companies, are required by law to go the competitive bidding route.)

The underwriting agreement between the issuer and the underwriting syndicate can take either of three common forms: a **firm commitment**, a **best efforts**, or a **standby** underwriting. Almost all underwriting deals are firm commitments by which the underwriters guarantee that they will sell a specified minimum quantity of the issuance at the offering price. If the underwriters fail to sell the guaranteed amount, they must take it themselves. The underwriter is viewed as buying the securities from the issuer for resale. Many debt deals are "bought"; i.e., the bankers do not have immediate buyers for all bonds. Virtually no common stock deal is bought—buyers have already been found for most common stock deals ahead of time. In a best efforts underwriting, the underwriters do not make a guarantee. They simply agree to do their best to distribute the securities, with the understanding that any unsold securities will be returned to the issuer. The standby underwriting is employed when the issuer offers the securities to existing shareholders through a rights offering and uses the underwriters only as a backup for any securities not taken through the rights offering.

The differences among these forms of underwriting are important. The firm commitment can be viewed as an insurance policy for the issuer; that is, no matter what happens, the issuer is assured that it will get the financing it requires. Thus, the risk of a failed offering is transferred from the issuer to the underwriter. Of course, this guarantee has value, and the underwriter expects to be compensated for providing the guarantee. The compensation generally takes the form of a wider underwriting spread on a firm commitment than on a best efforts underwriting. Additionally, the underwriters can be expected to have a bias toward underpricing the issue to assure themselves that it can be easily absorbed by the market without significant price concessions. The issuer, too, has views on the pricing of the security, and it wants to get the highest price it possibly can. Thus, there is a natural friction between the issuer and the underwriters. If possible, this conflict is resolved by either the negotiation or the competitive bidding process. But if it cannot be resolved, which usually means that the issuer demands a price for its securities that is higher than the underwriters feel they can accept, the only alternative is a best efforts offering. The risk then lies with the issuer.

There are two other important points to be made here. First, it is much easier to price a public offering than to price an initial public offering. For a public offering, the market has already established a fair price. Thus, public offerings are much less risky, and a higher percentage of the underwritings of these issues can be expected to take the form of a firm commitment. IPOs are a much more complicated matter. Pricing these issues requires the skill of experienced institutional investors who dominate marginal pricing decisions. Even so, the valuations arrived at by different potential underwriters can vary considerably.[4] And it has been repeatedly shown empirically that these issues tend to be undervalued at the offering, relative to subsequent market prices—underwriters may be protecting themselves, and/or the IPO discount may also be compensation to investors for buying a risky "unseasoned" security.

Another consideration in the underwriting process, particularly in the case of a firm commitment underwriting, is the behavior of the price of the issue during the underwriting period. Under rules established by the National Association of Securities Dealers or NASD (a self–regulating industry organization), underwriters and other members of the distribution syndicate cannot sell securities to the public for more than the offering price as stated in the prospectus. If the market turns soft, so that the security proves to be overpriced, the underwriters will get stuck with unsold inventory, which very likely will have to be sold at a lower price following the conclusion of the underwriting period. The loss comes directly out of the underwriting spread. On the other hand, if the market receives the securities well, or if its subsequent market price were to rise, even if significantly, the syndicate cannot raise the price of the securities and reap a windfall profit.

A standby underwriting has an altogether different structure, and the role of the underwriters is quite different. The standby underwriting revolves around **subscription rights**, which are relatively rare in the United States. In these cases, a firm in need of additional capital offers new securities to the public. It begins by granting subscription rights to existing shareholders in direct proportion to the number of shares they currently own. This is called a **rights offering**. A subscription right is a type of option; that is, a subscription right gives its owner the right to buy some quantity of stock directly from the issuer for some set period of time at a specified price, called the subscription price. (A subscription price is analogous to a strike price in a call option.)

---

[4] For discussion of issues concerning the pricing of IPOs, see Mauer and Senbet (1992); Welch (1992); Ruud (1991); Barry (1989); Bower (1989); Hegde and Miller (1989); Welch (1989); Johnson and Miller (1988); Tinic (1988); Miller and Reilly (1987); and Rock (1986). For discussion of issues concerning POs (seasoned equity), see Tripathy and Rao (1992); Slovin, Sushka, and Hudson (1990); Kalay and Shimrat (1987); Asquith and Mullins (1986); Booth and Smith (1986); and Masulis and Korwar (1986).

Consider an example. Suppose that a firm has two million shares of common stock outstanding and it wishes to distribute another one million shares. It might issue one subscription right to each shareholder for each share of stock currently owned. In our specific case, the issuer would require two rights to buy one share of stock. To encourage the shareholders to use the rights, the subscription price is generally set a little below the current market price. As a general rule, if the market price of the stock is above the subscription price, the rights will be exercised and the issuer will be able to distribute its stock without using an underwriter.

The logic behind subscription rights involves the issue of dilution. If existing shareholders are offered the right to buy into a new issue in the same proportion as their ownership interest in the existing outstanding shares, no shareholder can claim to have his or her ownership interest diluted by the new issue. Some states, and many corporate charters, contain provisions banning an arbitrary dilution of shareholders' ownership interests without their consent. Importantly, subscription rights are generally transferable. So, even if the recipient of the rights has no desire to use them, he can still sell them to someone else who will. Of course, like any option, the value of the right will depend on how deeply it is in– or out–of–the–money, how much time remains before it expires, and so on.

The problem with a rights offering is that there is no guarantee that the rights will be exercised. For example, continuing with our earlier scenario, suppose that at the time the rights are issued, the company's stock is trading at $20 a share. The rights have a subscription price of $19.50 a share, and they are good for 30 days. If, just before the rights are due to expire, the stock is trading for anything above $19.50, the rights will be exercised and the stock distribution will successfully take place. But if the stock is trading below $19.50 just before the rights are due to expire, they will not be exercised. Therein lies the problem.

To protect itself from the possibility of a failed rights offering, management can enter into a standby underwriting agreement with an investment bank. In essence, the investment bank guarantees that it will buy any and all stock that is not taken by the rights holders. If the standby underwriting is actually used, the underwriter will take the securities at an agreed–upon price, just as it would have done in a firm commitment underwriting. The underwriter will, in turn, resell the securities through its distribution channels. Of course, the investment bank takes a risk. If the rights offering fails, it is probably because the market price of the stock has declined. Thus, the underwriter may be forced to sell the securities below the offering price. To the degree that the underwriter is forced to mark down the price to move the securities, the difference will come out of the underwriter's pocket.

In exchange for its standby underwriting agreement, the investment bank collects a fee as a percentage of the size of the planned offering. This fee is payable irrespective of whether or not the underwriting becomes necessary. A standby underwriting agreement may be viewed as a put option for the issuer; that is, if the price of the stock declines, the agreement becomes valuable. The price of this put option will, of course, depend on many of the same things that determine the value of any option. The most important of these are the amount of the proceeds to the issuer and the time to expiration of the rights offering.

Returning to a firm commitment underwriting, once the securities have been approved by the SEC, the underwriting syndicate engages in its final negotiation with the issuer to set the underwriting terms. The day this occurs is called the **offering date**, and the final terms include the price of the offering, the size of the offering, and the gross spread. Immediately thereafter, the issuer files with the SEC an amendment to the prospectus to include the offering information. The **tombstone** is published the next day. Importantly, the tombstone does not constitute either an offer to sell securities or a solicitation of an offer to buy securities, and this is stated very clearly. The tombstone is merely a public notice (advertisement) that an offering is being made. The actual offering can be made only by the prospectus.

Distribution

New issues of securities are distributed through what is known as a **distribution syndicate**. As noted earlier, the distribution syndicate includes both the underwriting syndicate, which bears risk, and the selling group (if any), which does not bear risk. (The term *underwriting syndicate* is often used synonymously with the term *distribution syndicate*, but this is not technically correct.)

The primary purpose of forming a distribution syndicate is to distribute the securities as quickly as possible. Speed is important because, between the time of commitment to an offering price and the time of actual sale to the public, the underwriters run the risk that the market price might decline. As already noted, the underwriters will be injured by a price decline, but will not benefit from a price rise. Thus, the faster the distribution can be completed, the better off are the underwriters. This helps to explain why distribution syndicates are often very large. However, there is another good reason for syndicates to be large. Each participant receives a relatively small portion of the total issuance to distribute, but they can participate in many issuances. This means that the underwriters are essentially diversified across securities, and there is less risk associated with holding a diversified portfolio with a small investment in each security than there is in holding a large position in only a few securities.[5]

Structure of a Syndicate. The distribution syndicate can be large or small and, as already noted, it consists of both the underwriting syndicate and the selling group. The size will generally depend on the size and the type of the issuance. The underwriting syndicate consists of several distinct groups: the managers, the bulge bracket, the major bracket, the mezzanine bracket, and the submajor bracket. The managers are selected by the issuer, who also selects one of them to serve as lead manager. The lead manager (also called the book–running manager), in consultation with the issuer, forms the syndicate. It is important that the syndicate consist of members whose strengths complement one another in a fashion that will assure the success of the offering.

The different brackets of syndicate participants are usually grouped separately both on the tombstone and in the prospectus. The managers appear at the top of the list, and the lead manager's name is usually, but not always, printed first. The managers are followed by those bulge bracket firms (also called special bracket firms) that are participating but are not already listed as managers of the syndicate.[6] Next comes the

---

[5] With the smaller deals of the 1990s, the trend is to smaller and even no syndicates as firms acquire the ability to distribute entire deals themselves. Even where syndicates are still used, they sell smaller issues of stocks and bonds than in the 1980s.

[6] Carter and Manaster (1990) provide a listing of investment banks based on their position in tombstones listed in Investment Dealer's Digest from January 1979 to December 1983. The five top–bracket firms included First Boston, Goldman Sachs, Merrill Lynch, Morgan Stanley, and Salomon Brothers.

major bracket. These are large firms that generally have considerable distribution capability. Next is the mezzanine bracket. They are small firms but have special relations with either the issuer or the lead manager. The final group consists of the regional or the submajor bracket. The latter three groups will typically contain many boutiques or niche firms. A typical tombstone appears in Figure 3.1.

Distribution of Securities. Each member of the underwriting syndicate is allocated a share of the issuance to distribute. For purposes of allocating the revenues from the underwriting and distribution, the syndicate is divided into three groups: the managers, who also sell the majority of securities; the preferred group of dealers; and the nonpreferred dealers, or selling group. The preferred dealers, which include the managers, are designated as such by the syndicate and are responsible for the bulk of the distribution. The allocations get smaller as we descend through the brackets. This helps to spread the risk.

Among its duties in the syndicate, the lead underwriter is usually expected to place a **stabilizing bid** in the market. This is particularly important if the issuance is an IPO, because there is unlikely to be any other market making in the security. The stabilizing bid is set at the offering price and serves to guarantee, at least for a time, that investors can exit their positions in the securities for the same price that they paid for them. Following completion of the distribution, the lead underwriter will often continue to make a market in the security, particularly if it is not traded on an exchange or by over–the–counter dealers. This post

---

More recently, based on 1991 league tables covering the following types of offerings: (1) debt, (2) equity, (3) mortgage–backs, (4) asset–backs, (5) preferred stock, and (6) yankee bonds, the firms that best seem to fit the bulge bracket definition were Merrill Lynch, Goldman Sachs, Lehman Brothers, First Boston, Morgan Stanley, and Salomon Brothers. Our criteria were based on "full credit to the lead manager," considered only the top 10 firms in each offering category, and required that a firm be in the top five within at least two categories.

For international underwritings, rankings for three league tables from 1991 were utilized. These were international bonds, Eurobonds, and international equities. The firms that appeared at least once in the top five (including all three categories) were Nomura International, Credit Suisse/CSFB, Daiwa Securities, Deutsche Bank, Goldman Sachs, Paribas, S.G. Warburg Group, Lehman Brothers, and Merrill Lynch.

Figure 3.1

This announcement is neither an offer to sell nor a solicitation of offers to buy any of these securities. The offering is made only by the Prospectus.

September 23, 1993

6,000,000 Shares

codaenergy, inc

Common Stock

Price $5.75 Per Share

Copies of the Prospectus may be obtained from such of the undersigned and other dealers or brokers as may lawfully offer these securities in such State.

A.G. Edwards & Sons, Inc. — Johnson Rice & Company

Bear, Stearns & Co. Inc. — CS First Boston — Alex. Brown & Sons Incorporated — Dillon, Read & Co. Inc.

Kemper Securities, Inc. — Kidder, Peabody & Co. Incorporated — Merrill Lynch & Co. — Morgan Stanley & Co. Incorporated

Oppenheimer & Co., Inc. — PaineWebber Incorporated — Prudential Securities Incorporated

Salomon Brothers Inc — S.G. Warburg & Co. Inc. — Wertheim Schroder & Co. Incorporated

Advest, Inc. — Robert W. Baird & Co. Incorporated — J. C. Bradford & Co. — Burns, Pauli & Co., Inc.

Fahnestock & Co. Inc. — First Albany Corporation — First of Michigan Corporation

Interstate/Johnson Lane Corporation — Janney Montgomery Scott Inc. — Edward D. Jones & Co.

Ladenburg, Thalmann & Co. Inc. — Legg Mason Wood Walker Incorporated — Mabon Securities Corp.

McDonald & Company Securities, Inc. — Morgan Keegan & Company, Inc. — The Principal/Eppler, Guerin & Turner, Inc.

Rauscher Pierce Refsnes, Inc. — Raymond James & Associates, Inc. — Scott & Stringfellow, Inc.

Stifel, Nicolaus & Company Incorporated — Southwest Securities, Inc. — Sutro & Co. Incorporated

Tucker Anthony Incorporated — Wheat First Butcher & Singer Capital Markets

Black & Company, Inc. — Brean Murray, Foster Securities Inc. — Gaines, Berland Inc.

Huntleigh Securities Corporation — May Financial Corporation — Mesirow Financial, Inc.

Sanders Morris Mundy Inc. — Smith, Moore & Co.

Source: *The Wall Street Journal*, September 28, 1993.

offering market making provides liquidity but no longer serves a price–stabilizing role.

The fact that the lead underwriter will maintain a stabilizing bid—i.e., will buy at or very near the offering price—during the underwriting period suggests that the lead underwriter has a particularly strong incentive to underprice the security from the outset in its negotiations with the issuer. Also, because it will make a market in the security from the outset, the lead underwriter may find that the issue is well received and that demand exceeds its allocation. Given this possibility, the lead underwriter, as part of the underwriting agreement, will often have an **overallotment option** to purchase additional shares from the issuer at the offering price. This provision is called, in market slang, the **Green Shoe option**.[7] It usually allows the lead underwriter to purchase additional securities from the issuer up to some stipulated amount, 5 to 15 percent being typical. The overallocation option may be used to cover a short created in the initial offering phase by underwriters who oversell the securities. If fewer securities are sold than anticipated, then repurchases can be made to absorb the supply and cover the short. If more securities are sold than anticipated, the overallotment covers the short. In some cases, bankers will create additional repurchasing power by overselling more of the deal than the overallotment will cover ("naked short"). This exposes the banker to significant risk if the prices rise too quickly. The overallotment option can be used only to purchase additional shares made necessary by the underwriter's stabilization efforts.

Division of Revenues.   The members of the syndicate buy the securities from the issuer for resale to the public investor. Thus, they become principals to the transactions. As principals, the syndicate members cannot charge a commission; that is something only an agent can do. Thus, the syndicate members must derive their revenue from the difference between the offering price to the public and the proceeds to the issuer. As already noted, this is called the **underwriting spread** or the **gross spread**. The flotation cost to the issuer includes, but is not limited to, the gross spread. The flotation costs also include any underpricing and any miscellaneous fees that must be paid by the issuer.

---

[7] The term "Green Shoe option" stems from the origin of this technique. The first issuer to grant such an option was the Green Shoe Company.

For purposes of illustration, let's suppose that the fair market price for a firm's stock, which for an IPO is not determinable prior to issuance, is $52.75. The negotiation with the underwriters results in an agreement that the offering price will be $50, and the proceeds to the issuer will be $47.50. Thus, the gross spread is $2.50. Additionally, the issuer will be required to pay fees to cover the cost of SEC filings, legal fees, accounting fees, printing fees, and so on. Let's suppose that these amount to $0.75 per share. So, although the gross spread is $2.50, the flotation cost to the issuer is $6.00 ($2.75 underpricing + $2.50 gross spread + $0.75 other costs). This actual cost of $6.00 illustrates the importance of distinguishing between the **yield to an investor**, which is equal to the instrument's expected return as a percentage of the size of the investment made in the security, and the **all–in cost**, which is the cost to the issuer, stated as a percentage of the financing raised. All–in cost calculations do not ordinarily reflect the amount by which the security is believed to be underpriced; but in theory, at least, they should.

The gross spread is divided into three parts: the management fee, the underwriting fee, and the selling concession. The precise composition of these fees will vary from offering to offering, but the general rule of thumb is 20 percent, 20 percent, and 60 percent, respectively.

The **management fee** goes to the managers for their role in preparing the offering. In particular, the due diligence investigation places a special burden on the syndicate managers, particularly the lead manager(s), which is responsible for its adequacy and thoroughness. Thus, the management fee is, in part, compensation for this service. The management fee is divided among the managers, and the lead manager may receive a larger share, depending on the size, structure, and the role of the various managers in the transaction. This is consistent with the lead manager's role and responsibilities for allocating securities, accounting for costs, coordinating the road show, and so on.

The **underwriting fee** is the portion of the gross spread that is intended to cover the many miscellaneous costs associated with the underwriting, excluding those costs that the issuer must bear directly. The former include such things as advertising, legal expenses of the managers, stabilization expenses, postage and other correspondence, and so on. After the expenses have been met, any residual from the underwriting fee is divided on a pro rata basis among the members of the syndicate based on their level of participation. If the expenses exceed the underwriting fee, the members will be invoiced for the difference, again on a pro rata basis.

The **selling concession** is paid to the firms in the syndicate based on the number of shares they are responsible for selling. The actual sales will be made by each firm's registered representatives (reps). The reps are compensated for their efforts according to a well–established schedule that is based on the type of customer. For example, the reps typically receive 35 percent of the selling concession for sales to individuals, 20 percent for sales to small institutions, 15 percent for sales to midsized institutions, and 10 percent for sales to large institutions. These fees are in lieu of commissions (which the firms cannot charge, given their role as a principal in these transactions) and are normally greater than the commission that would have been earned by the reps on secondary–market brokerage business.

Let's consider a numerical example to see how the reps are compensated for their role. Let's suppose that a rep is going to sell 200 shares of the same stock discussed above to some individual investors. The gross spread is $2.50 and the selling concession is 60 percent of this, or $1.50. Since the sale will be made to individuals, the rep will get 35 percent, or $0.525, for each share sold.

While the syndicate consists of underwriters, the distribution may also involve other firms that either are not in the business of underwriting or choose not to act in the capacity of underwriters for purposes of the offering at hand. These firms make up the selling group. Members of the **selling group** buy securities from one or more of the underwriters and then resell them to their customers. For their participation, members of the selling group receive a significant portion of the selling concession. This portion is called a **reallowance**. The size of the reallowance can vary, but it often approximates one–half of the selling concession. The remainder of the selling concession is retained by the underwriting syndicate member. (Members of the selling group are sometimes called **nonpreferred dealers**, while members of the underwriting syndicate are sometimes called **preferred dealers**.)

To illustrate the source of revenue to the selling group, consider one last time the offering described above. The selling concession was $1.50 per share (60 percent of the gross spread). Of this, the selling group will get half, or $0.75 per share. The remaining $0.75 per share of the selling concession will be retained by the syndicate member that provided the securities from its underwriting allocation.

The degree of participation in a syndication by the underwriting syndicate members is determined in part by their willingness to make a commitment to buy the securities and in part by the total number of securities the syndicate is prepared to take. To help assure that it does not take a loss on its participation and to assure itself that it can resell its allotment very quickly, most members of a syndicate will presell securities to investors on a "not held" basis, even before the final agreement is reached between the underwriters and the issuer. Each dealer will have its reps contact customers and try to get commitments from those customers to take shares. Both the investor and the dealer reserve the right to back out. The investor will back out if it does not like the final terms, and the dealer might back out if (1) the deal never comes to fruition, or (2) the dealer's allotment is insufficient to cover the shares for which it has buyers. This process of obtaining commitments from customers prior to making a final underwriting commitment is called **preselling** the issue or **building a book**.

Obviously, from a rep's perspective, it is important to presell securities to investors that can be relied upon to take them when the time comes. If a customer reneges a few times, that customer will not be approached again. On the other hand, if the dealer oversells its allotment and cannot deliver all the securities it has promised, its reputation can be damaged among its customers. Thus, preselling is a delicate act requiring realistic expectations on everybody's part.

At the end of the underwriting period, generally one week from the offering date, a meeting is held between the underwriters and the issuer. At this meeting, which is called closing, the issuer delivers the shares and the underwriters, by way of the lead underwriter, make payment to the issuer.

Competitive Bidding in Syndications.   The process that we have described has concentrated on a negotiated underwriting agreement. But we also noted that there are times when the terms of the agreement are put up for competitive bid. This is common, for example, in the public utility industry, and it is intended to prevent abuses stemming from collusion between the utility managers and the underwriters. In these cases, the issuer announces, often by way of an advertisement in the financial pages of newspapers like *The Wall Street Journal*, that a security issue is being put up for competitive bid. Different syndicates bid on the required items. The best bid wins the business. With the exception of the competitive bidding on terms, as opposed to a negotiation of terms, the underwriting and distribution process is basically the same.

Competitive bidding is most common in debt issuances, and, with the exception of public utilities, negotiated underwriting agreements are most common in equity issuances.

Shelf Registration

One of the most significant developments in corporate finance in the 1980s, and there were many, was the advent of **shelf registration**. Shelf registration, known technically as **Rule 415**, was an experimental effort to streamline the public offering process. The experiment was an attempt to both reduce the cost of issuances in the United States and speed up the offering process. It was motivated, in part, by a rapidly increasing flow of new issuances to offshore markets. The experiment was launched in 1982 and proved so successful that it was made law the very next year.

In a shelf registration, called a **shelf**, in market slang, the issuer prepares an offering in the usual way—preliminary filing with the SEC, due diligence investigation, final filings with the SEC, and so on. However, under Rule 415, the filing is good for two years. This is in contrast to the traditional registration in which the filing is only good for a very short period of time, and the distribution begins within a day or two of the final acceptance by the SEC.

During this two–year period, the firm may "tap" the shelf repeatedly. For example, suppose that a firm feels it may need or want to issue bonds to finance future expansion or to take advantage of attractive "windows of opportunity" which might appear from time to time. It therefore works with an investment bank to prepare a filing with the SEC, or prepare the filing on its own, and it files under Rule 415. Once the shelf is accepted by the SEC, the firm may use it on as little as 24 hours notice to the SEC. During the life of the shelf filing, the firm can repeatedly amend the registration to reflect material changes in the firm or with respect to the offering, and it may amend the filing to reflect nonmaterial matters, such as a change of underwriters.

Consider a simple case. The XYZ Corporation happens to be in need of $200 million of financing. It decides to issue long–term bonds to meet this need. However, anticipating that it may need additional financing at a later date, it employs a shelf registration and obtains authorization to issue up to $500 million of new debt. Once approved, it negotiates or puts up for competitive bid $200 million of the offering with an underwriting syndicate. The $200 million is then distributed. Some time later, the firm decides to issue another $100 million of long–term bonds. It files the appropriate amendments, changing the terms as necessary to reflect current market conditions and any material changes involving the firm. It then negotiates a new agreement and brings out the additional bonds. The shelf can be repeatedly tapped in this way.

There are a number of advantages to a shelf. First, it allows the firm to get the costly and time–consuming part of the issuance process over and done with in one shot. Second, it allows the firm to come into the market on very short notice in order to meet unexpected needs and to exploit any windows of opportunity that might arise.

There are costs associated with the shelf registration process, just as there are with the regular registration process. One of these is filing fees that must be paid to the SEC as a percentage of the size of the offering. These fees can be considerable for a firm that registers an offering that is much bigger than it has any reasonable expectation of actually issuing. To get around this problem, the firm registers only what it reasonably expects to issue, and then, if necessary, amend the filing to increase the size of the offering. Of course, additional fees must be paid, but at least none are wasted.

For large firms that tap the capital markets regularly, the shelf registration process has become the method of choice since Rule 415 was made law.

Offshore Markets and Dual Syndications

Two additional important developments of the 1980s that had a signifi-cant impact on public offering strategies were the derivatives markets (primarily swaps) and the rapid growth of offshore markets—principally the Euromarkets. The extraordinary growth of the latter was, in large measure, a consequence of the development of the former. The derivative markets, described in a later chapter, allow a firm to raise money in almost any country and currency by selling securities to investors who are amenable to holding securities denominated in that currency, and then "swapping" these liabilities into the desired currency.

Let's start with a simple case. Suppose that a U.S firm can issue dollar–denominated debt in the Eurobond markets, called **Eurodollar bonds**. If it does not sell its securities to U.S. investors, it is not required to register them with the SEC. This saves considerable time and expense. The securities are distributed through a European syndicate. Securities distributed in this way may not provide as much protection for investors, since the due diligence investigation, if any, is unlikely to be as rigorous. Nevertheless, once the distribution is complete and the securities have traded for 90 days, the securities are considered to be **seasoned**, and American investors can then buy them.

The preceding example did not require any currency conversions, because the American firm denominated its securities in dollars. But it could just as easily have issued the securities in deutschemarks, pounds sterling, or yen, and then swapped the liability into dollars with the aid of a currency swap.

Given these opportunities, U.S. issuers were tempted to take their issuance business overseas, and Euromarket operatives were quite willing to accommodate. As the volume of Euromarket business exploded, more and more offshore markets opened to provide the same services. Collectively, these markets became known as **offshore markets**. The loss of business to the offshore markets led to two major regulatory responses in the United States. One was the shelf registration described earlier, and the other was the introduction of an offshore market in the United States. In the latter, securities are issued in the United States to non–American investors and do not require formal registration. After the securities are seasoned, however, American investors can buy them.

It is not uncommon today for U.S. firms, particularly large ones placing very large issuances, to employ a dual syndication. A **dual syndication** is one in which two separate syndicates are employed—one for distribution within the United States, and one for distribution outside the United States.

Since we have broached the subject of foreign markets, it is worth noting that foreign firms may issue in the United States, just as U.S. firms may issue securities outside the United States. If such foreign securities are to be sold to American investors, they must be registered with the SEC, just as a domestic issue must be registered. As an aside, the market has developed an interesting vernacular for bonds issued outside of the issuer's domestic market: Dollar–denominated bonds issued in the United States by non–American firms are called **yankee bonds**; yen–denominated bonds issued in Japan by non–Japanese firms are called **samurais**; and sterling–denominated bonds issued in the United Kingdom by non–British firms are called **bulldogs**.

The Syndication Department

Each major investment bank that is in the business of managing underwritings maintains a **syndication department**. The syndication department is responsible for assembling the underwriting syndicate and for helping to select the selling group in cooperation with the issuing firm. The syndication desk maintains close ties with many broker/dealer firms, known collectively as the **Street**. Although they may be competitors in other aspects of their business, when it comes to syndication, the firms perceive themselves as partners. Syndication departments play an important role in working out problems and conflicts that occasionally arise between members of syndicates.

Seasoned Public Offerings

We have described an initial public offering as a firm's first issuance of securities, usually stock, to the investing public. And we have described a public offering, also called a seasoned public offering, as a new offering of securities by a firm that has already issued securities to the public. There are, however, three distinct types of seasoned public offerings. These include **primary seasoned offerings, secondary offerings**, and **combined offerings**. A primary seasoned offering is an offering of a new issue of securities by a firm that has already done an initial public offering. The purpose of primary seasoned offerings is to raise new capital (financing) for the firm.[8]

---

[8] Ellis and Dunkelberg (1992) found that under some conditions, the prestige of the investment banker (bulge bracket bankers versus non–bulge bracket bankers) may influence how the market reacts to an announcement of a primary seasoned equity issue offering.

A secondary public offering, also called a **secondary placement**, is used by a firm's founders, and other prepublic owners, and some post–public holders of the securities to "cash out" of the firm; that is, the securities distributed in a secondary public offering are purchased by the underwriters directly from the prepublic owners and not from the firm.

A combined offering is partly primary and partly secondary; it is used to both raise new capital for the firm and to cash out some of the prepublic owners.

Secondary public offerings are necessary because underwriters discourage insiders from selling their own stock as part of an IPO. After all, it is hard to persuade investors that a stock is attractively priced when the firm's own managers and owners are selling out. Indeed, many underwriters will not handle an IPO that includes the sale of securities by the owners and/or managers.

As an alternative to a secondary public offering, the owners could simply sell their securities in the secondary market through broker/dealers. But this solution has complications: Sales of securities, particularly stock, by founders and other insiders often send a signal that they hold a negative view of the firm—irrespective of the motivation for the sale. Additionally, the SEC must be notified of such sales, and this information is made public and carefully scrutinized for abuse of inside information. The secondary public offering is a vehicle by which the owners can cash out (not necessarily completely) and not overly affect the market— because the underwriters are creating additional demand by marketing by securities and explaining why the sale is happening.

Private Placements

We had earlier described private placements as a vehicle that circumvents the public offering process and all the registration baggage that goes with it. Private placements are not appropriate for all financing, but when they are, they can be extremely effective—both in speed and in meeting idiosyncratic corporate needs.

The private placement, as an alternative to the public offering, was established in law by the Securities Act of 1933. That act made it clear that when a security is offered to a limited number of sophisticated investors, such as institutional investors, the need for formal registration is unnecessary. In essence, the responsibility for the due diligence investigation is transferred from the investment bank and issuer to the lenders. However, there was a question for many years as to how many potential investors could be solicited before a private placement ceases to be a private placement. In response, the SEC issued Regulation D in 1982. The rule allows for an unlimited number of potential investors to be solicited. However, the rule also imposes a test on investors in a private placement: specifically, the investors must be able to demonstrate both a capacity and an intent to hold the securities for an extended period of time. This test is motivated in part by the fact that such issues are not easily marketable and partly to prevent private placement investors from simply reselling the securities to less sophisticated investors.

Private placements are limited by both the number of investors involved and the sophistication level and size of those investors. Private placements work to the advantage of the issuers by reducing the time it takes to raise capital *and* the cost of raising that capital. The investors benefit because, in lieu of the protection afforded by registration, they can demand and will usually get a somewhat higher return on the securities than would be required in a public offering. To see that the issuer can pay more to the investor in a private placement and still come out a winner, imagine that the securities involved take the form of a bond issuance. Suppose that, if the bond is issued as part of a public offering, it would require a coupon of 9.50 percent to sell at par. However, the flotation costs, together with the subsequent administrative costs associated with managing the issue, would raise the real cost of the financing, called all–in cost, to 10.75 percent, if stated on an effective annual basis. Nevertheless, the return to the investors is the amount of the coupon—i.e., 9.50 percent. Suppose now that the private placement can be effected with a coupon of 10 percent, with the fees that would be payable to the investment banker raising the all–in cost to 10.40 percent. Thus, when comparing the cost to the issuer, the issuer gains by 35 **basis points** (100 basis points = 1 percentage point). When comparing the return to the investor, the investor gains by 50 basis points.

The cost savings, together with the greater speed with which the financing can be effected, largely explain the motivation for private placements. However, additional and very powerful motivations exist for private placements. There are times, for reasons we will not go into, when an issuer wants certain special features attached to its issuances that are not acceptable to most investors. These very features, however, may be acceptable to one very special, or a small number of very special, institutional investor(s) because of the peculiar characteristics of that investor's balance sheet. By direct negotiations, or negotiations via the intermediation of the investment bank, the issuer and the investors can agree on terms for the securities that would simply not be acceptable in a broad–based public offering.

Finally, private placements are useful when the debt is of less than investment–grade quality or is simply unrated for lack of a financial history. The latter case is typical in smaller LBO situations. Such bonds often involve an equity kicker. Additionally, in private placements, the securities may include a provision allowing for subsequent registration with the SEC to make the securities more marketable.

On occasion, the desire for a private placement originates with an investor rather than with an issuer. This is sometimes called a **reverse inquiry**. It highlights the fact that in private placements, where the terms are often complex, there is a need for an active negotiation between the issuers and the investors. The investment bank's role in this process is to identify potential issuers and potential investors and facilitate the process of security design and placements. This activity is the responsibility of a specialized group most often called the **private placement group**, which, depending on the organization of the investment bank, can be located within the corporate finance department, within the institutional sales and trading department, or within the high–yield group—or it may stand alone, occupying a spot within the bank somewhere between corporate finance and distribution.

The major investors in private placements are institutions which have relatively large and dependable cash flows. This is typical, for example, of insurance companies, private pension funds, and public pension funds. Not surprisingly, these are the firms that dominate the investment side of the private placement market. Because their cash flows are highly predictable, they can meet the intent and capacity requirements of the law with relative ease. Importantly, these institutions, particularly the insurance companies, have developed departments having specialists in the evaluation of such issues. Often, other institutional investors will wait until a major insurance company "signs on" before committing to a private placement. The approval of the insurance company gives the other investors the confidence they need to feel comfortable with the issue. In recent years, foreign investors, most notably the Japanese, have been involved in private placements, although this involvement varies considerably from year to year.

Increasingly, investment banks have commercial bank competition in the private placement market. Because private placements do not require the investment banking intermediary to "buy" the securities for resale, commercial banks or their securities subsidiaries can be involved in such activity, and their involvement continues to expand. This is one of the many areas where the traditional distinctions between investment banks and commercial banks are disintegrating.

Commercial Paper

Excluding the derivative and junk bond markets, which we shall take up in a later chapter, there is one more important component of the corporate finance operations of investment banks. This is the **commercial paper** market. Commercial paper, called in market slang either **paper** or **CP**, is a relatively short–term debt obligation of a corporation. Under SEC rules, corporate instruments having a maturity of 270 days or less are exempt from registration. Hence, commercial paper has, with rare exceptions, a maximum maturity of 270 days.

Corporations issue commercial paper for two fundamentally different financing purposes: long–term financing and to manage seasonal needs. Finance companies and other financial corporations issue commercial paper to meet long–term funding needs. While this sounds contradictory, it is not when one views the activity in the context of a broader funding strategy. As a general rule, interest costs are lower for short–term borrowing than for long–term borrowing. If one believes that the current yield curve configuration will remain relatively stable, and if short–term rates are lower than long–term rates, then financing in the short–term commercial paper market makes sense—even if the need is actually long–term. The firm can issue its paper and, when it matures, roll the paper over, called a **rollover** or a **refunding**. In essence, the proceeds from the new paper issue are used to pay off the old paper issue.

Long–term financing achieved with commercial paper is essentially floating–rate in character. With each rollover, the issuer must pay the then–prevailing rate. Thus, the rate can be viewed as reset at each rollover. Floating–rate financing can be converted to something approximating fixed–rate by use of fixed–for–floating interest rate swaps.

Investment banks assist firms in both commercial paper issuance, through their commercial paper departments, and with conversion to fixed–rate through their derivative product groups—but that is a later story.

There is one interesting advantage of structuring a long–term financing with commercial paper. This is particularly important in situations where the amount of financing varies considerably from period to period. For example, in financing automobile sales, a firm like General Motors Acceptance Corporation (GMAC) can reduce the amount of financing with each rollover to reflect both the portion of principal that has been repaid as required under the automobile–purchase loan agreement, and the portion of principal that is prepaid by the borrower. While the former is known, the latter is not. With frequent rollovers, the firm can make adjustments in the size of its issuances to adjust for principal prepayments.

The second major use of commercial paper is to deal with seasonal cash flow needs. These are temporary needs, and commercial paper is ideally suited to meet them. It is primarily industrial corporations that use the commercial paper markets to meet seasonal needs.

Because they are such regular users of commercial paper, financial corporations that depend on commercial paper for financing often, but not always, sell their paper directly to investors without the intermediation of investment banks. Industrial corporations, on the other hand, almost always place their paper using an investment bank's commercial paper dealers.

Commercial paper placed through dealers is sometimes called **dealer paper**. We concentrate on this form because it is the only form that involves investment banks. Commercial paper dealers cultivate relation-ships with issuers. Issuers tend to use a single dealer, and dealers do not, as a general rule, discuss their commercial paper business with one another. In the issuance of commercial paper, the dealer in essence acts as an agent in the sale of the paper to investors. However, as part of the agreement, the dealer will take for its own account any paper that it cannot sell. This is called **positioning**. Positioning paper is not the objective of a commercial paper dealer, but it is occasionally necessary. Paper that has been positioned can be resold to investors if market conditions permit, but never at such a time or in such a fashion as to have an impact on the primary market for paper. To do so would jeopardize the relationship between the issuer and the dealer.

There is no secondary market for commercial paper. However, to maintain good relations with commercial paper investors as well as the issuers that it services, a commercial paper dealer will generally buy back the paper of the issuers for which it distributes. Of course, the investment bank will require a small price concession from the investor. Historically, no more than 2 percent of paper is sold back to dealers. If an investor repeatedly sells paper back to the dealer, the dealer will become reluctant to do business with that investor.

Most commercial paper is placed with institutional investors. These include insurance companies, pension funds, money market mutual funds, and so on. Transactions are typically large, described as **wholesale**, and involve millions of dollars of paper. For its services, the investment bank charges a fee that is fairly standard. This is one–eighth of a point (percentage point) per dollar per year. For example, if the paper has a maturity of 180 days, the fee is one–sixteenth of a point—calculated as $180/360 \times 1/8 \times 1\%$ × principal amount. (Commercial paper transactions assume a 360–day year, and yields are quoted on a bank discount basis.)

The easiest way to calculate the CP dealer's fee is to state it on one–day basis per $1 million of principal. This is:

$$\frac{1}{360} \times \frac{1}{8} \times 1\% \times \$1 \text{ million} = \$3.47$$

Thus, a dealer earns $3.47 for each $1 million of paper distributed for each day of that paper's maturity. Dealers do not want to handle very short maturity paper. The fees earned from selling commercial paper having a maturity of only a few days are not sufficient to cover a dealer's costs. Nevertheless, for large customers who issue CP regularly, dealers will accommodate occasional short maturity needs to maintain good customer relations.

Commercial paper dealers respect one another's business and do not try to steal one another's clients, at least not overtly. This was also once true of the underwriting business, but no longer. Most investment banks will not handle the distribution of paper that is not rated, and some investment banks, such as CS First Boston and Salomon Brothers, will not handle paper with anything less than an investment grade rating. One way around this problem is for unrated firms, or firms with poor ratings, to secure a **letter of credit** (LOC) from a commercial bank. The letter of credit serves as collateral on the commercial paper. If the issuer is unable to meet its obligations when the paper matures, the commercial bank must do so. Such commercial paper is called **LOC paper**. Of course, for the letter of credit, the CP issuer must pay the bank a fee, which is stated as a percentage of the size of the issue.

As a side point, commercial paper is another area in which investment banks and commercial banks are increasingly in competition. Currently, dealing in commercial paper is still restricted to investment banks. But commercial banks often post rates on behalf of firms that place their paper directly with investors. Thus, although commercial banks do not deal in commercial paper, they assist direct issuers to bypass the investment bankers and, in the process, make themselves appear more full–service.

Summary

In this chapter, we have considered the role of the modern investment bank in corporate finance. Through their corporate finance divisions, private placement departments, and commercial paper operations, investment banks secure the long–term and short–term financing needed by large and small domestic and foreign corporations. In public offerings, the investment bank plays a number of roles: it helps prepare the issuance documents; it assembles the distribution network, including the underwriting syndicate and the selling group; and it assumes the risk of a failed issuance, thus providing a form of insurance to the issuer.

In private placements, the investment bank provides a somewhat different form of service. It assists firms in the design of special, often complex, issues of debt and preferred stock and helps place these issues with institutional investors. In the process, the investment bank identifies issuers and investors that meet each other's idiosyncratic needs. The private placement market is a market in which securities can be issued quickly, in which special features can be included in a security's indenture that might not be acceptable in a public offering, and in which securities of poorer quality and unrated debt can find a home.

The commercial paper market allows corporate issuers to tap short–term markets to meet seasonal needs and to structure long–term financing by coupling CP issues with over–the–counter derivative securities. Investment banks make the market in dealer–placed paper but do not make the market in directly placed paper. The dealers essentially serve a role in the CP market that is, in a sense, midway between underwriting and private placement. As in underwriting, the commercial paper dealer makes a commitment to buy the issuer's securities and accepts the risk that it might have to position any securities that it cannot sell. As in the private placement market, the investors in commercial paper are institutions, the market is essentially a wholesale market, and the securities are relatively nonmarketable. Also, as in the private placement market, the CP market hinges heavily on the investment banks' personal knowledge of both investors and issuers.

Through their underwriting, private placement, and CP activities, investment banks meet the financing requirements of corporations and the investment objectives of individual and institutional investors.

References and Suggested Reading

Allen, D. S., R. E. Lamy, and G. R. Thompson, "The Shelf Registration of Debt and Selection Bias," *Journal of Finance*, 15:1, March 1990, pp. 275–287.

Altschul, J. S., "Policing Off–Shore Dealing in U.S. Securities," *International Financial Law Review*, 5:3, March 1986, pp. 35–36.

Asquith, P. and D. W. Mullins, "Equity Issues and Offering Dilution," *Journal of Financial Economics*, 15:1,2, January 1986, pp. 61–90.

Auerbach, J. and S. L. Hayes, *Investment Banking and Due Diligence: What Price Deregulation?* Boston: Harvard Business School Press, 1986.

Bae, S. C. and H. Levy, "The Valuation of Firm Commitment Underwriting Contracts for Seasoned New Equity Issues: Theory and Evidence," *Financial Management*, 19:2, Summer 1990, pp. 48–59.

Barry, C. B., "Initial Public Offering Underpricings: The Issuer's View—A Comment," *Journal of Finance*, 44:4, September 1989, pp. 1099–1103.

Barry, C. B. and R. H. Jennings, "The Opening Price Performance of Initial Public Offerings of Common Stock," *Financial Management*, 22:1, Spring 1993, pp. 54–63.

Blackwell, D. W. and D. S. Kidwell, "An Investigation of Cost Differences Between Public Sales and Private Placements of Debt," *Journal of Financial Economics*, 22:2, December 1988, pp. 253–278.

Blackwell, D. W., M. W. Marr, and M. F. Spivey, "Shelf Registration and the Reduced Due Diligence Argument: Implications of the Underwriter Certification and the Implicit Insurance Hypothesis," *Journal of Financial and Quantitative Analysis*, 25:2, June 1990, pp. 245–259.

Booth, J. R. and R. L. Smith, "Capital Raising, Underwriting, and the Certification Hypothesis," *Journal of Financial Economics*, 15:1,2, March 1986, pp. 261–281.

Bower, N. L., "Firm Value and the Choice of Offering Method in Initial Public Offerings," *Journal of Finance*, 44:3, July 1989, pp. 647–662.

Carter, R. B. and F. H. Dark, "The Use of the Over–Allotment Option in Initial Public Offerings of Equity: Risks and Underwriter Prestige," *Financial Management*, 19:3, Autumn 1990, pp. 55–64.

Carter, R. and S. Manaster, "Initial Public Offerings and Underwriter Reputation," *Journal of Finance*, 45:4, September 1990, pp. 1045–1067.

Denis, D. J., "Shelf Registration and the Market for Seasoned Equity Offerings," *Journal of Business*, 64:2, April 1991, pp. 189–212.

Drake, P. D. and M. R. Vetsuypens, "IPO Underpricing and Insurance Against Legal Liability," *Financial Management*, 22:1, Spring 1993, pp. 64–73.

Ellis, M. E. and J. Dunkelberg, "The Effect of the Prestige of the Investment Banker on Positive Versus Negative Seasoned Equity Issue Announcements," presented at the Financial Management Association meetings, San Francisco, October 1992.

Frerichs, H., "Underwriter Due Diligence Within the Integrated Disclosure System—If It Isn't Broken, Don't Fix It," *Securities Regulation Law Journal*, 16:4, Winter 1989, pp. 386–412.

Hansen, R. S., B. R. Fuller, and V. Janjigian, "The Over–Allotment Option and Equity Financing Flotation Costs: An Empirical Investigation," *Financial Management*, 16:2, Summer 1987, pp. 24–32.

Hedge, S. P. and R. E. Miller, "Market–Making in Initial Public Offerings of Common Stocks: An Empirical Analysis," *Journal of Financial and Quantitative Analysis*, 24:1, March 1989, pp. 75–90.

Hess, A. C. and P. A. Frost, "Tests for Price Effects of New Issues of Seasoned Securities," *Journal of Finance*, 36:1, March 1982, pp. 11–25.

Johnson, J. J. and R. E. Miller, "Investment Banker Prestige and the Underwriting of Initial Public Offerings," *Financial Management*, 17:2, Summer, 1988, pp. 19–29.

Kadapakkam, P. R. and S. J. Kon, "The Value of Shelf Registration for New Debt Issues," *Journal of Business*, 62:2, April 1989, pp. 271–291.

Kalay, A. and A. Shimrat, "Firm Value and Seasoned Equity Issues: Price–Pressure, Wealth Redistribution, or Negative Information," *Journal of Financial Economics*, 19:1, January 1987, pp. 109–126.

Kidwell, D. S., M. W. Marr, and G. R. Thompson, "Shelf Registration: Competition and Market Flexibility," *Journal of Law & Economics*, 30:1, April 1987, pp. 181–206.

Klepetko, F. A. and D. A. Krinsky, "Raising Equity Capital—Untying the Knots in the Green Shoe," *Journal of Business Strategy*, 12:4, July/August 1991, pp. 56–59.

Masulis, R. W. and A. N. Korwar, "Seasoned Equity Offerings: An Empirical Investigation," *Journal of Financial Economics* 15:1,2, January 1986, pp. 91–118.

Mauer, D. C. and W. Senbet, "The Effects of the Secondary Market on the Pricing of Initial Public Offerings: Theory and Evidence," *Journal of Financial and Quantitative Analysis*, 27:1, March 1992, pp. 55–79.

Mechanics of Underwriting, Practicing Law Institute, 1992.

Miller, R. E. and F. K. Reilly, "An Examination of Mispricing Returns and Uncertainty for Initial Public Offerings," *Financial Management*, 16:2, Summer 1987, pp. 33–38.

Muscarella, C. J. and M. R. Vetsuypens, "A Simple Test of Baron's Model of IPO Underpricing," *Journal of Financial Economics*, 24:1, September 1989, pp. 125–135.

Ritter, J. R., "The Long–Run Performance of Initial Public Offerings," *Journal of Finance*, 46:1, March 1991, pp 3–27.

Rock, K., "Why New Issues Are Underpriced," *Journal of Financial Economics*, 15:1,2, March 1986, pp. 3–27.

Ruud, J. S., "Another View of the Underwriting of Initial Public Offerings," *Federal Reserve Bank of New York Quarterly Review*, 16:1, Spring 1991, pp. 83–85.

Saunders, A., "Why Are So Many New Stock Issues Underpriced?" *Business Review*, Federal Reserve Bank of Philadelphia, March/April 1990, pp. 3–12.

Slovin, M., M. Sushka, and C. Hudson, "External Monitoring and Its Effect on Seasoned Common Stock Issues," *Journal of Accounting and Economics*, 12, March 1990, pp. 397–417.

Sundaram, S., W. A. Ogden, and M. C. Walker, "Wealth Effects of Corporate Presentations to the New York Society of Security Analysts," *Financial Analysts Journal*, March/April 1993, pp. 88–89.

Tinic, S. M., "Anatomy of Initial Public Offerings of Common Stock," *Journal of Finance*, 43:4, September 1988, pp. 789–822.

Tripathy, N. and R. P. Rao, "Adverse Selection, Spread Behavior, and Over–the–Counter Seasoned Equity Offerings," *Journal of Financial Research*, 15:1 Spring 1992, pp. 39–56.

Welch, I., "Seasoned Offerings, Imitation Costs, and the Underpricing of Initial Public Offerings," *Journal of Finance*, 44:2, June 1989, pp. 421–449.

Welch, I., "Sequential Sales, Learning, and Cascades," *Journal of Finance*, 47:2, June 1992, pp. 695–732.

4

Public Finance: Federal, State, and Local

Overview

Just as the corporate sector has significant financing needs, so does the public sector. We include in the public sector the U.S. Treasury, agencies and sponsored corporations of the U.S. Government, and state and local governments.

We lump these into three categories: Treasury finance, agency finance, and municipal finance, respectively. The role of investment banks is different in each of these three areas, and this, in part, justifies our treating them separately. Unlike the corporate sector, which issues both debt and equity securities, the public sector issues only debt securities.

As always, our primary interest is in the role played by the investment bank and not in the investment characteristics of the specific securities that are issued. Of course, we need to have some understanding of the securities to fully appreciate the role of the investment banks, but such discussion will be kept to a minimum.

Investment banks are involved in the Treasury markets in four ways:

1. They participate in the primary market–making process.
2. They participate actively in secondary market making as dealers.
3. They trade the securities aggressively to earn speculative and arbitrage profits.
4. They often use Treasury securities to develop strategies and new instruments.

In agency finance, investment banks play a role that occupies a niche somewhere between that of an underwriter and a dealer. They also play a role in making a secondary market in agency issues and in advising agency issuers on the structure of their offering. As with agency issues, our principal concern with municipal finance is in primary market making. The principal ancillary services performed by investment banks in the municipal market again include advice on security design and secondary market making.

Treasury Finance

The U.S. Treasury issues debt instruments to finance current budget deficits and to carry the national debt. The market for Treasury securities is very liquid, and the instruments are relatively homogeneous. Treasury securities are called, collectively, **Treasuries**. Sometimes they are called **Governments** or **govies**, but these latter terms are also sometimes understood to include agency issues.

The primary market for Treasury debt is made by the Federal Reserve Bank of New York, which holds periodic auctions. Participating in this auction process as bidders are about 40 **primary government securities dealers**. These primary government securities dealers include both investment banks and commercial banks. All the bulge bracket firms are included among the primary government securities dealers. Among commercial banks, the primary government securities dealers are mainly major money center banks, such as Citibank, Chemical Bank, and Chase Manhattan Bank. Clearly, market making in government securities is another area in which investment banks and commercial banks compete.

The securities themselves consist principally of Treasury bills (T–bills), Treasury notes (T–notes), and Treasury bonds (T–bonds). The funds obtained from the sale of these securities are used to refund existing debt, called **refunding**, and to raise new money.

As part of the Fed's auction process, the primary government securities dealers enter competitive bids for the securities on behalf of themselves and their customers. The securities they purchase for themselves are then resold to other securities dealers and investors. Government securities dealers, including the primary government securities dealers, also make an active secondary market in Treasuries. As dealers, they buy and sell in an effort to profit from the difference between their bid and ask prices.

The government securities market is the least regulated of all securities markets in the U.S. For this reason, this market has often been the market of choice for those interested in experimentation and innovation. For example, the government securities market gave rise to the first widely accepted zero coupon products and also gave birth to the repo/reverse market.

The Instruments

Of all debt markets in the world, the market for Treasury securities is the largest and most homogeneous. It is also one of the safest, in terms of default risk. On top of this, Treasury securities are available in a near continuum of maturities out to a full 30 years. And, as already mentioned, the Treasury market is the least regulated of all securities markets in the United States. This unique combination of features makes this market (1) one of the most important for purposes of establishing the yields against which other instruments will be compared; (2) the market of choice for experimentation and innovation; and, (3) the market in which other positions can be offset for risk management purposes. Additionally, interest earned from holding Treasuries is exempt from state and local taxes, but it is subject to federal income taxation.

Treasury bills are issued in maturities of three months (13 weeks or 91 days), six months (26 weeks or 182 days), and one year (52 weeks or 364 days). In addition, the Treasury occasionally issues very short–term "cash management bills" to cover funding gaps. Unlike conventional notes and bonds, T–bills do not pay periodic interest coupons. Instead, they are sold at a discount from face value and redeemed at face value. The interest is the amount of the discount. For this reason, these instruments are correctly viewed as short–maturity zero coupon bonds.

Since 1977, T–bills have been issued exclusively in **book–entry** form. This means that there are no physical certificates evidencing ownership. Instead, ownership is evidenced by entries in a computer data file. The computer data file constitutes the "book." While the percentage varies, in recent years T–bills have represented about 40 percent of all outstanding Treasury debt.

T–bill yields are not quoted in the same way as bond and note yields. Yields on bills are quoted on a **bank discount basis** (also known as **discount basis** and sometimes as **bank basis**). As noted in the preceding chapter, this same method is used for quoting yields on commercial paper.

Discount basis understates the true yield for two reasons. First, the yield is calculated on the basis of the bill's face value, even though the investor actually pays less than face value. Second, interest is paid on the actual number of days the bill is held, even though the daily interest rate assumes that the year has only 360 days.

Note and bond yields are quoted on what is called a **semiannual bond basis**. Semiannual bond basis is the yield to maturity that equates the present value of the instrument's cash flows to its current price when the yield is stated on the assumption of semiannual compounding.

The difference between discount basis and bond basis yield quotations is substantial and should not be overlooked. For example, it would not be illogical to employ an arbitrage strategy requiring one to be long an instrument yielding 9.20 percent (discount basis) and short an instrument yielding 9.50 percent (bond basis). The uninitiated, however, would clearly think it foolish to hold an asset yielding 9.20 percent at a cost of 9.50 percent. Such exploitable situations are ready–made for the talents of an investment bank's financial engineers.

Treasury notes and bonds both pay semiannual coupons and are often referred to collectively as **coupons** to distinguish them from the Treasury's discount instruments. Treasury notes are sold with original maturities from 2 to 10 years. More specifically, they are sold with maturities of 2, 3, 5, and 10 years. There is a regular issue cycle for each of these maturities. For example, 2–year and 5–year notes are issued monthly and 10–year notes are issued quarterly. Treasury bonds have original issue maturities of 30 years and are issued semiannually as part of the Treasury's refunding cycle.

Because notes are issued frequently and in different maturities, there are multiple issues of similar maturity in the hands of investors and dealers at any given time. For example, a 5–year original maturity note has a 3–year maturity after two years. Of course, a new 3–year note also has a 3–year maturity. The most recently issued of any given maturity is considered the current issue and is referred to, in market jargon, as an **on–the–run** issue. The on–the–run issues are the most liquid, and trading in them is active. Additionally, trading is active in all maturities greater than 10 years.

Many investors and traders prefer to be in actively traded issues in order to be assured of the liquidity necessary to exit positions quickly and cost–effectively. Not surprisingly, the demand for the on–the–run issues is greater than the demand for off–the–run securities, and traders pay a premium to be in an on–the–run. Coupons bearing Treasuries with less than a year to maturity tend to be very illiquid. For this reason, those with an interest in trading short maturities are much more inclined to trade bills.

Because the interest income from Treasuries is not exempt from federal income tax, clearly the largest tax for most taxpayers, these securities are usually included among a broader category of securities called **taxable fixed income**. Taxable fixed income, or TFI, also includes corporate debt and mortgage–backed securities. TFI also includes the issues of government agencies, foreign debt securities, and issues of multinational agencies such as the World Bank.

The Role of Investment Banks in the Treasury Market

As noted in the Overview section of this chapter, investment banks are involved in the primary market for Treasury securities in their capacity as primary government securities dealers, in the secondary market as dealers, and as traders and new product innovators. Our concern in this chapter is with the first of these activities. Because the Treasury issues its securities under an Act of Congress, Treasuries are exempt from registration with the Securities and Exchange Commission.

Trading in Treasury notes and bonds in the secondary market takes place in terms of price stated as a percentage of par value to the nearest 32nd of a point. Nevertheless, the auctions are held in terms of yield. Typically, the Treasury announces a new auction at least one week in advance and then solicits competitive bids. Only primary government securities dealers can enter bids, but they can submit bids for both their own account and for the accounts of their customers—provided the customer has requested that the dealer do so.

The Treasury has long had rules in place to prevent any single primary government securities dealer from achieving a monopoly position in any single bond issue. This was achieved by placing limits on the total percentage of an issuance that such a dealer could bid for. For many years this limit was 35 percent, and the system seemed to work well.

As with corporate offerings, primary government securities dealers often presell a Treasury issue. That is, they line up customers to take the securities that they are planning to bid for, and based in part on the size of the presold book, they determine the quantity they will bid for. In addition to meeting its presold obligations, the investment bank would also want to obtain some inventory of each new issue for itself—an important requirement to be an effective full–service market maker in the secondary market.

Until recently, under the Treasury's rules, bidders submitted secret bids, in yield, to two decimal places—e.g., 8.63 percent—and in the quantities desired. The Treasury then awarded the issue to the lowest yield bidder first and progressed upward until the full issue was sold. The highest accepted bid (which translates to the lowest accepted price) was called the **stop out bid**, or, when translated to a price, the **stop out price**. The Treasury then set the issue's coupon to the next lowest one–eighth of a percentage point so that the average price paid was as close to par as possible without exceeding par. Each successful bidder was then charged a price that corresponded to its bid and the issue's coupon. Some bidders would pay a premium, others a discount, and some would pay par. The difference between the average bid and the stop out bid was called the **tail**. Noncompetitive bids from small investors (up to $1 million) were also accepted, and all noncompetitive bidders received their securities based on the average bid.

The Treasury's auction method was often criticized, but it seemed to work reasonably well most of the time. The system accommodated the Treasury's needs, and there was little evidence, at least as far as the public was concerned, of unfair trading practices. But, as noted in the introductory chapter, market makers in any security stand to profit by establishing a monopoly position in a security, and Treasury securities are no exception. Unfortunately, in the early 1990s, senior members of the Treasury desk at one of the most prestigious investment banks, Salomon Brothers, long renowned for its bond trading expertise, admitted to violating auction rules. The violations were apparently for purposes of securing a monopoly–like position in certain Treasury issues. In essence, Salomon's traders bid aggressively for the legal limit to which they were entitled—i.e., 35 percent of the offering—but then also submitted bids for customers. Bidding on behalf of customers for customers' accounts is a proper function of a primary government securities dealer; but in this case, the customers did not request that the bids be made and did not know that the bids were being made. Once the securities were purchased for customers, Salomon bought them from the customers' accounts for what the customers had paid, thus placing the securities in Salomon Brothers' own account. This practice seems to have made it possible for Salomon Brothers to gain control at times of considerably more than the allowed percentage of the issuance. For example, Salomon controlled 94 percent of the 2–year Treasury notes sold to competitive bidders in May 1991. If noncompetitive bidders are included, then Salomon controlled 86 percent of the $12.26 billion note issue.[1]

This illegal trading practice seems to have gone on at Salomon Brothers for some time before it was discovered. It appears that management was aware of irregular activity in the Treasury accounts but chose to ignore it. When it became apparent that the authorities were looking into irregularities in the Treasury trading practices at Salomon Brothers, senior management took a closer look and decided it would be best to "come clean." Senior management then reported what they had found to the authorities. Those directly responsible for the irregularities and those managers who were clearly aware of, who should have been aware of, or who tolerated the irregularities either resigned or were fired.

In the end, Salomon was fined $290 million to settle securities and antitrust charges by the SEC and Justice Department and another $4 million to settle charges levied by 39 states and the District of Columbia.[2] However, Salomon was not forced to plead guilty to any felonies. This concession was important, because a party convicted of a felony cannot, under the law, engage in securities business. But of greater importance than the fines, Salomon's reputation was badly damaged. This made it harder for Salomon to attract business and enter markets. To illustrate, (1) third–quarter 1992 earnings fell 93 percent, from $85 million in 1991 to $6 million in 1992; (2) Salomon had difficulty re–entering the municipal bond market in March of 1993, which it had left in April of 1987; and (3) Salomon's debt was downgraded in April of 1993.

---

[1] *The Wall Street Journal*, September 5, 1991, page C1.

[2] *The Wall Street Journal*, January 6, 1993.

Some feel that Salomon Brothers got off too lightly for its misdeeds. Others feel that the treatment was fair, in light of the fact that the firm's management itself brought the illegal activity to the attention of the authorities. This is undoubtedly an issue that will be debated for some time.

One of the consequences of what became known as the Salomon Brother's Treasury auction scandal was a decision by the Treasury to experiment with alternative auction methodologies. The first experiment to be tried was instituted in 1992. It is a Dutch auction system in which each competitive bidder bids, in yield, for a portion of the issue. After all the bids are counted, all the bidders receive the securities at the same yield, which is the highest accepted bid. At first glance, such a system would seem to work to the detriment of the issuer. After all, it awards every bidder the highest successful bid, irrespective of how low the bids were. The logic in this system is that it encourages bidders to enter low bids quite aggressively, since they will all get the securities at the highest accepted bid anyway. But the lower a firm bids, the more likely it is that the firm will get a share of the issue. If it bids high and the auction is oversubscribed (the usual case), the firm will not obtain any securities. If a firm fails to get sufficient securities to meet its presell obligations, the firm will have to buy the securities in the secondary market—probably at a higher price—to meet its commitments.

Once the auction is complete and the yield is established, the coupon is set in the old way and the dealers receive their securities in the usual fashion.[3] Noncompetitive bids are also accepted, and all noncompetitive bidders receive their securities at the same price as competitive bidders.

It is unclear whether or not the new auction system will be made permanent. In theory, at least, if markets are efficient, it really should not make any difference what system is used to auction the securities provided the system is fair to all participants. In other words, rational expectations should prevail and the same equilibrium should be achieved.

Investment banks derive revenue from participating in the Treasury's auction process from a number of sources. First, using their market savvy and trading expertise, they hope to buy securities at advantageous rates and then resell them to their presell books at a small profit. Although the

---

[3] Under the old auction system, the average yield and the coupon were very close. This is not necessarily the case under the experimental system.

profit may be small in terms of the yield differentials between their buying and selling prices, the transactions at this level are huge—in the hundreds of millions of dollars, and often in the billions. Even on small yield differences, such large transactions can produce handsome profits. Second, investment bankers need to build inventory for their secondary market making—i.e., dealer activity. Typically, a dealer's bid–ask spread on wholesale transactions, stated as price differentials, on actively traded Treasuries is about 1/32nd of a point. However, this can be as little as 1/64th of a point and as much as 1/8th of a point. Third, investment banks will use Treasuries to engage in various types of trading, hedging, and arbitrage strategies.[4] Some of these are exceedingly complex and beyond the scope of this book. Some of the simpler uses will be discussed in later chapters.

Agency Finance

The securities (debt issues) of federal agencies and sponsored corporations of the U.S. Government are called, in market jargon, **agencies**. From an investment perspective, they fill a niche somewhere between corporate debt securities and Treasury securities. For example, like Treasuries, many have the explicit backing of the federal government. Such backing is said to be *de jure*. Others do not have the explicit backing of the government, but they are implicitly backed. Investors understand that the government would not let the enterprise default on its obligations. Such backing is said to be *de facto*. The crisis in the FSLIC in recent years is a good example of the importance of this *de facto* backing. Also, like Treasuries, the interest income on some, but not all, agency issues is exempt from state and local income taxes. But, as with corporates, the distribution process involves the formation of a distribution syndicate rather than a Fed–managed auction. And the interest accrual method is of the corporate type (called 30 over 360) as opposed

---

[4] For discussion of some of these strategies and the role played by Treasuries in affecting them, see Marshall and Bansal (1992, 1993), Chapter 23.

to the Treasury type (called actual over 365).[5] Yet the settlement period is one business day, like Treasuries, rather than five business days, like corporate.

Agency issues trade at a yield premium to Treasuries, and yields are often quoted as a **spread over Treasuries** of equivalent average life.[6] With the exception of mortgage–related agency issues, this spread appears to be compensation for a lack of liquidity relative to Treasuries. In the case of the mortgage–related issues, the spread also includes compensation for bearing the prepayment risk associated with these instruments.

The issuers of agency securities include a number of major agencies and sponsored corporations. Some of these are mortgage market–related and others are not. The former include the Government National Mortgage Association (GNMA, called Ginnie Mae), the Federal Home Loan Banks (FHLB), the Federal National Mortgage Association (FNMA, called Fannie Mae), and the Federal Home Loan Mortgage Corporation (FHLMC, called Freddie Mac). In addition to the major issuers, there were, for many years, many minor issuers. These minor issuers lacked market clout and often upset the offering calendars of the major issuers and the Treasury. To rectify these problems, Congress created the Federal Financing Bank (FFB) in 1973. The FFB consolidates the issuances of all federal agencies except the major ones. Because agencies issue their securities, like the Treasury, under Acts of Congress, they are exempt from SEC registration.

Role of the Investment Bank in the Agency Market

Each federal agency appoints a **fiscal agent** to act as its representative. These fiscal agents are typically major investment banks or commercial banks. The fiscal agents assist in the design and pricing of the securities.

---

[5] Corporate coupon–bearing notes and bonds accrue interest on the assumption that each month has 30 days and each year has 360 days. Thus, such instruments do not accrue interest on the 31st day of a month, and they accrue three days' interest on February 28 in a non–leap year. Treasury coupons accrue one day's interest each day, every day. They treat each year as having 365 days.

[6] Average life is used in lieu of maturity because many agencies, particularly those established to fund the mortgage market, are amortizing, whereas Treasuries are always nonamortizing. In such situations, maturity is not a good comparative measure.

They do not sell the agency securities directly to investors; however, they are responsible for ancillary services, such as serving as paying agents and handling the routine clerical duties associated with managing the issue.

The actual sale (distribution) of the securities is handled by a dealer syndicate assembled for that purpose. The dealers perform the underwriting function; that is, they buy the securities from the agency for the purpose of reselling them to investors.

The underwriters in agency issues, particularly mortgage–related issuances, often repackage the securities to make them more attractive to investors. For example, investment banks will often purchase whole mortgages and then securitize them, through structures called **collateralized mortgage obligations**, for subsequent resale to investors. This transforms the issuance from a single–class asset to a multiclass asset and can add value for investors. The investment banks seek to exploit this added value—a form of arbitrage.

Investment banks may also add special financial engineering features to the securities, such as trailing floors in exchange for periodic caps on floating–rate issues. (We return to the financial engineering role of investment banks in Chapters 8 and 9.) These same dealers, generally, are active in the secondary market for the securities. The dealer syndicates include both investment banks and other broker/dealers.

Municipal Finance

The municipal market was once synonymous with the term **tax–exempt finance**. Due to the advent of private–project financings with a tax–exempt character, however, this is no longer literally true. Municipals include issuances of state governments, local governments, and certain other entities and political subdivisions, including such things as school districts and agencies of state and local governments. This market is large and grew very rapidly throughout the 1980s. By the start of the 1990s, the number of individual issuers numbered around 40,000. It is dominated, however, by the issues of a handful of states and their municipalities.

The investor's attraction to the municipal market is predicated, in large part, on the tax treatment of the interest these instruments pay. The interest payments are exempt from federal income tax (both corporate and personal) and may, depending on the residence of the investor, also be exempt from state and local income taxes.

The municipal market is a distinct segment of the fixed–income market and occupies a niche all its own. This is explained by more than just the tax treatment of the interest income thrown off by these securities. The issuers are organized differently and have an altogether different purpose for their existence. For these reasons, municipal issuers are generally serviced by a different group within an investment bank than are the corporate issuers.

Municipal issues include both notes and bonds. Issues having maturities up to three years are generally classified as notes, and those having maturities longer than three years are generally classified as bonds. These instruments fall into two general categories: general obligation bonds and revenue bonds. **General obligation bonds** are issued by states, cities, and other taxing jurisdictions. These bonds are secured by the general taxing authority of these jurisdictions. For some, like school districts, this taxing authority is often limited to taxes of one specific type, such as real estate. But in others, such as cities and states, it includes all forms of taxes. Obligations of those entities with broad taxing authority are sometimes called **full faith and credit obligations**.

Revenue bonds are issued by entities created for purposes of financing and operating special projects, such as bridges, tunnels, road systems, airports, colleges and universities, power projects, and so on. They are also sometimes used to finance industrial development projects, in which case the projects sometimes take on a mixed public/private character. Debt obligations issued to finance specific projects are typically serviced by the revenues, and only the revenues, generated by those projects. Thus, bonds sold to finance the construction of a bridge or tunnel, such as those issued by the Metropolitan Bridge and Tunnel Authority in New York, are serviced, and ultimately retired, by the tolls charged to users of those facilities; hence, the name revenue bond.

Sometimes taxing jurisdictions will issue bonds that are a combination of general obligation and revenue bonds. These issues are backed by the general taxing authority of the issuing jurisdiction but also encompass a claim to the revenues thrown off by certain specific projects. The revenue component will come into play in the event that the general taxing authority should prove inadequate to service the debt. At the other extreme, but still within the purview of taxing jurisdictions, are issues that limit the claim on taxing authority to certain forms of taxation. These obligations are called **limited–tax general obligation** bonds.

It is recognized, in most cases, that revenue bonds are riskier than general obligation bonds. The reason for this is simple. Debt service on revenue bonds is most often limited to a single revenue source and not backed by the general taxing authority of the issuing jurisdiction. If that source fails to generate the revenues that were anticipated when the project was planned, the issuer may prove unable to service its debt. A project may fail to generate anticipated revenues for a number of reasons: demand for the product or service provided by the project might have been overestimated; the project might become obsolete due to the advent of new technology; private competitors may offer a superior alternative product or service; the project might not be completed due to cost overruns and/or supervening illegality; or the project might have to cease operating due to a natural disaster, such as an earthquake.

Probably the best–known revenue bond default in the United States over the last 20 years is the failure of the Washington Public Power Supply System (WPPSS). WPPSS was established by the state of Washington to provide for the wholesale production of electric power for resale to municipal and private power companies in the American Northwest. In 1977, WPPSS issued revenue bonds to finance two new nuclear power plants, called Projects 4 and 5. These bonds were supported by sales contracts of the power that was to be produced. Unfortunately, the project experienced large cost overruns, and it became apparent that the growth in electric power demand for the Northwest had been overestimated. Based on these considerations, the Washington Public Power Supply Company terminated the construction of the plants in 1982. The holders of WPPSS Project 4 and 5 revenue bonds then brought suit against the issuing authority and the affiliated municipalities. In 1983, the Washington State Supreme Court ruled that the state and local authorities had no legal authority to repay the debt from other revenue sources. WPPSS then defaulted on $2.25 billion of bonds. The default, which came to be known as "WHOOPS," sent shock waves through the municipal market, causing the yields on revenue bonds, particularly for wholesale electric power projects, to rise considerably relative to general obligation bonds.

During the early 1980s, the volume of new tax–exempts exploded. In 1985, the volume of tax–exempt issuances exceeded the volume of taxable corporate debt issuances for the first time (as measured by par values). This was after the tax–exempt market nearly doubled in size from about $119 billion of new issuances in 1984 to $218 billion of new issuances in 1985. The rapid growth during this period was motivated in part by changes in federal law which allowed municipalities to issue tax–exempt securities to finance private projects, called **private–purpose tax–exempts**. Not surprisingly, the rapid increase in the volume of private–purpose tax–exempts attracted congressional attention, given its impact on tax revenues. In response, as part of the Tax Reform Act of 1986, Congress placed restrictions on private–purpose usage of the tax–exempt markets. Some purposes were banned altogether and others were limited in size. The supply of new issue private–purpose tax–exempts declined thereafter. Additionally, the 1986 Tax Act limited the flotation costs that an issuer of private–purpose bonds can incur to 2 percent of the proceeds raised. Not surprisingly, this restriction cut deeply into the investment banking communities' willingness to service the private–purpose tax–exempt market.

The U.S. Constitution specifically prohibits the federal government from interfering in the financing of state governments and, by extension, local governments. Consequently, municipal issues need not be registered with the SEC and are exempt from the disclosure requirements that apply to corporate issuances. As a result, there is considerable discrepancy between the level of disclosure provided by different issuers. Some, notably large regular issuers, generally provide considerable disclosure in the form of a detailed offering statement or prospectus. Other issuers, however, provide little more than summary credit information. A paucity of information tends to limit the market for the latter securities to investors in the geographic region of the issuer who know the entity reasonably well, who are comfortable with the risks involved, and who are satisfied with the capacity of the issuer to repay.

The Role of Investment Banks in the Municipal Market

Although they can, municipal issuers rarely attempt to sell securities directly to investors. There is a limited amount of private placement activity in the municipal market, but the underwriting route utilized in public offerings of corporate issues is most often employed for municipal issues. For most municipal issuances, an underwriting syndicate is formed. The issuer sells the issue to the syndicate for resale to investors. The underwriting agreement is usually negotiated, but competitive bidding involving several syndicates might be employed. Negotiated underwritings are the norm in the issuance of revenue bonds. Competitive bidding and negotiated underwritings are about equally common in general obligation issues. Some state laws require competitive bidding in cases where taxing authority will be used to service the issue. In any case, once the underwriting agreement is reached, the syndicate assumes the risks of a failed offering. The syndicate then reoffers the securities to potential investors.

The competitive bidding process is a bit different on municipal offerings from that on corporate offerings. First, rather than "invite" syndicates to participate, the municipality will publish an official notice of sale that specifies the size of the issuance, the maturity(s) of the bonds, the principal amount, any conditions or restrictions surrounding the issuance, and so on. The syndicates then formulate their bids, which can be a complex undertaking for underwriters given the myriad restrictions that can be placed on the issuance. For example, it is quite common for tax–exempt issuers to issue **serial bonds** (bonds which are divided into distinct tranches, with each tranche scheduled to mature on a different date). At the same time, there may be a constraint that requires that all coupons be set within several hundred basis points of one another. If the yield curve is particularly steeply sloped, it may not be possible to accomplish this objective without selling some of the bonds at a premium to par and others at a discount from par.

An interesting difference between corporate underwriting syndicates and tax–exempt underwriting syndicates concerns the types of participants involved. Under the Glass–Steagall Act, commercial banks are banned, in general, from participation in securities transactions. However, the Act specifically exempts banks from this provision when the securities are general obligation issues of state and local government units. Thus, the securities subsidiaries of commercial banks have always participated in the underwriting and distribution of municipal general obligation bonds. In 1968, as part of the Housing and Urban Development Act, the underwriting authority of commercial banks in the municipal market was further extended to include revenue bonds that were issued to fund housing and higher education. During most of the 1980s, several major commercial banks, most notably Citicorp, Bankers Trust, Morgan Guarantee, and Chase Manhattan, have held spots among the top 20 lead underwriters of municipal securities.

While tax–exempt issuers are not required to register their securities with the SEC, their issuances must still go through the three stages of issuance: origination, underwriting, and distribution. The origination phase, which involves preparing the securities for distribution— documentation, financial statements, preparation of the indenture, etc.—is handled by an investment bank's public finance banking department. The underwriting division takes responsibility for pricing. Distribution involves two steps: formation of the syndicate, with the aid of the bank's syndicate department, and distribution—a responsibility of sales and trading.

Until 1975, underwriters and distributors of tax–exempt securities were only subject to general antifraud provisions in federal securities law. However, evidence of high pressure, known as "**boiler room**," sales tactics eventually led Congress to create the Municipal Securities Rulemaking Board of MSRB in 1975. This body is a self–regulating organization for the industry with the power to make rules for participants in these markets. Enforcement of the rules is vested in the SEC.

An important function of investment banks, including the securities units of commercial banks, in municipal finance is the provision of financial advisory services. A survey by the Government Finance Research Center[7] lists a number of important advisory areas utilized by tax–exempt issuers. We have chosen to group these into four categories:[8]

1. advice on financial planning and debt policy
2. technical assistance in structuring new debt
3. information dissemination
4. monitoring

(Advisory services are discussed in more detail in Chapter 10.)

---

[7] Government Finance Research Center, *The Price of Advice*, Chicago: Government Finance Officers Association, 1987.

[8] Ronald W. Forbes, "The Tax–Exempt Market," in *Investment Banking Handbook*, New York: Wiley, 1988.

Who's Who in Municipal Underwriting

Many of the same names that dominate the league tables for corporate underwritings are also large players among municipal underwriters. But some other names appear as well. Specifically, using the 1991 league tables for municipal underwritings, and giving "full credit" to the lead underwriters, the dominant players were Goldman Sachs; Merrill Lynch; Lehman Brothers; First Boston; Smith Barney, Harris Upham; Bear, Stearns; and PaineWebber.

Summary

Just as private business must secure financing by tapping the capital markets, the public sector must also secure financing to achieve its purposes. The public sector consists of the U.S. Treasury, agencies and sponsored corporations of the federal government, and municipal issues. To some degree, the latter includes certain private–purpose tax–exempt issues.

To the extent that tax collections are insufficient to finance the federal government's expenditures and transfer payments, the Treasury must sell debt. It does this through primary market–making activities effected on its behalf by the Federal Reserve Bank of New York with the active participation of the primary government securities dealers.

Agency issues are distributed by dealer syndicates assembled by a fiscal agent appointed by the agency. The fiscal agent also performs various ancillary services for the issuer but does not itself become involved in the selling operation. The dealer syndicates perform the underwriting function in that they buy the securities for resale to investors. However, in many agency issuances, particularly the mortgage market, the underwriters alter the structure of the securities to make them more attractive to investors. This is an important financial engineering contribution.

In the municipal market, the investment banks underwrite and distribute both the general obligation and revenue bonds of states, municipalities, and other political entities. The underwritings may be either negotiated or competitive.

Unlike public offerings of corporations, public offerings of the public sector do not require registration with the Securities and Exchange Commission.

References and Suggested Reading

Buser, S. A. and P. J. Hess, "Empirical Determinants of the Relative Yields on Taxable and Tax–Exempt Securities," *Journal of Financial Economics*, 17:2, December 1986, pp. 335–355.

Chandy, P. R. and I. Karafiath, "The Effect of the WPPSS Crisis on Utility Common Stock Returns," *Journal of Business, Finance, and Accounting*, 16:4, Autumn 1989, pp. 531–542.

Corrigan, E. G., "Changes in the Government Securities Market," *Federal Reserve Bank of New York Quarterly Review*, 16:4, Winter 1991–92, pp. 6–11.

The Handbook of U.S. Treasury and Government Agency Securities: Instruments, Strategies, and Analysis, Frank J. Fabozzi, (ed.), Chicago: Probus Publishing, 1990.

Fortune, P., "The Municipal Bond Market, Part II: Problems and Policies," *New England Economic Review*, May/June 1992, pp. 47–64.

Hoffman, M. J. R., W. G. Mister, and J. R. Strawser, "The Tax Reform Act of 1986 and Tax–Exempt Financing: Analysis and Speculation," *Government Accountants Journal*, 37:4, Winter 1989, pp. 43–51.

Kuttner, R., "How Not to Deregulate Banking: The Fire Wall," *New Republic*, June 20, 1988, pp. 13–15.

Laber, G., "Market Reaction to Bond Rating Changes: The Case of WHOOPS Bonds," *Mid–Atlantic Journal of Business*, 24:1, Winter 1985/86, pp. 53–65.

Lasser, D. J., "New Issue Yield Spreads in the 30–Year Treasury Bond Market," *Financial Review*, 26:2, May 1991, pp. 237–247.

Marquette, P. R. and E. R. Wilson, "The Case for Mandatory Municipal Disclosure: Do Seasoned Municipal Bond Yields Impound Publicly Available Information?" *Journal of Accounting and Public Policy*, 11:3, Fall 1992, pp. 181–206.

Marshall, J. F. and V. K. Bansal, *Financial Engineering: A Complete Guide to Financial Innovation*, New York: New York Institute of Finance, 1992.

Marshall, J. F. and V. K. Bansal, *Financial Engineering*, 2e, Miami: Kolb Publishing, 1993.

Peavy, J. W. and G. H. Hempel, "The Effect of the WPPSS Crisis on the Tax–Exempt Bond Market," *Journal of Financial Research*, 10:3, Fall 1987, pp. 239–247.

Schaffer, L. S., "Who Is the Municipal Securities Rulemaking Board?" *ABA Bank Compliance*, 10:3, April 1989, pp. 19–24, 41.

Silber, W. L., *Municipal Revenue Bonds, Costs, and Bank Underwriting: A Survey of the Evidence*, New York: NYU, Graduate School of Business, Salomon Brothers Center for the Study of Financial Institutions, 1980.

Smith, C. W., "Economics and Ethics: The Case of Salomon Brothers," *Journal of Applied Corporate Finance*, 5:2, Summer 1992, pp. 23–28.

Umlauf, S. R., "Information Asymmetries and Security Market Design: An Empirical Study of the Secondary Market for U.S. Government Securities," *Journal of Finance*, 46:3, July 1991, pp. 929–953.

Zimmerman, D., "Tax–Exempt Bonds: A Sacred Cow That Gave (Some) Milk," *National Tax Journal*, 42:3, September 1989, pp. 283–292.

5

Secondary Market Making: Dealer/Broker Activity

Overview

The **secondary market** is the market in which previously issued (i.e., outstanding) securities trade among investors and between investors and dealers. This is quite distinct from the **primary market**, in which issuers distribute securities through underwriters to investors. In primary market transactions, the issuer of the securities receives the proceeds of the sale. In secondary market transactions, an investor or dealer, not the issuer, receives the proceeds.

At a purely theoretical macroeconomic level, secondary market making may not seem as important an investment banking activity as is primary market making. After all, primary market making allocates scarce financial resources among competing parties that have a need for such resources. In the process, financial claims—some equity and some debt—are created. Secondary market transactions transfer ownership of those claims without redirecting the allocation of the resources that were provided through the primary market transactions.

This macroeconomic view, however, is short–sighted. It overlooks the fact that resource allocation decisions—i.e., decisions to buy stocks and bonds from issuers—are made at a microeconomic level. In other words, the actual process of resource allocation is the product of thousands, often millions, of decisions by individuals and institutional investment managers.

It is highly unlikely that individual investors and money managers would be so willing to exchange their monetary assets for financial claims if they did not believe they could liquidate those claims (i.e., sell them to other investors) should they feel a need to do so. And there could be many reasons for them to do so: investment expectations change, unexpected financial needs arise, financial situations change, asset owners die, and so on. Without liquidity, a financial claim is much less attractive to an investor. Thus, an investor in an illiquid asset can be expected to demand a higher yield as compensation for the asset's illiquidity, and this higher yield would have to be borne by the issuer.

By their secondary market making, the broker/dealer operations of investment banks and other securities firms give financial claims greater liquidity. This benefits investors, who want an escape window; issuers, which can expect to pay lower yields; and the investment banks themselves—which earn profits from their broker/dealer activities.

In this chapter, we will consider the activities of broker/dealers. The term **broker/dealer** is understood to include the secondary market–making activities of investment banks, commercial banks (which make markets in exempt securities[1]), and independent securities firms. We begin by distinguishing between brokers and dealers. We then examine dealer activity in more detail. We follow with an examination of brokerage activity.

As an aside, for certain financial instruments, notably derivative instruments, there is no clear demarcation between the primary and secondary markets. Indeed, the terminology is hardly appropriate at all. With these instruments, the act of selling a contract (assuming one does not already own one) serves to create it. The act of buying a contract (assuming one is not already short) has the same result. The point is that we will lump transactions in the derivative markets (futures, options, and swaps) together with secondary market activity, because all such transactions involve dealers and brokers. Nevertheless, the transactions can be just as easily considered primary in nature.

Throughout this chapter we will use the term *dealer* to refer both to the securities firms that engage in this activity and also to the persons

---

[1] By "exempt securities," we are referring to securities that are exempt from the provisions of the Glass–Steagall Act such that they may be traded by commercial banks or their subsidiaries.

employed as dealers by the securities firms. The same dual usage will apply to the term *broker*.

Dealing versus Brokering

A **dealer** in securities is really little different from a dealer in anything else. A dealer buys and sells. In both cases, she is transacting for her own account; that is, she is a **principal** in the transactions. As such, she cannot charge a commission for her role as a dealer but must earn her living (and profits for her firm) from the difference between her buying price (called her **bid price**) and her selling price (called her **ask price** or **offer price**, also known as an **asked price**). The difference between the bid and ask prices is called the **bid–ask spread**. Because the transactions a dealer makes are for her own account, she bears the risk that the value of the securities might change while she holds them. This is called **price risk**.

Unlike a dealer, a **broker** in securities is not a principal to the transactions in which he is involved when he is acting in the capacity of a broker. Instead, he is acting as an **agent** on behalf of his customers. For his role as an agent, the broker collects a **commission** on each transaction he makes. Because he is not a principal to the transactions, the broker does not bear any price risk.

Many dealer markets, particularly in the over–the–counter stock market, involve individuals who serve as both brokers and dealers. As such, the broker must be clear, on each transaction to which he is a party, as to the capacity in which he is acting—that of a principal, or an agent.

In large investment banks, broker/dealer activity typically falls within a department called **sales and trading**. We distinguish here between sales (which encompasses both brokerage and dealer activity) and trading, which we take up in the next chapter.

Dealer Activity in the Financial Markets

Certain types of financial instruments trade only in an over–the–counter market. Such markets are known as **dealer markets**, because their existence depends on dealers that are willing to play the role of market maker. Swaps, mortgage–backed products, OTC options such as caps and floors, and guaranteed investment contracts are just some examples of the products that trade in dealer markets. Other instruments trade exclusively on exchanges. Futures are the best example of these. Still other instruments trade in both exchange markets and in dealer markets—stocks and bonds, for example.

Traditionally, an **exchange** is an organized, centrally located marketplace that lists specific instruments. The instruments are highly standardized so that all units of the same instrument are identical to one another. Buyers and sellers, or their agents, meet at designated locations on the floor of the exchange to trade the listed instruments.

The need for floor space to provide for physical meetingplaces for buyers and sellers has always placed a constraint on the number of securities that an exchange can list. The same is true, of course, for futures exchanges.

The rules for listing on an exchange are stringent. They are promulgated and enforced by the exchange and its affiliated self–regulating organizations, and by oversight and regulatory agencies like the Securities and Exchange Commission (SEC) and the Commodity Futures Trading Commission (CFTC). Trading rules generally require open outcry of all bids and offers with all market participants having equal opportunity to **hit a bid** or **take an offer**. In the United States, the best–known stock exchange is the New York Stock Exchange, and the best known futures exchange is the Chicago Board of Trade.

A dealer market is considerably less formal and much more decentralized than an exchange market. These markets are made by dealers, and trading is said to take place in an **over–the–counter (OTC)** environment. Consider the case of stocks and bonds. In the dealer market for stocks and bonds, any registered broker/dealer can appoint himself a dealer in a security, provided he conforms to the National Association of Securities Dealers (NASD) rules and can meet certain minimum financial and clearing standards. As a dealer, an individual must be prepared to take a position in all securities in which he makes markets. At any given point in time, these positions may be either long or short.

The dealer stands ready, at all times, to provide a **quote** and to **size the quote**. The quote includes both a bid price and an ask price, and the size is the maximum number of shares, in the case of stock, or the maximum amount of principal, in the case of bonds, for which the quote may be considered applicable. Each publicly traded stock is assigned a symbol (sometimes called a ticker symbol) consisting of two, three, or four letters. These symbols are unique in that no two stocks employ the same ticker symbol. In the case of bonds, each bond can be identified by its issuer, its maturity date, and its coupon rate. However, each bond issue also carries a cusip number, which serves as a unique identifier. All bonds of the same issue having the same terms share the same cusip number.

The OTC market in stocks has become increasingly automated through the efforts of the NASD. Today, any broker searching for securities for a client can simply punch the appropriate symbol into a computer network that was established and is operated by the NASD and immediately obtain bid and ask prices for almost any widely traded security. The system is called the National Association of Securities Dealers Automated Quotation System, or the NASDAQ system. If there are multiple dealers, the system will provide all current bids and all current asks and highlight the highest bid and the lowest ask. The broker then simply calls or telexes the dealer to "hit" the dealer's bid, on behalf of his client, or to "take" the dealer's ask, again, on behalf of his client. The client, i.e., broker's customer, will pay a commission to the broker but will not ordinarily see the bid–ask spread when she receives written confirmation of the trade unless she specifically requests it. Thus, the bid–ask spread is a part of the cost of transacting in a market, just as is the commission.

There have been significant moves in recent years to replace the physical trading facilities of stock and futures exchanges with computer-based systems. The New York Stock Exchange, for example, has introduced a computer system called the **designated order turnaround** (**DOT**) system to match buyers and sellers in large transactions. This system is critical to certain strategies, such as program trading, that depend on speed of execution to succeed. The Chicago futures exchanges have also introduced automated order–matching systems, which they continue to refine and improve. The dominant system, **GLOBEX**, has been licensed to other exchanges as well. As these systems become more and more sophisticated and more capable of mimicking the action on the floor of the exchange, the physical exchange floor, with all of its space–consuming baggage, becomes progressively less necessary. It also removes the constraints on the number of individual securities (or futures) that an exchange can list and trade. Interestingly, it would seem that the technology revolution is rapidly making the distinction between exchanges and OTC markets less clear.

Investment banks participate in the secondary markets as securities dealers for a number of reasons. First and generally foremost, securities dealing is a profit center for the bank. That is, dealers earn, or at least try to earn, profits for the firm from their bid–ask spread. In stable markets, the dealer's life is relatively easy. He buys, he sells, he buys or sells again. If his pricing is right, then his inventory will tend to be relatively stable. If his pricing is too high, more people will sell to him than buy from him, and his inventory will grow. This would suggest a need to lower his pricing. If, on the other hand, the dealer's pricing is too low, more people will buy from him than sell to him and his inventory will shrink—perhaps becoming negative (a short position). Neither an unplanned inventory buildup nor an unplanned inventory drawdown is desirable, so the dealer must monitor his position and adjust his prices accordingly.

The dealer's bid–ask spread varies based, in large part, on the level of trading in the security and the number of other dealers with whom the dealer competes. If the volume of trading is routinely heavy, it can be expected that a number of persons or firms will compete as dealers, and competition among them will tend to narrow the spread. For example, in heavily traded OTC stocks, spreads of as little as one–eighth of a point (the minimum possible) are not unusual for $40 stocks. On the other hand, in very lightly traded securities, where as little as 100 shares (one round lot) may be traded per week, a spread of $5 or more might occur on a $40 stock. For obvious reasons, the size of the bid–ask spread is considered a standard method for judging market liquidity.

Interestingly, the 1/8th point increments in which the prices of stocks in the United States move may soon change. The convention goes back to the early days of the markets and is based on the use of hand signals for trading. As trading becomes increasingly computer–based, the 1/8th minimum price change convention becomes progressively more obsolete. It merely guarantees that investors will have to absorb at least 1/16th of a point when they buy and 1/16th of a point when they sell (i.e., one–half of the bid–ask spread on each side of the transaction). This is in addition to any commissions that might have to be paid to brokers. Recent suggestions to change the minimum price change to 1 cent ($0.01) from 1/8th point ($0.125) have been met, not surprisingly, by jeers from dealers, who fear that such a change will cut into their revenues—particularly in more liquid securities, where the spread is rarely more than 1/8th point.

Besides the profit motive, there are other reasons that investment banks act as dealers in the secondary markets. One reason is to develop and maintain good pricing skills. This is a critical ingredient for effectively pricing issues of new securities in primary market making (underwriting and distribution). Thus, secondary market making supports primary market making. Additionally, because issuers need and want liquid markets for their securities, and because primary market making is a very relationship–driven activity, investment banks will generally make secondary markets in the securities that they underwrite—at least until other dealers have established a viable market. Closely related to this is the role of the lead underwriter in establishing and maintaining a stabilizing bid for a new offering throughout the offering period. The latter should not be regarded as a traditional dealer activity, however, because the lead underwriter does not generally adjust its price during the offering period to reflect market conditions.

To some degree, even exchange trading involves dealer activity, although it is generally not called that. For example, the New York Stock Exchange employs a specialist for each stock it lists. The **specialist** is an exchange member appointed by the exchange to serve the special functions and assume the special responsibilities of the specialist role. Among these responsibilities is to guarantee that there will always be a buyer and a seller, so that any member of the trading public can always get a market order filled—whether buying or selling. To accomplish this, the specialist will provide a bid price and an ask price. Any floor trader or floor broker interested in transacting in a stock can approach a trading post and solicit bids and offers from other traders. If there are no other bids and offers, the specialist is required to provide a quote. Thus, a portion of the specialist's income is derived from its bid–ask spread associated with its market making. Specialists perform other functions as well, but it is this dealer–type activity that is of interest here.

Specialists often work for specialist firms. These are firms that fill the role of specialist for many different stocks. By concentrating their energies in this type of activity, **specialist firms** try to become adept at managing their positions and securing the financing necessary to carry their positions.

In addition to specialists, there are other quasi–dealer activities that take place on exchange floors. For example, on stock exchanges, there are **odd–lot brokers** who buy and sell stock in lots of less than 100 shares. They typically provide a bid price a little below the current round–lot bid and an ask price a little above the current round–lot ask. While called odd–lot brokers, these people are actually dealers. On futures exchanges, too, there are traders who function as dealers. For example, there are traders called **scalpers** who will buy (sell) at a small price concession below (above) the last trade price, and so on.

The bond market is interesting in that bonds trade at two different levels. There is a **retail** market made by the New York Stock Exchange that services small investors who wish to buy bonds in small denominations (a few thousand dollars of par value, for example). But over 95 percent of par volume bond trading takes place at the **wholesale**, often called **institutional**, level, where dealers make markets in Treasury bonds, agency bonds, corporate bonds, municipal bonds, and mortgage–related products. There are also dealer markets for trading **high–yield**, sometimes called **junk**, bonds.

The wholesale markets for bonds and related fixed–income securities are divided into two broad categories: **taxable fixed–income** and **tax–exempt**. The taxable fixed–income securities include treasuries, agencies, corporates, mortgage–backs, asset–backs, and a few other areas. The tax–exempts include the issues of state and local governments and issues of certain other political jurisdictions. Although we should not generalize, within most investment banks, trading in taxable fixed–income occurs at type–specific desks: corporate desk, government desk, mortgage desk, and so on. Within each desk are found even more narrowly focused specialists. For example, at the government's desk, there are short–maturity traders (T–bills), intermediate–maturity traders (T–notes), and long–maturity traders (T–bonds). Similarly, at the corporate desk, trading in investment–grade bonds is separated from trading in high–yield bonds. Indeed, the latter is often housed at a separate desk altogether.

An interesting development during the 1980s was an explosion of custom–made financial products developed at, and introduced by, investment banks. There are many reasons for this, including the exploitation of arbitrage opportunities, meeting specific investors' special needs, guaranteeing a steady flow of underwriting business, and enhancing the firm's reputation as an innovator. However, one of the main motivations for product development is to create a monopoly or near monopoly position in a secondary market. Innovating firms **trademark** or **servicemark** the name, which is often an acronym, for each of their new products.[2] The firm then markets the product, which is referred to as a **proprietary product**, and creates a dealer–based secondary market for it. Investors who purchase the product and wish to resell it often have no choice but to do so through the investment bank that created it and which continues to make a market in it. Not surprisingly, the bid–ask spreads on such products tend to be higher than on the spreads of more generic products in which there are many dealers.

It must be remembered that, whether in primary market making or secondary market making, the revenue earned is transaction–based. More transactions mean more revenue. During the 1980s, the investment banking business became much more transaction–oriented—some would say **transaction–driven**. This development is explained, in part, by rapid advances in technology that made it possible to transact more cost–effectively, which resulted in a narrowing of the bid–ask spreads, and the rapid development of risk management techniques and instruments, which made it possible to carry large positions with relatively little risk.[3] This combination drove investment banks to focus on more and larger transactions and more product innovations, where the profit margins are higher.

Managing Dealer Risks

Dealers, whether in the stock, bond, currency, commodity, or any other market, must always be cognizant of the price risks that they bear. The act of being a dealer, by the very definition of the activity, requires the dealer to take positions.

Dealing is, strictly speaking, not a speculative activity. That is, dealers try to earn their profits from their bid–ask spread coupled with

---

[2] Examples of trademarked acronyms include CATS, TIGRs, LIONs, COUGARs, and so on.

[3] For example, some traders who employ Treasury yield curve strategies finance positions in repo markets and frequently achieve positions 50 times (or more) larger than their capital (margins).

frequent transactions. This is in contrast to **speculators**, who take positions based on price forecasts. In market slang, a forecast is called a **view**. Dealers will sometimes take speculative positions based on their "view" of the market, but when they do, they are no longer acting in their capacity as a dealer. Instead, they have assumed the role of a speculator. This is neither good nor bad, but it does highlight an important difference.

When acting in the capacity of a dealer, the dealer would, ideally, like not to have a net position. In other words, the dealer would always like to be buying and selling simultaneously the same number of units of a given security or instrument in which she is making markets. But buying and selling decisions on the part of investors are not coordinated, and, therefore, the dealer who is trying to make a market must accept that net positions (i.e., inventory) and inventory variations are necessary components of the business that she is in. Indeed, it is the very act of providing liquidity—i.e., bridging time gaps in the order flow—that is the essence of the value that dealers provide to investors and for which dealers earn their spread. Unfortunately, this same inventory exposes dealers to sizable risks, called **price risks**.

Price risk is the chance that the holder of a position will experience an unexpected change in the value of the position as a consequence of a change in the price level—a factor that is largely beyond the dealer's control—even when the dealer is in a monopoly situation. Managing price risks is critically important to being a successful dealer, and it involves three steps:

1. identify the risks
2. quantify the risks
3. manage the risks

The first step is to identify the risks. This means identifying all the risks to which a dealer is exposed from holding a particular security. In the case of a stock, this would seem, at first glance, to be rather straightforward. The price of the stock may go up or down. But all is not as it first seems. A change in the price of a stock may be associated with a change in the level of the stock market quite broadly and have nothing whatsoever to do with any specific event involving the firm. This tendency of stock prices to respond collectively to changing economic fundamentals is referred to as **systematic risk** or **market risk**. On the other hand, the price of a stock may change as a direct consequence of an event that is specific to the firm or industry, in which case the price change is not associated with a more general change in the overall level of the stock market (as measured by some broadly based stock index). This is referred to as **unsystematic risk** or **company– (or industry–) specific risk**.

The risks associated with fixed–income securities are considerably more complicated than those associated with stocks. Consider, for example, the risks associated with managing a bond position. First, there is **interest rate risk**, which is the sensitivity of the prices of fixed–income securities to changes in interest rate levels. This is a form of market risk, in the sense that it is not specific to any specific issuer. Simply put, when interest rates rise, bond prices fall, meaning that any bond dealer who is long bonds will suffer losses when interest rates rise. Although for most bond dealers interest rate risk is the dominant form of risk, it is far from the only form of risk with which bond dealers must contend. Other forms of risks are credit risk (the risk that the issuer's creditworthiness may deteriorate), call risk (the risk that the issuer may choose to retire the issue prior to maturity), prepayment risk (similar to call risk but applicable to mortgage–type debt securities), purchasing power risk (loss of purchasing power as a consequence of inflation), and tax rate risk (the risk that the tax treatment of an issue might change due to a change in the tax law or an unfavorable ruling by the tax courts).

The degree to which each of these types of risk is of concern to a specific dealer will depend on the type of fixed–income securities in the dealer's portfolio. For example, a dealer in Treasuries does not have to be concerned about credit risk or prepayment risk, but he does have to be concerned about interest rate risk (some Treasury issues are callable, so this risk might also be of some concern). A dealer in junk bonds, however, must be very much concerned about credit risk and call risk, in addition to interest rate risk. Junk bond values will change dramatically in response to changes in credit ratings and other judgments of credit–worthiness. Dealers in mortgage products must cope with significant prepayment risk exposures.

The point of this review is that dealers in securities must be aware of the risks to which they are exposed. They should also manage the risks. Failure to manage the risks can easily result in a dealer being forced out of business from an unexpected change in price levels—as happened in October 1987 and again, to a lesser degree, in October 1989.[4]

Before risks can be managed, they must be measured—i.e., quantified. This is important, because often the risks associated with one position and the risks associated with another position may be partially offsetting. This is sometimes called a **natural hedge**.

The simplest risks to manage are the market risks—that is, the risks associated with movements in the market as a whole. Let's consider a simple case of a dealer in the stock market. If the dealer makes a market in a single stock, he is bearing considerable company–specific risk. It is possible to hedge this company–specific risk with an option on the stock if (1) there is an option on the stock that is currently trading, and (2) the option market is sufficiently liquid that the cost of transacting in the option hedge does not cut too deeply into the dealer's market–making profits. An alternative, and generally superior, approach to hedge company–specific risks is available, but only for dealers who make markets in many stocks.

Consider such a dealer. Suppose that a dealer makes markets in 30, 40, or even 100 different stocks. It may be that a broker/dealer firm employs a number of people as dealers, each of whom is responsible for a handful of different stocks. For risk management purposes, we can, and should, look at the broker/dealer firm's aggregate position instead of at the positions of each employee–dealer individually. When looked at this broader level, the company–specific risks tend to cancel one another out. This is a natural consequence of diversification, and it is an integral part of modern portfolio theory.

The systematic risks associated with individual stocks are measured with the aid of what is known in portfolio theory as **beta** coefficients. The computation of these betas is not part of our discussion. Suffice it to say that each stock has its own idiosyncratic beta, and these betas are relatively easy to measure with standard statistical techniques. The overall beta of the broker/dealer's portfolio is simply a weighted average of the

---

[4] Dealers are usually forced out of the market well before bankruptcy. Unexpected changes in price levels may cause the value of the dealer's inventory to drop below regulators' capital requirements. The regulators will then step in and force the dealer out of business.

betas of the individual stocks in the portfolio. For a well–diversified dealer portfolio, then, the securities firm calculates the portfolio beta and selects a hedging instrument, such a stock index futures contract, like the S&P 500 futures contract traded on the Chicago Mercantile Exchange.

Let's consider a simple case. Suppose that a securities firm makes markets in 40 different securities. The firm's risk managers have calculated a beta for each stock in which the firm makes markets, and several times each day the risk managers calculate a portfolio beta by weighting each stock's beta by the sizes of the firm's positions in the securities. Let's suppose that the current portfolio size is $22.5 million and the portfolio beta is 1.25. This means that the firm's portfolio is 1.25 times as volatile, in terms of its systematic risk, as the S&P 500 (which has a beta of 1.00 by construction). Furthermore, let's assume the firm has decided to hedge its long position in stocks by using S&P 500 futures contracts, which are currently priced at $420 and employ a contract multiple of 500. The contract value is therefore $210,000, which is the product of the futures price and the contract multiple—i.e., 420 × $500.

The portfolio beta serves as the **hedge ratio**. A hedge ratio is the number of units of the hedging instrument needed to offset the risks associated with the cash position. The cash position, stocks in this case, is the position to be hedged.

The risk managers now calculate the size of the futures hedge needed to offset the risks associated with the dealer's portfolio, as follows:

$$\text{Size of Hedge} = \text{Hedge Ratio} \times \text{Size of Position}$$
$$= 1.25 \times \$22,500,000$$
$$= \$28,125,000$$

Finally, by dividing the above value by the value of each futures contract, the risk managers can determine the number of futures contracts necessary to hedge the dealer's overall cash position. The calculation is:

$$\text{Number of Futures} = \frac{\text{Size of Hedge}}{\text{Size of Futures}}$$

$$= \frac{\$28,125,000}{210,000}$$

$$= 133.9$$

Thus, the firm's risk managers will sell (go short) 134 S&P 500 futures contracts. Several times each day, the risk managers will recalculate the size of the hedge and the number of futures contracts required to keep the firm properly hedged. The hedge position will be increased or decreased accordingly.

The same kind of calculation is done to hedge a bond portfolio (and other fixed–income portfolios). In this case, the risk we want to hedge is the interest rate risk associated with changes in the level of interest rates. Again, the risk managers employ one or more of several different standardized measures of interest rate risk. The one that is best known is called **duration**, but the one that is most widely used is called the **dollar value of a basis point** (although it has several other names as well). The dollar value of a basis point (**DV01**) is defined as the dollar amount by which the market value of $100 of par bonds will change when the instrument's yield changes by one basis point (0.01%). This is computed for each bond. The firm's overall interest rate risk can then be found by aggregating the individual risks, as follows:

$$\text{Total Interest Rate Risk} = \frac{\Sigma \, \text{Size}_i \times \text{DV01}_i}{100}$$

where Size_i denotes the size (in par value dollars) of the i–th position and DV01_i denotes the DV01 of the i–th position. Next, the risk managers calculate the interest rate risk, again using DV01, associated with a futures contract. To complete our example, we will use Treasury bond futures for this purpose. Treasury bond futures cover $100,000 of par.

$$\text{Futures Contract Risk} = \frac{\text{DV01}_f \times \$100,000}{100}$$

Finally, the number of futures contracts required is calculated as:

$$\text{Number of Futures} = \frac{\text{Total Interest Rate Risk}}{\text{Futures Contract Risk}}$$

Thus, the process is essentially the same whether the risk managers are managing the risks associated with a stock or with a bond portfolio. Indeed, the process is the same regardless of the price risk we are managing and could just as easily have been a foreign exchange risk or a commodity price risk.

A properly structured hedge is critical to successful securities dealing. Only by keeping the price risks hedged can the dealer comfortably operate on a large scale with limited capital—essential to profitable operation in an intensely competitive world.

The same logic used to manage the risks associated with making markets in stocks and bonds, as outlined above, is used to manage risks when making markets in mortgage products, swaps, zero coupon bonds, and so on. We will touch on these subjects in later chapters.

Financing Dealer Inventory

Just as a securities dealer must hedge the risks associated with its positions, she must also finance her positions. For example, a major investment bank like Salomon Brothers holds many billions of dollars of securities to service its market–making functions. (These positions are separate from its speculative and arbitrage positions.) These positions must be financed. In the language of the markets, we say that the positions must be **carried**.

Consider a securities firm that makes wholesale markets in many different corporate bonds. Its customers are primarily financial institutions such as insurance companies and pension funds. To service these clients, the securities firm holds inventory positions (some short, but most long) in several hundred different securities. To carry these positions, the firm must borrow funds on a very large scale. Actually, the long positions require the firm to borrow funds and the short positions provide funds that can be lent. It is only the difference that must be financed (or lent).

Most financing of dealer positions today takes place in the **repurchase** and **resale** markets (i.e., the repo market). These same markets are also the source of securities that are sold short. Since its creation several decades ago, the repo market (and its counterpart, the dollar roll market, for mortgage–backed securities) have become a critical element of modern investment banking.

Let's see how the repo market works as a financing source for a securities dealer. For purposes of illustration, let's suppose we have a government securities dealer who has purchased, as part of his market–making activity, $10 million of par value T–bonds. The fair value of these bonds is currently 97–11/32, and the dealer bought them at his bid of 97–10/32, thereby picking up 1/32nd of a point for his trouble. At 97–11/32, the market value of the bonds is $9,734,375. When the dealer buys the bonds, he must also pay the seller the accrued interest on the bonds, which, we will suppose, is $125,000. Thus, the value of the bonds, including accrued interest, is $9,859,375 (i.e., $9,734,375 + $125,000).

To pay for the bonds, the dealer must borrow $9,859,375. He wants to keep the cost of this borrowing as low as possible, which, as a practical matter, means borrowing for a very short time and fully collateralizing the loan. The repo market is ideal for this purpose. The dealer "sells" the bonds in the repo market for $9,859,375 with a simultaneous agreement to "buy them back"—i.e., repurchase them—at a later date. This could be one day later, two days later, a week later, a month later, and so on.

Let's suppose that the dealer agrees to buy the bonds back one day later. As such, this is called an **overnight repo**. The agreement can either require that the dealer buy the securities back at the same price with "add–on" interest or, equivalently, to buy them back at a specific price that reflects the financing cost. For example, suppose that the overnight repo rate is 4 percent. The repo rate employs an actual/360–day count convention, so one day's interest is calculated as follows:

$$\text{One Day's Interest} = \$9,859,375 \times 4.00\% \times \frac{1}{360}$$

$$= \$1,095.49$$

Thus, the repo agreement could state that the dealer is selling the securities with the commitment to repurchase them the next day at $9,860,470.49 (i.e., $9,859,375 + $1,095.49), or it could simply require that the securities be repurchased the next day at $9,859,375 with $1,095.49 of interest (i.e., 4 percent). A repo transaction can be viewed two ways. First, it can be viewed as a sale and a repurchase, in which case the flat price would seem the correct way to state the repurchase terms. Alternatively, it can be viewed as a collateralized loan, in which case the add–on interest would seem the correct way to state the repurchase terms.

Both views of the transaction—sale and repurchase versus collateralized loan—are reasonable, and in fact the transactions are typically viewed as having characteristics of both of these forms. For example, during the time that the "lender" holds the securities, the borrower still bears all price risk associated with variations in the security's market value and the borrower is still entitled to all interest that accrues on the repo securities.

Because the dealer still accrues interest on the securities, he must consider the interest he earns relative to the repo interest cost of financing the securities. If the accruing coupon is greater than the repo costs, the net **cost of carry** may be negative. Of course, since the dealer still bears the price risks, he must keep the position hedged (probably in the futures market). The cost of hedging must also be factored into the analysis.

The repo markets can also be used to obtain securities for short sales. For example, suppose that a dealer has a customer who wants to buy $20 million of the same government bond discussed earlier. The fair market price is still 97–11/32. The dealer's ask price is 97–12/32. The dealer has $10 million of the bond in inventory. The dealer sells the $20 million to the client. Of this, $10 million is from inventory and the other $10 million is obtained in the repo market. In short, the dealer buys $10 million of the bonds (together with accrued interest) in the repo market with the promise to return (i.e., resell) the bonds to the other party at some specific future date.[5] In essence, the dealer has made a loan and taken the government bonds as collateral. He then uses these bonds to deliver on his short sale to his client. It will be noted that this transaction is the mirror image of the earlier transaction; that is, the dealer is a lender rather than a borrower. Not surprisingly, this transaction is called a **resale** (also known as **reverse repurchase agreement,** or simply a **reverse**). Of course, one party's repo is always another party's resale.

We can now summarize the key elements of effective dealer activity:

1. Price the securities so that the bid is slightly below and the ask is slightly above the fair market value.
2. Finance the securities, or obtain inventory, in the repo (resale) market.
3. Quantify the risks associated with each security in the book and hedge any residual risk in futures (or other derivatives).
4. Monitor the cost of carry.

Other Dealer Markets

In addition to stocks and bonds (including in the latter governments, corporates, and municipals), securities firms make markets in a variety of other instruments. For example, as strange as its sounds, investment banks make markets in repos and resales. In other words, they will quote both borrow rates (called **pay rates**) and lend rates (called **receive rates**) in the repo market. Their lending rate is typically about 15 to 20 basis points higher than their borrowing rate. Importantly, the repo operation is distinct from the bond operation, and each area is viewed within the investment bank as a separate profit center. Thus, when a bond desk

---

[5] The reader might be inclined to ask why the dealer does not simply buy the required $10 million of bonds from another dealer or customer. The answer is simple: If the dealer buys the securities, he will have to pay the other dealer's or customer's ask price. This will, in all likelihood, be the same as or higher than his own ask price, and therefore he makes no profit (and might even suffer a loss). Buy borrowing the securities, he preserves the opportunity to later cover the short sale through a purchase at his own bid price. If it should be necessary to roll the short position forward at the end of the resale agreement period, the dealer would simply enter into another resale for the same securities.

wants to tap the repo market for financing, it transacts with another department within the bank. The repo desk treats the bond desk just as it would treat any other customer.

While a 15 basis–point spread is rather small, when the transactions are large, as they typically are in the repo/resale market, the repo/resale desk can be a formidable profit center. On a $1 million repo transaction, 7.5 basis points (one–half the pay–receive spread) is about $2.08 per day in interest (.00075 × $1,000,000 × 1/360). Adding to this the $2.08 that the dealer picks up on the other side of the transaction, the operation nets $4.16 per million. For large shops, the repo desk may finance $10 to $20 billion a day in this market. Even at $10 billion, the repo desk may earn $41,600 a day.

Among the other important dealer markets in which investment banks are active are the swaps market, the mortgage–backed market, the junk bond market, and the tax–exempt market. With the exception of the tax–exempt market, which has already been discussed, we will talk about each of these markets in later chapters. To a lesser degree, investment banks also make markets in foreign exchange (this market is dominated by commercial banks). In each of these markets, the dealer's role is essentially the same: determine the fair market price, provide a bid and an ask on either side of fair value, finance the inventory, and hedge the position.

Brokerage Activity in the Financial Markets

As we already described, brokers are persons who act as agents for others—i.e., the principals—when the latter wishes to buy or sell securities or other instruments. Because they act as agents, brokers collect a commission from the principals for the service, called **broking**. (The terms *broking* and *brokering* are used synonymously; we will usually employ the former). Because they accept a commission for the service they provide, brokers have a fiduciary obligation to their clients to obtain the best fills possible on the orders they take. A fill is market slang for a completed transaction.

Within the securities industry, brokers are known as registered representatives, account representatives, account executives, investment executives, or some similar term that varies from shop to shop. To perform the functions of a broker in the securities industry, an individual must pass an exam known as the Series 7. The Series 7 exam is prepared by the National Association of Securities Dealers (NASD) but the administration of the exam is contracted to an outside party. Only employees of member firms of NASD and of the New York Stock Exchange (NYSE) are eligible to sit for the exam. In essence, the firm must sponsor its employee for the exam. The NYSE requires a candidate to be employed by the sponsoring firm for a minimum of 60 days to sit for the Series 7 exam, and to be employed for a minimum of 120 days to do business with a client. Other eligibility requirements may be imposed by the firm, and, in general, most firms require an individual to work for the firm for a minimum of six months. Similar rules apply in the futures industry, where a person must pass the Series 3 exam. The Series 3 exam is administered by the National Futures Association (NFA).

The mechanics of brokerage are fairly simple and clear. A public customer wants to place an order to buy or to sell something. The customer might specify that the order is a **market order** or a **limit order**. The former implies that the order is to be filled immediately at the best price currently available. Thus, the broker is authorized to hit the bid (if buying) or take the offer (if selling). Barring an unusual market situation, market orders can almost always be filled in seconds, and they are easy work for brokers. Limit orders are considerably more difficult. A limit order specifies a price. The order must be filled at the specified price, a better price, or not at all. If the order becomes fillable, a customer has a right to expect that it is filled. For example, suppose that the price of a stock is $40 a share, and a customer gives his broker an order to buy the stock at 39–1/2. Subsequently, the customer observes that the stock trades at 39–3/8 before closing for the day at 39–7/8. Because the price dipped below 39–1/2 at some point *after* the limit order was accepted by the broker, the customer has a right to expect that the order was filled. If it was not, the customer can hold the broker responsible for a fill. Importantly, if the stock were to trade at 39–1/2 *but not below* 39–1/2, the customer does not have a right to expect a fill. To understand why, it is important to trace an order.

For simplicity, let's suppose that the stock trades on the New York Stock Exchange. The account representative takes the order and relays it by phone or telex to a desk clerk on the floor of the exchange. The desk clerk hands the order to a runner, who takes it to an exchange member (only exchange members or their designees can trade on the exchange floor). The member, acting in the capacity of a **floor broker**, has the responsibility to fill the order. She would take the order to the trading post where that particular security trades and attempt to transact with either (1) another floor broker, (2) a **floor trader** trading for his own account, or (3) the stock's specialist. If the order is a market order, it can always be filled immediately. But if the order is a limit order, the floor broker will hand it to the specialist, who will record the order in the specialist's **order book**. Once the floor broker has handed the order over to the specialist, the floor broker may move on to other business.

The specialist book is a chronological notebook in which a specialist records all orders received for execution at specific prices. Specialists also record their own inventory in the book.[6] The contents of the book are not divulged to the public. For example, if XYZ is trading at $40 and the specialist receives an order to buy 200 shares of XYZ at 39–5/8 from Merrill Lynch, then the order is recorded as a buy at 39–5/8 or better for Merrill Lynch. Merrill's order is placed in the book immediately after any preceding orders to buy at 39–5/8. Orders are filled in the sequence in which they are placed in the book—first come, first served. Because orders are filled in sequence, it is possible for a buy order at 39–1/2 to be in the specialist's book and for the stock to trade at 39–1/2, but for the customer's order not to be filled. For the order not to be filled, it simply means that someone else had a prior order to buy and that an insufficient number of sell orders at 39–1/2 had been received to work down through the book to the customer's order. But if a trade is made at 39–3/8, the customer does have a right to expect a fill and to hold his broker responsible for a fill. After all, an order to buy at 39–3/8 should never be filled until every order to buy at 39–1/2 has been filled.

By taking, holding, and, one hopes, filling a customer's order, a specialist takes on the responsibility of the broker. Indeed, the specialist has become the broker for the broker, and is sometimes described as the brokers' broker. For his services, the specialist collects a fee (commission) from the brokerage firm whose order he fills—but only if the order is filled. Thus, the specialist has a powerful incentive to try to fill orders. Again, the account representative has a fiduciary obligation to get the best

---

[6] From the outset of the specialist system, specialists employed hard copy (i.e., paper) notebooks to track these orders. In recent years, specialists have increasingly switched to more efficient computer–based "books."

possible fills for his customers. That fiduciary responsibility passes to the floor broker and from the floor broker to the specialist. Each party can hold the next party down the order line responsible for any failure to perform.

In the case of stocks that do not trade on an exchange, an account representative passes limit orders on to dealers (market makers) in the securities. The dealers take them and hold them just as a specialist would.[7] Alternatively, the account representative can hold orders himself and keep checking the markets in the hopes of having opportunities to fill them. Of course, this is time–consuming and inefficient. An opportunity might arise and be missed. Thus, most orders are passed on to market makers.

Limit orders that are given to an account representative will often be held by the account representative and not passed along, but only if they are **away from the market**—meaning that the prices are so far away from the last trade price that the specialist and the dealers would not want to be bothered holding them. If the price is too far away from the market, the account representative will also not want to hold it.

Brokerage firms tend to be geared to either a retail business or an institutional business. As the terms imply, retail brokers provide services targeted to individuals. Institutional brokerage firms provide services targeted to institutional investors whose transactions tend to be large. Often, large transactions are described as **wholesale**. Examples of retail brokerage firms include Merrill Lynch, Shearson Lehman, and Prudential Securities. Examples of institutional brokers include First Boston; Bear, Stearns; Goldman Sachs; and Morgan Stanley. Firms with large retail brokerage businesses are called **wirehouses**. For the clientele they serve, all the firms mentioned above are full–service, meaning they can provide such services as advice on individual securities, financial planning, investment management, research, and order execution.

There are two specialty levels within the securities industry. These are **discounters** and **high net worth brokers**. The discounters, which include firms like Charles Schwab and Muriel Siebert, offer transaction services at commission schedules significantly below those of the full–service firms. But, as a general rule, many of the amenities provided

---

[7] More precisely, the NASDAQ system employs an open book in which limit orders are posted and can be filled by a dealer in the security.

by full–service brokers are lacking. High net worth brokers such as Kidder Peabody are at the opposite extreme. They occupy a niche between retail and wholesale. They offer their services to individuals who have a net worth of $500,000 or more (some have higher net worth cutoffs). They offer an extraordinary level of service but, as a general rule, also charge full–service level commissions.

Institutional brokers, and sometimes retail brokers, often specialize by type of security. This is particularly true for brokers that handle futures transactions and, sometimes, for those that handle options. Such specialized brokers often service institutions that use these instruments for hedging purposes.

Other Broker Services

Retail brokers provide many ancillary services to support their primary business of brokerage. They monitor margin accounts, offer investment management services, assist in structuring portfolios, and provide research and recommendations. The precise combination of services provided, and the fees charged for these services, vary from brokerage firm to brokerage firm. They also sometimes vary based on the client's net worth or the volume of trading activity in clients' accounts.

Let's consider some of these ancillary services in a bit more detail. When a customer opens a brokerage account with a brokerage firm, there are a number of types of accounts to chose from. First, the account can be a **regular account** or an **IRA** (or **Keogh**) account. The latter allows the investor to self–manage his IRA investments. All funds placed in an IRA account must conform to the rules governing IRAs. Regular accounts can be individual, joint, or custodial. There are several types of joint accounts, but in general any beneficial owner of a joint account, unless specified otherwise, has trading authority over the account. A **custodial account** is an account that is managed by one party for the benefit of another, usually a minor. Such accounts are most often created under the **Uniform Gift to Minors Act**. An account may also be **discretionary** or **nondiscretionary**. A discretionary account grants trading authority to the account representative. The account representative can then make trades on behalf of the account owner without obtaining the owner's approval. The final distinction concerns margin. A retail brokerage account may be a **cash account** or a **margin account**. A cash account limits the customer's transactions to purchases that he is prepared to pay for in full. That is, the broker will buy securities for the account owner but only to the degree that the client has sufficient funds to pay for them. In a margin account, the account owner may buy securities on **margin**. This means that the brokerage firm will lend a portion of the funds necessary for the purchase of the securities to the account owner. The account owner will be required to pay interest on the borrowed funds at a rate called the **broker loan rate**. The portion of the funds that can be borrowed is set by the brokerage firm, but the maximum percentage is set by the Federal Reserve. At present, for corporate securities, this is 50 percent. For Treasury securities, up to 90 percent of the purchase price can be borrowed. Margin accounts also permit short sales—i.e., the borrowing and selling of securities not currently owned by the seller. Importantly, the "margin" in a margin account is that portion of the funds which the account owner tenders himself, not the portion lent by the brokerage firm. This is often a point of confusion.

When securities are purchased on margin—i.e., a portion of the funds are borrowed—the brokerage firm must monitor the value of the account's securities, which serve as collateral on the broker loan. The maximum percentage that can be borrowed applies only to the **initial margin**. Once the securities have been purchased, secondary margin rules take over. The account must maintain a minimum level of margin, sometimes called **maintenance margin**. If price changes should result in an erosion in the value of the position, the owner's equity in the position may fall below the maintenance margin level, with the result that the account has insufficient collateral to maintain the position. At this point, the account representative will notify the account owners, usually by phone, that the margin has become insufficient and must be brought back up to the minimum required level. This is, of course, the proverbial **margin call** that most investors dread. The account owner must then (a) add sufficient collateral to the account to increase the account's margin to the required level, or (b) sell securities.

Margin accounts and short sales provide two additional sources of revenue for brokers. First, short sales allow brokers to earn commissions on transactions in which customers are betting that market prices will decline, as opposed to the more routine transactions in which investors bet that prices will rise. Second, the funds that a broker lends to customers are lent at a rate that is higher than the cost of those funds to the brokerage firm. Specifically, commercial banks lend funds to the brokerage firm at a rate of interest called the **call money rate**. This rate is very low, because the securities that are purchased with the money are used as collateral on these loans. The brokerage firm "marks up" the call money rate, and reloans the money at its **broker loan rate**. The difference between the broker loan rate and the call money rate typically ranges from 25 basis points to 150 basis points and can be a significant source of revenue to the brokerage firm. There are alternative sources of funds that brokers can lend to customers. For example, customer accounts often hold significant cash balances. These cash balances can be borrowed from customers with surplus cash and then relent to other customers. Again, the broker earns the difference between its borrow rate and its lending rate.

The second ancillary service we mentioned earlier was investment management services. This covers a lot of territory. For example, brokerage firms collect and process dividend and interest coupon payments. They also provide cash management services, such as debit cards and checking privileges, that allow funds to be withdrawn from brokerage accounts by simply using the debit card as a credit card would be used, or by writing a check. These brokerage functions are best described as **investment servicing activities**, to distinguish them from investment management proper. Investment management refers to investing other people's money for them and managing the investments by making buy, sell, and hold decisions.

Increasingly, brokerage firms offer portfolio management services through investment counselors or financial planners. These services are generally geared toward high net worth investors and are aimed at establishing lifelong relationships. Investment counselors begin by taking inventory of the client's assets and liabilities. The assets include the value of the client's real estate, stock and bond portfolios, mutual funds, life insurance policies, retirement accounts, and so on. The counselor will then map out a financial plan designed to "take the client from where he is to where he wants to be." This will generally mean structuring a rational portfolio and a lifetime plan that provides for the changing needs and situation of the client.

Achieving a status of "investment counselor" or "financial planner" requires more than just knowing the instruments and knowing the rules governing securities transactions. It requires a deeper understanding of financial theory and practice and a broader picture of financial instruments and how these instruments meet, or fail to meet, investors' needs. To achieve this higher level of sophistication, many brokerage firms have introduced professional development departments and repeatedly upgrade the level of education of their brokers. Kidder Peabody, for example, introduced a high–end training program that recruits experienced business practitioners and newly minted MBAs. These recruits are then put through an intensive training program that lasts from 8 to 12 weeks. The program employs accomplished financial consultants from major American universities to present the theory underlying the instruments and the strategies of modern investment management. This is backed up by visits from, and to, the trading desks within the firm and from visits by other experienced personnel. When the recruits successfully complete the program, Kidder bestows on them the title "Investment Executive" and sends them into the field to cultivate a high net worth and/or small to medium–size corporate clientele. As reported in *The Wall Street Journal*, this program has earned Kidder Peabody an excellent reputation in personnel training and has contributed significantly to the development of the firm's retail business.[8] The result has been a sizable contribution to Kidder's bottom line.

The final ancillary service we consider is research. Brokerage firms, particularly those with an institutional clientele, devote considerable resources to research. Research is typically organized along product lines. For example, there is fixed–income research, equity research, derivatives research, high–yield research, and so on. Research reports take a variety of forms. Some, particularly equity research reports, constitute buy/sell recommendations. Others are concerned with strategies. For example, there might be discussion of different strategies that can be used to achieve fixed–rate financing, or discussion of how derivative instruments can be used in asset/liability management in the savings and loan industry, and so on. Still others are simply intended to be educational in

---

[8] *The Wall Street Journal*, December 9, 1992, in an article entitled, "Kidder Has Made a Gallant Comeback," reports " . . . some Wall Street executives consider Kidder's 1,200 member brokerage force its corporate jewel. Kidder brokers cater to wealthy individuals, small businesses and institutions: the average Kidder broker generates about $350,000 in annual commissions, people familiar with the firm say, among the highest levels on Wall Street."

nature. These might describe a new product and its uses without any attempt to "sell" the product. Or the report might discuss different analytical approaches to price securities or to value an instrument. Of course, you have a much better chance of selling a product or a service to someone who understands what it is that you are trying to sell them. Thus, research reports, even those that do not constitute buy/sell recommendations, do have sales implications.

The First Rule of Brokerage: Know Your Customer

Rule 405 of the NYSE requires brokers to act in the best interest of their customers. This is simply an explicit recognition of the fiduciary relationship that exists between a broker and a client. It is difficult to act in the best interests of a customer, however, if one does not know anything about the customer. What is good for one client, for example, might not be good for another. Only by learning something about the client can the broker decide what is suitable for that client and what is not. The importance of getting to know the customer has become known within the trade as the "know your customer rule."

Every brokerage firm asks a number of basic questions about the customer when a new account is established in an attempt to satisfy the requirements of the law. These questions concern the client's income, wealth, and types and duration of experience in different types of investment and trading assets. For example, it would not be prudent to encourage an elderly person with no prior investment experience to invest all of his or her wealth in a single risky security coupled with considerable leverage (buying the stock on margin, for example).

Many broker/dealers go considerably beyond the basic know your customer rule and develop a detailed investor (client) profile for each of their clients. This is common, for example, for brokers who cultivate high net worth clientele. Kidder Peabody's Investor Profile document appears as an appendix to this chapter.

Possible Abuses

As in all industries that provide personal services to individuals and institutions, there are some unscrupulous firms and individuals in the securities industry, and the public has to watch out for them. After all, these firms are in the business of making large financial transactions on behalf of the public; consequently, there are few businesses in which more damage can be done to unsuspecting people in as short a period of time. Fortunately, the unscrupulous firms tend not to last very long. But this is little comfort to someone who has been fleeced.

Even within the most respectable and staid of old–line securities firms, an occasional bad apple will surface. Unfortunately, one serious case of misbehavior can undermine the reputation of an entire firm for a very long time.

The securities laws are intended, in large part, to make it as difficult as possible for a securities firm to take advantage of customers. Further, the laws provide for remedial action when it is established that a customer has been abused.

The brokerage side of the investment banking industry is monitored by self–regulating organizations (SROs) such as the National Association of Securities Dealers (NASD), the New York Stock Exchange (NYSE), the American Stock Exchange (AMEX), and the Chicago Board Options Exchange (CBOE). Over the last few years, these SROs have become tougher in their sanctions against brokers and brokerage firms. For example, during 1991 there were 1,041 disciplinary cases filed—an increase of 70 percent over the 614 cases filed during 1990. Fines for violations range from less than $5,000 to hundreds of thousands of dollars. Following are examples of the types of abuses that the SROs watch for.

Bucket shops: Bucket shops are securities firms, usually small, that take customer orders but do not immediately execute them. Instead, they wait to see if the price moves away from the price stipulated in the customer's order, and only if it does do they fill the order. The customer is told it was filled at the stipulated price, and the difference accrues to the bucket shop. For example, suppose that a stock is trading around $40. A customer places an order to buy at $40. As it happens, the order could be filled, but the firm does not execute the order. Later, the price declines to $39–1/2. Observing this, the firm fills the order by buying the stock at 39–1/2, and reports the fill to the customer at $40. The customer pays a commission and loses another one–half point besides. This practice is banned by the NASD.

Boiler rooms: Boiler room operations are firms that use high–pressure sales tactics to sell securities, often to naive investors. The securities, which might be a new issue or a seasoned issue, are touted with exaggerated claims of their probability of succeeding. In the worst cases, the securities are nonexistent, or a firm is created for the purpose of issuing worthless securities. When a new issue is being pushed, boiler room sales personnel will often get an extraordinary percentage of the offering price. For example, the boiler room, acting as "underwriter," might take half of the offering price or more.

Investors should always be wary of "once in a lifetime" deals, "sure things," or any other claim that sounds to good to be true. It probably is.

Churning: Churning refers to excessive trading of a customer's account when the primary motivation for the trading is to earn commissions or bid–ask spreads for the broker/dealer. Churning is much more likely to occur in accounts in which the client has granted the broker discretionary trading authority, but it can also occur in nondiscretionary accounts if the client routinely takes the broker/dealer's advice. Churning is difficult to prove because it rests on motivation. As a general rule, to prove churning, a client must demonstrate an inordinate number of trades involving the purchase and sale of securities within an unreasonably short period of time with no obvious economic rationale.

Suitability: As part of the "know your customer" doctrine, brokers have an obligation to limit their investment recommendations and to limit purchases of securities on behalf of customers to those securities that are appropriate for the customers. This is particularly important in the case of discretionary accounts. Securities that are appropriate for a particular customer are described as "suitable." It is important that the client fully understand the potential risks of the investments recommended to him or purchased on his behalf, and that the securities purchased be reasonable investments for that client. For example, options would probably not be a reasonable investment for an elderly investor living on a fixed income, even if the investor understands the options and the inherent risks.

The issue of suitability of an investment is not limited to individuals. The state of West Virginia has successfully held several investment banking firms liable for losses incurred by the state's consolidated fund from trading bonds, bond options, and other fixed–income securities. These trades were considered speculative and were therefore illegal under West Virginia law. Fines were imposed despite questions as to whether or not the investment banks provided any advice and notwithstanding the fact that West Virginia was permitted to keep the gains on profitable trades.[9]

Front running: Front running, also known as **trading ahead of a customer**, refers to transactions made by a securities firm for its own trading accounts in anticipation of trades that are to be made by a client. For example, if a broker/dealer receives an order to buy a large number of shares of stock or a significant amount of the par on a bond issue, the broker/dealer has reason to believe that the order will likely drive up the price. In anticipation of this, the broker/dealer may buy the stock or the bonds for its own account prior to filling the order for the customer. Then, as it fills the order for the customer and the price rises, the broker/dealer sells out its own position at the higher price. Front running is specifically prohibited by the rules and regulations of the securities industry. Importantly, it is sometimes possible to engage in **intermarket front running**. For example, a broker/dealer might take a large order to buy stock from an institutional client. If that stock is a component of an important market index and if futures contracts trade on that stock index, then the broker/dealer might buy stock index futures in anticipation of its client buying the stock. This is a grayer area than front running, but it is generally considered unethical.

Poor fills: A broker/dealer is entrusted by his customer to fill an order at the best possible price. This obligation passes from the account representative to the floor broker. There have been instances in which floor brokers, working in concert with floor traders trading for their own accounts, have deliberately transacted on behalf of customers at disadvantageous prices. This particular type of illegal trading at the expense of the public customer created a scandal in the futures industry in the late 1980s. To see how this might occur, suppose that a customer gives his account representative a market order to buy 10 T–bond futures contracts. At the time, the contract is bid at 94–27/32 and asked at 97–28/32. Because the order is a market order, the floor broker is authorized to pay

---

[9] See *The Wall Street Journal*, May 11, 1992, p. C13.

as much as is necessary to fill the order immediately. Now suppose that, after receiving the order, the floor broker signals to a floor trader with whom the floor broker is in cahoots. This is to let the floor trader know that the floor broker is holding a market order. The floor broker then calls for asks and receives a variety of offer prices from 97–28/32 to 97–30/32. His collaborator, the floor trader, offers to sell for 97–29/32. Of course, the floor broker should take the 97–28/32 offer, but instead he takes his collaborator's 97–29/32 offer. The floor trader then immediately turns to the other floor traders who offered to sell at 97–28/32 and takes their offer to close out his position. Thus, the floor trader goes short at 97–29/32 and offsets this transaction at 97–28/32, thereby picking up 1/32 ($31.25 per contract) on each of ten contracts. The public customer, of course, pays for this in the form of a higher transaction price.We do not mean to leave the impression that a thief lurks behind every door in the securities industry. Quite the contrary. The industry has ethical standards and, for the most part, the business is remarkably honest. Nevertheless, the public customer should be wary and remain vigilant. Any suspicious transactions should be investigated and explained to the customer's satisfaction.

Summary

In this chapter we have considered the role of brokers and dealers in secondary market making. This is the activity in which securities are transferred from one beneficial owner, who is not the issuer, to another beneficial owner. Secondary markets are essential to achieving liquidity. Without liquidity, investors would undoubtedly demand a higher yield on their investments and this cost would be borne, out of necessity, by the issuer.

Dealers are principals to transactions. They make a market by offering to both buy (at their bid price) and sell (at their ask price). When they buy, they add securities to their inventory. When they sell, they remove securities from their inventory. To be effective, a dealer must watch the size of his inventory, finance his positions at the lowest possible cost of carry, and keep his positions hedged against price risk.

Brokers act as agents for others—i.e., their customers or clients. The investor has the right to expect that a broker will always be acting in his best interests and that the broker will refrain from any self–serving transactions (called **self–dealing**) at the customer's expense. This fiduciary obligation passes to floor brokers and to any other party who enters the transaction as an agent of the broker. Brokerage firms perform a number of important services for their customers. Among these are account monitoring, investment management, portfolio structuring, and research and advice.

While most brokers are honest and obey both the letter and the spirit of the law, and most firms are reputable and eager to maintain their reputation for honesty and integrity, there are, nevertheless, both dishonest firms and dishonest brokers and dealers. The securities laws and the rules of the NASD and other self–regulating organizations have been designed to discourage unethical and dishonest behavior. The exchanges, too, participate aggressively in the process of policing their members. Nevertheless, customers need to be ever vigilant for abuses. The stakes are high and the temptation is great.

References and Suggested Reading

Baird, A. J., *Option Market Making: Trading and Risk Analysis for the Financial and Commodity Option Markets*, New York: Wiley, 1993.

Blume, M. E., "Soft Dollars and the Brokerage Industry," *Financial Analysts Journal*, March/April 1993, pp. 36–44.

Execution Techniques, True Trading Costs, and the Microstructure of Markets, Katruna F. Sherrerd, (ed.), Association for Investment Management and Research, 1993.

Falloon, W., "The Temptation of Front–Running," *Intermarket*, 5:1, October 1988, pp. 23–31.

Goggin, R., "Broker Sales Techniques Can Be Adapted for Trust Business," *Trusts and Estates*, 128:10, October 1989, pp. 35–42.

Labuszawski, J. W. and J. E. Nyhoff, *Trading Financial Futures: Markets, Methods, Strategies, and Tactics*, New York: Wiley, 1988.

Ray, C. I., *The Bond Market: Trading and Risk Management*, Burr Ridge, IL: Business One Irwin, 1993.

Rubenfeld, A., *The Super Traders: Secrets & Successes of Wall Street's Best and Brightest*, Chicago: Probus Publishing, 1992.

Schwager, J. D., *Market Wizards: Interviews with Top Traders*, New York: New York Institute of Finance, 1989.

Schwartz, R. A., *Equity Markets: Structures, Trading and Performance*, New York: Harper & Row, 1988.

Schwartz, R. A. and D. K. Whitcomb, *Transaction Costs and Institutional Investor Trading Strategies*, New York: Salomon Center, New York University, 1988.

Standards of Practice Handbook: The Code of Ethics and the Standards of Professional Conduct, Charlottesville, VA: Association for Investment Management and Research, 1992.

Wagner, W. H. and M. Edwards, "Best Execution," *Financial Analysts Journal*, January/February 1993, pp. 65–71.

Appendix

Investor Profile

CLIENT NAME _____

DATE _____

PREPARED BY _____

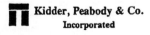

Kidder, Peabody & Co.
Incorporated

FAMILY INFORMATION

Husband's Name	Date of Birth	SS#
Wife's Name	Date of Birth	SS#
Children's Names	Date of Birth	SS# ☐ College
	Date of Birth	SS# ☐ College
	Date of Birth	SS# ☐ College
	Date of Birth	SS# ☐ College
Elders [Name]	Age	

Home Address

City   State   Zip   Home Phone [   ]

Business [Name]

Address

City   State   Zip   Business Phone [   ]

Attorney   Accountant

INCOME

Salary $ Investments $ Trusts & Estates $ Annuity Income $ Rental Income $

Tax Bracket   %   Liabilities Other Than Mortgage

Will: ☐ Yes ☐ No   Drawn by Attorney? ☐ Yes ☐ No   Executor   Beneficiary

Gifts (contemplated or given)

Trusts:

Grantor   Beneficiary

Trustee   Principal

Objective

Comments

Pending Inheritance

                                Total Income $

REAL ESTATE

Primary Residence	☐ Owned ☐ Rented	Estimated Value $	
	☐ Mortgage	Monthly Payment $	Years Until Paid
Other Real Estate	☐ Owned ☐ Rented	Estimated Value $	
	☐ Mortgage	Monthly Payment $	Years Until Paid
Other Real Estate	☐ Owned ☐ Rented	Estimated Value $	
	☐ Mortgage	Monthly Payment $	Years Until Paid

EMPLOYMENT, RETIREMENT PLANS AND BUSINESS INTERESTS

Husband	Wife
Employer	Employer
Position	Position
Years	Years
Anticipated Retirement Date / /	Anticipated Retirement Date / /
Pension Plan: Amount at retirement $	Pension Plan: Amount at retirement $
Profit Sharing Plan: Amount at retirement $	Profit Sharing Plan: Amount at retirement $
How Funded: (check one)	How Funded: (check one)
☐ Insurance ☐ Equities ☐ Split Funded	☐ Insurance ☐ Equities ☐ Split Funded
Other Employer Plans and How Funded	Other Employer Plans and How Funded
☐ Government Bonds ☐ Stock ☐ Mutual Funds	☐ Government Bonds ☐ Stock ☐ Mutual Funds
Person Responsible Phone	Person Responsible Phone
IRA and IRA Rollovers	IRA and IRA Rollovers
Current Balance $	Current Balance $
How Invested: ☐ Annuities	How Invested: ☐ Annuities
☐ CD's ☐ Mutual Funds ☐ Stocks ☐ Bonds	☐ CD's ☐ Mutual Funds ☐ Stocks ☐ Bonds
Keogh or Self-Employed Plans	Keogh or Self-Employed Plans
Current Balance $	Current Balance $
How Invested: ☐ Annuities	How Invested: ☐ Annuities
☐ CD's ☐ Mutual Funds ☐ Stocks ☐ Bond	☐ CD's ☐ Mutual Funds ☐ Stocks ☐ Bond
Business Buy-Sell Agreement: ☐ Yes ☐ No	Business Buy-Sell Agreement: ☐ Yes ☐ No
How funded	How funded
Affiliations (fraternal, business, civic organizations, philanthropic)	Affiliations (fraternal, business, civic organizations, philanthropic)

LIQUID ASSETS

Government Bonds: Type	Amounts $	
Government Bonds: Type	Amounts $	
Government Bonds: Type	Amounts $	
C.D.'s: Bank/Inst.	Amount	Maturity
C.D.'s: Bank/Inst.	Amount	Maturity
C.D.'s: Bank/Inst.	Amount	Maturity
Money Market Funds	Amount	Where
Money Market Funds	Amount	Where
Money Market Funds	Amount	Where
Checking Account: Bank	Balance $	
Checking Account: Bank	Balance $	
Savings Account: Bank	Balance $	
Savings Account: Bank	Balance $	
Savings Account: Bank	Balance $	

Secondary Market Making: Dealer/Broker Activity   **157**

STOCKS

Number of Shares	Corporation	Purchased		Current Price	Registered in Whose Name
		Year	Total Cost		

Total Securities Committed $

FIXED INCOME

Maturity	Par Value	Issue & Description	Taxable	% Interest	Purchased		Registered in Whose Name
					Year	Total Cost	

Total Bonds $

MUTUAL FUNDS

Name	Date of Purchase	Cost	Current Value

Total Mutual Funds $

UNIT INVESTMENT TRUSTS

Name	Trust #	Date of Purchase	Cost	Amount

Total Trusts $

DIRECT INVESTMENTS

Partnership Name	Industry	Investment Amount	Current Yield	Date of Purchase	Cash Flow	Gain/Loss

Comments

Total Direct Investments $

INSURANCE AND ANNUITIES

Medical Insurance: ☐ Yes ☐ No   Major Medical: ☐ Yes ☐ No   Salary Continuance: ☐ Yes ☐ No

Disability Insurance: Amount of Coverage $ Waiting Period

Insurance and Annuity Policies:

Insurance Face Amount	Company	Type	Issue Date	Cash Value	Beneficiary	Annual Premium

Comments

Total Life Insurance $

INVESTMENT EXPERIENCE

What are your investment objectives? _____

_____

_____

Risk Characteristics   ☐ Aggressive   ☐ Moderate   ☐ Conservative   Other _____

What is your present investment/asset allocation policy?

    ☐ Preservation of Capital   ☐ Current Income   ☐ Long-Term Growth   Other _____

What time frame do you consider adequate for performance evaluation?

    ☐ Less than 3 years   ☐ 3 years   ☐ More than 3 years   Other _____

What has been your worst investment? _____

What has been your best investment? _____

What investment would you not consider under any circumstance? _____

Is there any country, industry, company or any investment vehicle that would not be acceptable as a matter of principle?
☐ Yes ☐ No

Which one(s)? _____

Do you have any investment preferences? _____

What rate of return over inflation (as measured by the US Consumer Price Index) would be considered:

   Exceptionally good? ___ %   Acceptable? ___ %   Exceptionally poor ___ %

Have you had a Margin Account?   ☐ Yes ☐ No   When?_____

Have you traded Options?   ☐ Yes ☐ No   When?_____

Have you traded Commodities?   ☐ Yes ☐ No   When?_____

Have you ever owned any of the following?

   ☐ Oil & Gas   ☐ Real Estate   ☐ Venture Capital   ☐ Other Limited Partnerships _____

Would you consider them if appropriate?   ☐ Yes ☐ No

What is your short and long-term outlook for:

	Short-Term			Long-Term		
	Lower	Higher	Same	Lower	Higher	Same
Interest Rates	☐	☐	☐	☐	☐	☐
Stock Market	☐	☐	☐	☐	☐	☐
Interest Rates	☐	☐	☐	☐	☐	☐

Would you consider using the services of a professional investment manager?   ☐ Yes ☐ No

Why not? _____

Have you even used one? ☐ Yes ☐ No   Experience _____

NOTES

_____

_____

_____

_____

_____

_____

_____

_____

6

Trading:
Speculation and Arbitrage

Overview

Most, but not all, investment banks have trading operations. As we will use the term here, **trading** means taking positions in financial instruments, or commodities, in order to earn profits from either (1) a change in price levels, or (2) a discrepancy in relative values. The former is called **speculation** and the latter is called **arbitrage**. Investment banks typically have both proprietary trading operations and institutional trading operations. **Proprietary trading** is trading that is done for the investment bank's own account. **Institutional trading** is undertaken for the benefit of institutional clients of the investment bank and can be done on a profit–sharing or management fee basis. Proprietary trading and institutional trading are often handled by distinct groups within the investment bank in order to avoid even the appearance of a conflict of interest. In this chapter, we concentrate on proprietary trading. (Institutional trading by investment banks is discussed in Chapter 10 in the more general context of investment management.)

Trading is distinct from sales. Sales, which includes both the broking and the dealing activity discussed in the last chapter, generates revenue for the investment bank from the *act* of transacting. This revenue may come from the bid–ask spread or from commissions, but in all cases it represents compensation for transactional services—not from holding positions. Trading, on the other hand, involves taking positions to earn profits from the positions themselves. Not surprisingly, investment banks see their broker/dealers as distinct from their traders: the former are often called **salespeople** to distinguish them from the **traders**.

In this chapter, we specifically exclude hedging from our definition of trading. As we have already seen, hedging is done to manage risks; its purpose is not to generate transactional–services income or profits from positions. (The risk management role of hedging was demonstrated in the last chapter in the context of dealers hedging their positions.) Traders do hedge, and hedging is often an integral part of trading. But hedging is not the basis for trading. This will be demonstrated later.

Traders, particularly speculators, take risks—often big risks. Dealers do not take risks as a part of their dealer function. This does not mean, however, that dealers never take risks; they often do. But when they do, they have exchanged their dealer hat for a trader hat. To the degree that dealers engage in trading, it is usually within very narrow, management–defined, limits. Nevertheless, the fact that dealers sometimes act as traders should not blur the distinction between sales and trading. The proper function of a dealer is to make markets, and to earn a return from making markets. The proper function of a trader is to earn trading profits.

While most investment banks—particularly the larger ones—employ traders, the degree to which investment banking firms depend upon trading for their profits varies considerably from shop to shop. A few investment banks are renowned for the prowess of their traders. The most notable of these is Salomon Brothers, which employs traders in all market areas, but is legendary in the bond markets. Bear, Stearns is also a trading powerhouse.

In this chapter, we will examine a number of distinct types of trading activity that are common at investment banks. These include several forms of speculation and a number of forms of arbitrage. Arbitrage, while conceptually simple, is often mathematically complex. Indeed, Wall Street firms employ large numbers of Ph.D.–level mathematicians and physicists, in addition to finance types, in an effort to identify and exploit arbitrage opportunities.

Closely related to arbitrage is the creation of synthetic instruments. We will illustrate some of the trading uses for synthetic instruments in this chapter. A fuller discussion of synthetic instruments will be provided in later chapters, but not necessarily in the context of trading. Finally, we will consider what is often called **risk arbitrage**. Risk arbitrage is not a true form of arbitrage, but it is clearly a form of trading and is widely practiced by many investment banks. Unfortunately, we cannot do much more than touch on any of these subjects in this one chapter. As with the other topics we discuss, books the length of this one can be and have been written on each of the forms of trading described in this chapter.[1]

Speculation

Speculation means, quite simply, to take a position in anticipation of a change in price levels. (This can mean a change in absolute price levels or in relative price levels.) Thus, if a speculator thinks that a price will rise, she buys the instrument, hoping to sell it later at a higher price. If the speculator believes that a price will fall, she sells the instrument short, hoping to buy it back later at a lower price.

For the most part, professional speculators operate on the short side of the market with the same ease with which they operate on the long side of the market. This is generally difficult for the novice to understand. In some markets, such as futures and options, this is possible because the long side and the short side of the market are perfectly symmetric. In other markets, such as the bond markets, it is possible because a well–developed repurchase agreement (repo) market provides access to securities to be used for short sales.

Speculators are basically forecasters who act upon their forecasts in order to earn a return. *Keep in mind that true speculators do not see themselves as having control over prices.* Rather, prices are determined by the interaction of supply and demand. In an ideal market economy, each speculator, like each consumer and each producer, is very small relative to the market as a whole, and no individual speculator, consumer, or producer exerts enough market power to bring about a change in prices on his own. Thus, the speculator is a forecaster and not a manipulator of prices. If prices rise when the speculator is long or fall when the speculator is short, then the speculator profits from a correct forecast. If prices fall when the speculator is long or rise when the speculator is short, then the speculator suffers a loss from an incorrect forecast. We should note that even the best forecast—predicated on the best information and the best analysis—can go astray due to exogenous shocks: fires, floods, earthquakes, lawsuits, industrial accidents, legal problems, actions

---

[1] The References and Suggested Reading section at the end of this chapter includes examples of texts devoted to various types of trading.

by government agencies, and so on. Clearly, the nature of speculation is such that to earn speculative rewards, speculators must bear risk.

The real world of markets is not as perfect as basic economic theory would have us believe. Sometimes, for whatever reasons, an individual or a group acquires the power to manipulate a market. Such individuals are not speculators. They are market **manipulators**. By definition, a manipulator is one who uses his private power to bring about a rise or a fall in prices in such a fashion as to produce personal gain at the expense of others who are not parties to the manipulation. Manipulation of markets is inherently evil, in the sense that it undermines confidence in the pricing system and interferes with the efficient allocation of resources. For these reasons, market manipulation is also often illegal. It is not surprising, then, that manipulators try very hard to disguise themselves as something other than manipulators—usually as speculators. As a consequence, those injured by market manipulation often mistakenly blame speculators. (The Hunt brothers' manipulation of the silver market in the late 1970s and Ivan Boesky's recent shenanigans are cases in point and highlight the need for clear ethical standards for those who deal in the markets at any level.)

Speculators also often get bad press when they reap honest profits. The nonspeculator hears tales of speculators who made "windfall" gains because they were long oil when oil prices rose, or short the stock market at the time of the equities market collapse. The nonspeculator concludes that the speculator's gain came at the nonspeculator's expense, because the nonspeculator is paying higher prices for gasoline or heating oil, or his retirement stock portfolio has less market value. The nonspeculator is often unable to distinguish cause from effect. The speculator who was long oil did not cause the price of oil to rise, irrespective of the extent of his personal profit from the occurrence. He gathered and analyzed the information which led him to conclude that the price of oil would have to rise in order to clear the market.[2] On the basis of that analysis, he bought oil. The speculators who lose money—and there are typically

---

[2] "Clear the market" refers to the point where demand equals supply. In our example, oil prices are relatively low, causing the demand for oil to exceed the supply. As a result, oil prices rise, causing the demand to decrease and the supply to increase. Oil prices will continue to rise until the demand for oil equals the supply for oil, and the oil market "clears."

many more of these—do not ordinarily get much press, and their losses do not carry the same weight as the profits of the successful speculators in the minds of the nonspeculators.

While the buying and selling activities of individual speculators rarely have more than a negligible impact on market prices, the cumulative or aggregate effect of speculative buying and selling can have a very significant effect. This is not, however, bad. Speculative buying and selling are usually in response to information acquisition and analysis, and any price changes that subsequently result should represent movement toward market clearing. In the absence of speculation, market prices would respond more slowly to changing market conditions, and delays would mean less efficiency in resource reallocation.

But our purpose here is not to defend speculation as an institution; it is to explain how it is actually done. Nevertheless, it is important to appreciate that speculators serve at least three very useful offices in a market economy: they assist in price discovery, they assist in resource allocation across both space and time, and they willingly bear risks that others do not wish to bear.

Keep in mind that speculative profits as a reward for successful forecasting and speculative profits as a reward for risk bearing are not mutually exclusive and, indeed, are actually supportive. For example, hedgers' sales of risk management contracts (such as futures contracts) tend to depress the prices of those contracts. Speculators then forecast that prices will go up, and they buy the contracts. Prices subsequently rise as hedgers offset their risk management contracts upon termination of their cash positions, and speculators profit from the rise in prices. All other things being equal, the result should be a small transfer of wealth from hedgers to speculators.

Speculative Methods

It is often said that there are as many different speculative methods as there are speculators. While there is undoubtedly some truth in this, speculative methods of price analysis are generally divided into two broad categories called **fundamental analysis** and **technical analysis**. Despite the fact that users of one method often disavow the other, these two schools of thought are not mutually exclusive.

Fundamental analysts examine all information that bears on the underlying economic relationships—supply and demand—that ultimately determine all prices. They gather information on domestic and foreign production, read government reports, interpret federal reserve policy, estimate input costs and usage rates, monitor technological developments, analyze demographic data, and so on. From this information, they attempt to determine what the intrinsic market clearing price is and how that market clearing price is likely to change over time. A current price below the market clearing price represents an undervalued asset, and a current price above the market clearing price represents an overvalued asset. Undervalued assets are purchased, and overvalued assets are sold.

Although each type of instrument has its own special set of factors that must be considered, this same basic approach can be applied to all financial instruments, including commodities, stocks, debt securities, currencies, and so on. Fundamentalists' methods range from simple intuitive analysis of information to extremely elaborate and quantitatively sophisticated econometric models. As a general rule, the forecasting approach employed by these speculators takes a long–term view of the market. That is, fundamentalists are prepared to wait a considerable time for the market price to move to its fair value.

Technical analysis takes a very different approach to forecasting future prices. The technical analyst, or technician, accepts that the fundamental approach is founded on solid economic logic (theory) but often maintains that it is very difficult, if not impossible, to practice successfully. The technician argues that the fundamentalist simply cannot gather enough private information to consistently outperform the market. Instead, the technician focuses on one specific category of information called **transactions data**. Transactions data are any information associated with the record of past transactions (including the most recent ones). Transactions data consist of such things as transactional prices, trading volume, open interest, short interest, specialists' positions, odd–lot transactions, and so on.

The technician examines the transactions data for patterns that have predictive value. In other words, the technician searches through long histories of transactions data for patterns, called **formations**, which have repeatedly occurred in the past and which have frequently been followed by some specific directional movement. Then, by examining very recent and current price behavior, the technician tries to find similar formations and to take a position based on those formations prior to the oft–encountered subsequent price movements.

The technician's faith in the existence of patterns of activity revealed slowly over time hangs on the technician's belief that prices move in identifiable trends. It is not at all clear why such trends should exist, but a number of plausible reasons have been given, including:

1. the gradual, rather than rapid, dissemination of information (as in the case of the development of a drought, or a failure in a firm's product that might lead to an expensive recall);
2. the tendency of market psychology to swing only slowly in a new direction;
3. the tendency of a "herd instinct" to dominate investor psychology; and
4. the access of some market participants to information before the general market.

Technicians use a variety of methods and varying time horizons. Some limit their activities to visual, chart–type methods that employ bar and point–and–figure charts. Others use computer–based models that have been optimized by systematic search procedures. Still others operate by a seat–of–the–pants approach—buying at the first sign of an up–move and selling at the first sign of a down–move. Some technicians take a long–term approach, trying to exploit a long–term or primary trend. But most take a much shorter view of the market, looking to capture short– to intermediate–term trends.

Trading and Research

Traders depend heavily on research. Not surprisingly, there are synergies in having both a strong trading operation and quality research departments. But research departments serve two different constituencies: in–house trading personnel and brokerage clients. With respect to the first, traders are always looking for evidence of mispricings, and research personnel are often the first to uncover such evidence. All of the bulge bracket investment banks, and most of the majors, have research departments. In the bulge bracket firms, research is usually divided up into segregated departments: equity research, which supports the equity traders, retail brokers, and institutional sales desk; fixed–income research, which supports the shop's bond and mortgage–backed traders and its institutional sales desk; quantitative research, which develops complex and mathematically sophisticated trading—often arbitrage, strategies, usually for in–house use; and so on.[3]

The point is that trading and research are powerful allies. Similarly, trading and sales are natural allies. Sales personnel, including both brokers and dealers, assist traders in acquiring those assets that the traders believe are undervalued and in selling those assets that the traders believe are overvalued. Sales desks also feed off research, which the brokers and dealers—both retail and institutional—feed to their clients in the hopes of motivating transactions. Not surprisingly, many investment banks have pulled their sales, trading, and research departments together into integrated divisions.

Speculation: Absolute Value Trading

Let's return now to speculation. We will begin with **absolute value traders**. An absolute value trader is a trader who believes that the price of an asset is too high or too low and who takes an outright (unhedged) position in the asset. These traders are often said to position securities based on their "view."[4]

Suppose that an investment bank's research department, which analyzes securities on both a fundamental and a technical basis, concludes that a stock is undervalued and is positioned to move higher in the near term. The research department issues a report to this effect. An equity trader working for the investment bank, and who is in agreement with the research department's conclusions, would likely purchase the stock. Of course, equity traders also do their own analysis, ferret out their own information, and have their own hunches and instincts. Not surprisingly, an equity trader will not always agree with the recommendations of the bank's research staff and, when he doesn't, will not act on it.

---

[3] Because research departments support both the in–house traders and the firm's brokerage clientele, they often find themselves in a conflict–of–interest situation. For example, if an investment bank's research department turns bearish on a particular company's stock or bonds, is the bank's principal obligation to the in–house traders, to the brokerage clientele, or to the company whose securities are involved (which might be a client of the bank on the issuance side)? We will return to these issues when we address research in Chapter 12.

[4] A "view" is market slang for forecast.

Consider another example. Suppose that an investment bank is a dealer in an XYZ bond that is currently rated by Moody's and Standard & Poors (bond–rating agencies) as triple A. This is a top investment grade rating. Suppose now that the fixed–income research department concludes that the issuer's creditworthiness is deteriorating, or is very likely to deteriorate soon, and that a downgrade of the bond is likely. Of course, all other things being equal, a downgrade of the bond will cause its price to decline. The trader, acting on the research report, sells the bond short. If the bond is downgraded, or if a more widely held perception develops that the bond will soon be downgraded, the bond's price will decline. After the bond's price declines, the trader will buy the bond back and cover the short position.

These simple scenarios demonstrate the importance of an investment bank's research department to its traders. The traders take as input the analysis of the research department, and they transact through the firm's dealers. This helps to explain why sales, trading, and research, once viewed as stand–alone activities within an investment bank, have been increasingly integrated over the past 10 or 15 years. There are many other situations in which a trader might take an outright position in a security based on a particular view of a market or a view of a specific security. For example, a bond trader who believed that interest rates would soon rise would be inclined to go long bonds. A currency trader who believed that the Commerce Department would announce a greater than expected U.S. trade deficit would likely go short the dollar. A global equity trader who felt strongly that the Japanese stock market was due for a rally and that the yen would strengthen against the dollar would likely purchase Japanese equities or an equity index instrument (such as Nikkei warrants). Examples go on and on. We will consider some specifics of the analysis when we discuss research in Chapter 12.

Speculation: Relative Value Trading

Relative value trading is a form of trading that can and often does resemble arbitrage. If risks are fully hedged, it may, in fact, become arbitrage. The concept is perhaps most easily demonstrated in the context of a bond trading operation. To fully appreciate the arguments, we will need a short discourse on yield curves.

Yield curves depict the relationship between the yields (yield–to–maturity) and the terms (term–to–maturity) for a given class of fixed–income instruments. A class of instruments includes all securities which meet some specific criteria that make the securities reasonably comparable (except with respect to yield and maturity). For example, U.S. Treasury securities constitute a class; fully taxable triple A–rated corporate bonds of industrial corporations would constitute a class; and so on. The logic of yield curves is based on the observation that yields tend to be greater for longer–maturity instruments than for shorter–maturity instruments. The earliest attempts to explain this phenomenon noted that long–maturity instruments are more price–sensitive to changes in yield than are short–maturity instruments. Thus, maturity was perceived to be a good indicator of interest–rate risk. Greater risk implied greater return (yield) and, hence, the yield curve should be upward sloping.[5] And indeed, this was the usual case.

In 1938, a better measure of interest rate sensitivity, called **duration**, was developed. Like maturity, duration is measured in years. Today, it is not uncommon to depict yield versus duration rather than yield versus term.[6] Once one has plotted yield against term or yield against duration, one can "fit" a smooth line to the data points using nonlinear regression techniques. A typical yield curve is depicted in Figure 6.1, and a yield versus duration curve is depicted in Figure 6.2.

Once this line is observable (either visually or with the aid of a computer), the relative value trader steps into the picture. Consider a corporate bond trader working for an investment bank with a large corporate bond department. Next, suppose that the trader limits his trading to bonds within a homogeneous group (e.g., top investment–grade industrial bonds). For simplicity, the bonds are all **straight bonds**—that is, bonds that are neither callable nor convertible. Using the procedure described above, the bond trader looks for overvalued and undervalued bonds. While this will most often be done quantitatively, the graphic depiction helps us to visualize what is going on.

---

[5] This early explanation for the shape of the yield curve has come to be known as the liquidity premium theory. Today, it is only one of several competing theories that can explain this shape.

[6] In one special case, that of zero coupon bonds, duration and maturity are always identical. Thus, in these cases, one can plot yield versus term or yield versus duration and get the same result.

Figure 6.1
Yield vs. Maturity

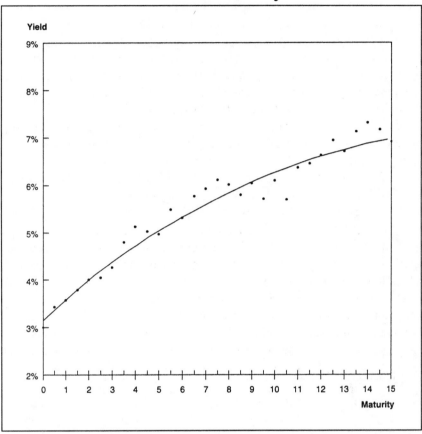

Now consider Figure 6.2. Notice that some of the yields, such as those of bonds A and C, lie above the curve. Others, such as B and D, lie below the curve. All other things being equal, the bonds whose yields lie above the curve are undervalued and the bonds whose yields lie below the curve are overvalued relative to one another. It is important to understand that the values are relative values, not absolute values. The bond trader is not making a forecast as to which way bond prices more

Figure 6.2
Yield vs. Duration

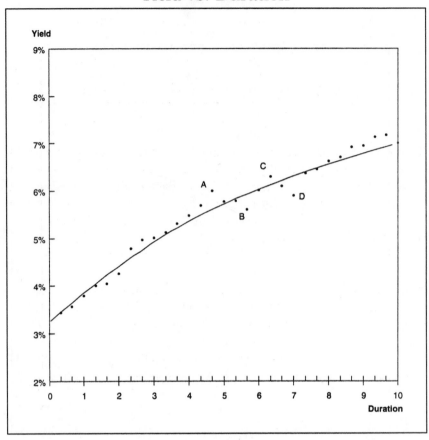

generally will move, only a forecast of how the prices of these bonds should move relative to one another.

The trader now buys the undervalued bonds (A and C) and sells the overvalued bonds (B and D). To make this more real, suppose the trader buys $5 million of A and $3 million of C and sells short $4 million of B and $4 million of D. These values are par values, and the transactions are made through the firm's bond dealers. Suppose that the market values (as a percentage of par) and the DV01s of the bonds are as given in

Table 6.1
Current Position

POS #MM	Bond	Price	DV01
5.0	A	96.375	0.0454
4.0	B	95.750	0.0524
3.0	C	97.250	0.0638
−4.0	D	102.875	0.0689

Table 6.1. Also assume, again for simplicity, that any unexpected shifts in the curve in Figure 6.1 take the form of parallel shifts.

The next thing the trader does is standardize the interest rate risk exposure by converting each bond position to a risk equivalent position in some **benchmark instrument** (often called a **baseline instrument**). This is usually a Treasury bond or note on which a futures contract is traded. Let's suppose that the DV01 of the T–bond futures happens to be $0.0975 per $100 of par. This is the benchmark DV01. Next, we can formulate the hedge ratios (HR) by dividing each bond's DV01 by the benchmark DV01 and multiplying by the bond's yield beta (we are assuming that the yield betas are all 1 for this particular example). These hedge ratios are then multiplied by the par values of the corresponding bonds to obtain the T–bond equivalent positions. This information is provided in the trader's risk management report depicted in Table 6.2.

Table 6.2
Relative Value Trader's Risk Management Report

POS #MM	Bond	Price	DV01	HR	Equivalent Position $MM
5.0	A	96.375	0.0454	0.4656	2.3282
−4.0	B	95.750	0.0524	0.5374	−2.1497
3.0	C	97.250	0.0638	0.6543	1.9631
−4.0	D	102.875	0.0689	0.7066	−2.8267
					Sum −0.6851

Finally, the T–bond equivalent positions are summed to get the T–bond risk equivalent of the bond trader's overall book. In this case, the book is equivalent, *for risk purposes only*, to a short position in $0.685 million of par value T–bonds. The corporate bond trader could hedge by taking a long position in $0.685 million of cash T–bonds or by purchasing T–bond futures. Since each T–bond futures contract covers $.1 million of par value, the bond book is hedged against interest rate risk by taking a long position in 6.8 T–bond futures contracts. For simplicity, we will assume that cash Treasuries are used as the hedging instrument.

The reader should recognize that this bond trader hedges his positions using the same methodology that the bond dealer used in the last chapter. But the dealer was attempting to profit from the transactional services that he provides, while the bond trader is attempting to profit from errors in relative valuation.

The bond trader's long positions have to be financed and securities must be obtained to deliver on the short sales. These needs are met via transactions in the repo market, the mechanics of which were discussed in the last chapter. In brief, the trader sells the bonds in the repo market with an agreement to buy them back the next day at the same price, with add–on interest. The cost of financing the positions is the repo rate paid. At the same time, the bonds that are sold short are acquired in the resale market. Specifically, the trader "buys" the securities in the repo market with the promise to sell them back the next day. This is equivalent to making a collateralized loan. The other party pays the trader the repo receive rate. Thus, the short positions earn repo interest. Not to be overlooked is the coupon interest earned on his long positions and the coupon interest paid on his short positions. In other words, the trader earns coupon interest on the corporate bonds that he is long but pays repo interest to finance them. The opposite is true for the short positions. Also, since the trader hedges in cash T–bonds, there may be a cost (positive or negative) to hedging. If so, this is equal to the difference between the coupon interest earned on the T–bonds and the repo interest paid to finance them. The bond trader's cost of carrying his relative value corporate bond book, then, is the sum of all coupon interest paid (including that from both corporate bonds and Treasury bond hedges) and all repo interest paid, less the sum of all coupon interest received and all repo interest received.

The corporate bond trader cannot overlook the cost of carrying his bond book. For example, if his relative value strategy is intended to earn a return of 12 basis points on the par value of his positions, but the cost of implementation, including the cost of carry and transaction costs, is more than 12 basis points, then the strategy is doomed to fail. If, on the other hand, the cost of carry is less than 12 basis points (and it can even be negative), then the strategy should prove profitable, barring unexpected value variations due to such things as unfavorable changes in bond ratings.

To complete the example, let's suppose that the bond trader expects to earn 12 basis points on market adjustments to fair value (after allowing for occasional losses due to unanticipated ratings changes) and that the strategy has a positive cost of carry of 5 basis points; then the expected profit on each position is 7 basis points. Of course, 7 basis points is only 0.07 percent and may not seem worth the effort, but this conclusion is premature.

Suppose that the trader's positions are held for about 10 days, on average, before prices correct and an opportunity to unwind the position appears. Let's also assume that at any given point in time, the trader has an aggregate position of $50 million. What, then, is the expected profit to the firm from the activities of this trader? Well, the firm would earn an average return of 7 basis points on $50 million over a 10–day period, and this could be turned over about 36 times in a year. The profit for the firm is thus $1,260,000 (i.e., 0.0007 × $50 million × 36). The trader would, of course, be compensated in the form of a performance bonus. That is, he can expect to receive some modest base salary plus a significant percentage of the profits he generates for the firm.

One might be inclined to say that this trader's performance was not really very good. After all, he earned a profit for the firm of $1.26 million (after all direct costs except his own compensation) while carrying positions having aggregate par values of $50 million. The return, as a percentage of the aggregate position, is only about 2.5 percent. If we allow for a base salary of $100,000 plus a bonus equal to 30 percent of profits, the investment bank's residual is $782,000. Finally, after allowing for indirect costs (support systems and other overhead), the firm might have $500,000 left and, after taxes, might have profits of only $300,000.

It would seem, then, that a $300,000 after–tax profit on $50 million of positions is a pretty poor return. Indeed, it is only 0.6 percent. But this completely overlooks the fact that all the money used in the trader's strategy came from outside the firm; none of the firm's own capital was used (although the firm's capital was at risk). This use of other people's money to hold positions is often described as **leverage**. No other industry uses as much leverage as does the securities industry, particularly the large trading firms like Salomon Brothers and Bear, Stearns. For these firms, the use of leverage can run to 50 times (or more) of the firm's own equity capital.[7] Thus, the real contribution of this trader, when restated in terms of the firm's return on equity, is 30 percent (50 × 0.6%). When seen in this light, the muscle of the major trading houses can be better appreciated. More important, it can be seen that the exploitation of even small mispricings can render substantial returns for the mathematically sophisticated trader.

In the example just presented, the corporate bond trader financed his positions and used cash Treasury hedges. The hedges were employed because the trader was a relative value trader and not a position trader; that is, he did not take a "view" on the general direction of the market. If the bond trader had a view on the direction of interest rates such that he felt that rates would soon rise, then he might not have hedged the residual interest rate risk in his corporate bond book. If rates rise, bond prices will fall—irrespective of their relative values. Since he is net short, as suggested by the sum of his T–bond equivalent positions, he would profit from a rise in rates. But this trader is not forecasting interest rates, and therefore he chooses to hedge.

Let's consider the trader's positions in a somewhat different light. First, his positions do not require any investment on the part of his firm, since the positions are fully financed in the repo market. Second, by having hedged the residual risk in cash T–bonds (or in T–bond futures), his positions do not expose him to any meaningful interest rate risk. This

---

[7] We have to distinguish between leverage in the form of long–term debt and leverage in the form of short–term debt. In a traditional corporate finance setting, leverage measures generally concentrate on the use of long–term debt (relative to equity). Among the bulge bracket firms, the ratio of long–term debt to equity varied (in the latest year for which data were available) from a high of 2.16 for Merrill Lynch to a low of 0.82 for PaineWebber. But this is really not the right way to measure leverage in a trading environment where most of the financing is done in the short–term repo market. It is this use of short–term borrowing/lending that generates multiplier effects of 50X or more for some firms.

comes close to being arbitrage. But it is not pure arbitrage (completely riskless), because the bond trader is still exposed to credit risk on his bonds. However, credit risk is a largely unsystematic form of risk; while some bonds might be unexpectedly downgraded, others might be unexpectedly upgraded. In a large portfolio, the upgrade and downgrade effects on value might be expected to cancel out.

Before leaving this example, we need to ask where the trader profits from this strategy. First, all other things being equal, the prices of the undervalued bonds should move up to their fair values, and the prices of the overvalued bonds should decline to their fair values. Thus, the strategy should accrue profit as the market adjusts to correct its pricing errors. These opportunities arise because of occasional imbalances in the demand for and supply of individual bonds. Of course, the trader must cover his financing costs in the repo market. As a general rule, the trader will pay a slightly higher rate on his financings in the repo market than on his lendings in the resale market. Additionally, the trader will earn coupon interest on the bonds he is long and pay coupon interest on the bonds he is short. These sources of interest income and interest expense must be factored into the dealer's profit forecast before any positions are put on to be sure that the expected profit is sufficient to cover any residual costs.

Speculation: Ratings Forecasts

The last example illustrated how some bond traders trade based on relative values. Other bond traders trade on the basis of ratings forecasts. For example, on March 11, 1993, Standard & Poors downgraded the debt of the three largest U.S. air carriers: AMR (the parent of American Airlines), United Airlines, and Delta Airlines. In justifying the downgrades, S&P stated that the move was based on industrywide overcapacity, weak overall demand, and "an adverse industry environment and a narrowed competitive advantage over second–tier airlines."[8] At the time, American had outstanding debt of $11.4 billion; Delta had outstanding debt of $5.7 billion; and United had outstanding debt of $4.3 billion.

Immediately following the S&P downgrades, the market values of most of the outstanding bond issues of the three carriers slipped. Of

---

[8] See *The Wall Street Journal*, March 12, 1993.

course, we must distinguish between a decline in price caused by a downgrade and a decline in price caused by other factors, such as a general rise in interest rates. As it happened, following the downgrades announcement, the yields on the three air carriers' bonds rose from 30 to 50 basis points relative to the yields on Treasuries of equivalent maturity—indicating that the yield changes were attributable to the downgrades.[9]

A bond trader who had correctly anticipated the downgradings could have sold the bonds short prior to the downgrades. Not surprisingly, fixed–income research departments of investment banks do engage in extensive credit analysis and attempt to forecast ratings changes. And some traders do trade on ratings–change expectations. Suppose that such a trader anticipates a downgrade of AMR bonds. In anticipation, she sells short $10 million of the bonds. Since she is betting on a yield change as a consequence of a downgrade and not making an interest rate forecast, she needs to protect herself from interest rate changes that are not associated with ratings changes. This is the same as the relative value trader who needs to protect himself from interest rate changes not associated with the relative value changes. Our ratings trader would, of course, be long bonds expected to be upgraded and short bonds expected to be downgraded.

Speculation: Complex Forecasts

The simplest type of fixed–income speculator takes a naked position (i.e., one in which the risk is not offset in another instrument) based on an interest rate forecast (i.e., a view). If the view is for rates to rise, he goes short. If the view is for rates to fall, he goes long.

Of course, a view on rates can be more complex than a simple projection that rates will rise or fall. For example, the trader might expect short–term rates to rise relative to intermediate and long–term rates. This would imply a flattening of the yield curve. Or the trader might forecast

---

[9] We are not aware of any formal event studies of this particular ratings downgrade. A formal study would be required before one can formally conclude that the yield changes on the airlines' bonds were, in fact, a consequence of the ratings changes. Nonetheless, the anecdotal evidence appears strong.

that short–term rates will decline relative to intermediate and long–term rates. This would imply a steepening of the yield curve.

Or consider another type of forecast. Suppose that the trader believes that corporate bond yields will rise relative to Treasury yields. This might or might not be associated with a forecast of a change in the steepness of the yield curves or the general direction of rates. Complex forecasts such as these can be exploited, but they tend to involve considerably more risk than the hedged strategies discussed earlier.

Arbitrage

Arbitrage is routinely defined as the simultaneous taking of positions in two or more markets in order to exploit pricing aberrations among them.[10] Those who practice arbitrage are often called, in market slang, **arbs**. The strategies employed by arbs are some of the most complex imaginable and often involve very sophisticated mathematics, lightning speed in execution, and considerable computer power. Program trading is one example, but not necessarily a very complex one. It is not surprising that those who develop and practice the more complex arbitrage strategies are often described as "quant jocks."

The academic definition of arbitrage demands that the strategy not require any of the arbitrageur's own funds and that it be entirely riskless. Indeed, when both of these conditions are satisfied, the arbitrage is described as **academic arbitrage** or **pure arbitrage**.

Arbitrage strategies take many forms: one can arbitrage value discrepancies across space, across time, and/or across instruments. One can also arbitrage tax asymmetries and risks. Let's consider examples of spatial and temporal arbitrage. We will save discussion of arbitrage across instruments and risks until we have examined derivative instruments and how they are used.

---

[10]Arbitrage rests upon the same mathematics and fundamental relationships as hedging. In fact, in some markets arbitrage is often conducted in conjunction with hedging.

Spatial Arbitrage

Spatial arbitrage is the simplest form of arbitrage. In spatial arbitrage, also known as **geographic arbitrage**, the arbitrager looks for pricing discrepancies across geographically separate markets. For example, suppose that a bond dealer in San Francisco is offering a bond at 102-15/32 and a dealer in New York is bidding 102-17/32 for the same bond. For whatever reason, the two dealers have not spotted the aberration in the prices, but the arb does. The arb immediately buys the bond from the San Francisco dealer and sells it to the New York dealer.

Of course, there is no reason that the arbitrage opportunity had to involve dealers in two different cities. It could have involved two dealers in the same city, two dealers in different countries, or two dealers standing right next to each other. All that is essential is that the dealers did not observe that one's ask price was lower than the other's bid price. These are the opportunities that spatial arbitrageurs try to exploit. The asset itself is irrelevant. It could be debt, preferred stock, common stock, a mortgage–backed security, a commodity, an equity index, and so on.

In the case of securities, the spatial arbitrageur can transfer owner-ship from the selling counterparty to the buying counterparty at near zero costs. This is generally not the case with commodities which must be transported to make deliveries. Thus, the arbitrageur must capture sufficient price differential to cover the transportation (and any transac-tion) costs and still have a profit.

The spatial arbitrage strategy can also involve the conversion of the asset that is the subject of the arbitrage from the delivery standard in one market to the delivery standard in the other market. For example, gold is traded in some markets in 95 percent purity but in other markets in 99 percent purity. The gold can be converted from one market standard to the other, but not without some additional cost. Thus, the pricing differential must cover the transportation costs, the transaction costs, and the conversion costs.

Temporal Arbitrage: Program Trading

Temporal arbitrage is arbitrage across time. It involves buying an asset for immediate delivery and selling it for later delivery in order to exploit a price discrepancy between the cash price and the forward price. The forward transaction is most often accomplished with a futures contract.

The strategy can also be reversed. That is, we can sell the cash asset (short) for immediate delivery and buy the futures contract.

This strategy is widely used by investment banks and other securities firms to exploit pricing discrepancies between cash stock prices and stock index futures prices. The strategy is often called **program trading**. The term program trading is sometimes used more broadly to describe a number of mechanical trading techniques. A more precise description is **cash/index arbitrage**. Nevertheless, we will call the strategy program trading.

In program trading, the arbitrageur, using live data feeds and high–speed information processing equipment, searches for opportunities in which a basket of stocks is either overvalued or undervalued relative to a stock index futures contract. The strategy is conceptually simple: when the cash stocks are cheap and the futures are rich, the arb buys the cash stocks (thereby synthesizing the index) and sells the stock index futures. The futures are rich, relative to the cash, if the difference between the prices is greater than the cost of carry. The latter is important, because the cash stocks must be carried forward in time until the position can be profitably unwound or until the stock index futures contract settles. The strategy is employed in reverse when the cash is rich and the futures are cheap.

Although the basic strategy is conceptually simple, it is difficult to effect, because the cash stock index that makes up one side, or leg, of the strategy does not actually exist. There is no such actual tradable thing as an "S&P stock index" or a "Major Market Index." Instead, one has to trade a basket of stocks that mimic the S&P 500 stock index or the Major Market Index. This basket of stocks is called a **proxy portfolio**. Once such a profitable portfolio has been identified, the transactions must be executed nearly instantaneously to capture the pricing discrepancy before it can evaporate.

Consider for a moment the actual mechanics of the operation. An investment bank's program traders continuously search (via their computers) for a proxy portfolio with a minimum of, let's say, 98 percent correlation with the S&P 500 stock index. They find many such portfolios but none that are so seriously mispriced as to represent a profitable opportunity. Nevertheless, they continue to search. Suddenly—probably following some significant news event that disrupts the current equilibrium and places stock prices and index futures prices in a temporary state of disequilibrium—an opportunity presents itself. A proxy portfolio is identified that offers a 98.5 percent correlation with the S&P 500 index and which is currently priced at $452.20 when the futures price is $454.40. As it happens, the futures contract is deliverable in two months. The stocks purchased are financed in the repo market at an annual rate of 4.80 percent (a monthly cost of 0.40 percent). While the stocks are held, they provide dividend income to the investment bank. This dividend income has the effect of reducing the cost of carry. Let's suppose that the annual dividend rate is 3 percent (a monthly rate of 0.25 percent). Then, the cost of carry is the interest expense less the dividend income. Denoting the periodic interest rate for two months as r and the periodic dividend rate as d, the fair futures price, relative to the proxy stock portfolio, should be 453.56. The calculation is depicted below.

$$F = S(1 + r - d)$$
$$= 452.2 \ [1 + 2(.004) - 2(.0025)]$$
$$= 452.20(1 + .008 - .005)$$
$$= 453.56$$

Since the futures price is $454.40, the futures contract is mispriced, and an opportunity seems to exist. Suppose the round–trip transaction costs (including the costs of transacting in both stocks and futures) amount to 0.06 percent, as a percent of the spot price S. Then, the transaction cost amounts to 0.27 (.06% × 452.20). The strategy has the potential to produce a profit of 0.57. This is calculated as 454.40 – 453.56 – 0.27. As a percentage of the spot price, this is a return of about 12.6 basis points (i.e., 0.57/452.20).

As a worst–case scenario, this return will be earned over a two–month period, because the cash index and the futures price must converge at the time of the futures contract's delivery. The return amounts to 12.6 basis points earned over two months, which, with luck, can be repeated six times in a year to yield a total return of about 75 basis points, or three–quarters of 1 percent. While this does not seem like much, it must be remembered that this is the return earned on someone else's money. The large program traders are capable of moving literally billions of dollars into and out of the stock market in their efforts to exploit such opportunities. Even a 12–basis–point return on, say, $500 million of someone else's money can be a handsome profit for the investment bank.

Investment banks engage in program trading for their own accounts but also on behalf of clients. Clients fall into two basic camps: unlevered and levered. The unlevered clients are those who put up their own cash to program trade: buy (sell) stocks and sell (buy) futures. Since no money needs to be borrowed, the goal is simply to have a riskless position but earn more than the risk–free rate. For example, let's suppose that the current two–month T–bill rate is 4.80 percent. The two–month repo rate happens also to be 4.80 percent. The unlevered program trading operation then buys the stocks at 452.20, sells the futures at 454.40, and sits for two months. During this time, the operation earns dividends on its stock holdings at an annual rate of 3 percent (the dividend rate). The end result is that the investors earn a total return of 5.92 percent before transaction costs. This total return consists of a 3 percent dividend rate plus a 2.92 percent gain rate, computed as [(454.40-452.20)/452.20] × 6. Assuming that transaction costs are the same as they were in the last example, the investor should earn an annual return of about 5.55 percent after transaction costs. And if the investor is willing to leverage up (i.e., use repo financing to enhance the return), the strategy could prove even more rewarding. The investment bank that handles this institutional trading for its clients will earn, for its efforts, transaction fees and management fees.

In sum, the program trading strategy, whether practiced by the investment bank for its own account or practiced for clients in exchange for the transactional–services compensation and/or a management fee, is essentially a strategy that replicates a riskless asset but is intended to return more than the riskless asset. Many arbitrage strategies, just like program trading, seek to replicate the risk character of T–bills and yet to return more than T–bills. Any time a portfolio strategy tries to replicate the risk characteristics of a T–bill, the portfolio is described as a **synthetic T–bill**. More generally, any portfolio of instruments designed to replicate the investment characteristics of a security is called a **replicating portfolio** or a **synthetic security**. The terms are used interchangeably.

Temporal Arbitrage: The Cash–and–Carry Synthetic

A cash–and–carry transaction involves the purchase of an instrument and the simultaneous sale of a futures contract (or other derivative) in order to create a synthetic short–term instrument. Such synthetic short–term instruments are created in order to earn low–risk short–term rates. The program trading strategy that we just examined is one example of a cash–and–carry synthetic transaction.

Let's now consider a cash and carry involving bonds. Suppose that the 20.5–year Treasury bond carries a coupon of 8 percent and is currently priced at 93-16/32. At this price, the instrument provides a yield to maturity of 8.684 percent (semiannual bond basis).[11] Also, assume that there is a six–month forward T–bond futures contract with a conversion factor of 1.000.[12] In other words, $100,000 of face value of this 20.5 year T–bond is deliverable per futures contract. At the time of delivery, the bond itself will have a maturity of 20 years. As it happens, the futures contract is currently priced at 93-2/32. What is the return to an investor who buys the bond and sells the futures?

To answer this question, we need to ask how much the investment bank's trader, or the client for which he is transacting, will earn from the transactions. First, the trader will receive a coupon payment of $4 in six months. This represents one–half of the annual 8 percent coupon. Second, the trader is going to sell the instrument (deliver on the futures contract) for 93.0625 (93-2/32). Thus, in six months the trader will have 97.0625 (i.e., 93.0625 + 4.000). Since the trader will have a terminal value of 97.0625 at a current cost of 93.50 (93-16/32), the return is 7.62 percent. The calculation, which follows, is simple in this case, because the holding period is exactly one–half of a year.

$$\text{return} = \left(\frac{97.0625}{93.5000} - 1 \right) \times 2 = 7.62\% \text{ (semiannual bond basis)}$$

---

[11] It is standard practice to state the yield on a bond on a semiannual bond basis. This is a yield to maturity that assumes semiannual compounding.

[12] Many different T–bonds can be used to make delivery on a T–bond futures contract. To make these bonds, which have different coupons and maturities, equivalent, the futures exchange publishes a table of conversion factors. For example, if a bond has a conversion factor of .9850, then one could satisfy the delivery obligation by delivering a bond having a face value of $98,500 per $100,000 of futures contract face value.

It is important to appreciate that while the trader has purchased a T–bond, which is a long–term instrument, the forward sale of the bond, through the medium of the futures contract, gave the overall position a short–term character (a synthetic T–bill). As such, the position earns a short–term rate (7.62 percent in this case) and not the long–term rate (8.684 percent) embodied in the bond's price. The upshot is that the cash–and–carry strategy creates a synthetic short–term investment which provides a short–term return.

We need to stress that the creation of a short–term synthetic from a long–term instrument will return a short–term rate and not a long–term rate. For example, at the time we observed the market prices used in this example, the 182–day T–bill rate was quoted at 7.24 percent (bank discount yield).[13] Of course, bank basis and bond basis yields are not directly comparable without first making a conversion. As it happens, the bond equivalent yield for this T–bill is 7.619 percent. This is virtually identical to the return from the synthetic.

Why did the synthetic T–bill return the same rate as the real T–bill? The answer is simple: If markets price assets efficiently, then all equivalent assets should return the same rate. Of course, market efficiency is itself a consequence of the intensive exploitation of the markets by speculators and arbitrageurs. However, this does not mean that opportunities to earn excess returns never arise. In fact, they do—and quite often. It is unrealistic to believe that markets can be perfectly efficient at all times. If they were, arbitrageurs and speculators would be unable to earn a fair return for their efforts and would withdraw from the markets. But if they withdrew from the markets, how could the markets continue to be efficient?

A synthetic T–bill can also be created by applying the cash–and–carry strategy to other assets. For example, we could do the same with a corporate bond. In the case of a corporate cash–and–carry—i.e., buy corporate bonds and sell T–bond futures (since there are no corporate bond futures)—the strategy produces a synthetic short–term

---

[13] T–bill yields are routinely quoted on a bank discount basis (often called bank basis), which employs an actual/360–day count convention and discounts the instrument's price to reflect the interest. In contrast, T–bonds are quoted on a bond basis, which employs an actual/365–day count and does not discount the instrument's price to reflect interest. Instead, interest is added on.

instrument, but the yield is not as certain as it is with the Treasury cash–and–carry. The reason is that the corporate bond is not deliverable against the T–bond futures. Instead, the arbitrageur would sell the corporate bond and offset the futures contract just before the futures contract was due to be delivered. But, since the corporate bond yield does not track the T–bond yield perfectly, there is a positive variance to the return from such a strategy. This is essentially a manifestation of what is called, in hedging theory, **basis risk**, even though the futures position was not undertaken as a hedge. This particular form of basis risk is sometimes called a **quality spread risk**. Because it is not riskless, the corporate cash–and–carry often offers a greater short–term return than the Treasury cash–and–carry.

Whether a cash–and–carry strategy is superior to a real short–term instrument depends on whether the futures to be used are cheap or rich. When they are cheap, the cash–and–carry strategy will be unattractive. When they are rich, the cash–and–carry strategy will be attractive. When properly priced, which (all other things being equal) we would expect to be the normal situation, the two strategies should produce identical returns. As a historic observation, money market investors would have done consistently better during most of 1981 and most of 1982 by investing in synthetic T–bills. During this period, T–bond futures were rich. The opposite was true during 1983 and most of 1984. Since 1984, there has been less consistency, so that futures are sometimes rich and sometimes cheap, but neither tends to prevail for a long period of time.

The lesson in this is that portfolio managers should evaluate all of their alternatives before selecting (or constructing) their investment vehicle. And investment bankers can be very helpful in this regard. Clearly, the prohibitions against trading futures that are often imposed on such managers, out of a mistaken belief that such instruments are purely speculative, are misplaced. It also points up once again the importance of distinguishing between relative value and absolute value.

Cash and Carry in Arbitrage: Enhancing Portfolio Return

We have demonstrated how the cash–and–carry strategy can be used to create synthetic T–bills. We have also argued that, if markets were always efficient, synthetic T–bills should return the same rate as real T–bills. In practice, however, synthetic securities sometimes offer a greater return and sometimes a lower return than real securities due to imperfection in the markets. We now focus on how investment bankers can enhance portfolio returns with synthetic instruments for themselves and for their clients.

While portfolio managers—particularly money market portfolio managers—should compare the returns on real T–bills to the returns on synthetic T–bills, the problem is a little different for the arbitrageur. Arbitrageurs, by definition, attempt to finance their positions. The very large positions which they take and carry are taken with borrowed funds. Today, these positions are most often financed in the repo market, and this is the key to understanding how arbitrage can enhance portfolio returns.

Recall the example we used to illustrate the Treasury cash–and–carry strategy in the preceding section: The arbitrageur can buy the 20.5 year T–bond and sell the T–bond futures to create a synthetic T–bill, thereby earning a certain return of 7.62 percent. This rate is identical to the 7.62 (7.619) percent return on real T–bills. It would appear that the arbitrageur could invest equally profitably in either market. But this is not necessarily the case. The real question is what is the **implied repo rate** at which the two positions can be financed.

To illustrate this issue, suppose that the T–bonds can be financed in the repo market at 7.34 percent and the T–bills at 7.42 percent. In other words, under current market conditions the arbitrageur can purchase T–bonds and then use them as collateral in the repo market to obtain the funding used to purchase the bonds at a cost of 7.34 percent. Also under current market conditions, the arbitrageur can purchase T–bills and use them as collateral in the repo market to obtain the funding needed to purchase the bills at 7.42 percent. In this case we have the following situation:

Strategy	Repo Rate	Return	Net Profit
Cash and Carry	7.34	7.62	28 bps
Buy T–bills	7.42	7.62	20 bps

Under this scenario, the cash–and–carry (synthetic T–bill) is the superior investment for the arbitrageur since it returns 8 basis points (bps) more than the real T–bill. It is worth noting that while 28 basis points might not seem like very much—after all, it is only a little more than one–quarter of a percentage point—it is actually a very handsome return for an investment that is riskless and requires almost no investment of the arbitrageur's own funds. For example, suppose that the trade involves $10 million of synthetic bills and only $50,000 of the arbitrageur's own money. The strategy would return $14,000 over the course of six months. This translates to a per annum return of 56 percent (compounded semiannually) on the arbitrageur's investment. Not so insignificant a return as it first seems!

Let's take this example just a little further. Suppose that the real T–bill returns 7.66 percent, while the synthetic T–bill returns 7.62 percent. All the other information is the same as above. For a money market portfolio manager, there is no question that the real T–bill offers greater relative value (7.66 percent versus 7.62 percent). But for the arbitrageur, the synthetic T–bill offers greater relative value (28 bps versus 24 bps). Clearly, for the arbitrageur, the repo rate, which represents the financing cost, cannot be ignored. This is why the term "implied repo rate" is used to describe the return on the synthetic security. As such, it is the financing rate at which the arbitrageur would break even. In the example just used, the implied repo rate is 7.62 percent.

Risk Arbitrage

The term risk arbitrage is inherently contradictory. True arbitrage, as we have earlier defined it, is riskless. Nevertheless, the term is very descriptive of this particular type of activity.

Risk arbitrage is associated with mergers and other forms of corporate ownership restructurings. Most, if not all, major investment banks and many specialty shops have risk arbitrage departments or operations. As originally used, the term risk arbitrage meant to buy the stock of a target firm in a takeover and to sell the stock of the acquiring firm. Consider a simple example. Corporation X announces that it would like to acquire Corporation Y by way of an exchange of stock. Let's suppose that Corporation Y offers one share of its stock for two shares of Corporation X's stock. At the time, Corporation Y's stock is trading for $68 a share and Corporation X's stock is trading for $30 a share. The risk arbs will buy two shares of X's stock (at a total cost of $60) and sell short one share of Y's stock at $68. Assuming that the takeover is successful on the original terms, the risk arbs stand to earn $8 from the simultaneous buying and selling. Of course, once the deal is consummated, the risk arbs receive one share of Y for the two shares of X that they tendered. They then use the share of Y they receive to cover their earlier short sale. Of course, the aggressive buying of Corporation X's stock by risk arbs will drive its stock price up and the short sales of Corporation Y's stock will tend to drive its price down until the two are in equilibrium. Equilibrium, however, does not necessarily mean equal. As long as there is a risk that the deal will fall through, the market price of two shares of X will tend to stay somewhat below that of one share of Y. The greater this risk, the greater the disparity will be.

Investment banks are natural players in the risk arbitrage game. First, they have experienced mergers and acquisitions groups that are expert at assessing and identifying potential takeover targets, undervalued assets, weak managements, and so on. They are also often privy to information—through advisory relationships, underwriting relationships, investment relationships, and so on—that gives them a special insight into companies that are likely to be "put in play." Investment banks also have the support of their research departments, which can and often do spot special situations.

While these special relationships give investment banks a competitive advantage in the risk arb business, they also create potential conflicts of interest. A client that is being advised by an investment bank on an acquisition or defensive measures in an effort to ward off an acquirer does not want its investment bank involved in an arb strategy that may work to the client's disadvantage.

For these reasons, once an investment bank becomes involved in an advisory capacity with a party that is involved in a takeover, or even engages in discussions to become an adviser in a takeover, the investment bank's risk arbs are usually told that the firms involved are off–limits. In addition, to avoid the appearance of a potential exploitation of inside information, most major investment banks will not become involved in a risk arb deal until the takeover effort has been announced publicly by a published tender offer. These are called **announced deals**.

Despite the origins of the term risk arbitrage, the term is understood today to encompass all activities associated with speculation and arbitrage involving the securities of firms involved in takeovers. For example, simple speculation in a stock based on the expectation that the corporation will be or is a takeover target, or positions taken in the belief that a current bid by an acquirer will be raised through negotiation or by competitors, or positions taken in the belief that the takeover effort will fail, are all lumped together today and included under the heading "risk arbitrage."

Risk arbitrageurs become key players in many takeover situations. Indeed, it is not unusual for risk arbs, at some stage in a takeover battle, to hold as much as 25 percent or more of the outstanding shares.

Efficient Markets: Friend or Foe?

Some years ago, academicians proffered a theory which became known as the efficient markets hypothesis.[14] The efficient markets hypothesis maintains that market pressures brought about by intense competition among speculators and arbitrageurs to exploit information and aberrant price relationships will ensure that competitive markets are, at all times, informationally efficient—i.e., that all market prices fully reflect all available information. As such, it is not possible to consistently earn a return in excess of a fair return commensurate with the risks involved.

The efficient markets hypothesis has been the subject of intense and often heated debate and the subject of innumerable empirical investigations. From the late 1960s through the early 1980s, academicians repeatedly reported on scientific studies which could find no evidence of exploitable market opportunities.[15] The investment community, however, never accepted the efficient markets hypothesis. To do so, it seemed, would be to reject the very foundation on which much of the profession rests.

---

[14] See Fama (1965).

[15] The first major survey paper on the subject which summarized all literature through 1970 was published by Fama (1970). Most of this research dealt with the behavior of stock prices. Subsequent literature focused on commodity prices. For a partial review of the latter, see Marshall (1989, Chapter 9).

In the early 1980s, two respected academicians persuasively rebutted the underlying logic of the efficient markets hypothesis.[16] They argued that it was inconsistent to believe that market efficiency could be the product of speculation and arbitrage, which are privately costly activities, and yet also to believe that speculation and arbitrage would not be rewarded. If there were no reward for speculation and arbitrage, then these activities would cease. And if they ceased, how could the markets continue to be efficient?

The question of market efficiency, or lack thereof, is critically important to traders—whether they work for investment banks or otherwise. The answer, which was also offered by these academicians, is to accept that there is an equilibrium degree of inefficiency. That is, there is enough inefficiency, at least on occasion, to provide a return to speculation and arbitrage, but not so much inefficiency that the return is excessive. Thus, there is an incentive to develop new strategies that can better (more effectively) exploit whatever inefficiencies exist. More sophisticated tests applied to the markets over the last few years have indeed found subtle, although usually very temporary, exploitable opportunities.[17]

There is no doubt that speculation and arbitrage make prices more efficient, and there is also no doubt that the financial engineers who work for investment banks have themselves contributed to making the markets more efficient. But efficiency is not the friend of the trader or the financial engineer—at least not most of the time. As markets become ever more efficient, fewer exploitable opportunities remain, and ferreting out those that do requires more effort. This has led to the age of the quant jock to whom we made reference earlier. Quant jocks employ sophisticated quantitative techniques, build elaborate valuation relationships, and sift through enormous quantities of data in their unending search for exploitable opportunities. When they find one, they quickly turn their resources or those of their firm to it, and in the process they help to eliminate it. While this is not the intent, it is the inevitable result.

---

[16] This argument was first made by Grossman and Stiglitz (1980).

[17] See for example, Reinganum (1981), and Keim (1983). Related research includes Anderson (1986), Joy (1986), Keane (1986, 1991), and Miller (1987).

Summary

Trading encompasses two related activities: speculation and arbitrage. Investment banks engage in these activities to earn trading profits for themselves and for their institutional clients. The degree to which investment banks depend on trading for their profits varies considerably from shop to shop. For some firms, trading is the dominant activity. Such firms include Salomon Brothers and Bear, Stearns. For other firms, trading profits represent only a small component of their revenue. Without question, however, firms that depend heavily on trading profits will experience very volatile profit histories.

Trading profits depend on exploitable market opportunities. The extent of such opportunities depends greatly on market volatility. During periods of quiet markets, opportunities may be scarce. But during volatile periods, very profitable opportunities may appear—and often.

Speculation implies either a view on the direction of a market or an effort to exploit relative values. The latter can, if fully hedged, take on the character of arbitrage. Arbitrage involves simultaneous transactions in multiple markets to exploit price discrepancies. To be true arbitrage, the activity must not involve any of the arbitrageur's own funds and must be riskless. Real world arbitrage, however, is not always so perfect. Arbitrageurs attempt to exploit pricing aberrations across both space and time, and the strategies range from the extremely simple to the exceedingly complex.

Speculation and arbitrage serve a useful office in a market economy. By their transactions, traders serve to reallocate resources to those areas where they have the greatest value. The efficient allocation of resources is one of the principal virtues of a market–based economic system, and trading pushes this process to its absolute limit.

References and Suggested Reading

Allingham, M., *Arbitrage: Elements of Financial Economics*, New York: St. Martin's Press, 1991.

Anderson, S. C., "Closed–End Funds Versus Market Efficiency," *Journal of Portfolio Management*, 13:1, Fall 1986, pp. 63-65.

Barnhill, T. M., "Quality Option Profits, Switching Option Profits, and Variation Margin Costs: An Evaluation of Their Size and Impact on Treasury Bond Futures Prices," *Journal of Financial and Quantitative Analysis*, 25:1, March 1990, pp. 65-68.

Basu, S., "The Investment Performance of Common Stocks in Relationship to Their Price Earnings Ratio: A Test of the Efficient Markets Hypothesis," *Journal of Finance*, 32:3, July 1977, pp. 663-682.

Belongia, M. T. and G. J. Santoni, "Interest Rate Risk, Market Value, and Hedging Financial Portfolios," *Journal of Financial Research*, 10:1, Spring 1987, pp. 47-55.

Bierwag, G. O., *Duration Analysis: Managing Interest Rate Risk*, Cambridge, MA: Ballinger, 1987.

Brennan, M. J. and E. S. Schwartz, "Arbitrage in Stock Index Futures," *Journal of Business*, 63:1, part 2, January 1990, pp. S7–S31.

Castelino, M. G., "Basis Volatility: Implications for Hedging," *Journal of Financial Research*, 12:2, Summer 1989, pp. 157-172.

Douglas, L. G., *Yield Curve Analysis: The Fundamentals of Risk and Return*, New York: New York Institute of Finance, 1988.

Fama, E. F., "The Behavior of Stock Prices," *Journal of Business*, 38:1, January 1965.

Fama, E. F., "Efficient Capital Markets: A Review of Theory and Empirical Work," *Journal of Finance*, 25:2, May 1970.

Fama, E. F., *Foundations of Finance: Portfolio Decisions and Securities Prices*, New York: Basic Books, 1976.

Francis, J. C., *Management of Investments*, 3e, New York: McGraw–Hill, 1993.

Gastineau, G. L., "From the Board: A Short History of Program Trading," *Financial Analysts Journal*, 47:5, September/October 1991, pp. 4-7.

Grossman, S. and J. Stiglitz, "On the Impossibility of Informationally Efficient Markets," *American Economic Review*, June 1980.

Hill, J. M., "Program Trading of Equities: Renegade or Mainstream?" *Business Horizon*, 32:6, November/December 1989, pp. 47-55.

Hill, J. M. and F. J. Jones, "Equity Trading, Program Trading, Portfolio Insurance, Computer Trading and All That," *Financial Analysts Journal*, 44:4, July/August 1988, pp. 29-38.

Hilliard, J. E. and S. D. Jordan, "Hedging Interest Rate Risk Under Term Structure Effects: An Application to Financial Institutions," *Journal of Financial Research*, 15:4, Winter 1992, pp. 355-368.

Joy, O. M. and C. P. Jones, "Should We Believe the Tests of Market Efficiency?" *Journal of Portfolio Management*, 12:4, Summer 1986, pp. 49-54.

Kaufman, G. G., G. O. Bierwag, and A. Toevs, *Innovations in Bond Portfolio Management: Duration Analysis and Immunization*, Greenwich, CT: JAI Press, 1983.

Kawaller, I. G., *Financial Futures and Options: Managing Risk in the Interest Rate, Currency, and Equity Markets*, Chicago: Probus Publishing, 1992a.

Kawaller, I. G., "Choosing the Best Interest Rate Hedge Ratio," *Financial Analysts Journal*, 48:5, September/October 1992b, pp. 74-77.

Keane, S. M., "The Efficient Markets Hypothesis on Trial," *Financial Analysts Journal*, 42:2, Mar/April 1986, pp. 58-63.

Keane, S. M., "Paradox in the Current Crisis in Efficient Market Theory," *Journal of Portfolio Management*, 17:2, Winter 1991, pp. 30-34.

Keim, D. B., "Size–Related Anomalies and Stock Return Seasonalities: Further Empirical Evidence," *Journal of Financial Economics*, 12:1, pp. 13-32, 1983.

Lindahl, M., "Minimum Variance Hedge Ratios for Stock Index Futures: Duration and Expiration Effects," *Journal of Futures Markets*, 12:1, February 1992, pp. 33-53.

Marshall, J. F., *Futures and Option Contracting: Theory and Practice*, Cincinnati: South–Western, 1989.

Miller, E. M., "Bounded Efficient Markets: A New Wrinkle to the EMH," *Journal of Portfolio Management*, 13:4, Summer 1987, pp. 4-13.

Miller, J. D., M. Miller, and P. J. Brennan, *Program Trading: The New Age of Investing*, New York: J. K. Lasser, 1989.

Ray, C. I., *The Bond Market: Trading and Risk Management*, Burr Ridge, IL: Business One Irwin, 1993.

Reinganum, M. R., "Misspecification of Capital Asset Pricing: Empirical Anomalies Based on Earnings Yields and Market Values," *Journal of Financial Economics*, 9:1, March 1981.

Toevs, A. L. and D. P. Jacob, "Futures and Alternative Hedge Ratio Methodologies," *Journal of Portfolio Management*, 12:3, Spring 1986, pp. 60-70.

Wheeler, L. B., "The Oscillation of Systems: The Missing Link Between Volatility and Market Efficiency," *Financial Analysts Journal*, 45:4, July/August 1989, pp. 7-11.

7

Corporate Restructuring: Mergers, Acquisitions, and LBOs

Robert P. Yuyuenyongwatana[1]

Overview

Corporate restructuring is an umbrella term that includes mergers and consolidations, divestitures and liquidations, and battles for corporate control. At its most general level, the term **corporate restructuring** can mean almost any change in operations, capital structure, and/or ownership that is not part of the firm's ordinary course of business. Our interest in restructuring focuses on the role played by the investment bank's mergers and acquisitions department and other departments or divisions of the bank that are involved in effecting corporate restructuring strategies. Mergers and acquisitions departments are known in the trade as M&A departments.

We are going to focus most of our attention on issues involving ownership and control. This leads logically to the subject of leveraged buyouts by both corporate outsiders and corporate insiders. While corporate mergers, consolidations, takeovers, and acquisitions have historically occurred in waves lasting from five to ten years and going at least as far back as the late 1800s, the leveraged buyout is unmistakably a product of the 1980s. It was during the 1980s that many of the new tools which made leveraged buyouts possible, including high–yield or junk bonds, found favor. The 1980s also witnessed a more accommodat-

[1] Robert P. Yuyuenyongwatana is Assistant Professor of Finance in the Graduate School of Business of St. John's University, New York.

ing regulatory environment and a tax environment more conducive to capital formation and corporate restructuring.

We will begin this chapter with a brief examination of the various activities which fall under the corporate restructuring umbrella. Following this, we will focus more narrowly on the issues of going private and the role of the leveraged buyout in achieving this private status. We will then address the sources of value in corporate restructurings. As we examine the many issues involved, we will repeatedly stop to consider the investment banker's role in restructuring activity. The role of the investment banker in corporate restructurings overlaps other topics addressed in this book. Consequently, the role of the investment bank in restructurings is also addressed in the chapters on securities issuances (Chapter 3) and advisory services (Chapter 10), and to a lesser degree in other chapters.

Corporate Restructuring

The term corporate restructuring encompasses three distinct but related groups of activities: **expansions**—including mergers and consolidations, tender offers, joint ventures, and acquisitions; **contractions**—including sell–offs, spin–offs, equity carve–outs, abandonment of assets, and liquidation; and **ownership and control**—including the market for corporate control, stock repurchase programs, exchange offers, and going private (whether by leveraged buyout or other means). All of these activities require the talents of experienced M&A personnel, and, because no two "deals" are exactly the same, these personnel must possess appropriate financial engineering skills.

As a general rule, an investment bank's M&A department tends to have a great deal of autonomy vis–a–vis the rest of the organization. Nevertheless, M&A must work closely with the bank's other areas, including the capital markets group, the corporate finance group, and the merchant banking group. Each of these latter groups has a role to play if a deal, particularly a contested one, is to be successful.

We will briefly look at each of the three major categories of restructuring in the sections which follow, beginning with expansions.

Expansions

Expansions include mergers, consolidations, acquisitions, and various other activities which result in an enlargement of a firm or its scope of operations. There is a lot of ambiguity in the usage of the terms associated with corporate expansions. For example, there are legal distinctions between those corporate combinations which constitute mergers and those which constitute consolidations. Technically, a **merger** involves a combination of two firms such that only one survives. Mergers tend to occur when one firm is significantly larger than the other, and the survivor is usually the larger of the two. A **consolidation**, on the other hand, involves the creation of an altogether new firm owning the assets of both of the first two firms—and neither of the first two survive. This form of combination is most common when the two firms are of approximately equal size. Despite this legal distinction, however, the terms "merger" and "consolidation" are often used interchangeably to describe any combination of two firms.

A merger can be horizontal, vertical, or conglomerate. A **horizontal merger** involves two firms in similar businesses. The combination of two oil companies, or two solid waste disposal companies, for example, would represent horizontal mergers. A **vertical merger** involves two firms involved in different stages of production of the same end product or related end products. The combination of a waste removal company and a waste recycler or the combination of an oil producer and an oil refiner would be examples of vertical mergers. A **conglomerate merger** involves two firms in unrelated business activities. The combination of an oil refiner and a solid waste disposal company would be an example of a conglomerate merger. These distinctions can be important in understanding the sources of value in business combinations.

Not all business expansions lead to the dissolution of one or more of the involved firms. For example, holding companies often seek to acquire equity interests in other firms. The target firm may or may not become a subsidiary of the holding company (50+ percent ownership) but, in either case, continues to exist as a legal entity. The **joint venture**, in which two separate firms pool some of their resources, is another such form that does not ordinarily lead to the dissolution of either firm. Such ventures typically involve only a small portion of the cooperating firms' overall businesses and usually have limited lives.

The term **acquisition** is another ambiguous term. At the most general level, it means an attempt by one firm, called the **acquiring firm**, to gain a majority interest in another firm, called the **target firm**. The effort to gain control may be a prelude to a subsequent merger, to establish a parent–subsidiary relationship, to breakup the target firm and dispose of its assets, or to take the target firm private by a small group of investors.

There are a number of strategies that can be employed in corporate acquisitions. In the **friendly takeover**, the acquiring firm will make a financial proposal to the target firm's management and board. This proposal might involve the merger of the two firms, the consolidation of the two firms, or the creation of a parent/subsidiary relationship. The existing shareholders of the target firm would receive cash and/or stock of the acquiring firm, or, in the case of a consolidation, stock in the new firm in exchange for their stock in the target firm. In a friendly takeover, managers in the target firm usually retain their positions after the acquisition is consummated.

At the other extreme is the hostile takeover. A **hostile takeover** may or may not follow a preliminary attempt at a friendly takeover. For example, it is not uncommon for an acquiring firm to embrace the target firm's management in what is colloquially called a **bear hug**. In this approach, the acquiring firm's board makes a proposal to the target firm's board. The target firm's board is required to make a quick decision on the acquiring firm's bid. The target firm's board may also be apprised of the acquiring firm's intent to pursue a tender offer[2] if its bid is not approved. In such a situation, the acquiring firm looks to replace the noncooperating directors. The alternative to the bear hug is for the acquiring firm to appeal directly to the target firm's shareholders without any preliminary proposal to the target firm's board. Whether made explicit or not, it is understood that in a hostile takeover, current management can expect to be replaced by management of the acquiring firm's choosing.

---

[2] A tender offer is a formal proposition to the stockholders of a corporation offering to buy their shares at a specific price, usually set above the market price at the time the tender offer is made. The buyer ordinarily assumes all costs but reserves the right to accept all, none, or only some of the shares presented to it.

Defenses

The same M&A departments that advise acquiring firms on takeovers also advise target firms on defenses against them. These specialists have engineered a number of strategies which often have such bizarre nicknames as **shark repellents** and **poison pills**—terms which accurately convey the genuine hostility involved. In this same vein, the acquiring firm itself is often described as a **raider**. One such strategy is to employ a **target block repurchase** with an accompanying **standstill agreement**. This combination is sometimes described as **greenmail**. That is, the target firm agrees to buy back the acquiring firm's stake in the target firm's stock (the target block repurchase) at a premium to the current market price of that stock. In return, the raider is required to sign an agreement to the effect that neither the raider nor groups controlled by the raider will acquire an interest in the target firm for some specified period of time (the standstill agreement).

Not surprisingly, the legality (and ethics) of greenmail and standstill agreements have been questioned. One has to ask if it is fair to the other shareholders of a firm for management to use company resources to buy out one specific shareholder particularly when the perception is that that one shareholder represented a potential threat to management's control. If a clear case can be made to demonstrate that a buyout was in the collective interests of the shareholders, then management would seem to have satisfied its fiduciary obligations to them. But if the only motive behind the buyout and standstill agreement is to preserve management's own lucrative positions, then an important fiduciary relationship would seem to have been violated, and management could and should be held accountable. As of this writing, the legal and ethical issues have not been fully resolved.

Other defenses against hostile takeovers include **leveraged recapitalizations** and **poison puts** (versions of the shark repellant and poison pill strategies alluded to above). The leveraged recapitalization, or "recap," strategy was developed by Goldman Sachs in 1985 in an effort to fend off an attempted takeover of Multimedia, Inc. The strategy is also known as a **leveraged cash–out**, or LCO. In this strategy, the firm borrows heavily (issues debt) and uses the funds to pay outside share-holders a large one–time cash dividend. At the same time, the firm pays its inside shareholders (managers and employees) their dividend in the form of additional shares of stock. This has two simultaneous effects:

1. It increases the target firm's use of leverage and thereby decreases its attractiveness to the acquiring firm—as the latter might have planned its own "leveraging up" of the target firm's assets.
2. It concentrates stock in the hands of insiders, thereby making it more difficult for an outsider to gain a controlling interest.

Leveraged cash–outs bear more than surface similarities to leveraged buyouts in that both involve the use of a great deal of financial leverage in order gain or maintain control. We will return to this point later.

Corporate takeovers and other forms of change in effective control often result in a deterioration of the target firm's creditworthiness. This can be extremely costly to bondholders and other creditors of the firm. One way to deal with this is to grant debtholders protective poison put covenants, which allow the debtholders to "put" the debt they hold back to the corporation or the acquiring firm in the event of a transfer of control. This can be extremely costly to the acquiring firm and, hence, decreases the attractiveness of the target. While it would seem that poison puts are a genuine form of investor protection, this is not necessarily the case. Such puts often grant the bondholders the right to put the bonds *if and only if* the takeover is hostile. Consequently, friendly takeovers and management buyouts do not, generally, make the put exercisable—even if the takeover or buyout originated as a response to an earlier hostile takeover attempt. Whether it be friendly or hostile, a takeover can cause credit deterioration and thus the poison puts may be more for the protection of current management than for the protection of the debt–holders.

A very appealing defensive measure against a hostile takeover attempt is for the target firm's management to seek a **white knight**. A white knight is a second acquiring firm with which the target firm can negotiate a more favorable and "friendly" takeover. An alternative to the white knight is for management itself to attempt a takeover—usually through a management–led leveraged buyout. A management–led leveraged buyout is sometimes called a **management buyout**, or MBO.

There are several advantages to a friendly takeover relative to an unfriendly one. First, the target firm's resources are not wasted in an effort to fend off the acquiring firm. Second, there is a greater chance that the management of the combination will have a more harmonious working relationship and more easily meld the operations of the two firms. Finally, employee morale, the importance of which is often underestimated, is less likely to suffer in a friendly takeover than in an unfriendly one.

Contractions

Contraction, as the term implies, results in a smaller firm rather than a larger one. If we ignore the abandonment of assets (occasionally a logical course of action), corporate contraction occurs as the result of disposition of assets. The disposition of assets, sometimes called **sell–offs**, can take either of three broad forms: spin–offs, divestitures, and carve–outs. **Spin–offs** and **carve–outs** create new legal entities, while divestitures do not.

In a spin–off, the parent company transfers some of its assets and liabilities to a new firm created for that purpose. The shareholders of the original firm are then given shares in the new firm on a proportional basis to their ownership in the original firm. After the sell–off, the original shareholders have the same equity interest but it is now divided between two separate entities. The shareholders are then free to transfer their stocks into one or both firms or to keep them, as they see fit. By creating a new firm with its own assets, its own management, and separate ownership, the spin–off represents a genuine transfer of control. This was the approach taken when American Telephone & Telegraph (AT&T) was broken up into a group of individual regional phone companies.

There are a number of variations on the spin–off, including the **split–off** and the **split–up**. In a split–off, some of the shareholders are given an equity interest in the new firm in exchange for their shares of the parent company. In a split–up, all the assets of the parent company are divided up among spin–off companies and the original parent ceases to exist. Spin–offs, regardless of their form, may be and have been described as stock dividends. It is important to observe that in all forms of spin–offs, the parent company receives no cash from its transfer of assets to the new firm(s).

In contrast to the no–cash transfer of assets in a spin–off, a **divestiture** involves an out–and–out sale of assets, usually for cash consideration. In other words, the parent company sells some of the firm's assets for cash to another firm. In most cases, the assets are sold to an existing firm so that no new legal entity results from the transactions.

An equity **carve–out** is a form of contraction between a spin–off and a divestiture. It does bring cash to the original firm, but it also disperses assets and ownership in the assets to nonowners of the original firm. In this arrangement, the original firm forms a new firm and transfers some of the original firm's assets to the new firm. The original firm then sells equity in the new firm. The purchasers of this equity may or may not be the owners of the original firm. Like a divestiture, an equity carve–out brings cash to the firm and, like a spin–off, creates a new legal entity.

Ownership and Control

The third major area encompassed by the term "corporate restructuring" is that of ownership and control. Actually, this is closely related to both expansion and contraction activities. For example, a hostile takeover is effected by acquiring ownership and wresting control from the current board. Similarly, once ownership and/or control have been wrested from the current board, the new management will often embark on a full or partial liquidation strategy involving the sale of assets. Despite this overlap, however, our concern in this section is not so much with expansion or contraction, but rather with strategies intended to transfer ownership and/or control to a new group.

Let's first consider some steps that might be taken by current management to make the transfer of ownership and/or control more difficult. One strategy often employed involves the adoption of anti–takeover amendments to the corporate by–laws in order to make an acquisition more difficult and more expensive. Some common attempts include (1) staggering the terms of the members of the board so that an acquiring firm must wait a considerable period before it can replace a sufficient number of board members to get its way; (2) applying supermajority voting provisions to matters involving mergers—such as requiring a 75 or 80 percent favorable vote; and (3) providing current management with **golden parachutes**—sizable termination payments—in the event that management is terminated following a change in the control of the firm.

Current management starts off with a considerable advantage over dissident shareholders. First, as a general rule, management nominates new board members, who are often rubber–stamped by the majority of the firm's shareholders. The board, in turn, reappoints management. But dissident shareholders are not without weapons of their own. One such weapon is the proxy contest. In a proxy contest, dissident shareholders attempt to secure the proxies of other shareholders in an effort to install their own people on the board and to lessen the control of the incumbents. Proxy contests are often used by major shareholders who lack a controlling interest but who nevertheless wield enough weight to have a reasonable prospect of attracting sufficient proxies to swing a vote. Proxy fights per se do not involve a transfer of ownership, but they do involve an effort to alter control of the firm.

The alternative to gaining or retaining control via proxy battles is to alter the very structure of ownership. We have already considered the more traditional ways by which ownership is passed to new parties via the merger or consolidation of firms, but the really unique development of the 1980s was the advent of the leveraged buyout. The leveraged buyout preserves the integrity of the firm as a legal entity but consolidates ownership in the hands of a small group. We look at **leveraged buyouts** more closely in the next section.

Going Private: The Leveraged Buyout

While corporate restructurings are not new, they do tend to occur in waves, as was experienced in the 1980s. The major restructuring wave of the 1980s witnessed all the traditional forms of restructuring including mergers, acquisitions, consolidations, spin–offs, divestitures, and proxy battles. But it also saw the advent of a major new trend. In the 1980s, many large, publicly traded firms went private, and most employed a similar strategy called a leveraged buyout, or LBO.

A number of economic and financial factors converged to make the leveraged buyout an attractive concept. All that was lacking was the means. The advent of junk bonds, bridge financing, venture capital firms, and merchant banking, all of which are products of financial engineering at investment banks, provided those means. We begin with a look at the economic and financial factors that created an environment conducive to going private. We then consider the various means enumerated above, and finally we consider the sources of value that leveraged buyouts seek to capture.

The Economic and Financial Environment

A period of prolonged and accelerating inflation began in the 1960s and continued until the early 1980s. This extended period of inflation had the effect of dramatically reducing the ratio of the market value of U.S. corporations to the replacement cost of those corporations' assets. The ratio of market value to replacement cost of assets is called the q–ratio. When the q–ratio is less than one, it is cheaper to buy capacity by acquiring a going firm than it is to build capacity by purchasing real assets. Over the period from 1965 to 1981, the average q–ratio of American industrial corporations declined from about 1.3 to about 0.5.[3] The q–ratio did not start to rise again until 1982, when a bull market in U.S. equities began.

The inflation also had the effect of reducing the average corporation's real leverage. This occurred because both the interest and principal on preexisting debt was not indexed for inflation. Thus, in real terms, the inflation reduced both the amount of real debt on corporate balance sheets and the cost of servicing this debt. The unintentional decline in the pre–1980s use of leverage created an opportunity for corporate managers to enhance equity returns by **leveraging up** the firm, or, more accurately, *re*–leveraging the firm. Any firm which failed to leverage up on its own became a potential target for a takeover by others who would leverage up once they had control.

Restructuring activity was also stimulated by a succession of favorable changes in the tax law. One particularly conducive piece of legislation was the Economic Recovery Tax Act (ERTA) of 1981. ERTA permitted old assets to be **stepped up** for depreciation purposes upon purchase by another firm and for the higher basis to be depreciated at an accelerated rate. It also enhanced the role of **Employee Stock Ownership Plans** (ESOPs) by making deductible both the interest and the principal on money borrowed from banks to purchase company stock for these plans. A subsequent change in the tax law increased bank willingness to lend for this purpose by allowing banks to deduct one–half the interest they received on these ESOP loans.

It also became clear in the 1980s that the government had adopted a more permissive attitude toward horizontal and vertical business

---

[3] See Weston, Chung, and Hoag (1990), Chapter 16.

combinations. This new attitude stimulated interest in exploiting production and marketing efficiencies made possible by product and market extensions.

The final economic factor setting the climate in the 1980s was real economic growth. In the end, a merger, a consolidation, or a leveraged buyout can be successful only if (1) its assets can be disposed of at a profit, or (2) the ongoing concern that has been acquired has healthy cash flows. Beginning in 1982, corporate earnings grew rapidly and nearly continuously throughout the decade. This earnings strength was sufficient to convince many that successful deals could be engineered.

The Tools for Going Private

While the economic climate in the 1980s was undoubtedly right for a wave of mergers and consolidations, leveraged buyouts—in which a small group of investors acquires most or all of a firm's outstanding equity and then takes the firm private—required new and very special financing tools. These tools soon appeared and were put to work quite aggressively. Most of them were engineered by investment banks, but they were often coupled with **secured acquisition** loans from banks. The principal additional tools are junk bonds, private placements, bridge financing, venture capital, and merchant banking.

Junk bonds are perhaps the most controversial of the tools used in leveraged buyouts. These bonds were pioneered by Michael Milken of the investment banking firm of Drexel Burnham Lambert and soon propelled Drexel to near–bulge–bracket status in the investment banking industry. Other investment banks soon followed Drexel's lead into the high–yield market. By 1989, the $200+ billion junk bond market consisted of more than 2,000 issues representing some 800 companies in 100 industries.[4]

Many issues of junk bonds have a **reset provision** or belong to a category of **deferred–payment instruments**. These are designed to enhance the bond yields to the investors—but at a higher cost to the issuers. A reset provision forces the issuer to increase the interest rate it pays to the bondholders if the bond fails to trade at or above par by a stipulated date.

---

[4] See Farrel (1989), p. 85.

The two most common deferred–payment securities are the **pay-ment–in–kind** (PIK) and the **deferred–coupon bond**. A PIK holder receives additional bonds in lieu of cash payments up until the cash–out date, when the investor receives more interest payments from holding more bonds. In the deferred–coupon bond, an investor buys the bond at a discount (typically about 35–40 percent) and begins collecting interest several years into the life of the bond.

Private placements represent issues of debt that are not offered to the general public. Instead, they are placed with a small group of institutions, such as insurance companies, pension funds, and other sophisticated investors that do not need the protection afforded by registration with the Securities and Exchange Commission. All other things being equal, the holders of privately placed debt generally receive a higher return than do the holders of publicly offered debt. Nevertheless, private placements can be less costly to the issuer (since the costly registration process is avoided). Furthermore, private placements can be effected much more quickly, since the due diligence investigation required for registration can be avoided. (Private placements are more fully discussed in Chapter 3.)

Private placements and junk bond offerings differ from secured bank–acquisition loans in that the former are typically unsecured and subordinated forms of debt. On the other hand, as debtholders, these investors have a claim senior to that of shareholders. Because they stand between the secured debt of the banks and the very risky residual claims of the shareholders, private placements and junk bonds used to finance leveraged buyouts are often called **mezzanine money**. In addition to receiving a higher rate of interest than that payable on the secured debt, the providers of mezzanine money often also receive a portion of the equity—called an **equity kicker**.

In **bridge financing**, the investment bank makes a loan to the buyout group as interim financing until more permanent financing can be arranged. While the investment bank earns interest on its bridge financing, its primary motivation is usually the M&A advisement fees and the underwriting fees that it receives from its other involvements in the deal. These fees are far more likely to be earned if the deal can be closed before other parties have a chance to counter the buyout group's bid, or the target firm has the chance to adopt defensive strategies that can make the buyout more costly. The bridge loan allows the deal to be effected far more quickly and, therefore, with a greater probability of success. The investment bank's intent is to retire the bridge loan as quickly as possible and remove it from its books. But deals can go bad, and the investment bank can get stuck with the loan. The Campeau Corporation's default in the late 1980s on its bridge loan obligations after its successful takeover of Allied Stores, Inc., left its investment banker, The First Boston Corporation, with sizable losses.

Venture capital firms can play several roles in a leveraged buyout. First, they can take and hold a portion of the privately placed debt. Second, they can act as members of the buyout group, taking a portion of the equity. It is not uncommon, and indeed is rather typical, for venture capital firms to take both debt and equity in the target firm. By definition, venture capital firms specialize in taking substantial risks in their effort to earn substantial rewards. Some have been immensely successful.

The last tool mentioned above is that of **merchant banking**. Merchant banking is a relatively new endeavor for investment banks. In merchant banking, the investment bank takes a portion of the target firm's equity on its own books, becoming, in effect, an equity partner in the leveraged buyout. In merchant banking, the investment bank puts its own money at risk in the deal, and it plays a very high–stakes game. This is far riskier than making bridge loans, which are intended to be retired quickly. (Merchant banking is discussed in greater detail in Chapter 10.)

Sources of Value in a Leveraged Buyout

The M&A groups within investment banks, which both assist in effecting leveraged buyouts and often inspire them, argue that leveraged buyouts can and do create value. Others, particularly displaced managers, tend, not surprisingly, to disagree. This is an important issue. It is important to those whose personal wealth is affected by the creation of value and to the investment banks that profit from LBO activity. It is also a potential public policy issue. For these reasons, it is worth our effort to consider the arguments on both sides of this issue.

In a typical leveraged buyout, the acquiring group consists of a small number of persons or organizations. This group, using the financing tools described in the preceding section, acquires all or nearly all of the outstanding stock of the target firm and then takes the target firm private. The buyout group may or may not include current management of the target firm. If it does, the buyout is sometimes described as a management buyout or MBO. Nevertheless, it is still a leveraged buyout, and we will not distinguish between nonmanagement LBOs and MBOs.

Once the LBO has been completed, the firm, now private, might continue to operate in its original form, or it might sell off some or all of its assets. If it continues to operate, it might go public again after a few years, or it might be sold privately to a new group of investors in a second leveraged buyout. As odd as these latter courses may seem, they are not unusual paths for an LBO to take. If the LBO owners' intent in going public again or in selling to a new LBO group is to get their money out, the strategy is called **cashing out**. Cashing out in an LBO does not imply that the firm is in trouble (as it often does in sales of securities by managers in more traditional corporate structures). It implies only that the extraordinary returns possible with an LBO cannot continue without a re–leveraging of the firm. This will become clearer later, after we run through a complete example.

In order for the acquiring group to gain a controlling interest in the target firm, they must make a tender offer for the firm's stock. The only exception to this is if enough of the firm's stock already rests in a few hands, and those holders can be persuaded to become parties to the LBO. In all other cases, the acquiring group must bid for the stock at a premium to its current market price.

Since a successful LBO often involves bids at premiums ranging to 50 percent or more of the market price prevailing just before the takeover was launched and the buyout group expects to profit handsomely from taking the firm private, one wonders about the source(s) of value in an LBO. After all, the current shareholders cannot be bought out at a price significantly above market (thus receiving excess value) and the buyers subsequently also earn significant profits unless (1) the current market price significantly understates the current value of the firm, (2) some value is created by taking the firm private, or (3) value is transferred to the selling shareholders and the buyout group from other interested parties.

No issue has been more thoroughly discussed and more carefully examined in corporate restructurings than these sources of value—and for good reason. Market efficiency was long an accepted tenet of academic theory. This theory holds that all competitive markets price assets efficiently. In its purest form, the theory implies that a stock's current market price accurately reflects the value of all relevant information concerning the firm. Thus, if the source of the value in an LBO is simply a mispricing of the firm's stock, then the market could not have been efficient to begin with. While evidence developed during the 1980s has demonstrated that markets may not be as efficient as once believed, it does not support mispricings on the scale necessary to justify LBOs at the kinds of premiums they typically command. Therefore, the source of the value must lie with one of the other two explanations.[5]

Let's first consider the possibility that the act of taking the firm private creates value from several possible sources. The first source is the **agency problem** that stems from the separation of ownership and control. In a typical publicly held corporation, management and ownership are vested in different groups of people. Theory holds that managers will, at all times, make decisions and act in the best interests of the owners for whom they work. After all, managers are agents of the owners. But practice will often differ from theory, and managers may be inclined to make suboptimal decisions—particularly if they perceive benefits to themselves from doing so. Indeed, managers may do this unconsciously while convincing themselves that they are acting in the best interests of the shareholders. Suboptimal decisions can take many forms and range from the obvious—such as excessive perks for management—to the not so obvious—such as keeping unproductive assets.[6] The difference in the firm's value when the owners are the managers and when the owners are not the managers represents the agency cost. By taking the firm private, ownership and control become one and the same. This eliminates, or greatly reduces, the agency costs, and the reduction in agency costs is the source of the value gain associated with the LBO.

Another argument made for why going private can add to a firm's value concerns efficiency. There are several dimensions to the efficiency argument. The first is decision–making efficiency. The managers do not have to engage in extensive and time–consuming studies, prepare detailed

---

[5] We should not ignore the possibility, however, that managers may possess superior information to that possessed by the firm's shareholders. It is possible that managers involved in an LBO are merely exploiting nonpublic information.

[6] Managements sometimes hold on to unproductive assets in order to avoid the appearance of having made an earlier mistake in their decision to acquire them.

reports, and provide volumes of evidence to a skeptical board before making a decision to either launch a major new project or to terminate an existing one. Further, for those decisions involving approval of the firm's shareholders, the managers do not have to convince a diverse body of shareholders and wait for the annual meeting before gaining approval to take the firm in a new direction. The inefficiencies in the decision–making process introduced by the separation of ownership and control decrease the value of the firm. Such firms often lose the ability to move quickly in response to rapidly changing circumstances.

Another efficiency issue involves the publication of sensitive information. A publicly held firm is required to publish certain types of information, which can include competitively sensitive material. A nonpublic firm has no such requirement. In addition, the private firm does not have to absorb the expenses associated with periodic filing and compliance matters that are required of a publicly held firm.

A final argument, which also sometimes passes under the efficiency label, involves production and portfolio efficiencies. For example, some LBO deals involve specialized LBO firms.[7] In deals of this type, there can be synergistic benefits such that the sum of the parts is greater than the whole, and there can be the risk–reducing benefits that accompany diversification.

The last potential source of value gain from going private involves tax benefits. This particular benefit unquestionably exists. First, the asset step–up for depreciation purposes, which was discussed earlier in the general context of takeovers, applies equally to leveraged buyouts. Second, the tax savings that accompanies the payment of interest (relative to dividends) is considerable in leveraged buyouts, since the source of the leverage is the considerable debt that is employed. Finally, there are the benefits, also detailed earlier, that are associated with ESOPs. It is not surprising, therefore, that ESOPs play a significant role in many LBOs.

These value gains associated with an LBO are all, with the possible exception of the tax benefits, positive explanations for the value gains

---

[7] Examples of LBO specialist firms including Kohlberg, Kravis, Roberts & Company and Forstmann Little & Company. A number of interesting books on takeovers and takeover firms have been published in the popular press in recent years, including Anders (1992), Barmash (1988), Bartlett (1991), Burroughs and Helyar (1990), Lampert (1990), Rothchild (1991), Silver (1990), and Smith (1990).

achieved by the pre–buyout and post–buyout shareholders. The tax benefits can be construed, on the other hand, as either positive or negative depending on one's viewpoint. The alternative, but not mutually exclusive, explanation for the value gains to shareholders is decidedly more negative in nature. This view holds that the gains achieved by the shareholders come at the expense of other interested parties—particularly the firm's debtholders. That is, the gains to the shareholders are earned at the expense of others having a legitimate stake in the fortunes of the firm. For this reason, the value gain is described as a **wealth transfer**.

In addition to the firm's pre–buyout debtholders, others with a pre–existing stake in the firm—sometimes described collectively as **stakeholders**—include the firm's employees, preferred stockholders, suppliers, and federal and local government. The latter derive tax revenues from the profits of the firm and the payroll taxes of the employees. The loss of tax revenue is included in the value creation argument, and we will not consider it again. The stake of the firm's employees takes the form of career commitments and pension benefits. It is not unusual, for example, for new owners of a firm to seek more favorable arrangements with the firm's workers or to trim excess employees. On the other hand, the employees can also be major beneficiaries of leveraged buyouts, as the new owners often see it in their own best interests to give the employees an even greater stake in the fortunes of the firm—a potentially useful motivating tool. The real issue, then, is the effect of the buyout on the firm's debtholders, and we concentrate the remainder of our discussion on this group.

The pre–buyout debtholders of the firm may or may not have protective covenants which are activated in the event of a change in control or the issuance of additional debt. The new debt, issued to finance the leveraged buyout, undoubtedly is not good for the pre–buyout debt-holders. The firm's increased use of leverage makes it that much more risky. All other things being equal, the increase in the riskiness of the firm reduces its creditworthiness, and the market price of the firm's outstanding debt can be expected to reflect this decrease. This is particularly likely to be the case if the new debt, used to finance the leveraged buyout, is not subordinated to the pre–buyout debt or if it has a shorter duration than the pre–buyout debt.

The empirical evidence on the wealth transfer hypothesis as the explanation for the value gain by shareholders in a leveraged buyout is mixed. Some studies have shown no significant loss of value to debt–holders,[8] while others have shown statistically significant losses.[9] In no case, however, has a study been able to show that the cumulative losses to the debtholders are equal to or greater than the cumulative gains to shareholders. One may conclude from this that while wealth transfer is a possible—indeed, probable—explanation for some of the value gains to shareholders, it is not sufficient in and of itself to account for all the gains.

It seems reasonable that all of the explanations offered for the value gains to shareholders in leveraged buyouts contain an element of truth and constitute parts of the total explanation. In other words, the value gains to shareholders are partly a consequence of wealth transfer and partly the result of efficiency gains, tax benefits, better information, and a reduction in agency costs. In any case, empirical evidence suggests that LBOs do create gains for the parent–companies' shareholders. Further–more, LBO firms tend to exhibit superior performance after the leveraged buyout.[10]

Critics of LBOs argue that a leveraged buyout can (1) cause layoffs of the target firm's employees, as the new management/owners streamline the firm's operations, (2) damage the debt markets, resulting in higher costs for debt capital all around, (3) force post–LBO management to concentrate on short–term goals—e.g., to service the firm's debt by reducing the advertising and research and development budgets to the detriment of long–term growth, and (4) result in bankruptcy due to the firm's inability to service its debts. All of these, it is further argued, adversely affect the economy, and serve to reduce the nation's ability to

---

[8] See Lehn and Poulsen (1988) for example. Marais et al. (1989) found nonconvert-ible debt had only "minimal reaction to buyout, but nonconvertible preferred stock and convertible debt increased."

[9] See Travlos and Cornett (1990), for example.

[10] See Bull (1989) and Hite and Vetsuypens (1989).

compete globally.[11] Furthermore, several studies have suggested that firms are not more efficient post–LBO than they are pre–LBO.[12]

Increasingly, there are legislative pressures and court rulings to curb the excesses of leveraged buyouts. The primary target for legislation is the tax deductibility of borrowings specifically undertaken to finance these deals. In 1986, the courts began applying a legal concept known as **fraudulent conveyance** to LBOs that resulted in bankruptcies. Using fraudulent conveyance arguments, the courts can order a return of part of the proceeds from an already–completed LBO transaction to the unsecured creditors if it can be reasonably shown that there was an intent to defraud creditors. This might occur, for example, if the loan proceeds are used to buy out existing shareholders rather than to continue to operate the firm. An example of such an action involved the Chapter 11 proceedings of Revco.[13]

A Typical Leveraged Buyout

It might be instructive to consider the entire process involved in a typical leveraged buyout. The example we present is hypothetical and not meant to describe any particular LBO but rather to capture the essence of the process by incorporating elements that tend to be rather typical. Capturing the essence requires simplification—without loss of too much realism.

At the end of 1988, the balance sheet of XYZ Corporation showed current assets of $4 million, depreciable fixed assets of $12 million, and nondepreciable fixed assets of $2 million. The depreciable assets had

---

[11] See Gart (1990) and Waddel (1990).

[12] See Tomic and Yuyuenyongwatana (1992, 1993). Lichtenberg and Siegel (1990) also found no change in productivity for LBOs that occurred during 1981–82, but they did find a significant increase in productivity for 1983–86 firms. Briston et al. (1992) obtained results that contradicted those of Hite et al. (1989) and found that mean return and variance did not change significantly after the MBO announcement. Along the same lines, Chatterjee (1992) found that takeover gains were due to restructuring that the firm could do itself, not to synergy. But Torabzadeh et al. (1992) found that merged firms have larger excess returns than corresponding LBOs. This latter study supports synergy beyond restructuring.

[13] See Kolod (1990) and Michel and Shaked (1990).

been fully depreciated but were still in good and quite usable condition. The replacement cost of these assets was estimated at about $10 million. The firm had current liabilities of $1.5 million, long–term debt of $2.5 million, and common stock equity (including retained earnings) of $2 million. There were 1 million shares of common stock outstanding. The balance sheet is given in Figure 7.1.

The firm's sales were very stable and its earnings had been very consistent. Given this, management suggested that the firm increase its use of debt and decrease its use of equity capital. This was rejected by the firm's board on the grounds that the firm's shareholders were too conservative to take kindly to a dramatic increase in leverage. At the time, the firm's short–term notes had a cost of 10 percent, and its long–term debt had a cost of 12 percent. As a result, 1988's interest expense was $0.35 million. The firm's profit and loss statement for 1988 appears as Figure 7.2.

Figure 7.1
XYZ Corporation Balance Sheet—1988
(all values in millions)

Assets			Liabilities & Equity		
Current assets:			Current liabilities:		
Cash	0.20		Accruals	0.25	
Marketable securities	1.55		Accounts payables	0.75	
Inventory	1.75		Notes payable	0.50	
Receivables	0.50				1.50
		4.00			
			Long–term debt		2.50
Fixed assets:			Equity:		
Depreciable	12.00		Common stock	0.50	
Less cum. dep.	(12.00)		Retained earnings	1.50	
Net	0.00				2.00
Nondepreciable	2.00				
		2.00			
Total Assets		6.00	Total Liabilities & Equity		6.00

Figure 7.2
XYZ Corporation Profit & Loss—1988
(all values in millions)

Sales	$15.00
Cost of goods sold	8.00
Gross profit	7.00
Selling and administrative	5.50
Operating profit before depreciation	1.50
Depreciation	0.00
Operating profit	1.50
Interest expense	0.35
Earnings before taxes	1.15
Taxes (40 percent)	0.46
Earnings after taxes	0.69

Cash Flow = earnings after taxes + depreciation
= $0.69 million + $0.00 million
= $0.69 million

In 1988, the firm's earnings per share (EPS) was $0.69 and the firm's stock was selling at about $8 a share, or about 11.6 times earnings. Management had long believed that it could improve the firm's performance if freed from the dictates of the overly conservative board. However, management had been reluctant to attack the board's conservatism too aggressively out of fear of losing their jobs. In lieu of the better salaries and bonuses that might accompany better performance, management had settled for various perks, including such things as unnecessarily lavish offices and substantial fringe benefits. In late 1988, partly in response to rumors that a takeover attempt by a rival firm was in the works, management secured the services of a leading investment bank in the hopes of taking the firm private. On the advice of the investment bank, the management group set up a shell corporation to act as the legal entity making the acquisition. This company was called XYZ Holdings.

With the aid of its investment banker, XYZ Holdings made a tender offer at $12 a share (17.4 times earnings) for all the stock of XYZ Corporation. In the end, XYZ Holdings' bid was successful, and all the stock was purchased at $12 a share (deemed a fair value by the firm's investment bank). The two firms were then merged, with XYZ Holdings representing the surviving entity.

The acquisition cost to XYZ Holdings was $12 million ($12 per share × 1 million shares). Of this, $5 million was raised with the aid of a secured bank–acquisition loan at a cost of 12 percent, and $4 million was raised through the sale of bonds at a cost of 18 percent. The investment bank took a 40 percent equity stake by putting up $1.2 million of its own money and the management group put up the remaining $1.8 million. Management retained a buyout option with the investment bank to acquire the bank's equity after five years at a price which would afford the investment bank an annual compound return of about 40 percent. (This translates to a price of about $6.45 million.)

Upon taking control, XYZ Holdings stepped up the depreciable basis of the acquired assets to $10 million. The revised balance sheet is given in Figure 7.3.

Figure 7.3
XYZ Holdings Balance Sheet (revised)—1988
(all values in millions)

Assets			Liabilities & Equity		
Current assets:			Current liabilities:		
Cash	0.20		Accruals	0.25	
Marketable securities	1.55		Accounts payables	0.75	
Inventory	1.75		Notes payable	0.50	
Receivables	0.50				1.50
		4.00			
			Long–term debt		11.50
Fixed assets:			Equity:		
Depreciable	10.00		Common stock	3.00	
Less cum. dep.	(0.00)		Retained earnings	0.00	
Net	10.00				3.00
Nondepreciable	2.00				
		12.00			
Total Assets		16.00	Total Liabilities & Equity		16.00

The new owners immediately moved their offices to less expensive quarters and took other steps to reduce the firm's overhead expenses. The net effect was to reduce the firm's selling and administrative expenses by $1.5 million a year. Management was also in a position to recoup taxes paid in previous years by XYZ Corporation. A decision was made to depreciate the firm's depreciable assets using accelerated methods in order to enhance cash flow. The firm used all cash flow over the first four years to retire its debt. Its higher–cost bonds were retired first. A portion of the cash flow in the fifth year was used to retire debt, bringing it back to the level it stood at before the buyout. The earnings of XYZ Holdings over the next five years appear in Figure 7.4 together with the

Figure 7.4
XYZ Holdings Profit & Loss
(all values in millions)

	1989	1990	1991	1992	1993	1994*
Sales	$15.00	$15.00	$15.00	$15.00	$15.00	$15.00
Cost of goods sold	8.00	8.00	8.00	8.00	8.00	8.00
Gross profit	7.00	7.00	7.00	7.00	7.00	7.00
Selling and administrative	4.00	4.00	4.00	4.00	4.00	4.00
Operating profit before dep.	3.00	3.00	3.00	3.00	3.00	3.00
Depreciation	2.50	2.50	2.25	2.00	0.75	0.00
Operating profit	0.50	0.50	0.75	1.00	2.25	3.00
Interest expense	1.67	1.35	0.99	0.72	0.46	0.35
Earnings before taxes	(1.17)	(0.85)	(0.24)	0.28	1.79	2.65
Taxes (40 percent)	(0.47)	(0.34)	(0.10)	0.11	0.72	1.06
Earnings after taxes	(0.70)	(0.51)	(0.14)	0.17	1.07	1.59
Dividend	0.00	0.00	0.00	0.00	0.00	1.27
Cash flow:	1.80	1.99	2.10	2.17	1.82	1.59
Debt remaining:						
Short term (10%)	0.50	0.50	0.50	0.50	0.50	0.50
Long–term bank (12%)	7.50	7.50	5.61	3.44	2.50	2.50
Bonds (18%)	2.20	0.21	0.00	0.00	0.00	0.00
Cumulative retained earnings	(0.70)	(1.21)	(1.35)	(1.18)	0.64	0.96

*projected

projections for the sixth year (1994). The sixth year's earnings were considered sustainable with an 80 percent dividend payout.

At the end of five years, management exercised its right to buy out the investment bank's equity interest in the firm at the agreed price of $6.45 million. Management then took the firm public again in what is called a **secondary initial public** offering, or SIPO, and sold its equity interest at 15 times projected 1994 earnings. This brought the management group $23.85 million before flotation costs and $22.25 million afterward. After deducting the $6.45 million paid to the investment banking partner, the management team was left with $15.80 million on its initial investment of $1.8 million. This translates to an average annual compound rate of return of about 54 percent.

Let's consider for a moment the sources of the gains generated by this LBO. First, there were tax benefits from stepping up the acquired assets of the firm, from the deductibility of the interest on the funds used to finance a large portion of the original purchase, and from the carryback of losses in 1989, 1990, and 1991. Second, there was a reduction in agency costs apparent from the cost cutting in 1989, when management gave up some of its perks (the fancy offices and some fringe benefits). There were also the benefits afforded by the management group's extensive use of leverage—which is not as high–risk as it might first seem if we take into consideration the stability of the firm's earnings and expenses.

The Investment Bank in the LBO

Notice in our hypothetical LBO described in the preceding section that it was not necessary for XYZ Holdings (the post–buyout firm) to exhibit a significant immediate improvement in earnings in order to produce great value for the buyout group. Indeed, the buyout actually resulted in a sharp deterioration in after–tax earnings for the first four years. The key to understanding the viability of a leveraged buyout is clearly not profit but, rather, cash flow. Cash flow is the sum of earnings after taxes and noncash expenses. (Noncash expenses include such things as depreciation, depletion, and the amortization of intangible assets.)

The investment banking team that does the preliminary analysis and that, in the end, structures the deal concentrates its energy on understanding the size, source, and stability of the target's cash flows. The cash flows will be used to reduce debt, acquire other assets (possibly other firms), and/or pay large cash dividends to the shareholder group. The team's job is largely one of analyzing the cash flows and structuring a deal that can best exploit them. This leads to such questions as the following:

1. How sensitive are the cash flows to changes in the underlying assumptions (sales growth, for example)?
2. How much can the buyout group pay for the firm and still hope to make their target return?
3. What kinds of debt and how much debt can the firm support?
4. Should an ESOP structure be employed and, if so, how aggressively?
5. At what point should the buyout group—including the investment bank—look to cash out?

The leveraged buyout is a fascinating application of financial engineering since it brings together many elements of theory (the conceptual tools) and many of the new instruments (the physical tools) developed over the last 15 years. It also demonstrates the importance of tax and accounting rule changes as well as the influence of the regulatory environment in determining the shape and form of the end product.

Other Roles in Corporate Restructuring

We have discussed a number of areas in which investment banks play a role in corporate restructurings and we will touch on still others in later chapters. There are, however, a few areas that we should highlight here. Two in particular stand out. One is the fairness opinion, and the other is the role of the investment bank in bankruptcy workouts.

A **fairness opinion** is a statement issued by an investment bank, in exchange for a fee, as to the fair value of a firm's assets or its stock. In corporate restructurings, investment banks are often asked to provide such opinions. In fact, it is quite common for a firm's management to solicit fairness opinions from several different investment banks. Fairness opinions are very important when companies are taken private, because minority shareholders will be forced out and paid off in cash (or some other asset). To avoid charges that the buyout group has taken advantage of the minority shareholders, the buyout group will solicit fairness opinions and then pay off the minority shareholders based on these independent "expert" judgments.

While we have not addressed it in this chapter, corporate workouts of business failures (e.g., bankruptcies) are another important area for investment bank involvement in corporate restructurings.[14] In bankruptcy procedures, investment banks often provide expertise and assist in negotiations between corporations and the holders of those corporations' debt and equity. The goal is to bring about a viable reorganization under the applicable bankruptcy codes. Investment banks also assist in the retirement of debt and the replacement of securities that are often necessary in these situations. During the recession of the early 1990s, for example, corporate workout departments saw a tremendous increase in business (and revenue), while M&A departments saw a sharp contraction. Because the skills needed in these areas are similar, many M&A specialists were transferred to workout groups during this period.

Summary

The 1980s bore witness to a decade of aggressive mergers, acquisitions, and takeovers. The hands of the investment banks were all over these corporate restructurings, and the work continues. M&A teams search for, find, and exploit value. This value is split between those who hold the target firm's stock before the restructuring, those who hold the target's stock after the restructuring, and the investment bank that structures the deal. A portion of this value comes from a reduction in agency costs—which can only be applauded. But a portion may come at the expense of other stakeholders in the firm. The latter raises serious questions that have yet to be fully resolved.

The leveraged buyout activity of the 1980s took many publicly held firms private. The principal instruments used to accomplish this were junk bonds, private placements, bridge financing, venture capital, and merchant banking. All of these are tools in the bag of today's investment bank.

---

[14] For an interesting discussion of this period, see Rosenberg (1992).

References and Suggested Reading

Adams, W. and J. W. Brock, *Dangerous Pursuits: Mergers and Acquisitions in the Age of Wall Street*, New York: Pantheon, 1988.

Ainina, M. F. and N. K. Mohan, "When LBOs Go IPO," *Journal of Business Finance & Accounting*, 18:3, April 1991, pp. 393–403.

Alkhafaji, A. F., *Restructuring American Corporations: Causes, Effects, and Implications*, New York: Quorum, 1990.

Ambrose, B. W. and W. L. Megginson, "The Role of Asset Structure, Ownership Structure, and Takeover Defenses in Determining Acquisition Likelihood," *Journal of Financial and Quantitative Analysis*, 27:4, December 1992, pp. 575–588.

Amihud, Y., (ed.), *Leveraged Management Buyouts: Causes and Consequences*, Homewood, IL: Dow Jones Irwin, 1988.

Anders, G., *Merchants of Debt: KKR and the Mortgaging of American Business*, New York: Basic Books, 1992.

Ang, J. S. and A. L. Tucker, "The Shareholder Wealth Effects of Corporate Greenmail," *Journal of Financial Research*, 11:4, Winter 1988, pp. 265–280.

Auerbach, A. J., (ed.), *Corporate Takeovers: Causes and Consequences*, Chicago: University of Chicago Press, 1988.

Barmash, I., *Macy's for Sale*, New York: Weidanfeld & Nicolson, 1988.

Bartlett, S., *The Money Machine: How KKR Manufactured Power & Profits*, New York: Warner Books, 1991.

Bhagat, S. and R. H. Jefferis, "Voting Power in the Proxy Process: The Case of Antitakeover Charter Amendments," *Journal of Financial Economics*, 30:1, November 1991, pp. 183–225.

Bhagat, S., A. Shleifer, and R. W. Vishny, "Hostile Takeovers in the 1980s: The Return to Corporate Specialization," *Brookings Papers on Economic Activity*, 1990, pp. 1–84.

Blair, M. M., (ed.), *The Deal Decade: What Takeovers and Leveraged Buyouts Mean for Corporate Governance*, Washington: Brookings Institute, 1993.

Bowers, H. M. and R. E. Miller, "Choice of Investment Banker and Shareholders' Wealth of Firms Involved in Acquisitions," *Financial Management*, 19:4, Winter 1990, pp. 34–44.

Briston, R. J., B. Saadouni, C. A. Mallin, and J. A. Coutts, "Management Buyout Announcements and Securities Returns: A U.K. Study," *Journal of Business Finance & Accounting*, 19:4, June 1992, pp. 641–655.

Bruner, R. F., *The Poison Pill Anti–Takeover Defense: The Price of Strategic Deterrence*, Charlottesville, VA: The Research Foundation of the Institute of Chartered Financial Analysts, 1991.

Bruner, R. F. and L. S. Paine, "Management Buyouts and Managerial Ethics," *California Management Review*, 30:2, Winter 1988, pp. 89–106.

Bull, I., "Financial Performance of Leveraged Buyouts: An Empirical Analysis," *Journal of Business Venturing*, 4, July 1989, pp. 263–279.

Burroughs, B. and J. Helyar, *Barbarians at the Gate: The Fall of RJR Nabisco*, New York: Harper & Row, 1990.

Carroll, C. A., "Acquisitions of the 1980s: A Multiple Logit Analysis of Leveraged Buyout Candidates," *Review of Business & Economic Research*, 24:1, Fall 1988, pp. 20–30.

Chang, P., "A Measure of the Synergy in Mergers Under a Competitive Market for Corporate Control," *Atlantic Economic Journal*, 18:2, June 1988a, pp. 59–62.

Chang, P., "Economies of Scope, Synergy, and the CAPM," *Journal of Financial Research*, 11:3, Fall 1988b, pp. 255–263.

Chatterjee, S., "Sources of Value in Takeovers, Synergy or Restructuring Implications for Target and Bidder Firms," *Strategic Management Journal*, 13:4, May 1992, pp. 267–286.

DeAngelo, H. and L. DeAngelo, "Management Buyouts of Publicly Traded Corporations," *Financial Analysts Journal*, May/June 1987, pp. 234–243.

DeMong, R. F. and J. W. Peavy, (eds.), *Takeovers and Shareholders: The Mounting Controversy*, Charlottesville, VA: The Financial Analysts Research Foundation, 1985.

Eckbo, B. E., "Valuation Effects of Greenmail Prohibitions," *Journal of Financial and Quantitative Analysis*, 25:4, December 1990, pp. 491–505.

Farrel, C., "The Bills are Coming Due," *Business Week*, September 11, 1989.

Frankfurter, G. M., "Management Buyouts: The Sources and Sharing of Wealth Between Insiders and Outside Shareholders," *Quarterly Review of Economics & Finance*, 32:3, Autumn 1992, pp. 82–95.

Gart, A., "Leveraged Buyouts: A Re–Examination," *Advanced Management Journal*, 55, Summer 1990, pp. 38–46.

Hanly, K., "Hostile Takeovers and Methods of Defense: A Stakeholder Analysis," *Journal of Business Ethics*, 11:12, December 1992, pp. 895–913.

Harlow, W. V. and J. S. Howe, "Leveraged Buyouts and Insider Nontrading," *Financial Management*, 22:1 Spring 1993, pp. 109–118.

Harzel, L. and R. W. Shapro, *Bidders and Targets: Mergers and Acquisitions in the U.S.*, Cambridge, MA: Blackwell, 1990.

Hayn, C., "Tax Attributes as Determinants of Shareholder Gains in Corporate Acquisitions," *Journal of Financial Economics*, 23:1, June 1989, pp. 121–153.

Hite, G. L. and M. Vetsuypens, "Management Buyouts of Divisions and Shareholder Wealth," *Journal of Finance*, 44, 1989, pp. 953–970.

Hunter, W. C. and M. B. Walker, "An Empirical Examination of Investment Banking Merger Fee Contracts," *Southern Economic Journal*, 56:4, April 1990, pp. 1117–1130.

Israel, R., "Capital Structure and the Market for Corporate Control: The Defensive Role of Debt Financing," *Journal of Finance*, 40:4, September 1991, pp. 1391–1400.

Kaplan, S., "The Effects of Management Buyouts in Operating Performance and Value," *Journal of Financial Economics*, 24:2, October 1988, pp. 217–245.

Kaplan, S. N. and J. C. Stein, "How Risky Is the Debt in Highly Leveraged Transactions?" *Journal of Financial Economics*, 27:1, September 1990, pp. 215–246.

Kim, W. S. and E. O. Lyn, "Going Private: Corporate Restructuring Under Information Asymmetry and Agency Problems," *Journal of Business Finance & Accounting*, 18:5, September 1991, pp. 637–648.

Kluegar, R. F., *Mergers and Acquisitions: A Practical Guide to Taxation, Corporation, and Securities Law*, New York: Executive Enterprises Publications, 1988.

Knoeber, C. R., "Golden Parachutes, Shark Repellents, and Hostile Tender Offers," *American Economic Review*, 76:1, March 1986, pp. 155–167.

Kolod, A., "LBO as Fraudulent Transfers," *Real Estate Finance*, 7, Fall 1990, pp. 35–39.

Lampert, H., *True Greed: What Really Happened in the Battle for RJR Nabisco*, New York: New American Library, 1990.

Lehn, K., J. Netter, and A. Poulsen, "Consolidating Corporate Control: Dual–Class Recapitalizations Versus Leveraged Buyouts," *Journal of Financial Economics*, 27:2, October 1990, pp. 557–580.

Lehn, K. and A. Poulsen, "Leveraged Buyouts: Wealth Created or Wealth Redistributed?" *Public Policy Towards Corporate Takeovers*, M. Weidenbaum and K. Chilton, (eds.), New Brunswick, NJ: Transaction Publishers, 1988.

Lichtenberg, F. R. and D. Siegel, "The Effects of Leveraged Buyouts on Productivity and Related Aspects of Firm Behavior," *Journal of Financial Economics*, 27:1, September 1990, pp. 165–194.

Marais, L., K. Schipper, and A. Smith, "Wealth Effects of Going Private for Senior Securities," *Journal of Financial Economics*, 23:1, June 1989, pp. 155–191.

Marren, J. H., *Mergers and Acquisitions: A Valuation Handbook*, Burr Ridge, IL: Business One Irwin, 1993.

McLaughlin, R. M., "Investment–Banking Contracts in Tender Offers: An Empirical Analysis," *Journal of Financial Economics*, 28:1,2, November/December 1990, pp. 209–232.

McLaughlin, R. M., "Does the Form of Compensation Matter? Investment Banker Fee Contracts in Tender Offers," *Journal of Financial Economics*, 32:2, October 1992, pp. 223–260.

Michel, A. and I. Shaked, "The LBO Nightmare: Fraudulent Conveyance Risk," *Financial Analysts Journal*, March/April 1990, pp. 41–50.

Michel, A., I. Shaked, and Y. T. Lee, "An Evaluation of Investment Banker Acquisition Advice: The Shareholders' Perspective," *Financial Management*, 20:2, Summer 1991, pp. 40–49.

Muscarella, C. J. and M. R. Vetsuypens, "Efficiency and Organizational Structure: A Study of Reverse LBOs," *Journal of Finance*, 65:5, December 1990, pp. 1389–1413.

Rosenberg, H., *The Vulture Investor: The Winners and Losers of the Great American Bankruptcy Feeding Frenzy*, New York: Harper Business, 1992.

Rothchild, J., *Going for Broke: How Robert Campeau Bankrupted the Retail Industry, Jolted the Junk Bond Market, and Brought the Booming Eighties to a Crashing Halt*, New York: Simon & Schuster, 1991.

Ryngaert, M., "The Effect of Poison Pill Securities on Shareholder Wealth," *Journal of Financial Economics*, 20:1,2, January/March 1989, pp. 377–417.

Schandler, F. P. and J. E. Karns, "The Unethical Exploitation of Shareholders in Management Buyout Transactions," *Journal of Business Ethics*, 9:7, July 1990, pp. 595–602.

Scholes, M. S. and M. A. Wolfson, "The Effects of Changes in Tax Laws on Corporate Reorganization Activity," *Journal of Business*, 60:1, January 1990, pp. S141–S164.

Servaes, H., "Tobin's Q and the Gains from Takeovers," *Journal of Finance*, 46:1, March 1991, pp. 409–420.

Seyhun, H. N., "Do Bidder Managers Knowingly Pay Too Much for Target Firms," *Journal of Business*, October 1990, pp. 439–464.

Shoven, J. D. and J. Walfogal, (eds.), *Debt, Taxes, and Corporate Restructuring*, Washington: Brookings Institution, 1990.

Silver, A. D., *The Inside Trade*, New York: Harper & Row, 1990.

Siper, R. M., (ed.), *ESOPS in the 1980s: The Cutting Edge of Corporate Buyouts*, New York: AMA Membership Publication Division, 1988.

Smith, R. C., *The Money Wars: The Rise and Fall of the Great Buyout Boom of the 1980s*, New York: Dutton, 1990.

Stoughton, N. M., "The Information Content of Corporate Merger and Acquisition Offers," *Journal of Financial and Quantitative Analysis*, 23:2, June 1988, pp. 175–197.

Tomic, I. and R. P. Yuyuenyongwatana, "Performance of LBO Mergers," *Midwestern Business and Economic Review*, 16, Fall 1992.

Tomic, I. and R. P. Yuyuenyongwatana, "Performance of Leveraged Buyouts, Mergers and Non–Merged Firms," *New York Economic Review*, forthcoming 1993.

Torabzadeh, K. M. and W. J. Bertin, "Leveraged Buyouts and Shareholder Returns," *Journal of Financial Research*, 10:4, Winter 1987, pp. 313–319.

Torabzadeh, K. M. and W. J. Bertin, "Abnormal Returns to Shareholders of Firms Acquired in Business Combinations and Leveraged Buyouts," *Journal of Accounting, Auditing, and Finance*, 7:2, Spring 1992, pp. 231–239.

Travlos, N. C. and M. M. Cornett, "Going Private Buyouts and Determinants of Shareholder Returns," *Journal of Accounting, Auditing and Finance*, 1990.

Varaiya, N. P. and K. R. Ferris, "Overpaying in Corporate Takeovers: The Winner's Case," *Financial Analysts Journal*, May/June 1987, pp. 246–252.

Waddell, W. M., "Leveraged Buyouts: Clever Leveraging or Badly Bet Debt?" *Secured Lender*, 46, November/December 1990, pp. 34–40.

Wansley, J. W., W. R. Lane, and H. C. Yang, "Abnormal Returns to Acquired Firms by Type of Acquisition and Methods of Payment," *Financial Management*, 12:3, Autumn 1983, pp. 16–22.

Wansley, J. W., W. R. Lane, and H. C. Yang, "Gains to Bidder Firms in Cash and Securities Transactions," *Financial Review*, 22:4, November 1987, pp. 403–414.

Weston, J. F., K. S. Chung, and S. E. Hoag, *Mergers, Restructuring, and Corporate Control*, Englewood Cliffs, NJ: Prentice Hall, 1990.

8

Financial Engineering I: Zeros and Mortgage-Backed Securities

Overview

In this chapter, we are going to look at two examples of financial engineering that have had a significant impact on the business of investment banking. These are the development of zero coupon securities (zeros) and the development of mortgage–backed securities. While these two classes of instruments look very different, they are in fact products of a similar process. This process is called **conversion arbitrage**. In conversion arbitrage, the investment bank takes one (or more) financial instruments and, through a process of composition or decomposition, creates one (or more) very different financial instruments.

In the case of zeros, a single–class conventional bond is used to create a strip of individual zero coupon bonds. Although all zeros possess common properties, each zero is nevertheless different from the others in the strip. Similarly, mortgage–backed securities are created by taking either single–class whole mortgages or single–class mortgage passthrough certificates and using them as the fodder to create multiclass mortgage–backed securities called collateralized mortgage obligations. A similar process is employed to create asset–backed securities.

These examples of conversion arbitrage are singled out for discussion in this chapter because (1) they are illustrative of an important way by which investment banks add value for issuers and investors, and (2) they have become important sources of investment bank profits. We begin with a look at zero coupon bonds.

Zero Coupon Securities

The engineering of zero coupon securities is undoubtedly one of the most interesting innovations of the last 15 years. While simple in design, these instruments are a very useful vehicle for achieving portfolio return objectives, hedging complex risk exposures, and structuring a wide variety of synthetic instruments. Zero coupon securities, particularly those derived from conventional Treasury debt issues, have a number of unique properties of particular interest to financial engineers, and these properties are worth elaboration. We begin, however, with definitions and a historic overview.

A **zero coupon bond**, or **zero**, is a debt instrument that is sold at a deep discount from face value. As the name implies, these instruments do not pay periodic coupons. Instead, interest accrues via a gradual rise in the value of the instruments as they approach maturity. At maturity, zeros are redeemed for full face value.[1]

Although the advent of Treasury–based zero coupon products gave a major boost to the general market for zero coupon bonds, corporate and municipal experimentation in zeros had occurred earlier. The volume of this early activity was minimal, and we do not consider it further. We would be remiss, however, if we failed to point out that municipal zeros (munis) offer many of the benefits of Treasury–based zeros (discussed below), with the added benefit of providing tax sheltered income. Consequently, zero coupon munis have become an important factor in the municipal bond market.

The first zero coupon products involving Treasury securities and having a maturity greater than one year were actually derivative products and not Treasury securities at all. These were introduced in 1982 by Merrill Lynch, which called its product Treasury Investment Growth Receipts, or TIGRs. The creation of TIGRs was a three–stage process. First, Merrill Lynch purchased conventional coupon–bearing Treasury securities and removed the coupons, thereby separating the coupons and

---

[1] Actually, zero coupon instruments are not as new as widely believed. The U.S. Treasury has long issued discount instruments of short maturity, the best known of which are Treasury bills (T–bills) of 13–week, 26–week, and 52–week maturities. These instruments are just as surely zero coupon products as are the longer–maturity instruments to which the term is more often applied.

the final redemption payment into separate cash flows. Second, these individual cash flows, each corresponding to a different maturity, were then used to created irrevocable trusts with a custodial bank. As the final step, the custodial bank issued units in the trusts. These units were the TIGRs that Merrill Lynch then marketed to its clients. Although the TIGRs were not themselves issues of the Treasury, they were fully collateralized by Treasury obligations and nearly equivalent to Treasuries in terms of default risk.[2]

To understand the appeal of Treasury–based zeros, we need a brief review of the various forms of risk to which a holder of a fixed–income security is exposed. These include interest rate risk, default risk, reinvestment risk, call or prepayment risk, and purchasing power risk. **Interest rate risk** is the risk that the value of a security will change after its purchase in response to changes in interest rates generally and the instrument's yield more specifically. This risk is most often measured with the aid of duration. Interest rate risk is of greatest concern to holders of fixed–income securities who might have to sell the securities prior to their maturity.

In conventional fixed–income securities markets (i.e., absent zeros), interest rate risk can be managed in several ways. The first is to match the maturity of the instrument to the investor's investment horizon. This maturity/horizon matching approach, however, poses a **reinvestment risk problem**. This is the risk that the periodic coupons received will be reinvested at rates which differ from the yield prevailing on the bond at the time of its purchase. Fluctuations in the reinvestment rate create the potential for terminal wealth to differ from expectations, and therefore constitute a form of risk. The second way to manage interest rate risk is to invest only in instruments having a maturity shorter than that of the investor's horizon, and then to roll over into other instruments, also of short maturity, with the final rollover having a maturity date identical to the investor's horizon. This approach is particularly useful if the investor's horizon is uncertain, or if the investor feels that an earlier–than–expected liquidation might be necessary. By investing in short–maturity instruments, interest rate risk is minimized, because the

---

[2] While default risk is near zero in this structure, the possibility remains that the custodial bank might fail. Should the custodial bank fail, the holders of the TIGRs might experience delays and legal costs in enforcing their claims.

market values of short–maturity instruments are less sensitive to interest rate fluctuations. The final approach using conventional instruments is to purchase an instrument having a maturity greater than the investor's horizon, but then to hedge the interest rate risk in futures, forwards, or some other derivative instrument.

While the three approaches to managing interest rate risk can all be used to reduce risk exposure, none is perfect. The reason is simple: the ever–present reinvestment risk. In the first strategy (maturity/horizon matching), the periodic coupons must be reinvested. In the second strategy (short–term rollovers), while the maturity proceeds of each rollover are known at the time of the instrument's purchase, the reinvestment rate on the next rollover is not known in advance, and hence the reinvestment risk problem is amplified. The final approach (hedging) also fails to address the reinvestment risk problem.

The strategies described above have other failings as well. For example, the rollover strategy will produce a suboptimal return in an upward sloping but stable yield curve environment, and the hedging approach may involve a cost to the hedger.

Another risk investors in fixed–income securities are exposed to is **default risk**. Default risk is the risk that the issuer of the security will default on its financial obligations so that the holder of the instrument does not receive full payment of interest and/or principal in a timely fashion. It is generally accepted that the debt–rating agencies provide very good relative estimates of default risk, but empirical evidence has shown that the market does an excellent job of assessing default risk on its own.[3]

Just as the interest rate risk management problem can be handled in several ways, the default risk problem can also be managed in several ways. The simplest way is to invest in individual securities having an extremely low risk of default. This would certainly include obligations of the U.S. Treasury but might also include investment–grade corporate and municipal issues. An alternative approach is to hold a diversified portfolio

---

[3] For discussion and/or empirical evidence with respect to market assessments of default risk versus bond ratings, see Ederington (1985), Ederington, Yawitz, and Roberts (1987), Gentry, Whitford, and Newbold (1988), Hawley and Walker (1992), Hsueh and Kidwell (1988), Liu and Moore (1987), Ogden (1987), Perry, Liu, and Evans (1988), Reilly and Joehnk (1976), Sarig and Warga (1989), and Sorensen (1980).

of low–grade debt issues. While the securities in the portfolio may individually be high risk, the overall portfolio will tend to be of lower risk. This does not completely eliminate default risk, but the excess yield on these instruments—which can be viewed as a "default risk premium"—should be, in an efficient market, just sufficient to compensate the holder for the default risk he bears. Interestingly, there is empirical evidence to indicate that, in practice, the return on speculative–grade debt of the junk bond variety has actually provided a return in excess of a fair default risk level for extended periods.[4]

Treasury instruments are ideal for the management of both interest rate risk and default risk. First, they are available in every conceivable maturity from a few days out to 30 years, and they are very liquid. This means that any investor can easily find an issue with a maturity that matches his or her investment horizon and can acquire the issue at minimal transaction costs. Second, Treasuries are as close to default–free as any instrument can get, so the investor can disregard default risk.

Despite these appealing features, conventional Treasury issues still expose their holders to substantial reinvestment risk. It is this risk that zeros remove. By definition, a zero does not pay a periodic coupon, and consequently there is no reinvestment risk for the investor who matches the bond's maturity to his or her investment horizon. Thus, the purchaser of zero coupon Treasuries who matches maturity with his investment horizon is freed from interest rate risk, default risk, and reinvestment risk.

There are two other sources of risk associated with fixed–income securities. These are call risk and purchasing power risk. **Call (or prepayment) risk** is the risk that the investor is repaid the loan principal, in whole or in part, prior to the security's maturity date. This risk may be viewed as a form of reinvestment risk, because proceeds received earlier than expected must be reinvested at the then–prevailing rate. There is the added complication, however, that the time of repayment is itself unknown at the time of the instrument's purchase.[5] **Purchasing power risk** is the risk that the terminal proceeds will have more or less

---

[4] See, for example, Altman (1990) and Regan (1990).

[5] While some Treasury issues are callable, most are not. In creating zero coupon bonds from Treasury bonds, only noncallable Treasuries can be used.

purchasing power than expected because of unforeseen changes in the rate of inflation.

Zero coupon bonds can be structured to eliminate both call risk and purchasing power risk. For example, zero coupon bonds that are created from noncallable Treasury bonds, the usual case, are themselves noncallable. Purchasing power risk elimination is another matter. While it is possible to engineer zeros having a terminal value indexed to inflation, inflation–indexed bonds are not yet popular in the United States. Such bonds have, however, found a welcome home in the European markets.

In the past, in addition to their risk management uses, zero coupon derivatives also afforded interesting tax benefits. At the time of their introduction, the tax code provided for the taxation of interest when received. Consequently, because zeros pay all of their interest at maturity, the taxation of the interest on zeros was deferred. Deferral of taxation, while not as attractive as tax exemption, is desirable because it allows the investor to enjoy the use of the funds that would otherwise have been paid to the taxing jurisdiction. Note that this tax treatment no longer applies. Instead, interest on these instruments is taxed in the year in which it accrues, whether or not received.

Given the many benefits of zeros to investors, it is not surprising that Merrill Lynch's TIGRs soon had competition as other investment banks created their own zero coupon Treasury derivatives. These products, which traded under various acronyms, called trademarks, included such names as CATS, LIONs, COUGARs, DOGs, and EAGLEs, to mention just a few. The secondary market for each of these proprietary products was rather illiquid, since the only dealer for each product was the investment bank that created it. In an effort to address this problem, a group of government securities dealers, led by The First Boston Corporation, created a generic, Treasury–based, zero coupon product called **Treasury receipts**.

The risk management uses and the tax benefits of zeros combined to make these derivative products very attractive to investors. Although the tax benefits were eliminated by changes in the tax law that became effective in 1982, the instruments remained popular, and by 1985 the par value of outstanding zeros reached $100 billion. The value of outstandings has increased even more dramatically in the years since 1985. For the investment banks, the incentive for creating zero coupon products is twofold. First, the investor benefits afforded by zeros are reflected in their prices, so that the strip of zeros that can be created from a conventional bond can have a collective value that exceeds that of the conventional bond from which the strip is created.[6] Thus, stripping bonds can be a source of arbitrage profit for an investment bank. (This is discussed in more detail in the next section.) Second, the investment banks, acting in the their role of bond dealers and brokers (i.e., salesmen), stand to profit from making markets in these securities, just as they would do with any other type of bond.

The U.S. Treasury was a major beneficiary of the popularity of Treasury–based zero coupon products. The demand for the zeros created a demand for the bonds that are the raw material for making zeros. This demand for strippable bonds by investment banks and other government securities dealers drove up the prices and drove down the yields on these issues. The Treasury then benefited from the lower yields. Nevertheless, until June of 1982, the Treasury objected to the stripping of bonds and actively tried to dissuade investment banks from engaging in the practice. The Treasury's objections were based on the tax–deferral opportunities made possible by zeros. With the change in the tax law noted earlier, the Treasury dropped its objections, and in 1984 the Treasury created its own program for stripping bonds. The program, called **Separate Trading of Registered Interest and Principal of Securities (STRIPS)**, allowed the stripping of specially designated note and bond issues. The program proved popular and was later extended to allow the stripping of all noncallable coupon issues with original maturities of 10 years or more. These zero coupon bonds are direct obligations of the U.S. Treasury and, hence, completely default–free. All such securities are held in book–entry form.

---

[6] Arbitrage pressure has largely eliminated the pricing difference between a strip of zeros and the equivalent conventional bond. However, occasional opportunities still arise, and investment banks are quick to identify and exploit them. Additionally, under current rules (discussed later), arbitrageurs can also arbitrage between a higher collective value for a conventional bond than for an equivalent strip of zeros.

Zeros and Conversion Arbitrage

The creation of zero coupon bonds from conventional bonds is a classic example of conversion arbitrage. In **conversion arbitrage**, an instrument (or group of instruments) with a given set of investment characteristics is converted into an instrument (or group of instruments) that has a different set of investment characteristics. The most important of these investment characteristics is usually the amount and the size of the cash flows, but other characteristics can be important as well. Included among these characteristics are the risk and tax features of the cash flows. A general model of conversion arbitrage appears as Figure 8.1.

Zero coupon bond generation from conventional bonds is illustrated in Figure 8.2. The reader should verify that the conversion arbitrage model is satisfied in the creation of zeros.

Figure 8.1
Conversion Arbitrage Model

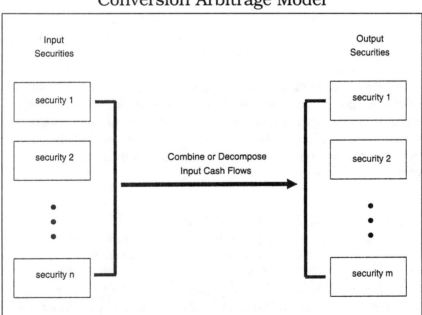

Figure 8.2
Zero Coupon Bond Generation
from Conventional Bonds

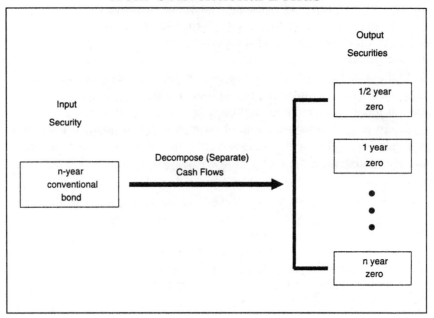

Conversion arbitrage can take several forms. In the case of the creation of zero coupon bonds from conventional bonds (and the creation of multiclass mortgage–backed securities discussed later in this chapter), the conversion arbitrage takes the form of "maturity intermediation"—a service long performed by financial institutions in their more traditional role of borrower/lender.

The Zero Coupon Yield Curve

It has long been common practice to plot the yields on debt instruments against their maturities. The plot of yields on conventional Treasury instruments against their maturities is now called the **conventional yield curve**. If the plot is based on conventional bonds trading near par value, the curve is sometimes called a **par yield curve**. Both practitioners and academicians alike, however, have long pointed out that such a yield curve is imprecise at best, because it implicitly assumes that maturity is the sole determinant of yield. In an early effort to rectify this failing, analysts began to plot a yield–to–duration curve for conventional Treasury instruments. The argument in favor of such a plot is that duration is a better measure of a debt instrument's interest rate sensitivity than is its maturity.[7] As appealing as this argument is, the **yield–to–duration** plot never supplanted the well–established conventional yield curve.

This is where zeros come in. The yield on a zero is the purest measure of the demand/supply conditions for lendable funds of a given maturity, since each zero provides a single payment at one and only one point in time. The introduction of the STRIPS program produced a well–defined and highly standardized zero coupon product with a continuum of maturities. An interesting feature of zeros—which is unique to zeros—is that their maturity and duration are identical. As such, a yield curve drawn with respect to zero coupon bonds is a pure depiction of the demand/supply conditions for lendable funds across a continuum of durations and maturities. Not surprisingly, the **zero coupon yield curve**, sometimes called a **spot yield curve**, has become an important analytical tool in both financial analysis and financial engineering.

A zero coupon yield curve can be plotted from direct observation on Treasury STRIPS. But the zero coupon bonds used to generate this yield curve are not as liquid as the conventional bonds from which they are created. This fact has led to the argument that the observable spot yield curve is not necessarily representative of the true zero coupon yield curve. To deal with this situation, those who have need of a reliable zero coupon yield curve have developed a simple arithmetic method for backing an implied zero coupon yield curve out of the par yield curve. This procedure, called **bootstrapping**, can be used to obtain an implied zero coupon yield curve for Treasuries, for corporates, for municipals, or for swaps.[8] (The latter is widely used today for pricing, for repricing, and for hedging swap products. This is discussed in the next chapter.)

---

[7] The logic of this was discussed in Chapter 6.

[8] For a detailed discussion of the derivation of the spot yield curve for swaps, see Bansal, Ellis, and Marshall (1993).

Table 8.1
Conventional Bond Yields

Maturity (years)	Coupon Rate	Periodic Coupon	Conventional Yield
0.5	8.000	4.0000	8.000%
1.0	8.250	4.1250	8.250
1.5	8.375	4.1875	8.375

The bootstrapping procedure for generating an implied zero coupon yield curve needs to be explained. Let's suppose that we have 6–month, 12–month, and 18–month conventional bonds trading near par (we will assume for illustration that they are all trading at par). These bonds are listed in Table 8.1.

We know that a yield is the discount rate that equates the present value of the future cash flows to the current market price of the bond. In this approach, all the cash flows are assumed to be discounted at the same rate—the bond's yield to maturity. This relationship is given by Equation 8.1.

$$\Sigma \ \frac{CF_t}{(1 + k/2)^t} = \text{price} \qquad (8.1)$$

In this equation, the value CF_t is the cash flow to be received in period t; $t = 1$ for the cash flow to be received in 6 months, $t = 2$ for the cash flow to be received in 12 months, and $t = 3$ for the cash flow to be received in 18 months. The value k is the yield to maturity (stated, by convention, on a semiannual bond basis).

But a conventional bond can also be viewed as a series of zero coupon bonds. If viewed this way, then the individual cash flows should each be discounted at the yields applicable to zeros of equivalent maturities. This relationship is given by Equation 8.2. Thus, the two present–value models should produce the same market price.

$$\Sigma = \frac{CF_t}{(1 + y_t/2)^t} = \text{price} \qquad (8.2)$$

In this model, the values y_t are the corresponding zero coupon yields, stated semiannual bond basis, for cash flows to be received at time t, $t = 1, 2, 3$.[9] Now, since the bond with six months to maturity has already paid all cash flows but the last, its yield to maturity is also the zero coupon yield for a six–month zero. Thus, y_1 is 8.000 percent. We can use this information to "back out" the implied one–year zero coupon rate by using the 12–month conventional bond. The calculation, which makes use of the left–hand side of 8.2, is shown below:

$$4.125 \times (1.0400)^{-1} + 104.125 \times [1 + (y_2/2)]^{-2} = 100$$

With a little arithmetic, we can solve for y_2, which is 8.255 percent. The reader should verify this. Now that we know the 6–month implied zero coupon rate and the 12–month implied zero coupon rate, we can use this information to get the 18–month implied zero coupon rate. The calculation is shown below:

$$4.1875 \times (1.0400)^{-1} + 4.1875 \times (1.0413)^{-2}$$

$$+ 104.1875 \times [1 + (y_3/2)]^{-3} = 100$$

The reader should be convinced that y_3 is approximately 8.384 percent. Our results are summarized in Table 8.2. The same procedure is then used to get all implied zero coupon yields out to the limit of the maturities on the conventional issues.

---

[9] It is customary to state zero coupon bond yields on a semiannual bond basis. This is the same convention used to quote the yields on conventional bonds. Semiannual bond basis means "an annual rate with semiannual compounding."

Table 8.2
Conventional Bond Yields

Maturity (years)	Coupon Rate	Periodic Coupon	Conventional Yield	Implied Zero Coupon Yield
0.5	8.000	4.0000	8.000%	8.000%
1.0	8.250	4.1250	8.250	8.255
1.5	8.375	4.1875	8.375	8.384

Zeros in Financial Engineering

Zero coupon bonds and zero coupon yield curves have become two of the most important tools employed by the financial engineering staffs of investment banks. There are good reasons for this. As discussed earlier, a zero coupon bond entitles its holder to a single payment at a pre-specified point in time. Both the initial purchase price and the cash flow at maturity are known at the time of purchase. By stringing together an appropriate assortment of zeros, a financial engineer can replicate the cash flow pattern of a great many conventional and nonconventional forms of debt. Alternatively, very complex financial structures can be decomposed into elemental components, and the cash flows associated with these elemental components can then be valued with the zero coupon yield curve.

For example, the process by which zeros are created can be reversed, and the conventional Treasury bond can be re–created. Such a strategy would be profitable if a real conventional bond of some maturity is priced above the cost of synthesizing it from a strip of zeros. The investment bank can also use this process to duplicate the cash flow pattern of mortgage debt, or to amortize corporate debt involving a grace period, and so on. This process is depicted in Figure 8.3.

Mortgage–Backed Securities

Mortgage lending was, at one time, a very routine affair. Using customer deposits as their primary source of funds, banks and thrifts originated mortgages that they then placed in their portfolios. These mortgages were

Figure 8.3
Cash Flow Patterns of Mortgage Debt

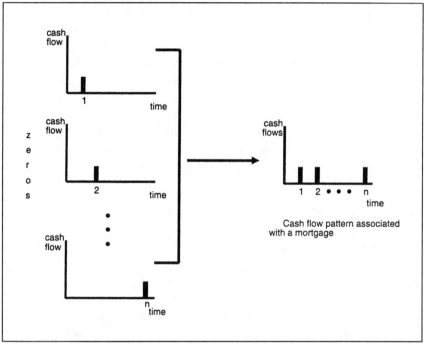

Cash flow pattern associated with a mortgage

serviced by the originating institution and held by that same institution until maturity. Of course, with its funds tied up in existing mortgages, the institution was unable to originate additional mortgages until it had either collected sufficient repayments from existing mortgagors or attracted additional deposits.

In an effort to add liquidity to the secondary mortgage market, Congress sponsored the creation of several organizations, the last of which was the Government National Mortgage Association (GNMA), more popularly known by its nickname, "Ginnie Mae," which was created in 1968. Since 1970, GNMA has provided a vehicle for the pooling and guaranteeing of mortgages. But the securities issued by these mortgage pools, called **passthrough certificates**, are single–class instruments which fail to address certain important investor concerns. In response to these concerns, investment banks applied financial engineering techniques—learned from their experience in creating zero coupon bonds—to convert single–class mortgage assets into multiclass mortgage–backed securities.

We begin this section with a brief look at the mortgage instruments that are the raw material from which mortgage–backed securities (MBS) are created. We then consider the structure of mortgage passthrough certificates. Next, we look at collateralized mortgage obligations (CMOs), some of the now–common CMO variants, and some relevant CMO math.

Investment banks today are big players in the MBS markets. They assist originating institutions in structuring and distributing these instruments; they structure and originate the instruments on their own; they make aggressive markets in the instruments; and they arbitrage the instruments whenever opportunities present themselves.

The Mortgage Instrument

A **mortgage** is a loan secured by real property, such as a building or land. In the residential mortgage market, the subject of this section, the borrower approaches a mortgage lender for a loan. If the borrower is approved, the lender provides sufficient funds for the purposes of the borrower (usually funds to purchase property), and the borrower signs a document agreeing to repay the loan, together with interest, according to some payment schedule. Since most mortgage lending involves amortization of the loan principal, the payment schedule is sometimes called an **amortization schedule**. The document constitutes the mortgage. The borrower is called the **mortgagor** and the lender is called the **mortgagee**. Over the course of its life, the mortgage must be serviced. That is, mortgage payments must be collected and recorded, real estate taxes must be collected and passed along to the appropriate taxing jurisdictions, and foreclosure proceedings must be instituted in the event of a default.

In a conventional mortgage, the mortgage rate is fixed for the life of the mortgage, and the mortgage payments are all of equal size. For these reasons, such mortgages are often called **level–payment mortgages**. Conventional mortgages typically have a term of 30 years, but shorter maturities are not uncommon. Payments on residential mortgages are usually made monthly, but other payment frequencies are possible.

Since each payment includes some repayment of principal, the mortgage balance declines with each payment, making conventional mortgages self–amortizing forms of debt. As a result of the declining mortgage balance and the fixed payment schedule, each subsequent payment must include less interest and more principal. Portions of a typical mortgage amortization schedule appear in Table 8.3.

As can be seen in Table 8.3, the early mortgage payments are mostly interest, while the latter mortgage payments are mostly principal. Mortgagors are usually permitted to make payments on their mortgages in excess of that which is required. Such excess payments are called prepayments and are credited directly against the mortgage balance. The right of the mortgagor to prepay the mortgage principal constitutes an **embedded call option**. Like all options, this option has value.

Table 8.3
Conventional Mortgage Amortization Schedule

Payment Number	Total Payment	Principal Component	Interest Component	Principal Balance
1	1,755.15	88.48	1,666.67	199,911.52
2	1,755.15	89.22	1,665.93	199,822.30
3	1,755.15	89.96	1,665.19	199,732.33
—	—	—	—	—
180	1,755.15	390.84	1,364.31	163,326.60
—	—	—	—	—
251	1,755.15	704.51	1,050.64	125,371.88
—	—	—	—	—
358	1,755.15	1,712.10	43.05	3,453.35
359	1,755.15	1,726.37	28.78	1,726.98
360	1,741.37	1,726.98	14.39	0.00

Notes: Starting principal on loan: $200,000
          Mortgage rate: 10.00 percent
          Term: 30 years, monthly payments

Source: *A–Pack: An Analytical Package for Business.**

A–Pack: An Analytical Package for Business is an inexpensive DOS–based, menu–driven package containing a wide variety of analytical techniques with a great many financial applications. It is published by MicroApplications, 516–821–9355.

In recent years, mortgage lenders have been discouraging borrowers from taking out conventional fixed–rate mortgages in favor of **adjustable–rate mortgages**, known colloquially as ARMs. There are many variants of ARMs, but they all share one common characteristic: the mortgage rate may change in response to changing market conditions. To persuade borrowers to take these mortgages, the originating institution often provides an artificially low mortgage rate for the first year or so. This initial low rate is aptly described as a "teaser rate." Following the period in which the rate is artificially held below market, the rate adjusts to a market level. Thereafter, the rate periodically adjusts to keep pace with market conditions. Such mortgages often have "caps" on each rate revision as well as lifetime caps. These caps are intended to protect the mortgagor from excessive changes in mortgage rates.

ARMs are themselves a product of financial engineering, but the engineering did not stop with adjustable rates. Indeed, financial engineers have been active in the mortgage markets and have produced an interesting assortment of mortgage variants, including graduated payment mortgages, graduated equity mortgages, pledged account mortgages, shared appreciation mortgages, and reverse annuity mortgages.

Passthrough Certificates: The Pooling Process

The mortgage pooling process, introduced in 1970 by the Government National Mortgage Association, provides a vehicle by which mortgage originators can move mortgages off their balance sheets while retaining the servicing rights. This provides an ongoing source of funding to lending institutions to originate new mortgages. The process itself is fairly simple. The GNMA specifies mortgage standards. Any institution employing these standards in its mortgage originations can pool the mortgages, purchase a performance guarantee from GNMA, and then issue passthrough certificates in the pools. The distribution process employs a mortgage passthrough broker/dealer syndicate, assembled by an investment bank. The GNMA guarantee covers the full and timely payment of both interest and principal. The passthrough certificates, also called **participation certificates**, are sold to investors and represent **pro rata** claims on the pool.

Variations of the basic mortgage passthrough are also issued by other federally sponsored organizations including the Federal Home Loan Mortgage Corporation (FHLMC) and the Federal National Mortgage

Association (FNMA), and by a number of private parties—usually large commercial banks. The nature of the guarantee provided by these organizations varies. FHLMC, for example, guarantees the timely payment of interest and the ultimate, but not necessarily timely, payment of principal. Private issuers of passthroughs may or may not purchase payment guarantees (insurance). The rest of our mortgage–oriented discussion will concentrate on GNMA passthroughs.

The pooling process separates the mortgage from the mortgage servicing function. The mortgage originator may keep the servicing rights or may sell them to another institution. The servicing rights have value because of a fee collected by the servicing agent. For example, in the GNMA pool, the servicing fee is set at 44 basis points (calculated on the principal balance) and is deducted from the mortgage interest. Six additional basis points are paid as a fee (premium) to GNMA for its guarantee. Together, these deductions total 50 basis points (one–half of 1 percent). Thus, a 10.75 percent mortgage coupon will return, if sold at par, 10.25 percent to investors in the passthroughs. This rate is called the passthrough rate.

In addition to the revenue derived from mortgage servicing fees, the mortgage originator also derives profit from the points it charges the borrower to originate the mortgage. A point is defined as 1 percent of the mortgage principal. The funds made available by the sale of the mortgages can be used to originate additional mortgages which, in turn, produce additional revenue from points collected on the new originations and from new servicing fees.

The pooling of mortgages has dramatically transformed the mortgage market. It is now routine for banks and thrifts to originate mortgages, pool them, and sell off the pools (either keeping the servicing rights for themselves or selling the servicing rights to another institution). While the pools themselves are large ($1 million is the minimum size and most are considerably larger), the passthroughs can be purchased in denominations as small as $25,000. Thus, they appeal to many private investors. The structure of the passthrough market is depicted in Figure 8.4.

Because mortgage passthroughs represent undivided claims on the mortgage pool—meaning that each passthrough owner holds a pro rata claim to all interest and principal repayments—the investor in pass-throughs is subject to both reinvestment risk and substantial prepayment risk. Further, if an investor sells a passthrough prior to its maturity, she

Figure 8.4
The Structure of the Passthrough Market

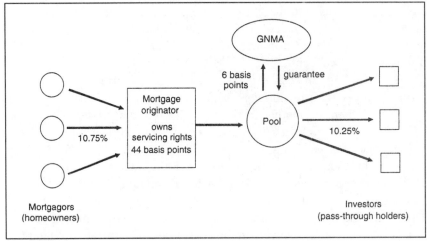

is also exposed to considerable interest–rate risk. The source of the interest–rate risk is the same as for any other debt instrument; therefore, we do not discuss it further. The reinvestment risk and the prepayment risk, however, require a little more explanation.

Recall that mortgages are amortizing forms of debt. That is, the investor receives periodic payments that include principal as well as interest. Since the periodic payments on amortizing debt are larger than the periodic payments on nonamortizing forms of debt, the reinvestment risk is greater on passthroughs than on coupon–bearing Treasury bonds and corporate bonds. The prepayment risk stems from the fact that the mortgagors have the right, which they frequently exercise, to prepay all or part of the mortgage balance. In other words, they may pay back the principal before they are required to do so. These prepayments are passed along to the holders of the passthroughs, who must then reinvest, often at a lower interest rate. Prepayments occur for a variety of reasons, including the sale of the home, a sudden availability of funds for the homeowner, the death of the homeowner, or a refinancing of the mortgage in response to lower interest rates. The last of these reasons accounts for the greatest number of prepayments on mortgages that are written during periods of high interest rates. A great deal of research has gone into modeling prepayment behavior.[10]

Collateralized Mortgage Obligations

While the financial engineering that led to the introduction of mortgage passthrough certificates added considerable liquidity to the mortgage market, the appeal of passthrough certificates is nevertheless limited by the "single–class" nature of the instruments. The pool arrangement allows for the passthrough of all interest and principal repayments to investors on a pro rata basis; thus, all investors in the same passthrough instrument hold identical securities with identical cash flows, identical maturities, and identical rights. This single–class structure does not suit the needs of all potential mortgage investors. The prepayment risk problem, in particular, has been a bane to investors.

In June of 1983, in an effort to address the prepayment risk problem, investment banks, led by The First Boston Corporation and Salomon Brothers, introduced collateralized mortgage obligations. Collateralized mortgage obligations were a dynamic innovation and quickly captured a major portion of the mortgage market. The instrument was adaptable, and many variants soon evolved. The original CMO product, however, had certain drawbacks. For example, while it did qualify for debt treatment under the then–existing tax code, it did not qualify for flow–through tax treatment, and thus added considerable debt to the balance sheet of issuing institutions.[11] To remove the debt from the balance sheet, issuing institutions employed grantor trust and owner trust structures. These structures, however, were less than ideal. They limited the issuer's flexibility and gave rise to other potentially adverse tax consequences.

The deficiencies of the CMO product under then–existing tax law eventually led to inclusion of special provisions in the Tax Reform Act

---

[10] Carron (1988) provides a very good starting point for anyone interested in mortgage prepayment models. For an updated discussion, see Kang and Zenios (1992).

[11] Debt treatment means that an instrument is recognized by debt of the issuer (not equity), and therefore payments are deductible expenses of the issuer. Flow–through treatment means that specific assets held as the payment source on debt are precisely matched to the debt, and the debt is defeased. This allows both the debt and the assets supporting the debt to be removed from the issuer's balance sheet.

of 1986 (TRA) for the creation of a CMO–like product that qualifies for flow–through tax treatment. Specifically, the legislation allows for the creation of **Real Estate Mortgage Investment Conduits**, or REMICs. Since their introduction, REMICs have largely supplanted CMOs as the operational vehicle for generating multiclass mortgage–backed securities from single–class mortgages, and the term CMO is now generally understood to include REMICs.[12]

From a financial engineering perspective, CMOs are another example of conversion arbitrage. The investment bank purchases mortgage pass-throughs (or whole mortgages) and then issues special bonds that are collateralized by the mortgages (hence the name). The bonds are divided into a series of distinct "tranches." The cash flows on each of the tranches are different, and hence the CMO structure allows a single–class instrument (the mortgage or passthrough) to be transformed, via maturity intermediation, into a multiclass instrument (the CMO).

In the basic or plain vanilla CMO, each tranche is entitled to receive a pro rata share of interest, just as with a passthrough, *but only one tranche at a time receives principal*. For example, at the beginning, only the first tranche receives principal. This tranche, called the **fastest–pay tranche**, receives all principal collected by the servicers, whether paid on time or prepaid, until all of the tranche's principal has been amortized. The tranche is then retired and the second tranche becomes the fast-est–pay tranche. The number of tranches on any one CMO may be as few as four or as many as 10 or more. The structure of the CMO, using passthroughs or whole mortgages as the collateral source, is depicted in Figure 8.5 for a four–tranche situation with the second tranche as the fastest–pay tranche (the first tranche has already been retired).

Many variants of the basic CMO have evolved since this product was first introduced. Some have structures considerably more complex than that depicted in Figure 8.5. For example, there are CMOs in which more than one tranche receives principal at a time, there are zero coupon–like CMO tranches, and there are CMOs based on adjustable–rate mortgages.

Consider, for example, zero coupon–like CMOs. On these CMOs, one or more of the tranches take the form of accrual bonds. An **accrual bond**, also called an **accretion bond** or a **Z–bond**, is a deferred interest

---

[12] For a review of the benefits of REMICs, see Levitin (1987), Duett (1989), and Parks (1992).

Figure 8.5
The Structure of the CMO

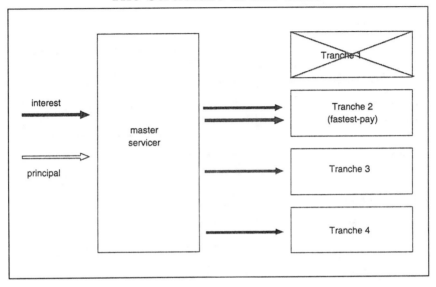

obligation resembling a zero coupon bond. The accrual bond does not receive any interest or principal until such time as the preceding tranches are fully retired. In the interim, the interest that would normally flow to the tranche accrues. Once all preceding tranches are retired, the accrual bond receives interest and principal in the usual way. The accrual bond structure is depicted in Figure 8.6, with the fourth tranche being the one and only accrual bond in this particular case.

While the CMO does not completely eliminate prepayment risk, it does greatly reduce it. The structure of the tranches guarantees that the first tranche will have a very short life, that the second tranche will have a somewhat longer life, that the third tranche will have a still longer life, and so on. Thus, a long–term instrument—the mortgage or passthrough—is used to create a series of distinct instruments, the tranches, that have short, intermediate, and long lives. The investor can pick the tranche that most closely mirrors his needs. Because investors can purchase need–specific securities and, hence, have less risk than that associated with whole mortgages or passthroughs, they are willing to pay a little

Figure 8.6
CMO with Accrual Bond Tranches

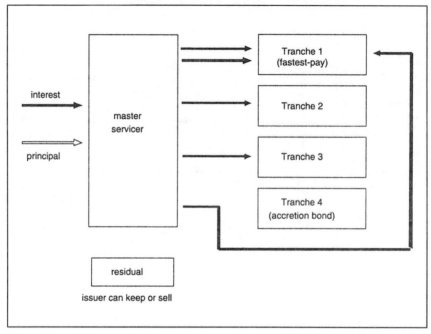

more for these instruments. The collective value of the CMO tranches can then be more than the value of the mortgages (or passthroughs) used to create them. This value difference is the source of a portion of the investment bank's profit. The investment bank also makes the secondary market in CMOs, acting as a dealer, and derives profit from the bid–ask spread.

CMOs, particularly those with accrual bond tranches, give rise to residuals—which are another interesting feature of the product. Consider, for example, a situation in which the accrual bondholders have been promised a return of 9 percent. Now suppose that the reinvestment rate on the proceeds received by the grantor trust (into which the mortgage collateral has been placed) exceeds 9 percent. Then, upon the retirement of the final tranche, there will be excess value. This excess value is called the **residual**. Of course, if the reinvestment rate averaged less than 9 percent, the residual would be negative. To deal with this latter possibility, the CMO trustee uses very conservative reinvestment rate assumptions and overcollateralizes the CMO bonds. These precautions assure that the residual will be positive, but the amount is still uncertain.[13]

The CMO issuer can retain the residual or sell it to an investor willing to bear the risk of the uncertain terminal value. The latter course has become the general, although not universal, rule. By selling the residual up–front, the CMO issuer is relieved of this source of uncertainty.

The issuance of CMOs requires filing and registration with the Securities and Exchange Commission. This entails considerable delay in any offering and considerable expense for the requisite due diligence investigation. However, the process has been streamlined in recent years by the advent of shelf registration. (Shelf registration was discussed in Chapter 3.) CMOs can be developed in several ways. One way is for a financial institution (such as an investment bank) to buy whole mortgages or passthroughs and then use these to create its own CMO products. Alternatively, mortgage bankers, thrifts, and commercial bankers that originate mortgages may develop their own CMOs. In this latter scenario, the securities are developed and distributed with the aid of investment bankers serving in their traditional role as underwriters. Some of the larger mortgage bankers have gone this latter route. Additionally, smaller originators who lack the volume to efficiently generate their own mortgage–backed securities can "rent" an existing conduit—i.e., sell their mortgages to another institution with an established market presence and a volume sufficient to exploit the economies of scale. As a result, relatively few issuers have filed registration statements, but those who have tend to be high–volume originators.

In the decade following the introduction of the now–generic CMOs, these mortgage–based products have evolved into many different forms that are sometimes described, collectively, as **derivative mortgage**

---

[13] The most conservative reinvestment rate assumption is to assume a reinvestment rate of 0 percent. Such an assumption literally guarantees that the residual will never be negative.

products, or **mortgage derivatives.**[14] (The term "derivative mortgage products" is often used more narrowly to connote high–yield, high–risk products. We employ the broader meaning here.) Since we have mentioned some of these derivative mortgage products in passing, it would perhaps be wise to offer a fuller description of a few. Specifically, we will briefly describe planned amortization classes (PACs), targeted amortization classes (TACs), interest–only (IOs) and principal–only (POs) securities, and floating–rate CMOs.

As already noted, CMOs were a major breakthrough in the management of the prepayment risk associated with mortgages. While generic tranches did not eliminate the prepayment risk in its entirety, they did allow the mortgage derivative investor to get a better grip on the paydown of the principal. A later development, designed to further reduce the prepayment uncertainty, was the introduction of **planned amortization classes.**[15] These CMO tranches guarantee a rate of amortization similar in nature to the way a sinking fund on a bond guarantees a bond's amortization. In general, PACs guarantee a fixed paydown schedule so long as the prepayment rate stays within some range. Such a range is called a **prepayment band.** The cash flow uncertainty is completely removed as long as the prepayments stay within the designated range.

Because the prepayment risk is further reduced by PAC and PAC–like CMO tranches, the investors in these tranches are willing to accept a lower yield or, equivalently, pay a higher price for a given coupon. But, of course, there are few free lunches. To provide one tranche with greater certainty, other tranches must accept greater uncertainty. A PAC can be issued as any tranche in the CMO. Regardless of where it is issued, the PAC tranche gets precedence over the other tranches (called **companion bonds,** which are issued only as part of CMOs having PACs) to the extent necessary to guarantee its paydown rate. As a consequence, the coupon rate will have to be higher on the other tranches in a CMO, relative to a generic form.

---

[14] For a more thorough discussion of mortgage derivatives, see Carron (1992) and Spillenkothen (1992). The market for these instruments was reported to exceed $1 trillion in 1992. Carron cites the figure $1.2 trillion.

[15] For a review of PACs, see Bykhovsky (1992) and Goodman (1992). Bykhovsky reports that as of January 1992, more than $225 billion in PACs had been issued.

Targeted amortization classes are CMO tranches that are scheduled to receive a specific monthly principal repayment. Excess principal received in any month is distributed to the non–TAC tranche classes. Should principal repayments be insufficient to fully meet the target, then the payments fall short and the average life of the tranche lengthens.

Interest–only and **principal–only** securities are created by separating the principal and interest components of mortgage payments. The claims on interest are sold to one set of investors and the claims on principal are sold to another set of investors. When interest rates decline, mortgagors prepay principal rapidly, which is then passed through to the PO investors. At the same time, however, this rapid prepayment of principal results in smaller interest payments, and so the cash flows to the IO investors diminish when interest rates decline. POs have long effective durations and are attractive investments for bullish investors (i.e., ones who feel that interest rates will decline). In other words, for a given promised future payment, the sooner one gets it, the better.[16] IOs appeal to bearish investors for the opposite reasons.

Value of the Embedded Option

Mortgage–backed securities are generally quoted in terms of a spread over Treasuries of similar average life.[17] The average life of an MBS,

---

[16] Do not confuse this with the reinvestment risk or call risk problem. Essentially, a PO holder has purchased the right to receive specific principal sums (no interest) at specific points in the future. If these same sums are received sooner than scheduled, the PO investor enjoys a windfall gain in time value. For example, if the PO holder is entitled to receive $100 in five years but receives the $100 after only three years (due to prepayment), then the proceeds can be reinvested for the remaining two years with greater terminal value even if the rates have fallen.

[17] Average life is a widely used measure of the average time to the full repayment of an instrument's principal. The average life of a nonamortizing instrument is identical to its maturity. For amortizing instruments, average life is shorter than maturity. The formula for average life is as follows:

$$AL = \sum_{t=1}^{mn} \frac{P_t \times t}{IP} \times \frac{1}{m}$$

however, is not known with certainty. The best we can do is estimate it based on our prepayment assumptions.[18] Nevertheless, given some prepayment assumptions, we can estimate an average life for a mortgage–backed security, and then we can compare the yield on the security to Treasuries of similar average life in order to determine the spread over Treasuries. For example, suppose that, shortly after issue and under appropriate prepayment assumptions, GNMA 9s originated in 1990–91 have an average life of 10 years. We observe that these MBSs are priced to yield 9.11 percent. We compare this yield to that on 10–year Treasuries, which, like all nonamortizing instruments, have an average life identical to their term to maturity. We observe that the 10–year Treasuries are yielding 8.14 percent. We conclude, then, that the GNMA 9s are trading at a spread of 97 basis points over Treasuries, which is said to be "97 over the 10–year."

As discussed earlier in this chapter, the right of the mortgagor to prepay the mortgage principal constitutes an embedded call option. This feature suggests that the spread over Treasuries may be misleading, because it fails to consider the value of the embedded option. Since an option has value, the party that sold the option (the mortgagee) must be compensated for it in some form. In the case of mortgages, this takes the form of additional yield. Thus, the spread over Treasuries includes some number of basis points that merely compensates the mortgagee for the option it has written. To deal with this, mortgage valuation techniques incorporate adjustments for the value of the embedded option.

There are two specific option adjustments that we would like to point out. The first is referred to as the **option–adjusted spread**, which is a restatement of the spread over Treasuries with the value of the embedded option deducted. For example, let's suppose that the embedded option has a value of 25 basis points. Then the option–adjusted spread over

---

where AL denotes average life, t denotes the period number, P_t is the principal repaid at the end of period t, IP denotes the initial principal, m denotes the number of periods per year, and n denotes the maturity of the instrument.

[18] There are a number of standard methods for estimating prepayment rates on mortgages. One of the most commonly employed is the PSA method, developed by the Public Securities Association. More sophisticated methodologies have been developed by a number of investment banks, particulary the First Boston Corporation and Salomon Brothers.

Treasuries is 72 basis points rather than 97 basis points. In the language of the mortgage markets, the option–adjusted spread is sometimes called an effective spread.

The second adjustment involves duration. The potential for greater prepayment, should rates decline dramatically, also shortens the effective duration. For this reason, players in the MBS market often calculate an **option–adjusted duration**. As expected, an option–adjusted duration is shorter than an unadjusted duration. (We usually use modified duration rather than Macaulay duration in these calculations.) Option–adjusted durations are also called effective durations. Suppose that, after adjusting for the option component, the effective duration is 5.4 years. The characteristics of the 10–year Treasury and the GNMA 9s are compared in Table 8.4.

Asset-Backed Securities

The fundamental logic in the engineering behind collateralized mortgage obligations is not specific to mortgages. Given the success of the CMO product, it is not surprising, then, that financial engineers soon looked for other payment streams that could benefit from the collateralization, often called **securitization**, process. A number of such payment flows have since been used as collateral on debt issues. These later debt issues are now known, collectively, as **asset–backed securities**, or **asset–backs**

Table 8.4
Treasury versus GNMA Characteristics

	10–Year Treasury	GNMA 9s due 2020–21
Maturity	10 years	30 years
Average life	10 years	10 years
Bond equivalent yield	8.14 percent	9.11 percent
Spread over Treasuries	0	97 bps
Option–adjusted spread	0	72 bps
Modified duration	6.7 years	5.7 years
Effective duration	6.7 years	5.4 years
Prepayment rate	N.A.	% PSA

(ABS). The term "asset–backed" securities refers to any securities backed by loans, leases, or installment contracts on personal property. Personal property is all property other than real estate and would include such things as computers and automobiles.

While any payment stream can be used to back a debt issue, the most frequently used are automobile, computer, and credit card receivables.[19] The structure of asset–backed securities is similar to that of mortgage–backed securities. They may be single–class instruments, like mortgage passthroughs, or multiclass instruments, like CMOs. Specialized boutiques have evolved to service the asset–backed market—both in structuring securities and in providing guarantees. The best known of these is probably Capital Markets Assurance Corporation (CapMAC).

As with mortgage–backed securities, the main risk to the holders of asset–backs is the prepayment risk associated with early prepayment of principal. Lack of knowledge concerning prepayment and reinvestment adds to the investor's uncertainty and makes it difficult to estimate the instrument's yield and effective maturity. These uncertainties will, of course, be reflected in an instrument's return.

Investment banks participate in the asset–backed market by structuring the securities and the collateral, managing the underwriting process, handling the distribution or private placement, and making the secondary market in the instruments.

Summary

Financial engineering has become an important and profitable undertaking for investment banks. In addition to enabling investment banks to develop new products and markets, it allows these firms to better intermediate between the needs of issuers and the needs of investors. Zero coupon bonds, mortgage–backed securities, and asset–backed securities are just three examples of financial engineering. The shared characteristic of these products is that they are all products of conversion arbitrage—a now–standard technique in the toolbox of financial engineers.

---

[19] Kavanagh, Boemio, and Edwards (1992) describe asset–backed commercial paper, Brady (1990) describes securitization in the Euromarkets, and Haley (1987) describes asset–backed consumer receivables.

Zero coupon bonds were first created by physically stripping conventional bonds against the wishes of the Treasury, but later they were stripped with the assistance of the Treasury. Mortgage–backed securities began with the development of passthrough certificates. The pooling process solved some problems but not all, which eventually led to the development of CMO and REMIC structures. Asset–backed securities, created by "securitizing" receivables and similar assets, represent a straightforward extension of the process by which CMOs were created.

In the next chapter, we continue our discussion of the role of investment banks in financial engineering by examining the development of over–the–counter derivatives.

References and Suggested Reading

Altman, E. I., "Current Issues: Junk Bonds—How 1989 Changed the Hierarchy of Fixed–Income Security Performance," *Financial Analysts Journal*, 46:3, May/June 1990, pp. 9–12, 20.

Arak, M., L. S. Goodman, and J. Snailer, "Duration Equivalent Bond Swaps: A New Tool," *Journal of Portfolio Management*, 12:4, Summer 1986, pp. 26–32.

Bansal, V. K., M. E. Ellis, and J. F. Marshall, "The Spot Swaps Yield Curve: Derivation and Use," *Advances in Futures and Options Research*, 6, 1993, pp. 279–290.

Becketti, S., "The Role of Stripped Securities in Portfolio Management," *Economic Review: Federal Reserve Bank of Kansas City*, 73:5, May 1988, pp. 20–31.

Becketti, S., "The Prepayment Risk of Mortgage–Backed Securities," *Economic Review: Federal Reserve Bank of Kansas City*, 74, February 1989, pp. 43–57.

Becketti, S. and C. S. Morris, *The Prepayment Experience of FNMA Mortgage–Backed Securities*, New York: NYU Salomon Center, 1991.

Belton, T. M., "The New Breed: Option–Adjusted Spreads," *Secondary Mortgage Markets*, 5:4, Winter 1988/89, pp. 6–11.

Brady, S., "The Year of the Asset–Backed Eurobond," *Euromoney*, February 1990, pp. 18–19.

Bykhovsky, M., "Anatomy of PAC Bonds," *Journal of Fixed Income*, 2:1, June 1992, pp. 44–50.

Carron, A. S., *Prepayment Models for Fixed and Adjustable Rate Mortgages*, New York: First Boston, Fixed Income Research, August 1988.

Carron, A. S., "Understanding CMOs, REMICs, and Other Mortgage Derivatives," *Journal of Fixed Income*, 2:1, June 1992, pp. 25–43.

Duett, E. H., "An Economic Analysis of REMICs," *Real Estate Review*, 18:4, Winter 1989, pp. 66–72.

Duett, E. H., *Advanced Instruments in the Secondary Mortgage Market: An Introduction to CMOs, REMICs, IOs & POs and Other Derivative Instruments*, New York: Harper & Row, 1990.

Ederington, L. H., "Classification Models and Bond Ratings," *Financial Review*, 20:4, 1985, pp. 237–262.

Ederington, L. H., J. B. Yawitz, and B. E. Roberts, "The Informational Content of Bond Ratings," *Journal of Financial Research*, 10:3, 1987, pp. 211–226.

Fisher, L., I. E. Brick, and F. K. W. Ng, "Tax Incentives and Financial Innovation: The Case of Zero–Coupon and Other Deep–Discount Bonds," *Financial Review*, 18:4, 1983, pp. 292–305.

Gentry, J. A., D. T. Whitford, and P. Newbold, "Predicting Industrial Bond Ratings with a Probit Model and Funds Flow Components," *Financial Review*, 23:3, 1988 pp. 269–286.

Goodman, L. S., "Facts About PACs," *Financial Managers' Statement*, 14:1, January/February 1992, pp. 20–23.

Gregory, D. W. and M. Livingston, "Development of the Market for U.S. Treasury STRIPS," *Financial Analysts Journal*, 48:2, March/April 1992, pp. 68–74.

Haley, W. J., "The Securitization of Consumer Receivables," *Bank Administration*, 63:7, July 1987, pp. 32–36.

Hawley, D. D. and M. M. Walker, "An Empirical Test of Investment Restrictions and Efficiency in the High–Yield Debt Market," *Financial Review*, 27:2, May 1992, pp. 273–287.

High Yield Handbook (1989), High Yield Research Group, The First Boston Corporation, January 1991.

Hsueh, L. P. and D. S. Kidwell, "Bond Ratings: Are Two Better Than One?" *Financial Management*, 17:1, 1988, pp. 46–53.

Kang, P. and S. A. Zenios, "Complete Prepayment Models for Mortgage–Backed Securities," *Management Science*, 38:11, November 1992, pp. 1665–1685.

Kaufman, H. M., "FNMA's Role in Deregulating Markets: Implications from Past Behavior," *Journal of Money, Credit & Banking*, 20:4, November 1988, pp. 673–683.

Kavanagh, B., T. R. Boemio, and G. A. Edwards, Jr., "Asset–Backed Commercial Paper Programs," *Federal Reserve Bulletin*, 78:2, Feb. 1992, pp. 107–116.

Levitin, C. M., "REMICs: Removing Tax Obstacles to More Efficient Trading of Mortgage–Backed Securities," *Real Estate Review*, 17:3, Fall 1987, pp. 26–34.

Liu, P. and W. T. Moore, "The Impact of Split Bond Ratings On Risk Premia," *Financial Review*, 23:1, 1987, pp. 71–86.

Livingston, M. and D. W. Gregory, *The Stripping of U.S. Treasury Securities*, New York: NYU Salomon Center, 1989.

Madura, J. and C. Williams, "Hedging Mortgages with Interest Rate Swaps vs. Caps: How to Choose," *Real Estate Finance Journal*, 3:1, Summer 1987, pp. 90–96.

Ogden, J. P., "Determinants of the Ratings and Yields on Corporate Bonds: Tests of the Contingent Claims Model," *Journal of Financial Research*, 10:4, 1987, pp. 329–340.

Page, D. E. and C. F. Sirmans, "Secondary Mortgage Market Yields: An Empirical Investigation of FHLMC Commitments," *Akron Business & Economic Review*, 17:2, Summer 1986, pp. 6–11.

Parks, J. T., "The ABCs of CMOs, REMICs, and IO/POs: Rocket Science Comes to Mortgage Finance," *Journal of Accountancy*, 171:4, April 1992, pp. 41–51.

Perry, L. G., P. Liu, and D. A. Evans, "Modified Bond Ratings: Further Evidence on the Effects of Split Ratings on Corporate Bond Yields," *Journal of Business Finance and Accounting*, 15:2, 1988, pp. 231–242.

Regan, P. J., "Junk Bonds—Opportunity Knocks?" *Financial Analysts Journal*, 46:3, May/June 1990, pp. 13–16.

Reilly, F. K. and M. D. Joehnk, "The Association Between Market–Determined Risk Measures for Bonds and Bond Ratings," *Journal of Finance*, 31:5, 1976, pp. 1387–1403.

Sarig, O. and A. Warga, "Some Empirical Estimates of the Risk Structure of Interest Rates," *Journal of Finance*, 44:5, December 1989, pp. 1351–1360.

Smith, D. J., "Collateralized Mortgage Obligations: An Introduction," *Real Estate Review*, 16:1, Spring 1986, pp. 30–42.

Smith, D. J. and R. A. Tagart, "Bond Market Innovations and Financial Intermediation," *Business Horizons*, 32:6, November/December 1989.

Sorensen, E. H., "Bond Ratings Versus Market Risk Premiums," *Journal of Portfolio Management*, 6:3, 1980, pp. 64–69.

Spillenkothen, R., "Statement to Congress," *Federal Reserve Bulletin*, 78:7, July 1992, pp. 492–495.

Understanding Securitized Investments and Their Use in Portfolio Management, Charlottesville, VA: Financial Analysts Research Foundation, 1991.

Wertz, W. F. and A. Donadio, "Collateralized Mortgage Obligations," *The CPA Journal*, 57:11, 1987, pp. 68–71.

9

Financial Engineering II: Derivative Instruments

Overview

In all the history of financial markets, no markets have ever grown or evolved as rapidly as have the derivative markets. Investment banks have played a major role in the development of these markets.[1] They innovate new products and act as dealers for the products. Indeed, so successful have been the dealer operations of these institutions at promoting the use of derivatives that these instruments are now used by industrial corporations, financial corporations, thrifts, banks, insurance companies, world organizations, and sovereign governments. Derivatives are used to reduce the cost of capital, manage risks, exploit economies of scale, arbitrage the world's capital markets, enter new markets, and create synthetic instruments. New users, new uses, and new variants emerge almost daily.

The term "derivative" has different meaning to different people. Technically speaking, at the broadest level, **derivative** includes any instrument or security whose value is derived from the value of some other asset, called the underlying asset. At this level, derivatives include exchange–traded products like futures and listed options; over–the–counter derivatives like swaps, caps, floors, and exotic options; mort-gage–backed and asset–backed products; and a slew of "structured" and

---

[1] Derivatives have been an important area of competition between commercial banks (both foreign and domestic) and investment banks from the inception of these products. Everything we say in this chapter with respect to investment banks is equally applicable to commercial banks. For discussion, see Brown and Smith (1988).

"hybrid" securities. In this chapter, we will limit ourselves to a narrower meaning which includes only swaps and over–the–counter options (caps, floors, exotics, etc.). We will start with a look at swaps, the cornerstone of the derivatives trade[2] and then turn our attention to options. In all cases, we limit our discussion to the simplest forms of these instruments—often referred to as "plain vanilla." These basic forms can be modified in an amazing number of ways, and they can be combined to structure, or engineer, sophisticated solutions to very complex problems.

History of the Swap Product

Quite simply, a **swap** is a contractual agreement in which two parties, called counterparties, agree to exchange a series of payments over a period of time. The first swaps were currency swaps. These were followed by interest rate swaps, commodity swaps, and equity swaps. Most recently, even more novel structures have been tried or proposed, including swaps pegged to real estate indexes, macroeconomic indexes, insurance claim rates, and environmental pollution rights.[3]

The first currency swap was engineered in London in 1979. During the two years that followed, the market remained small and obscure. This obscurity ended when, in 1981, Salomon Brothers put together what is now considered the landmark currency swap. This swap involved World Bank and IBM as counterparties and Salomon served the role of broker. The stature of the parties gave long–term credibility to currency swaps.

It was a short step from currency swaps to interest rate swaps. Like the currency swap, the first interest rate swap was engineered in London. This took place in 1981. The product was introduced to the United States the following year when the Student Loan Marketing Association (Sallie Mae) employed a fixed–for–floating interest rate swap to convert the interest rate character of some of its liabilities.

---

[2] The reader interested in a more detailed discussion of swaps and their uses, swap variants, swap pricing, swap documentation, and the management of a swap portfolio should see Kapner and Marshall (1990, 1991, 1993) or Marshall and Kapner (1992, 1994).

[3] See, for example, Marshall, Bansal, Herbst, and Tucker (1992).

Once established, the market for currency and interest rate swaps grew rapidly. From under $5 billion in notional principal outstandings at the end of 1982, the market grew to over $5 trillion by the end of 1992.[4]

The financial institutions that originated the swap product first saw themselves in the role of brokers. They would find potential counterparties with matched needs and, for a commission, would assist the parties in the negotiation of a swap agreement. The broking of swaps proved difficult because of the need for the contracting parties to reach agreement with respect to each and every contract provision. It wasn't long, however, before these institutions realized their potential as dealers; that is, they could make a more liquid market by playing the role of a counterparty. This was possible because of the existence of a large cash market for U.S. Treasury debt and well–developed futures markets in which the swap dealers could hedge their risk exposures.

By 1984, representatives from leading swap dealers began work on standardizing swap documentation. In 1985 this group organized itself into the International Swap Dealers Association (ISDA) and published the first standardized swap code. The code was revised in 1986. In 1987, the standardization efforts of the ISDA culminated in the publication of standard form agreements. Standardization of documentation dramatically reduced both the time and the cost of originating a swap. The ISDA documentation efforts have continued, and revised codes and forms capable of handling the latest swap market innovations continue to be developed.

Commodity swaps were first engineered in 1986 by the Chase Manhattan Bank. Their legality, however, was soon questioned by the Commodity Futures Trading Commission (CFTC), and for a time, a cloud hung over the market. The intervention of the CFTC brought that agency

---

[4] The true size of the swaps and related derivatives markets is not known. The only figures available are those compiled by the International Swap Dealers Association, recently renamed the International Swaps and Derivatives Association (ISDA), which periodically surveys its member firms. For a number of reasons, these figures significantly understate the true size of the markets. For example, the ISDA figures do not reflect the activity of nonreporting members, nonmember dealers, and swaps done directly between end users. In addition, many reporting dealers underreport the size of their derivative portfolios. The $5 trillion dollar figure reported here is taken from ISDA. Estimates of the true size of the market, including all types of swaps and other notional contracts, range from $7 to $15 trillion.

into conflict with the ISDA. At the same time, those institutions already involved in commodity swaps moved the bulk of their activity overseas.

In July of 1989, the CFTC reversed itself and granted swap contracts "safe harbor," provided that certain criteria were met. These criteria were of little consequence as, for the most part, they reflected current industry practice. By the end of 1989, the volume of commodity swaps outstanding was nearly $8 billion. While still small in comparison to interest rate and currency swaps, there appears to be tremendous potential for this market. Indeed, by the end of 1992, the market had grown in size to several hundred billion dollars.

Even faster growth accompanied the introduction of equity swaps. These were introduced by Bankers Trust Company in 1989. The new product soon attracted a number of major investment and commercial bank competitors, including Salomon Brothers, First Boston, J.P. Morgan, Morgan Stanley, and many others.

The Structure of a Generic Swap

All swaps are built around the same basic structure. Two parties, called **counterparties**, agree to make a series of payments to each other for some period of time, called the swap's tenor, or maturity. Typically, one party agrees to pay a fixed price on some quantity of underlying assets, called **notionals**, while the other party agrees to pay a floating price on the same or different notionals. These payments represent **service payments** in the same sense that interest is paid to service a loan. In addition to the service payments, the notionals themselves might be exchanged.

A swap may involve one exchange of notionals, two exchanges of notionals, a series of exchanges of notionals, or no exchanges of notionals. Most often, a swap involves one hypothetical exchange of notionals at the commencement of the swap and a hypothetical re-exchange of notionals upon the swap's termination. This is the basic or "plain vanilla" structure. By modifying the terms appropriately and/or adding specialty provisions, this simple structure can be converted to dozens of variants to suit specific end user needs.

The term **notionals**, which is used to describe the underlying assets on a swap, is itself intended to convey the hypothetical nature of the underlying assets and to distinguish them from real assets that are exchanged in the cash markets. The latter are called **actuals**. Notionals may take the form of quantities of money, in which case they are called **notional principals**, or quantities of a commodity.

It is very difficult to arrange a swap directly between two end users. A much more efficient structure is to involve a financial intermediary that serves as a counterparty to both end users. This is where the investment banks, in their role of dealers, come into the picture. A swap dealer becomes a counterparty to every swap it originates. On some swaps the swap dealer is the fixed–rate payer (floating–rate receiver), and on other swaps the dealer is the fixed–rate receiver (floating–rate payer). The swap dealer profits from the bid–ask spread it imposes on the swap coupon. For purposes of illustration, we will call one of the end–user counter-parties Counterparty A and the other Counterparty B.

The cash flows associated with a typical swap are illustrated in Figures 9.1, 9.2, and 9.3. Figure 9.1 depicts the initial exchange of notionals, which can be dispensed with on those swaps in which the exchange is purely hypothetical (most swaps); Figure 9.2 depicts the periodic service payments; and Figure 9.3 depicts the re–exchange of notionals, which, like the initial exchange of notions, can be dispensed with in those cases in which the notionals are purely hypothetical.

A swap by itself would generally not make much sense. But swaps do not exist in isolation. They are used in conjunction with appropriate cash market positions or transactions. There are three such basic transactions:

Figure 9.1
Swap: Initial Exchange of Notionals

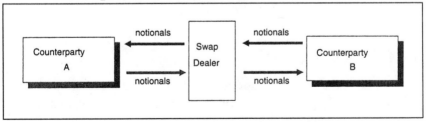

Figure 9.2
Swap: Periodic Service Payments
(required)

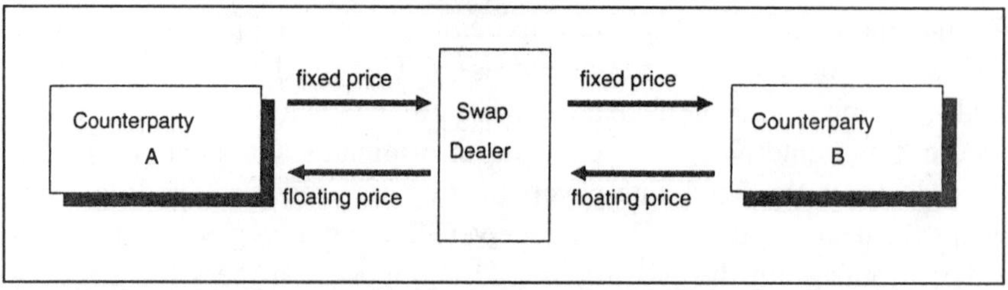

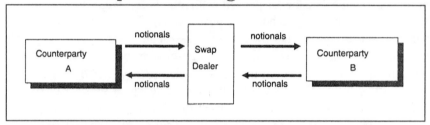

Figure 9.3
Swap: Re-exchange of Notionals

1. obtain actuals from the cash market;
2. make (receive) payments to (from) the cash market; or
3. supply actuals to the cash market.

These possibilities are summarized in Figure 9.4. The cash markets depicted in Figure 9.4 may be the same or different. By combining the cash market transactions with an appropriately structured swap, we can engineer a great many different outcomes.

Rate Swaps

Interest rate and currency swaps are often discussed together—in which case they are collectively called **rate swaps**. Since the inception of rate swaps, the floating–rate side has most often been tied to the London

Figure 9.4
Cash Market Transactions

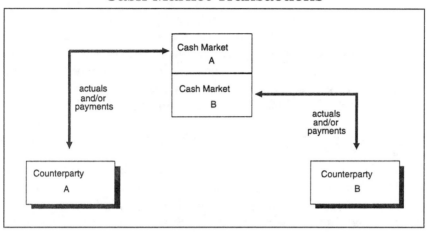

Interbank Offered Rate, known by the acronym **LIBOR**. LIBOR is the rate of interest charged on interbank loans of Eurocurrency deposits. While it is rarely made explicit, LIBOR is understood to be a quote on dollar deposits (Eurodollars). But nondollar LIBORs are also quoted. Deutschemark LIBOR, for example, would be denoted DEM LIBOR. All references to LIBOR in this chapter and elsewhere in this book are references to dollar LIBOR unless specifically indicated otherwise.

LIBOR quotes are available for various terms, including one–month deposits (1–M LIBOR), three–month deposits (3–M LIBOR), six–month deposits (6–M LIBOR), and one–year deposits (12–M LIBOR). Regardless of the length of the deposit, LIBOR, like all interest rates, is quoted on an annual basis.[5] The fixed–rate side of a rate swap is called the **swap coupon**.[6] It is important to note that differences between the yield conventions used to quote floating rates and fixed rates mean that these

---

[5] LIBOR is quoted on a money market basis; i.e., it is quoted on the assumption that a year consists of 360 days but the instrument pays interest each and every day.

[6] The swap coupon is usually quoted on a bond basis. This yield quotation method assumes that a year has 365 days and it pays interest each and every day.

two rates are not directly comparable without first making some conversions.

The floating–rate side of a swap need not be tied to LIBOR. It can be tied to some other readily identifiable rate that is not easily manipulated by an interested party. The rate can and often is tied to a rate index or based on an average of observations on a short–term rate or a rate index. Frequently used rates include certificates of deposit, commercial paper, T–bill, Fed funds, and the Twelfth District cost of funds. Nevertheless, the floating–rate side of most rate swaps are LIBOR–based.

Interest Rate Swaps

In interest rate swaps, the exchangeable notionals take the form of quantities of money and are, consequently, notional principals. In such a swap, the notional principals to be exchanged are identical in both currency and amount, and, therefore, can always be dispensed with. Furthermore, since the periodic service payments—called interest in this case—are also in the same currency, only the interest differential needs to be exchanged on settlement dates.

Interest rate swaps are often motivated by a desire to reduce the cost of financing. In these cases, one party has access to comparatively cheap fixed–rate funding but desires floating–rate funding, while another party has access to comparatively cheap floating–rate funding but desires fixed–rate funding. By entering into swaps with a swap dealer, both parties can obtain the form of financing they desire and simultaneously exploit their comparative borrowing advantages. For example, suppose that Party A is in need of 10–year debt financing. Party A has access to comparatively cheap floating–rate financing but desires a fixed–rate obligation. For purposes of illustration, assume that Party A can borrow at a floating rate of 6–M LIBOR + 50 bps, or at a semiannual (sa) fixed rate of 11.25 percent. As it happens, Party B is also in need of 10–year debt financing. Party B has access to comparatively cheap fixed–rate financing but desires a floating–rate obligation. For purposes of illustration, assume that Party B can borrow fixed rate at a semiannual rate of 10.25 percent and can borrow floating rate at 6–M LIBOR.

The swap dealer stands ready to enter a swap as either fixed–rate payer (floating–rate receiver) or floating–rate payer (fixed–rate receiver). In both cases, the dealer's floating rate is 6–M LIBOR. Suppose that, under its present pricing, if the dealer is to be the fixed–rate payer, it will pay a swap coupon of 10.40 percent (sa). If the dealer is to be the fixed–rate receiver, it requires a swap coupon of 10.50 percent (sa).

The financial engineers working for the swap dealer suggest that Party A issue floating–rate debt and Party B issue fixed–rate debt, and that they both enter into swaps with the swap dealer. Party A, now called Counterparty A, enters a swap, with the swap dealer acting as floating–rate payer; and Party B, now called Counterparty B, enters a swap, with the swap dealer acting as fixed–rate payer. While there are no exchanges of notional principals in these swaps, there are still three types of exchanges if we include the borrowings in the cash market. The full set of cash flows are illustrated in Figures 9.5, 9.6, and 9.7. Figure 9.5 depicts the initial borrowings in the cash markets; Figure 9.6 depicts debt service in the cash markets and the cash flows with the swap dealer; and Figure 9.7 depicts the repayment of principals in the cash market.

Figure 9.5
Interest Rate Swap with
Cash Market Transactions
(initial borrowing of principals)

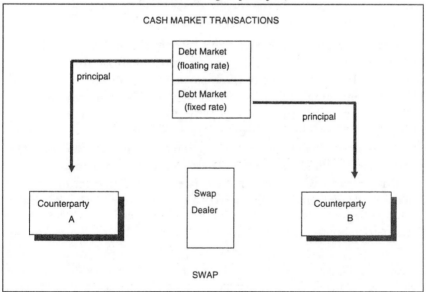

Figure 9.6
Interest Rate Swap with
Cash Market Transactions
(debt service payments with swap service payments)

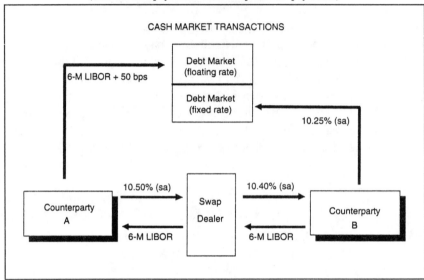

Examine Figure 9.6. Notice that Counterparty A pays LIBOR + 50 bps on its cash market obligation and receives LIBOR from the swap dealer. The LIBOR portions of these payments are, therefore, offsetting. The only remaining obligation of Counterparty A is to pay the swap dealer 10.50 percent. Thus, Counterparty A's final cost is approximately 11 percent.[7] Since direct borrowing of fixed rate in the cash market would have cost Counterparty A 11.25 percent, it is clear that Counterparty A has benefited by about 25 basis points by employing the swap.

Counterparty B is paying a fixed rate of 10.25 percent on its cash market borrowing and receiving 10.40 percent from the swap dealer.

---

[7] This is an approximation, because, as noted earlier, the 50–basis–point LIBOR differential is not directly comparable to the fixed rate. It must first be adjusted by multiplying by 365/360. After this adjustment, we see that the real cost to Counterparty A is closer to 11.01 percent.

Figure 9.7
Interest Rate Swap with
Cash Market Transactions
(repayment of principals)

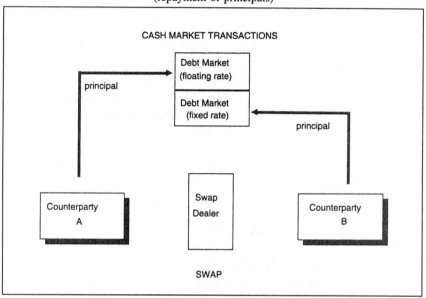

Thus, Counterparty B is ahead by 15 basis points. In addition, Counter-party B is paying the swap dealer LIBOR. Thus, the total cost of Counterparty B's debt is approximately LIBOR—15 basis points. Had Counterparty B borrowed floating rate directly, it would have paid LIBOR. Thus, we find that the swap has saved Counterparty B 15 basis points.

As a side point, notice that the swap dealer earns 10 basis points for its services in making a liquid swap market. This 10 basis points is the difference between the swap coupon received from Counterparty A and the swap coupon paid to Counterparty B. This bid–ask spread is the principal source of an investment bank's profit from making markets in swaps. Note also that the investment bank did not need to employ any of its own funds to derive this revenue, because the dealer is merely a conduit through which funds flow.

Interest rate swaps have many important uses besides lowering the cost of financing, but we do not have space to explore these in this book. Suggested reading is provided at the end of this chapter for those interested in more detailed discussion of swaps.

Currency Swaps

In a currency swap, the currencies in which the principals are denominated are different and usually (but not always) need to be exchanged. A currency swap is viable whenever one counterparty has comparatively cheaper access to one currency than it does to another. To illustrate, suppose that Counterparty A can borrow deutschemarks for seven years at a fixed rate of 9 percent and can borrow seven–year dollars at a floating rate of one–year LIBOR. Counterparty B, on the other hand, can

Figure 9.8
Currency Swap with
Cash Market Transactions
(initial borrowings and exchange of notional principal)

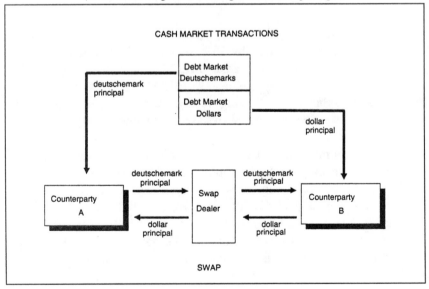

borrow seven–year deutschemarks at a rate of 10.1 percent and can borrow seven–year floating–rate dollars at a rate of one–year LIBOR. As it happens, Counterparty A needs floating–rate dollar financing and Counterparty B needs fixed–rate deutschemark financing.

The investment bank's financial engineers work out a solution using deutschemark–for–dollar currency swaps. The dealer is currently prepared to pay a fixed rate of 9.45 percent on deutschemarks against dollar LIBOR, and it is prepared to pay dollar LIBOR against a fixed rate of 9.55 percent on deutschemarks. The counterparties borrow in their respective cash market—Counterparty A borrows fixed–rate deutsche-marks and Counterparty B borrows floating–rate dollars—and then enter a swap. Figure 9.8 depicts the initial borrowings in the cash markets and the initial exchange of notional principals at the commencement of the swap. Figure 9.9 depicts the debt service in the cash markets and the

Figure 9.9
Currency Swap with
Cash Market Transactions
(debt service with swap payments)

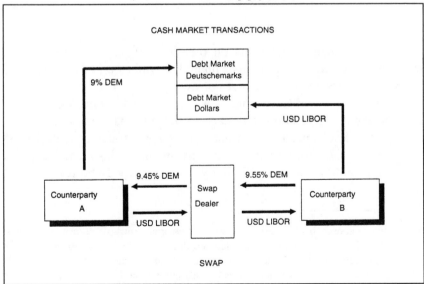

Figure 9.10
Currency Swap with
Cash Market Transactions

(repayment of actuals and re–exchanges of notional principal)

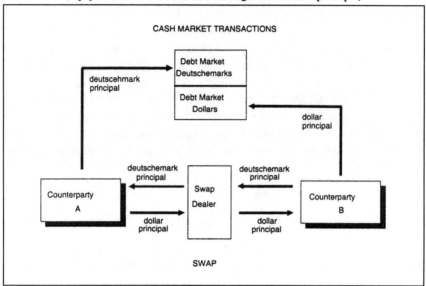

exchanges of interest payments on the swap. Figure 9.10 depicts the re–exchange of notional principals upon the termination of the swap and the repayment of the cash market borrowings.

Notice that while Counterparty A borrows deutschemarks, the swap converts the deutschemarks to dollars. Notice also that these dollars have a floating–rate character with a net cost of approximately LIBOR—45 basis points. This represents a 45 basis–point savings over a direct borrowing of floating rate.[8] Similarly, Counterparty B borrows dollars

---

[8] For purposes of this example, we are assuming that deutschemark interest differentials and dollar interest differentials are directly additive. We also assume that fixed–rate differentials and floating–rate differentials in the same currency are directly additive. Neither of these treatments is technically correct, but little is lost in employing these treatments for purposes of illustrating the concepts involved. The necessary

but uses the swap to convert the dollars to deutschemarks. These deutschemarks have a net cost of 9.55 percent. This represents a 55 basis–point savings over a direct borrowing of fixed–rate deutschemarks. Thus, we see that a swap can be used with the appropriate cash market transactions to convert both the currency denomination of a financing and the character of the interest cost.

Commodity Swaps

In a commodity swap, one counterparty makes periodic payments to the other at a fixed price for a given quantity of notional commodity, while the second counterparty pays the first counterparty a floating price (usually an average price based on periodic observations of the spot price) for the same quantity of notional commodity. As with interest rate swaps, no exchanges of notionals take place as part of the swap.

Consider a simple case. A crude oil producer (Counterparty A) wants to fix the price he receives for his oil for five years—his monthly production averages 8,000 barrels. At the same time, an oil refiner and chemicals manufacturer (Counterparty B) wants to fix the price he pays for oil for five years—his monthly need is 12,000 barrels. To obtain the desired outcomes, they enter into commodity (oil) swaps with a swap dealer but continue their transactions in actuals in the cash markets.

At the time these firms enter their swaps with the swap dealer, the swap dealer's midprice for setting the fixed–price leg on the appropriate grade of crude oil for swaps of this tenor is $18.25 a barrel. Counterparty B agrees to make monthly payments to the dealer at a rate of $18.30 a barrel and the swap dealer agrees to pay Counterparty B the average daily price for oil during the preceding month. At the same time, Counterparty A agrees to pay the swap dealer the average daily spot price for oil during the preceding month in exchange for payments from the dealer at the rate of $18.20 a barrel. As can be seen in Figure 9.11, these payments have the effect of fixing the price of crude oil for both the oil producer and the oil refiner.

The difference in the notional quantities in these two swaps raises an interesting point. If Counterparty A and Counterparty B had attempted a

---

adjustments are fully described in Kapner and Marshall (1990).

Figure 9.11
Commodity Swap with
Cash Market Transactions

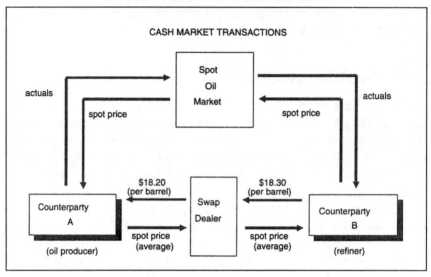

CASH MARKET TRANSACTIONS

swap with each other directly, the swap would likely have failed, since the parties have different notional requirements. But by using a swap dealer, both swaps are viable. The swap dealer can offset the risk from the mismatched notionals by entering a third swap as fixed–price payer on 4,000 barrels. And, until an appropriate counterparty can be found, the swap dealer can hedge in futures.

Equity Swaps

Equity swaps are swaps in which at least one leg is pegged to the return on a stock index. The other leg can be pegged to a floating rate of interest (such as LIBOR), can be fixed, or can be pegged to a different stock index. These swaps allow an end user to receive an equity return without holding equity; to hold an equity portfolio and yet to receive a fixed rate of return; or to hold a portfolio of domestic stocks and yet to receive an equity return from a portfolio of foreign stocks. Indeed, there are hundreds of uses to which such swaps can be put. Each of these three scenarios is depicted in Figures 9.12, 9.13, and 9.14, respectively.

Investment banks market equity swaps to portfolio managers as part of asset allocation strategies, to index fund managers who try to achieve a return identical to the return on a particular stock index, to institutions that are not permitted to hold stocks but who nevertheless desire an equity return, and so on.

Variants

There are two basic ways to create a swap variant. The first is to enter two or more separate commitments. Both might be swaps, or only one might be. For example, by entering a fixed–for–floating deutschemark/

Figure 9.12
Converting a Fixed Income Return
to an Equity Return

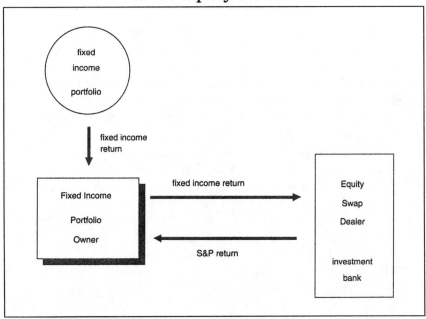

Figure 9.13
Converting an Equity Return
to a Fixed Income Return

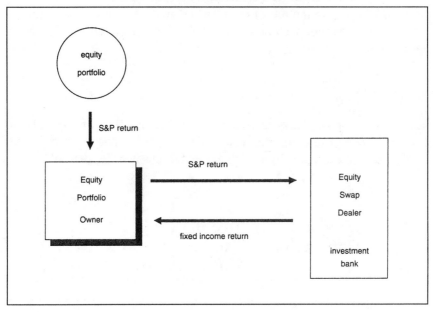

dollar currency swap as floating–rate dollar payer and simultaneously entering a dollar–based interest rate swap as floating–rate receiver, a counterparty can convert a fixed–rate deutschemark obligation to a fixed–rate dollar obligation. If both floating legs are tied to LIBOR, then this particular combination is called a **circus swap**. For all practical purposes, a circus swap creates a fixed–for–fixed currency swap.

The circus swap is depicted in Figure 9.15. Only the interest flows are shown in this exhibit, and only those flows between Counterparty A and the swap dealer. The end result, after cancellation of the two floating–rate sides, is that the fixed–rate deutschemark obligation has been converted to a fixed–rate dollar obligation.

The second way to create a swap variant is to alter the terms of the swap itself. There are a great many ways by which a swap can be tailored to suit some specific end user need. For example, while the notionals are

Figure 9.14
Converting a Foreign Equity Return
to a Domestic Equity Return

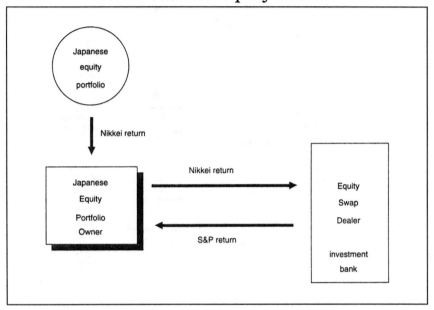

normally nonamortizing over the life of a swap, they can be made amortizing; swap agreements can be written with options to extend or to shorten their tenors; swaps can be entered with delayed setting of the swap coupon; and so on.[9]

The point of this discussion is that all swap structures are predicated on the same basic model. By varying the terms of a swap, by combining swaps, or by combining swaps with other instruments, a great many novel structures can be engineered.

---

[9] For a discussion of some of the many swap variants, see Abken (1991).

Figure 9.15
The Circus Swap

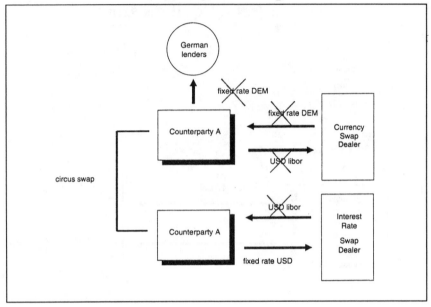

Swap Dealer's Role

The explosive growth of the swaps trade would not have been possible had the investment banks that first entered the business as swap brokers not transformed themselves into swap dealers. The swap dealer stands ready to enter a swap as a counterparty and, with equal willingness, to play the role of fixed–rate payer or fixed–rate receiver.

For many years, the swap dealers who operated out of investment banks backed their positions with the general credit of their firms. But after some concern arose about the creditworthiness of several investment banks, following the demise of Drexel and the troubles at Salomon Brothers (after the Treasury auction scandal), many investment banks spun their swap operations off into wholly owned subsidiaries. These subsidiaries, such as Salomon Brothers' Swapco unit,[10] are typically overcollateralized to win the highest possible credit rating. Further, they are often domiciled offshore to circumvent burdensome U.S. regulatory restrictions and potential future regulatory restrictions.

Unlike a swap made directly between two end users, a swap dealer does not need to match all terms of the first swap with Counterparty A to the second swap with Counterparty B. Moreover, the swap dealer does not require an immediately available Counterparty B in order to enter a swap with Counterparty A. The trick is for the swap dealer to keep the overall exposure associated with its swap book[11] properly hedged. In other words, the swap dealer strives to maintain a balanced book, but insofar as any imbalances exist, the swap dealer will hedge them.

In order to hedge effectively, swap dealers need a liquid debt market trading a very low–risk form of debt and having a continuum of maturities. The one debt market that meets all of these requirements is the market for U.S. Treasury debt. Thus, if a swap dealer enters an interest rate swap as fixed–rate payer against 6–M LIBOR, it could simply short the appropriate quantity of six–month T–bills and use the proceeds to purchase intermediate– or long–term Treasury notes or bonds.

Consider an example. Suppose that a swap dealer, such as Swapco, is approached by a client firm in need of a $25 million fixed–for–floating interest rate swap having a five–year tenor. The client wants to be the floating–rate payer (fixed–rate receiver). The dealer agrees to pay the client 9.26 percent (sa) on $25 million in exchange for the client paying the dealer 6–M LIBOR on $25 million. The dealer immediately hedges by selling $25 million (face value) of T–bills and uses the proceeds from this short sale to purchase $25 million (face value) of five–year Treasury notes, as depicted in Figure 9.16. The dealer is now hedged.

---

[10] Swapco was created to provide Salomon Brothers with a triple–A (AAA) rated entity from which to conduct the bank's derivatives business (see *Investment Dealers' Digest*, February 15, 1993). Swapco is supported by a large capital base ($175 million as of February 1993). Interestingly, it was created with a clause that provides for forced liquidation in the case of certain "trigger" events. For a more general discussion of termination provisions as they pertain to swaps, see Kapner and Marshall (1990).

[11] As mentioned in an earlier chapter, the term "book" is the investment banking community's term for a portfolio and should be read as such.

Figure 9.16
Dealer's Position with Hedge in Cash Markets

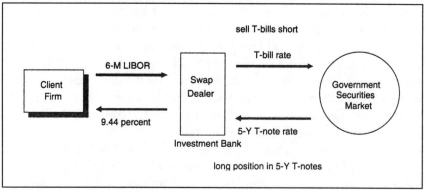

As a practical matter, a swap dealer will generally hedge in Treasury futures or Eurodollar futures, but cash market hedges, as depicted here, can be used as well. Notice that the hedge leaves the swap dealer with some risk on the floating–rate side, because the dealer is receiving LIBOR and paying the T–bill rate. To the degree that the changes in LIBOR and the changes in the T–bill rate are not perfectly correlated (and they are not), there is some residual risk.

When a swap dealer identifies a matched swap, or at least matches a portion of the notional principal on the first swap, it will lift an appropriate portion of its hedge in Treasuries (or futures). Thus, by continuously adjusting its cash or futures market positions, a swap dealer can effectively run a swap book without becoming overly concerned about matching individual swaps.

The use of the Treasury markets to hedge a swap book helps explain why most of the early swap dealers were also primary government securities dealers. Of course, almost all primary government securities dealers are either investment banks or commercial banks.

Over–the–Counter Options

We now turn to options. Investment banks, acting through their derivatives groups (the same groups that make markets in swaps), have become heavily involved in engineering an incredible variety of options.[12] These options are often tailored to meet very specific client needs; therefore, an over–the–counter (OTC) environment is the proper setting for such a market. The OTC options market competes, to some degree, with the listed markets in standardized exchange–traded options.

As usually defined, an **option** is a "right without an obligation." Most often this is a right to buy or sell some asset at a set price for a specified period of time. The former are called **call options** and the latter are called **put options**. The set price at which the option can be exercised is called its strike (or exercise) price. The asset on which the option is written is called the underlying asset.

Derivatives dealers make markets in call and put options, and these options are similar to the more standardized options that trade on options exchanges. But derivatives dealers also write more sophisticated options that are quite different from anything that trades on an exchange.

Most OTC options are cash settle, as opposed to providing for the physical delivery of the underlying asset. This means that at the end of the option's life (called expiration), or on its settlement date(s), the option seller, called the **writer**, and the option purchaser, called the **holder**, settle up in cash for the amount by which the option is in–the–money. The option writer must give this sum to the option holder. In the case of a call option, the option is in–the–money by the amount that the current market price of the underlying asset exceeds the strike price of the option. In the case of a put option, the option is in–the–money by the amount that the strike price exceeds the current market price of the underlying asset.

The attractive feature of options is that the payoff to the option holder on the option's expiration date or settlement date can never be negative. If the option is out–of–the–money on the option's expiration or settlement date, the option holder has no obligation to pay anything. Thus, the option holder can win but cannot lose. Indeed, the value of an option at its expiration is given by a "Max" function of the form: Max[in–the–money, 0]. This means that the option's payoff to the holder is the larger of the amount by which the option is in–the–money or zero.

---

[12] For a more detailed discussion of options, see Baird (1993), Kawaller (1992), Tucker (1991), Marshall (1989), Bodurtha and Courtadon (1988), and Ritchken (1987).

The opportunity to win gives an option value, and, of course, there are no free lunches. Thus, the option purchaser must pay an up–front fee to the option writer for the right conveyed by the option. This fee is called the **option premium** and represents the purchase price of the option.

Most options purchased from (or sold to) investment banks in the OTC markets are transacted at a wholesale level. The clients are usually institutional investors, and the transactions are very large. There are a number of common motivations for these transactions: Many options are bought or sold to synthesize some other type of asset. For example, the proper combination of assets can synthesize the underlying asset. And at times, it might be more cost–effective to synthesize the underlying asset than to purchase (or sell) it directly. By this same logic, and as demonstrated earlier with swaps, a corporation will sometimes find it cheaper to finance itself using synthetic structures than by issuing the desired liability directly. Another common corporate use of options is to hedge other positions on the firm's balance sheet. A firm often has an exposure to a price risk (including interest rate risk and exchange rate risk), and options can be used to hedge the firm against unfavorable changes in this price while, at the same time, preserving the opportunity to benefit from favorable price changes. Sometimes the nature of a firm's assets and/or liabilities results in the firm possessing the equivalent of an option, but one that is embedded in its other assets. These embedded options have value for the firm, but the firm might not need them. The firm can often "monetize" the embedded option by writing an option (i.e., selling it to an investment bank) that has the same characteristics as the one that is embedded in its balance sheet. This generates immediate cash for the firm. Investment banks' derivatives groups assist firms in identifying these embedded options.

Investment banks are also heavily involved in the design and issuance of "structured securities" through their structured products groups. **Structured securities** are engineered by combining a number of different instruments in order to create a single instrument with a unique set of investment characteristics. Structured securities often have at least one option component, and the structured products group that designs and assembles these securities often purchases (or sells) the option components from the investment bank's derivatives group. Thus, the derivatives group and the structured products group work closely together.

The valuation of options is an extremely complex undertaking requiring the most sophisticated statistical and quantitative skills.[13] Indeed, derivative groups, and other investment banking areas where options play an important role, employ many highly skilled experts with advanced degrees in finance, mathematics, statistics, engineering, and physics.

In addition to their cash settlement nature, many options written/purchased by an investment bank's derivatives group are multiperiod in nature. These are quite different from the single–period calls and puts that trade on options exchanges.

Multiperiod options are particularly interesting, because they are easily combined with other instruments, such as swaps, to engineer interesting outcomes (called payoff profiles) and to achieve very specialized solutions to financial problems. We will look at some of the ways that options can be combined with swaps later in this chapter. We now take a brief look at some of the more common option types traded by investment bank derivative groups.

Interest Rate Caps

From the perspective of the hedger, cash–settled options, like those written on stock indexes, are limited in their usefulness to those situations in which the hedger is concerned about fluctuations in prices over a short span of time. Think of this span as a single period. In other words, a single cash settlement will terminate the option on its expiration date. But suppose that the firm has a risk exposure that spans multiple periods, one following another. Such a situation might, for instance, occur if the firm is paying a semiannual floating rate of interest on its long–term debt and is concerned about a rise in rates.

Theoretically, this exposure can be hedged by stringing together a series of single–period interest rate options—one expiring every six months. But this is impractical for two reasons. First, it assumes that each contract expiration month will be sufficiently liquid so that the firm can

---

[13] The reader interested in the mathematics of option pricing should consider several of the following: Ritchken (1987), Cox and Rubinstein (1985), Kutner (1988), and Tucker (1991).

roll over its option contract into a new contract without substantial liquidity costs. Second, it assumes that options with every required expiration month into the very distant future are currently available. Both assumptions are unrealistic. In practice, only the front one or two contract months tend to be liquid—if indeed any are liquid—and conventional calls and puts are almost never written with expiration dates more than a year into the future.

The solution to this problem involves special over–the–counter options traded in dealer markets. These options are called interest rate caps and interest rate floors. We begin with **interest rate caps**, known more simply as **caps**. The writer of a cap pays the cap holder each time the contract's reference rate of interest is above the contract's **cap rate** of interest (also called the **ceiling rate** and, more generically, the **contract rate**) on a settlement date. The cap rate serves the same function as the strike price on conventional single–period options. By its structure, a cap provides a multiperiod hedge against increases in interest rates. It is important to note that even though caps are multiperiod options, the full premiums are ordinarily paid up–front.

Let's take a few moments to examine the structure of a cap and the settlement procedures more carefully. The cap dealer and the dealer's customer enter an agreement in which they specify a term for the cap (such as two years or five years), a reference rate of interest (RR), a cap rate (CR), the cap's notional principal (NP), and the settlement dates. As with swaps, the term of the cap is called its tenor. On the first settlement date, the cap writer pays the cap holder a sum determined by Equation 9.1. This sum is recalculated on the calculation date that precedes each settlement date. If the dealer is the cap writer, the dealer will pay the customer any amount due. If the dealer is the cap holder, the customer will pay the dealer any amount due.

$$\text{Dealer Pays} = D \times \text{MAX}[RR - CR,\, 0] \times NP \times LP \qquad (9.1)$$

In Equation 9.1, D denotes a dummy variable that takes the value +1 if the dealer is the cap seller and −1 if the dealer is the cap purchaser; MAX denotes the "MAX function," NP denotes the notional principal, and LP denotes the length of the period. The value LP will depend on the choice of reference rate and the frequency of payments. For example, LIBOR is quoted actual over 360. Thus, LP for 6–M LIBOR will typically be between 181 days and 184 days, expressed as a fraction of a year; i.e., 181/360 and 184/360. If the calculation results in a positive value (which can happen only if the dealer is the cap writer), then the dealer pays the client. If the calculation results in a negative value (which can happen only if the dealer is the cap purchaser), then the client pays the dealer. If the calculation produces the value zero, then no payments are made.

We can use Equation 9.1 to determine the payoff profile for a cap. A **payoff profile** is a visual depiction of the financial outcomes from holding an option (other financial instrument). The payoff profile is drawn for a single settlement date, but it looks the same for each settlement date covered by the cap. From the cap purchaser's perspective, such a payoff profile appears in Figure 9.17.

Figure 9.17
Payoff Profile for a Cap Purchaser
(per settlement period)

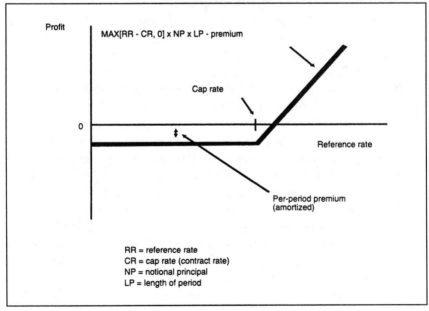

RR = reference rate
CR = cap rate (contract rate)
NP = notional principal
LP = length of period

Those readers familiar with options will recognize that a cap's payoff profile looks identical to that for a long call. But this is misleading. A call option usually depicts "price" rather than "rate" on the horizontal axis. If price is substituted for rate on the horizontal axis of the cap's payoff profile, the payoff profile actually looks like that of a long put on a debt instrument. The reason for this is that rates (yields) and prices are inversely related. This demonstrates that caps are analogous to put options for purposes of developing hedge positions and can accurately be described as multiperiod puts. (Nevertheless, because of the shape of the payoff profile, they are most often described as multiperiod calls.)

The premiums on multiperiod options are typically stated as a percentage of the notional principal and paid up–front. For example, a four–year semiannual cap having an appropriate cap rate might be available for a premium of 1.85 percent of the notional principal. Since the premium is paid up–front in a single lump sum, the payoff profile must reflect the amortized premium to be truly representative.

Most cap dealers, like swap dealers, operate out of the derivative groups of investment banks and commercial banks. Dealers both buy and sell caps and profit, as usual, from a spread between the bid price and the ask price. For example, consider a dealer making a market in 3–year 6–M LIBOR caps with a cap rate of 8 percent. The dealer might bid 1.28 percent and offer 1.34 percent. In other words, the dealer will write a cap for a premium of 1.34 percent and buy a cap for a premium of 1.28 percent. The difference between the bid and ask, 0.06 percent (6 basis points), is the dealer's bid–ask spread.

The following example shows an interest rate cap at work. Suppose that it is currently February 15, 1993. A firm in need of a 5–year interest rate cap on 6–M LIBOR approaches an investment bank's derivatives group, which makes markets in caps. The firm and dealer agree to a cap rate of 5 percent, notional principal of $50 million, and settlement dates of August 15 and February 15. The firm pays the dealer the up–front fee (i.e., premium) for writing the cap. Now suppose that the reference rate (6–M LIBOR) at the time of rate setting for the first payment is 5.48 percent. Since the reference rate exceeds the cap rate, the dealer must make a payment to the firm. The amount of this payment is determined by Equation 9.1. Substituting the values +1 for D, 5.48 percent for the reference rate, 5 percent for the cap rate, $50 million for the notional principal, and 181/360 for the LP, we obtain a payment of $120,667. The

Table 9.1
The Series of Payments on the Cap

Payment Date	Value of the Reference Rate	Value of the Cap Rate	LP	Payment
15 Aug 1993	3.56	5.00	181/360	$0
15 Feb 1994	4.24	5.00	184/360	0
15 Aug 1994	4.89	5.00	181/360	0
15 Feb 1995	4.78	5.00	184/360	0
15 Aug 1995	5.48	5.00	181/360	120,667
15 Feb 1996	5.18	5.00	184/360	46,000
15 Aug 1996*	5.94	5.00	182/360	237,611
15 Feb 1997	7.34	5.00	184/360	598,000
15 Aug 1997	6.08	5.00	181/360	271,500
15 Feb 1998	4.67	5.00	184/360	0
				$1,273,778

*Note: 1996 is a leap year, and thus there is one extra day in the 15 August 1996 payment formula.

full set of payments to the firm on this particular cap might look something like that depicted in Table 9.1. (In Table 9.1, the indicated values for the reference rate are for illustrative purposes only and do not represent actual rates on any specific dates.)

Since caps are multiperiod options, the simplest way to price a cap is to decompose it into the actual series of single–period options to which it is equivalent. This series of single–period options is sometimes called a **strip**. The fair value of each of the options in the strip can then be determined by using an appropriate single–period option pricing model. The sum of these fair values is the fair value of the cap. The dealer would then add (or subtract) a sum to this fair value to obtain the price at which it would sell (or buy) such a cap. As noted earlier, the difference between the dealer's bid and ask prices is just another bid–ask spread.[14]

---

[14] As an aside, recognition that a cap is equivalent to a strip of single–period options is also the basis for amortizing the cap premium for purposes of accurately portraying the payoff profiles.

As already noted, caps are priced as a percentage of the notional principal. Thus a cap, like the one just described, priced at 1.85 would require an up–front payment by the dealer's customer of $925,000 (i.e., $50 million × 0.0185). On this particular cap, the dealer ultimately paid out a total of $1,273,778. There was no way, of course, to know in advance what the total payout would be. It could easily have been much less than $925,000, and it also could easily have been much more.

There are many uses for interest rate caps, but the most common is to impose an upper limit to the cost of floating–rate debt. For example, suppose a firm raises debt capital by issuing a 5–year floating rate note paying 6–M LIBOR plus 80 basis points. The firm's management decides that it can handle an annual interest expense up to 10.8 percent but cannot afford to go above that figure. To limit the potential interest expense on this floating–rate note, the firm buys the cap described here from a cap dealer. Any time 6–M LIBOR exceeds 10 percent on the rate reset date for the note, the firm must pay more than 10.8 percent to its lenders. But with the cap in place, the dealer will pay the firm a sum equal to the excess over the 10.8 percent cost; therefore, the firm's net interest expense on its floating–rate note is limited to a maximum of 10.8 percent. On the other hand, when LIBOR is below 10 percent, the firm is paying less than 10.8 percent to its lenders, and so it does not need

Figure 9.18
Capped Floating Rate Debt

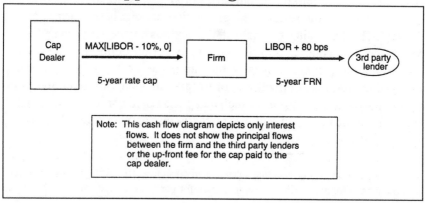

Note: This cash flow diagram depicts only interest flows. It does not show the principal flows between the firm and the third party lenders or the up-front fee for the cap paid to the cap dealer.

Figure 9.19
A Rate–Capped Swap

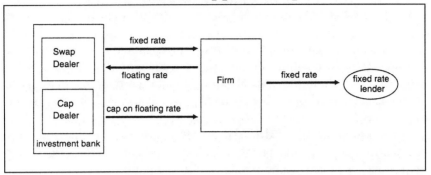

offsetting payments from the dealer. These cash flows are illustrated in Figure 9.18.

Financial engineers often combine interest rate caps with interest rate swaps and/or currency swaps. This produces **rate–capped swaps**. Consider a simple example. A firm wants rate–capped floating–rate debt, but the firm has a comparative advantage in the fixed–rate market. It can thus reduce its borrowing cost if it borrows at a fixed rate, swaps its fixed–rate payments for floating–rate payments with a swap dealer, and then caps its floating–rate payments to the swap dealer with an interest rate cap. The interest payment flows associated with these transactions are depicted in Figure 9.19. For obvious reasons, there are economies of scale for swap dealers to make markets in rate caps also.

Interest Rate Floors

An **interest rate floor** or, more simply, a **floor**, is a multiperiod interest rate option identical to a cap except that the floor writer pays the floor purchaser when the reference rate (RR) drops below the floor rate (FR). (As with interest rate caps, the floor rate is sometimes called the **contract rate**.) Let's again assume that the dealer is the seller of the option, and a customer of the dealer is the purchaser. In this case, the dealer will pay the customer a cash sum, based on a settlement formula, whenever the reference rate is below the floor rate on a rate reset date. The cash settlement formula, which is repeated on each settlement date, is given by Equation 9.2.

$$\text{Dealer Pays} = D \times \text{MAX}[FR - RR, 0] \times NP \times LP \qquad (9.2)$$

Notice that Equation 9.2 is identical to Equation 9.1 except that we have reversed the positions of the strike price (cap rate in the case of the cap and floor rate in the case of the floor) and the reference rate in the formula. The payoff profiles associated with Equation 9.2 are depicted in Figure 9.20.

The premium depicted in the payoff profile for the floor, like the premium depicted in the payoff profile for the cap, is a single–period equivalent obtained by amortizing the full premium paid at the time the floor is purchased.

Just as with interest rate caps, financial engineers find many uses for interest rate floors. The most common usage is to place a floor on the

Figure 9.20
Payoff Profile for a Floor Purchaser
(per settlement period)

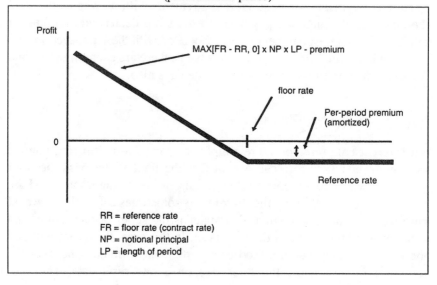

interest income from a floating–rate asset. Let's consider a simple case. An insurance company has obtained funds by selling 7 percent 10–year fixed–rate annuities. These annuities constitute fixed–rate liabilities. Because the insurance company's managers believe that interest rates will rise, they decide to invest the proceeds from the sale of the annuities in floating–rate assets (six–month T–bills) that are currently yielding 7.25 percent. Management's plan is to sell the floating–rate assets after rates rise and then invest the funds in fixed–rate assets.

While management's plan seems quite rational— i.e., fix interest costs now by the sale of the annuities while interest rates are low, invest in floating–rate assets until rates rise, and then move to fixed–rate assets—management still runs the risk that its interest rate projections might prove wrong. To deal with this risk, a financial engineer suggests the purchase of an interest rate floor. The firm buys a 10–year floor from a floor dealer with a floor rate of 7 percent and the six–month T–bill rate as the reference rate. For this floor, the firm pays the dealer an up–front premium of 2.24 percent, which, we'll suppose, is equivalent to an annual percentage cost of 0.34 percent. The firm is now protected from declines in rates. The cash flow diagram associated with this structure is depicted in Figure 9.21.

Figure 9.21
Using an Interest Rate Floor to Protect Return

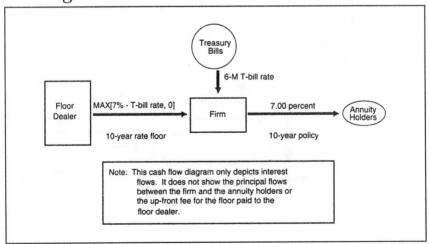

As it happened, management's interest rate projections proved wrong—at least for a time. Rates declined and stayed below the floor rate for four years. During this time, the insurance company received payments from the dealer. These payments made it possible for the insurance company to meet its obligations to the holders of its annuity policies. About four and a half years after the commencement of the floor, interest rates began to rise, and about five years after the commencement of the floor, the insurance company converted its floating–rate assets into five–year fixed–rate assets yielding 8.375 percent. At the same time, the insurer sold what remained of the floor back to the dealer for 0.82 percent. While the insurance company held it, the floor performed exactly as required. It spared the firm serious financial damage by guaranteeing a minimum return on its floating–rate assets.

Like interest rate caps, interest rate floors can be, and often are, combined with swaps. A typical cash flow diagram for a swap/floor combination is depicted in Figure 9.22.

Figure 9.22
Using a Floor to Achieve a Minimum Return

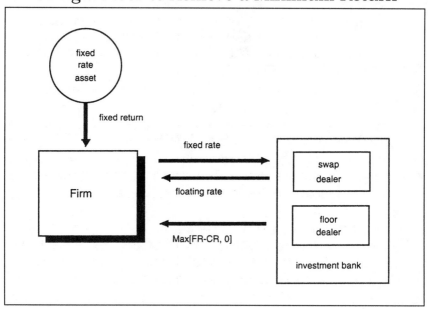

As depicted in Figure 9.22, a firm has purchased a fixed–rate asset and then used a swap to convert it to a floating–rate asset. To assure itself of a minimum level of return on its synthetic floating–rate asset, the firm has purchased a floor.

The examples we used to illustrate the cap and the floor both involved end users who were purchasers of these interest rate options. Not all end users will be purchasers. One interesting situation, in which the end user is a floor seller, involves a combination of a cap and a floor known as a **collar**. We consider this type of interest rate option in the next section.

Interest Rate Collars

An **interest rate collar** is a combination of a cap and a floor in which the purchaser of the collar buys a cap and simultaneously sells a floor. Collars can be constructed from two separate transactions (one involving a cap and one involving a floor) or they can be combined into a single transaction. A collar has the effect of locking its purchaser into a floating rate of interest that is bounded on both the high side and the low side. This is sometimes called "locking into a band" or "swapping into a band."

Consider an example. Suppose that a firm holds fixed–rate assets that are yielding 10 percent. These assets are funded with floating–rate liabilities tied to the prime rate. The current rate on these liabilities is 8 percent, and the firm wants to cap the cost at 9.5 percent (called a **prime cap**). But, as it happens, the cap dealer wants an up–front premium which translates into an effective annual percentage cost of 0.5 percent for the prime cap. The firm feels that this is too high a price to pay. The firm discovers, however, that it can sell a prime floor with a floor rate of 7 percent for a premium equivalent to an effective annual percentage return of 0.45 percent. Since the firm is the seller of the floor, it receives the premium. The firm decides to buy the cap and sell the floor—effectively purchasing a collar.

When prime rises above 9.5 percent, the dealer pays the firm the difference. When prime falls below 7 percent, the firm pays the dealer the difference. From the firm's perspective, its annual costs are now bounded between 7 percent and 9.5 percent. Since its interest revenue exceeds its interest cost, it has locked in a source of net revenue for the firm, although the amount of the net revenue can vary within the bounds

Figure 9.23
Payoff Profile for a Collar Purchaser
(per settlement period)

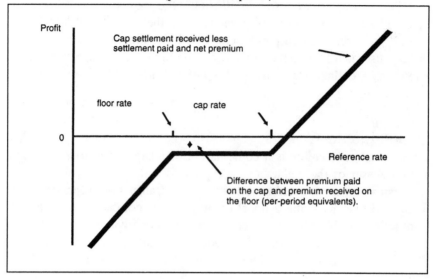

Profit

Cap settlement received less
settlement paid and net premium

floor rate

cap rate

0

Reference rate

Difference between premium paid
on the cap and premium received on
the floor (per-period equivalents).

Figure 9.24
An Interest Rate Collar at Work

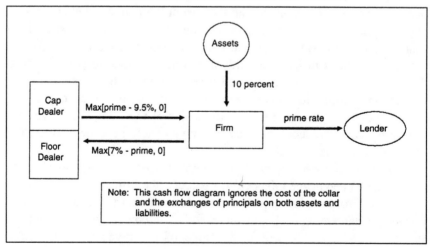

Assets

10 percent

Cap
Dealer

Max[prime - 9.5%, 0]

Firm

prime rate

Lender

Floor
Dealer

Max[7% - prime, 0]

Note: This cash flow diagram ignores the cost of the collar
and the exchanges of principals on both assets and
liabilities.

dictated by the collar. The payoff profile for the interest rate collar is depicted in Figure 9.23, and the cash flow diagram is depicted in Figure 9.24.

By entering a collar, the firm is able to place an interest rate cap on its floating–rate liabilities while simultaneously reducing the cost of the cap with the premium received from the sale of the floor. The cost to the firm, of course, is the payouts the firm must make to the floor dealer should the reference rate fall below the floor rate. This potential payout by the firm in a low–rate environment is often of less concern than its uncapped payouts in a high–rate environment, and, consequently, the collar is considered an attractive way to cap floating–rate debt.

Just as financial engineers often combine caps and floors with swaps, so also can collars be combined with swaps. Such a combination is called a **collar swap** or **mini–max swap**. The cash flow diagrams for a collar swap are depicted in Figure 9.25.

An investment bank making markets ("running a book") in caps, floors, and collars has an obvious interest in hedging the exposures associated with its positions in these instruments. The design of these hedging strategies is also the work of financial engineers. The hedging strategies employed by derivatives dealers are analogous to those employed by the investment bank's bond dealers and relative–value traders discussed in earlier chapters.

Figure 9.25
A Collar Swap at Work

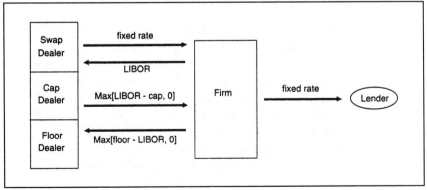

Miscellaneous Interest Rate Options

Investment banks' derivatives groups routinely make markets in a great number of other types of options. Some of these are options on other derivative instruments. Others are complex options quite different from anything that came before. We will briefly consider just a few of these, including participating caps, captions, swaptions, Asian options, and lookback options.

A **participating cap** is structured for the end user who is in need of an interest rate cap, but who is unable or unwilling to pay the up–front cost of the cap. The end user could reduce the cost of the cap by entering into a collar, but the collar reduces the benefits from a decline in rates, and the end user may not be willing to pay this price. One solution, the participating cap, is for the purchaser to pay the dealer a portion of the difference between the reference rate and the cap rate when the reference rate is below the cap rate, and for the cap writer to pay the cap purchaser the usual full difference between the reference rate and the cap rate when the reference rate is above the cap rate. The payment formula for the participating cap appears as Equation 9.3.

$$\text{Dealer Pays} = D \times \{\text{MAX}[RR - CR, 0] + (-PF \times \text{MAX}[CR - RR, 0])\} \times NP \times LP \tag{9.3}$$

Here, RR denotes the reference rate, CR denotes the cap rate, and PF denotes the percentage factor. All other notation is the same as that used earlier for caps and floors.

Let's consider a simple case. A firm in need of a five–year cap on a floating–rate liability tied to 1–year LIBOR approaches a cap dealer. The firm wants its rate capped at 10 percent on notional principal of $40 million. The dealer agrees to sell such a cap for an up–front premium of 2.75 percent. The firm cannot afford to pay such a large up–front fee, so the dealer suggests a participating cap. The firm will pay the dealer 30 percent of the difference between the reference rate and the cap rate (10 percent) whenever the reference rate is below the cap rate. In return, the dealer will pay the firm the full difference between the reference rate and the cap rate whenever the reference rate exceeds the cap rate. The firm agrees.

One year later, on the first settlement date, the reference rate (1–year LIBOR) stands at 9.42 percent. (The value of the reference rate is set on the prior reset date.) Plugging the values into Equation 9.3, we obtain the sum – $70,566.67.

$$
\begin{aligned}
\text{Dealer Pays} &= + 1 \times \{\text{MAX}[9.42\% - 10.00\%, 0] + \\
&\quad (-30\% \times \text{MAX}[10.00\% - 9.42\%,0])\} \\
&\quad \times \$40 \text{ million} \times 365/360 \\
&= -\$70,566.67
\end{aligned}
$$

Since this value is negative, the firm is paying the dealer. This calculation is repeated for each settlement period for five years.

The second special type of interest rate option is actually an "option on an option." Technically, it is a call option on a cap. This type of interest rate option, called a **caption**, was introduced in the mid 1980s.[15]

The question that immediately occurs is "why an option on an option?" The answer is surprisingly simple. Sometimes a firm wants to lock in the right to interest rate risk protection but is not really sure that it will need the protection, or the firm may feel that a better alternative may become available if it waits awhile. In these situations, financial engineers will suggest a caption or a caption–like instrument.

Consider an example. The chief financial officer (CFO) of a firm is considering a seven–year floating–rate financing. He will be making a pitch to the firm's board for permission to go ahead. The CFO knows that the board will be concerned about the firm's exposure on a floating–rate financing, and so the firm will need an interest rate cap. The CFO's investment bank, which makes markets in options, assigns a financial engineer to work with the CFO. This engineer suggests a 10 percent interest rate cap currently available for an up–front premium of 2.25 percent. But the CFO does not know if the board will approve his funding plans, so he cannot commit immediately. The board will decide in two weeks. But by the time the board does approve the plan, the cost of the cap may have risen. To deal with this problem, the investment

---

[15] The term "caption" is a registered servicemark of Marine Midland Bank.

bank's financial engineers suggest an option on the cap that is good for three weeks. For this option, the CFO agrees to pay the investment bank a premium of, say, 0.15 percent.

If the board approves the funding proposal, the CFO can notify the investment bank that he is exercising the firm's option on the cap. The investment bank then commits to a cap on the original terms—i.e., an up–front fee of 2.25 percent. If the board rejects the funding plan, the CFO lets the option on the cap expire.

Just as an investment bank can make a market in options on caps, it can also make a market in options on floors. These are not nearly as widely used as options on caps, however, and so we will not address them.

Another interesting and widely used option is the **swaption**. A swaption is an option on a swap. Such options can be written on interest rate swaps, currency swaps, commodity swaps, and equity swaps. The concept is nearly identical to an option on a cap. The end user and the swap dealer agree to the terms of a swap. The end user, however, cannot or does not want to make an immediate commitment to the swap. At the same time, the end user cannot afford to take the chance that the market will evolve unfavorably between now and the time when the end user can commit. To lock in the terms of the swap, the end user agrees to purchase a swaption from the swap dealer. Thus, the dealer guarantees the terms of the swap for some period of time—perhaps one month, for example—during which the end user can choose to exercise the swaption or simply let it expire. Of course, the end user will be required to pay a premium for the swaption. This premium must be paid whether the end user chooses to exercise the swaption or not.

In recent years, investment banks have become very creative in developing and customizing options. Many of these options are so different from anything that came before that they are called exotic options. Examples of **exotic options** that investment banks' derivative groups are actively involved in trading include Asian options, lookback options, and many others. **Asian options** (also called **average rate options**) are options in which the payoff on a settlement date is based on the average value of the reference rate over the applicable period; a **lookback option's** payoff on a settlement date is based on the highest (or lowest) value of the reference rate over the applicable period.

Credit Risk

Derivative positions expose investment banks to **credit risk**. This is the risk that a dealer's counterparty to a swap or an option (if the dealer bought the option) might default, and that such a default will result in financial injury to the investment bank. Derivatives dealers manage these credit risks in a number of ways. First, the dealers conduct thorough **credit analyses** of all potential counterparties and set limits on their exposure to any one counterparty. Second, dealers include special **default provisions** in their contract documentation to provide for the orderly liquidation of contracts that are likely to cause financial injury before such injury can be realized. Third, dealers employ various **credit enhancements** to improve the credit quality of their counterparties when necessary. Finally, dealers price credit risk into their products. The latter step is in recognition of the fact that no matter what steps are taken to protect against default losses, some will occur. By pricing in credit risk, the excess profit made on nondefaulting positions offsets the losses on defaulting positions.[16]

Summary

Investment banks are heavily involved in the financial engineering and marketing of derivative products, and the structuring of solutions to corporate problems that make use of derivative products. Investment banks profit from their market–making activities and from selling advisory services. They also trade derivatives when profitable opportunities present themselves and use derivatives to synthesize other securities. Transactions are handled by the investment bank's derivative products group. The principal derivative products are swaps and over–the–counter options.

Since their introduction, the swaps market has grown in size to many trillions of dollars. Swaps are contracts in which two parties agree to make payments to each other at regular intervals for some period of time.

---

[16] For further discussion of credit risk in the context of derivative instruments, see Briys, Crouhy, and Schobel (1991), Cooper and Mello (1991), Simons (1989), and Wall (1988).

Typically, one party agrees to pay a fixed rate and the other party agrees to pay a floating rate. Both payments are based on some hypothetical quantity called notional principal. Many variants of the basic swap structure have evolved since their introduction in the late 1970s. These are grouped into four major categories: currency swaps, interest rate swaps, commodity swaps, and equity swaps, but additional forms are under development. Swaps have many uses and are extremely flexible. Uses include reducing the cost of capital, hedging price risks, arbitraging markets, synthesizing other instruments, entering new markets, and many more.

The derivative groups of investment banks are now making active markets in a wide and growing variety of over–the–counter options. These options are usually cash settled and often multiperiod. Investment banks assist client firms in identifying situations in which the use of these options is appropriate, and investment banks stand ready to both buy and sell options, profiting from an appropriate bid–ask spread.

The derivative products groups of investment banks work closely with other groups within the bank. In particular, they work very closely with structured products groups, which often employ options (and swaps) in structuring new investment vehicles and securities having very special investment properties.

Investment banks must manage the risks associated with running derivative portfolios. The mathematics involved in pricing these instruments and managing the risks associated with running these portfolios are complex and require individuals with extraordinary expertise, including intimate knowledge of products and theory, specialized accounting skills, credit experience, and quantitative skills. Not surprisingly, the advent of derivative products has helped transform investment banking from a business in which one could succeed based on whom one knew into one in which one succeeds on the basis of what one knows.

References & Suggested Reading

Abken, P. A., "Beyond Plain Vanilla: A Taxonomy of Swaps," *Economic Review*, March/April 1991, reprinted in the 1991–92 Supplement to *The Swaps Handbook*, K. R. Kapner and J. F. Marshall, (eds.), New York: New York Institute of Finance, 1991.

Arak, M., A. Estrella, L. Goodman, and A. Silver, "Interest Rate Swaps: An Alternative Explanation," *Financial Management*, Summer 1988, pp. 12–18.

Aspel, D., J. Cogen, and M. Rabin, "Hedging Long–Term Commodity Swaps with Futures," *Global Finance Journal*, Fall 1989, pp. 77–93.

Baird, A. J., *Option Market Making: Trading and Risk Analysis for the Financial and Commodity Option Markets*, New York: Wiley & Sons, 1993.

Beder, T. S., "Equity Derivatives for Investors," *Journal of Financial Engineering*, 1:2, September 1992, pp. 174–195.

Bicksler, J. L. and A. H. Chen, "An Economic Analysis of Interest Rate Swaps," *Journal of Finance*, July 1986, pp. 645–655.

Bodurtha, J. N. and G. R. Courtadon, *The Pricing of Foreign Exchange Options*, New York: Salomon Center, New York University, 1988.

Briys, E., M. Crouhy, and R. Schobel, "The Pricing of Default–Free Interest Rate Cap, Floor and Collar Agreements," *Journal of Finance*, 46:5, December 1991, pp. 1879–1892.

Brown, K. C. and D. J. Smith, "Recent Innovations in Interest Rate Risk Management and the Reintermediation of Commercial Banking," *Financial Management*, 17:4, Winter 1988, pp. 45–58.

Cooper, I. A. and A. S. Mello, "The Default Risk of Swaps," *Journal of Finance*, 46:2, June 1991, pp. 597–620.

Cox, J. C. and M. Rubinstein, *Options Markets*, Englewood Cliffs, NJ: Prentice Hall, 1985.

Degler, W., "Selecting a Collar to Fit Your Expectations," *Futures Magazine*, 18:3, March 1989.

Fall, W., "Caps Vs. Swaps Vs. Hybrids," *Risk*, 1:5, April 1988.

Felgren, S., "Interest Rate Swaps: Use, Risk, and Prices," *New England Economic Review*, Federal Reserve Bank of Boston, November 1987, pp. 22–32.

Figlewski, S., "What Does an Option Pricing Model Tell Us About Option Prices?" *Financial Analysts Journal*, 45:5, September/October 1989, pp. 12–15.

Haghani, V. J. and R. M. Stavis, "Interest Rate Caps and Floors: Tools for Asset/Liability Management," Bond Portfolio Analysis Group, Salomon Brothers, May 1986.

Hull, J., *Options, Futures and Other Derivative Securities*, Englewood Cliffs, NJ: Prentice Hall, 1989a.

Hull, J., "Assessing Credit Risk in a Financial Institution's Off–Balance–Sheet Commitments," *Journal of Financial and Quantitative Analysis*, 24:4, December 1989b, pp. 489–501.

Jarrow, R. A. and A. Rudd, *Option Pricing*, Burr Ridge, IL: Irwin, 1983.

Kapner, K. R. and J. F. Marshall, *The Swaps Handbook*, New York: New York Institute of Finance, 1990; and Supplements 1991–92 (1991) and 1993–94 (1993).

Kawaller, I. G., *Financial Futures and Options: Managing Risk in the Interest Rate, Currency, and Equity Markets*, Chicago: Probus Publishing, 1992.

Kutner, G. W. "Black/Scholes Revisited: Some Important Details," *Financial Review*, 23:1, February 1988, pp. 95–104.

Litzenberger, R. H., "Swaps: Plain and Fanciful," *Journal of Finance*, (Presidential Address) 47:3, July 1992, pp. 831–850.

Marshall, J. F., *Futures and Option Contracting: Theory and Practice*, Cincinnati, OH: South–Western, 1989.

Marshall, J. F. and V. K. Bansal, *Financial Engineering: A Complete Guide to Financial Innovation*, New York: New York Institute of Finance, 1992.

Marshall, J. F. and V. K. Bansal, *Financial Engineering*, 2e, Miami: Kolb Publishing, 1993.

Marshall, J. F., V. K. Bansal, A. F. Herbst, and A. L. Tucker, "Hedging Business Cycle Risk with Macro Swaps and Options," *Journal of Applied Corporate Finance*, 4:4, Winter 1992, pp. 103–108.

Marshall, J. F. and K. R. Kapner, *The Swaps Market*, Miami: Kolb Publishing, 1992.

Marshall, J. F. and K. R. Kapner, *Understanding Swaps*, New York: John Wiley, 1994.

Marshall, J. F., E. H. Sorensen, and A. L. Tucker, "Equity Derivatives: The Plain Vanilla Equity Swap and Its Variants," *Journal of Financial Engineering*, September 1992.

Melnik, A. L. and S. E. Plaut, "Currency Swaps, Hedging, and the Exchange of Collateral," *Journal of International Money & Finance*, 11:5, October 1992, pp. 446–461.

Ritchken, P., *Options: Theory, Strategy, and Applications*, Glenview, IL: Scott, Foresman, 1987.

Simons, K., "Measuring Credit Risk in Interest Rate Swaps," *New England Economic Review*, November/December 1989, pp. 29–38.

Smith, C. W., C. W. Smithson, and L. M. Wakeman, "The Market for Interest Rate Swaps," *Financial Management*, Winter 1988, pp. 34–44.

Titman, S., "Interest Rate Swaps and Corporate Financing Choices," *Journal of Finance*, 47:4, September 1992, pp. 1503–1516.

Tompkins, R., "The A–Z of Caps," *Risk*, 2:3, March 1989.

Tucker, A. L., *Financial Futures, Options, and Swaps*, St. Paul, MN: West Publishing, 1991.

Wall, L. D. "Interest Rate Swaps: A Review of the Issues," *Economic Review*, Federal Reserve Bank of Atlanta, 73:6, November/December 1988, pp. 22–40.

Yaksick, R., "Swaps, Caps and Floors: Some Parity and Price Identities," *Journal of Financial Engineering*, 1:1, June 1992, pp. 105–115.

10

Advisory Services, Investment Management, and Merchant Banking

Overview

In Chapters 3 through 9, we examined many of the principal revenue–generating activities routinely undertaken by modern investment banks. In this, the final chapter of this section, we focus on three more revenue–generating activities: advisory services, investment management, and merchant banking. These activities either have been discussed in some specific context in earlier chapters, or they build on one or more activities that have already been discussed. Each, however, is important enough to focus a bit of attention on it directly.

Advisory services include any activity in which an investment bank provides advice, recommendations, or opinions in exchange for a fee. Such activities give rise to fiduciary relationships between the advisers and the clients. However, the nature of the advice provided often places the investment bank in a difficult situation, because its advice may be at odds with its own financial interests, which thus represents a potential conflict of interest.

Investment management, by definition, involves the investment of other people's (or institutions') money. Investment banks act as investment managers for a wide variety of investment vehicles, including real estate partnerships, venture capital pools, money market funds, and all sorts of mutual funds. They also structure and manage many specialty investment vehicles issued through beneficial and owner trusts. These latter instruments make up a segment of what are known as structured products.

Merchant banking involves the direct investment of the investment bank's own funds in some asset not directly related to the investment bank's traditional businesses. While merchant banking has long been associated with some investment banks, it truly came into its own during the 1980s. This move into merchant banking was, in large part, a consequence of two distinct developments. One of these, merger and acquisition activity (including leveraged buyouts), was discussed in Chapter 7. The other was an increased demand for venture capital fostered by rapid advances in technology and the realization that merchant banking, besides being profitable in its own right, helped to cement relationships that could lead to additional demand for more traditional investment banking services.

Advisory Services

In earlier days, advice was something that investment banks gave away, usually in conjunction with some other service (such as underwriting) that they were marketing. But the increasing complexity of the financial markets, the explosion in financial instruments, the intricacies of many strategies, and the complexity of legal, accounting, and tax issues have given expert advice an ever–greater value. Over the years, investment bankers have learned to capitalize on the value of their advice, and many investment banks now sell advice with the same savvy with which they sell securities.

Investment banks sell many types of advice. They will advise on restructuring a client's balance sheet for asset/liability management purposes or to hedge risks; they will advise on alternative ways to achieve a desired form of financing, including the duration of the financing, the interest rate character (fixed vs. floating), and the currency denomination of the obligations created; they will advise suitors seeking acquisitions, and they will advise targets of such suitors on countermeasures (i.e., defenses); they will provide valuation opinions in a variety of situations; they will give advice on taking public companies private, taking private companies public, and divesting or acquiring assets; they will assist in bankruptcy workouts; they will advise on the structuring of deals so as to minimize tax consequences; and much more.

Compensation for advisory services may take the form of transactional fees associated with implementing the deal on behalf of the client. At other times, the advisory services are performed free of charge in a goodwill effort to establish a relationship. But increasingly, compensation for advisory services is explicitly charged in the form of a fee for the service itself. These charges are as likely to be called **structuring fees** or **engineering fees** as they are to be called **advisory fees**, but in any case, it comes down to a fee paid for advice. Let's consider a few of the areas in which an investment bank may act in an advisory capacity.

Risk Management

Every firm, large or small, carries assets financed by liabilities and equity. Assets are carried because they generate revenue. Liabilities (another name for debt), on the other hand, entail a cost. Equity earns a return equal to the after–tax difference between the revenues provided by the assets and the costs associated with the liabilities. To the extent that a dollar of assets provides a return greater than the cost of a dollar of debt, the owners' return is enhanced. Thus, the use of debt can "leverage up" the returns to the owners of the firm.

But liabilities also involve risks, as do assets. To the degree that the risks associated with the assets and the risks associated with the liabilities are offsetting, the owners are protected. Hence, a profit may be earned by helping firms manage their asset/liability risks. This is called **asset/ liability management**. In a nutshell, the goal of asset/liability management is to structure the asset portfolio and the liability portfolio so that the risks are offsetting—or, alternatively, so that the financial risks are well understood and acceptable.

Good asset/liability management requires a keen understanding of financial risks. Some of these risks are straightforward, such as a price risk associated with inventoried commodities or an interest rate risk associated with a fixed–/floating–rate mismatch between assets and liabilities. But other risks can be exceedingly complex. For example, balance sheets are sometimes peppered with options. Sometimes these options are explicit assets (or liabilities) of the firm, but other times they are embedded in some other instrument. The valuation of these options and the measurement of the risks associated with them requires very specialized financial engineering skills, which most corporate managers lack. Also complicating the risk picture are the currencies in which assets and liabilities are denominated. As the corporate world becomes ever more global, currency mismatches between asset and liability denominations and between cash flow streams become an ever–greater source of risk.

Into this world step investment bankers, ready to analyze the balance sheet, decompose the revenue stream, identify the options, find the risks, and so on. Investment bankers are also ready to offer advice, for a fee, on how to improve the financial profile of the firm by either reducing risk or augmenting return. To the extent that the mix between assets and liabilities is poor but cannot be altered due to contractual commitments, the investment banker will offer hedging strategies. Some strategies will require the skills of the bank's derivatives group, which is also probably involved in the advisement process.

Rarely does risk management advice give rise to conflicts of interest between the investment bank and its client firm. Only to the degree that the investment bank actually sells the financial instruments used to manage the risks is there likely to be a potential source of conflict. For example, the investment bank may want to move some particular instrument off its own books. Or it may want to better balance its derivative portfolio, and is inclined, therefore, to push one solution relative to another. If the investment bank's role is limited to advice only, conflict of interest is not likely.

Mergers and Acquisitions

A second important area in which investment bankers are heavily involved in advice giving—and often *only* advice giving—is corporate restructuring. Operating out of M&A departments, investment bankers become involved in the restructuring advice game in a number of different ways. Sometimes an acquiring firm approaches the investment bank looking for advice on how to acquire a specific target firm or how to divest itself of certain of its businesses. Similarly, a potential target firm may approach an investment bank looking for advice on how to be acquired on the most favorable terms or how to fend off an unwanted suitor. At other times, a potential acquirer approaches the investment bank expressing an interest in making acquisitions but without any specific target in mind. Finally, the investment bank itself may approach firms—generally firms with which the investment bank has an established relationship—and suggest the acquisition trail either with or without particular targets in mind.

Most typically, potential target firms are those firms which are significantly undervalued by the market or those whose value can be enhanced through synergistic association with a particular acquiring firm. Valuation is, at the same time, both straightforward and complex. It is straightforward in that a firm's value is simply the discounted value of all future after–tax cash flows that it will generate. But it is also complex, because the assets of the firm may generate greater cash flows in someone else's hands, or there may be significant opportunities for cost–cutting, thereby enhancing cash flows even if the assets stay in the hands of the existing firm.

Investment banks offer advice to these firms that includes valuation opinions, acquisition strategies, defense strategies, financing strategies, and so on. So prized are some M&A advisers that they can survive even if separated from the investment banks that employ them. The best example of this in recent years was the team of Bruce Wasserstein and Joseph Perella. During their heyday at First Boston (late 1970s to 1987), Wasserstein and Perella, co–heads of M&A, built a powerful machine that identified, advised, and executed all variety of corporate restructurings. Repeatedly, the group (consisting of fewer than 150 people) contributed profits to First Boston completely out of proportion to their numbers.[1] More important, most of the deals the group structured were successful, resulting in very happy clients who then came back to Wasserstein and Perella over and over again.

In 1987, Wasserstein and Perella left First Boston over a dispute involving allocation of the firm's resources. They immediately launched their own firm. The strength of Wasserstein and Perella's reputation was such that some of First Boston's largest clients chose to abandon the large and powerful First Boston in favor of the experience and skill of Wasserstein and Perella. In essence, Wasserstein and Perella became a boutique investment bank specializing in M&A advice but dependent for execution on large, well–financed investment banks.

---

[1] Average employment at First Boston over the period was probably between 3,500 and 4,000. During many quarters, M&A contributed, either directly or indirectly, more than 25 percent of the firm's profits.

Advisement fees on successful M&A deals can run into the many millions of dollars. And, of course, if the adviser's shop also gets to execute the deal (which may involve the purchase of large quantities of stock, the issuance of bonds and/or stock, and the provision of bridge financing), the rewards can be particularly sweet. But even if the investment bank's role is limited to advisement, the fees earned for the firm can be substantial.

Similarly, the investment bank can earn significant advisement fees for assisting the target firms in their defense against unwanted suitors. They advise on tactics to make the target firm less attractive (using strategies described in Chapter 7), they seek out preferred acquirers if a "white knight" is called for, and they advise management on buying out the firm if an LBO is the preferred alternative.

It is important to note that M&A advisement often creates a conflict of interest situation for the investment bank. For example, the bank may have existing relationships with the target firm when it is approached by the acquiring firm. Or the investment bank may have a substantial position in the stock or bonds of either the target or the acquirer. Or the investment bank's own risk arbitrageurs may be looking to exploit either the anticipated success or failure of a particular deal—and so on. The investment bank must be vigilant in identifying and disclosing possible conflicts. Clients have a right to know when their adviser stands to benefit from either their success or their failure, beyond the agreed fees to be paid.

Fairness Opinions

A great many financial activities require fairness opinions. For example, in taking a company private, whether through an LBO or some other strategy, the minority shareholders that chose not to sell their stock into the tender offer will likely be bought out by the majority shareholders. The majority shareholders cannot simply assign an arbitrary value to the shares of the minority shareholders for purposes of buying them out. Indeed, they cannot (or at least should not) even try to set a value on their own, because they are interested parties and their opinions are surely suspect. Into this situation steps the investment bank, fully prepared, for a fee, to provide an estimate of fair value. This is the **fairness opinion**.

The purpose of the fairness opinion is to determine whether or not the price being paid for the asset in question is financially reasonable.

The opinion does not state whether the offer should be accepted or whether the offer is in the best interest of the firm or the shareholders. The opinion states only whether or not the offer is "financially fair."

A fairness opinion is not legally required, and the deductibility of the cost of a fairness opinion as an "ordinary and necessary expense" is questionable.[2] Furthermore, providing a fairness opinion does not relieve the board of directors of the responsibility for the decision to accept or not accept the offer. After all, an offer may be financially fair but not be in the long–term best interest of the firm's employees, management, and/or shareholders. However, not having a fairness opinion opens the door for potential litigation by shareholders. Consequently, management will often obtain more than one—often three—such opinions from different investment banks. These valuations will differ, often considerably, based on different assumptions made by the opinion giver and different valuation methodologies. The managers then pay the minority shareholders either the average of the valuations or something above the average. By so doing, the managers try to protect themselves from unfavorable shareholder reactions.

Many other situations require fairness opinions. Bankruptcy workouts, dissolution of investment companies, limited partnerships, thrifts, and valuation of nonpublic firms for estate tax purposes are but some examples. When the investment bank provides a fairness opinion, it charges for its time and expertise in preparing the opinion, for the potential for later litigation over its opinion, and, of course, for its profit—the extent of which will likely vary with its reputation. Again, the investment bank must be wary that there are no conflicts of interest associated with its role in providing a fairness opinion.

Investment Management

By definition, investment management means managing other people's money.[3] This involves deciding what types of assets to invest in and precisely what to buy (and when) and what to sell (and when). Invest-

---

[2] See Freidrich (1992), for discussion on this point.

[3] In market slang, investment management is sometimes called "running money."

ment funds can be managed for the beneficiary (beneficial owner) either as part of a pool (in which funds of different investors are commingled) or separately for a single client. The mutual fund structure is but one example in which investor funds are pooled for management purposes. Investment banks (and other securities firms) often become involved in investment management for a fee. Most often, this fee is a fixed percentage of the assets under management, but increasingly the fee is based on performance, or some combination of asset value and performance.

To Manage or Not to Manage

Investment banks are divided on the issue of whether or not investment management is a business in which they want to become involved. Some shops have avoided becoming involved in investment management, while others have made this a core component of their business. Among the latter, Merrill Lynch is probably the premier player, but other shops, including Kidder Peabody and Donaldson, Lufkin & Jenrette, are also important players. Of those that have gotten into the investment management business, some have purchased investment management companies, while others have built their businesses from scratch.

Narrowly defined investment banks (i.e., those that limit their investment banking activity to the traditional role of raising capital) can find little synergistic benefit from engaging in investment management but plenty of opportunities to antagonize traditional issuer clients. For example, if an underwriter is seen to place a large portion of its underwriting commitment into pools it manages, it runs the risk of being perceived as giving preferential treatment to the investors whose funds it manages and/or manipulating the size of the offering. Also, when the investment manager's opinion of a stock turns bearish and it seeks to remove the stock from its investment portfolio, it runs the risk of antagonizing the issuer of the stock—who may be a client of the investment bank. There is also the potential for a conflict of interest to develop over the use (or abuse) of inside information. Thus, the investment management group must be kept distinct (literally isolated from) the corporate finance group.

While narrowly defined investment banks may enjoy little benefit from investment management, broker/dealers can enjoy considerable benefit from investment management activities. But they, too, must be wary of conflicts of interest. By entering the investment management business, broker/dealers can exploit their firm's research skills, utilize their co–workers' quantitative trading skills, and capitalize on their established presence and reputation in the securities markets for effective marketing of their investment management services.

Among the potential conflicts of interest faced by broker/dealers involved in investment management, whether real or perceived, are account churning and angering the firm's best customers. Whether the investment funds under management are handled through a pool vehicle or through discretionary trading accounts, there is a risk that the broker/dealer might be perceived as making trades with no legitimate economic motive. This is particularly true if the trading results in commissions for the broker/dealer. Many investment managers deal with this by limiting the quantity of brokerage business they funnel through their own firm. The second concern involves the broker/dealer's best customers—its institutional investors, which may perceive themselves to be in direct competition with the broker who is also managing funds.

The latter concern has led some broker/dealers to specialize in strategies not likely to be used by their institutional clientele. These often involve sophisticated risk management techniques, the creation of synthetic securities, and the use of derivative instruments. One excellent example of this sort of activity is program trading conducted on behalf of clients (as opposed to proprietary trading). Another example is portfolio insurance strategies. The former is designed to synthetically create risk–free positions and yet to earn a return above the risk–free rate. The latter is intended to guarantee a minimum investment return while preserving upside potential.[4]

Assets, Strategies, and Fees

Investment managers have an amazing array of possible investment assets from which to choose. Equity investors can invest in growth stocks, blue chips, new issues, income stocks, particular industry groups, the stocks of particular nations or regions, or they can invest globally. Fixed–income

---

[4] The interested reader may wish to refer to J. F. Marshall and V. K. Bansal, *Financial Engineering: A Complete Guide to Financial Innovation*, for further discussion of these and other trading techniques.

investors can invest in municipal bonds, Treasury and agency bonds, investment–grade corporate bonds, high–yield corporate bonds, collateralized mortgage obligations, foreign bonds, money market instruments, etc. Furthermore, they can leverage up, or down, with appropriate futures and options positions.

Investment managers can also structure funds that specialize in venture capital investments (we will focus on these in the next section of this chapter), or that invest in commercial real estate, oil–producing properties, or agricultural investments. These funds usually, but not always, take the form of limited partnerships or unit trust structures rather than common stock. Whatever they choose to invest in, it is important that the investor know the objectives of the investment managers and the types of investments the investment managers might make.

Just as varied as the types of assets in which investment managers might invest is the investment strategy that they pursue. The managers might take a fundamental approach to the markets—i.e., trying to identify undervalued and overvalued assets; or they might take a technical (market timing) approach. Some will rely on the tenets of modern portfolio theory, which presupposes that assets are efficiently priced, and thus pursue an indexing strategy.

The fees levied by investment managers tend to vary both by the value of the assets under management and by the level of intensity of the investment management strategy. In general, the fee structure will step down as the value of the assets under management gets larger. For example, the fee might be 75 basis points on the first $20 million under management, 50 basis points on the next $30 million, and 25 basis points on everything over $50 million. Fees will generally be lower on passive strategies—such as index matching—than on active strategies—such as identifying overvalued and undervalued securities.

Performance fees, as an alternative to fees levied on asset values, were authorized by the SEC in 1985. Prior to this, value–based fees were the rule. Under the new rules, performance–based fees can be utilized on portfolios having more than a threshold market value but not on portfolios having less. The threshold value was originally set at $500,000.

Merchant Banking and Venture Capital

Merchant banking refers to taking debt or equity positions for the investment bank's own account in businesses that are not part of the investment bank's core businesses. In other words, the investment bank invests its own money in the securities of other firms but not as part of its broker/dealer activity, its risk arbitrage activity, or a long–run diversification plan. These investment positions can be motivated by the following factors:

1. The expectation of a rapid increase in the value of the investment.
2. To cement relationships with the issuing firm.
3. As partial compensation for traditional investment banking services.
4. To generate opportunities for investment management income.
5. As a window into technological developments.

In this section, we will consider the what, the why, and the how of merchant banking and how merchant banking is related to venture capital. Let's begin by combining the first and the last.

Venture capital is high–risk investment in start–up companies— often high–tech start–up firms.[5] Venture capital investing is not limited to investment banks. Indeed, there are private venture capital firms and publicly traded venture capital funds, neither of which is necessarily associated with an investment bank. Only when the venture capital investment is made directly out of the investment bank's own funds is the activity considered to be merchant banking. Furthermore, merchant banking does not necessarily require that the investments be of a venture capital nature—that is, the investments need not be in start–up companies; many of these investments originate from LBO and other corporate restructuring strategies in which the investment bank participated. These activities were discussed in Chapter 7, so we will focus most of our attention in this section on venture capital investing.

---

[5] Venture capital is also called **risk capital**.

Why Merchant Banking/Venture Capital?

At the start of this section, we gave five reasons why investment banks engage in merchant banking activity. Let's consider each of those reasons in detail. The first was that merchant banking is undertaken to provide significant returns in the form of a rapid increase in the value of the investment. This return is a combination of capital appreciation and carried interest.

Typically, the investment bank plays the role of a general partner in a venture capital pool. Generally, the investment bank is required to invest only a small sum, often as little as 1 percent of the pool equity. In addition to its pro rata share of profits, the investment bank, as general partner, organizer, and manager of the pool, is typically entitled to receive 20 percent (called **carried interest**) of the profits earned by the pool. Of course, the investment bank may contribute more than 1 percent of the pool equity if it wishes. But this additional investment grants the investment bank no special treatment relative to other investors. The carried interest is usually split between the investment bank and the people hired by the investment bank to manage the pool.

Consider the following scenario. Suppose that an investment bank organizes a $20 million venture capital pool. The bank contributes 1 percent ($200,000) of the equity from its own funds. The pool has a target life of five years. At the end of that time, the assets of the pool are to be sold off and the proceeds divided among the pool investors. As it happens, the venture capital pool's assets increase in value to $75 million over the five–year period. This is equivalent to an average annual return (after compounding) of 30.2 percent [i.e., $(75/20)^{1/5} - 1$]. However, since the investment bank is entitled to 20 percent of the pool's profits, its share is $11 million [i.e., $(75-20) \times 0.2$].

Now let's suppose that the profits are divided evenly between the investment bank and those hired by the investment bank to operate the pool. Thus, the investment bank keeps a total of $5.5 million of the carried interest. Of course, it also receives 1 percent of the disposition value of the pool, because it has a 1 percent equity interest in the pool. The latter is $640,000, which is arrived at by deducting $11 million from $75 million and multiplying the difference by 1 percent. Thus, the terminal value (after five years) for the investment bank is $6.14 million [i.e., $5.5 million + 0.64 million] on an initial investment of $0.2 million, for an annual compound return on investment (ROI) of about 98 percent [i.e., $(6.14/0.2)^{1/5} - 1$]. It is in this light that the investment banking industry's interest in venture capital and merchant banking must be seen.

Of course, not all venture capital pools will pay off as handsomely for the merchant banking operation as the one just described. But since the investment bank's risk is limited to its 1 percent investment, even a small percentage of successful venture capital investments will compensate for many that turn out badly. Of course, all is not as rosy for the other venture capital partners. While they, too, stand to benefit, the rewards are not proportional.[6]

It is important to note that investment banks may have difficulty convincing others to invest in venture capital pools if their own investment is limited to 1 percent while their rewards are locked in at 20 percent of profit. To alleviate this justifiable apprehension, investment banks often take a larger–than–required equity interest in the pool. For example, in the case described above, a 10 percent interest in the pool would have resulted in an annual compound ROI of 43 percent, i.e., $(\{5.5 + [(75 - 11) \times 10\%]\} \div 2)^{1/5} - 1$.

A related issue involves the ability of the investment bank to influence the success of the funded venture capital firms. The single most common cause for a start–up business to fail, assuming that it had good product potential and adequate capital, is poor management. It is quite common for start–up companies (especially those that are as high–tech as so many venture capital–backed companies are) to be run by the scientists and technicians who founded them. While the technological skills are essential for corporate success, technological expertise does not equate with management expertise. Thus, investment banks often insist, as a condition for providing capital, in having significant control over the selection of management. Competent management—or, at the very least,

---

[6] The reader should consider the return to one of the limited partners in the venture capital pool. From the $75 million terminal value of the pool, we must first deduct the 20 percent carried interest that goes to the investment bank and its pool manager. This, we showed, was $11 million. Thus, after payment to the investment bank, the terminal value of the pool was $64 million. A limited partner who invested 1 percent in the pool ($200,000) would be entitled to 1 percent of the terminal value, which was $640,000. The reader should confirm that this is equivalent to an annual compound return on investment of 26 percent.

one or more positions on the board—can dramatically increase the likelihood of success.

The second reason investment banks engage in venture capital/ merchant banking activity is to cement relationships. It should be remembered that investment banking has long been a relationship– oriented business, albeit less so today. With positions on the boards (or moral suasion), the investment bank is in a strong position to steer future securities issuances of the funded companies to the investment bank's corporate finance department. Winning more traditional investment banking business from these companies can, in and of itself, be sufficient motivation for venture capital investments. For example, through its relationships, the investment bank can earn fees by helping the start–up companies obtain mezzanine financing, providing advice, handling the initial public offering and subsequent offerings of securities, and so on.

The third reason we noted for investment bank involvement in merchant banking activity is as partial compensation for traditional investment banking services. This is quite common in LBO situations. In these deals, a small group of managers or others seek to take a firm private. They require the services of a well–connected investment bank to raise the capital and develop and implement the strategy. The investment bank may itself take partial equity in the LBO firm, either as compensation for services rendered or by buying its way in. Often, this equity stake must be held for some minimum period, after which it may be sold back to the LBO group. Because the investment bank involved in structuring the transaction has a great deal of intimate knowledge about the LBO's prospects for success, it may want an equity stake. What's more, the bank is in a powerful position to demand and obtain that equity stake.

The fourth reason for investment bank involvement in venture capital and merchant banking concerns generating investment management income. This has already been touched upon in the 20 percent carried interest typical in venture capital deals. But there are also other ven- ture–capital investment structures that provide investment management fees, including the operation of public venture capital pools. Some of these alternative structures will be discussed shortly.

The final reason we noted for merchant banking/venture capital activity concerned a window into technological developments. Investment banks operate in a fiercely competitive world where information is often the key to success. Intimate involvement in venture capital firms at the cutting edge of technology provides a unique window on technological developments as they occur. This gives the investment bank a very special ability to place in context the developments at other firms, and it enhances the quality of the investment bank's research reports—a key ingredient in attracting institutional clientele.

Steps Involved in Venture Capital Investing

The venture capital/merchant banking business requires a special and intimate knowledge of corporations and their managements. Few, if any, industries are in as strong a position to possess this knowledge as are investment banks. The process of exploiting this situation involves a number of steps. First, the investment bank or its merchant banking affiliate must identify potential investment opportunities. Second, the potential investments must be analyzed and evaluated. Third, the investment vehicle that will be used to exploit these investment opportunities must be structured. Fourth, the investments must be managed. And finally, the investments must be sold off after they have achieved their potential, or upon the mandatory dissolution of the investment vehicle (if it has a stipulated life, for example). Let's review these steps in a bit more detail.

First, most large investment banks (and many smaller ones as well) maintain active research departments. These research departments, which will be discussed in Chapter 12, employ highly competent and well–trained professionals who tend to specialize by industry. Thus, a major investment bank will have one or two equity researchers who specialize in the transportation industry and a few who specialize in the computer industry, the biotechnology industry, and so on. These researchers are expected to know virtually all that is knowable about the industry and the firms that are in it. They read the trade journals, monitor regulatory changes, follow industry trends, investigate technological breakthroughs, interview managements, and talk to researchers, scientists, and academics. The merchant banking unit exchanges information with the research department and often obtains leads and contacts concerning new or potential start–up companies from the research department. Additionally, the merchant banking unit maintains its own contacts among accountants, lawyers, and others who are privy to information concerning new businesses. Finally, many start–up companies approach investment banks directly in search of venture capital. From these various sources, as well as a considerable amount of their own snooping and, sometimes, by encouraging executives and scientists to go off and start their own firms, the merchant banking departments identify potential investments.

The next step is analysis and evaluation of each potential investment. At the very least, this means assessing the following:

1. The product or potential product under development.
2. The likelihood of further technological breakthroughs.
3. The patentability of new products and the enforceability of those patents.
4. The ease with which competitors can enter the market with similar products.
5. The marketability of the products including pricing and costs of production.
6. The competence of management.

The time horizon involved in taking the product from the development and testing stage to actual large-scale production is also critical. Based on these considerations, and some intuition, the merchant banking team will estimate funding requirements and future cash flows. These, in turn, are used to project the future value of the firm.

The third consideration is structuring an investment vehicle through which venture capital investments will be made. There are two dimensions to this. The first involves the types of securities that will be issued by the venture capital-backed companies (these represent the uses to which funds are put). The second involves the form of the venture capital pool (this represents the source of the funds). In general, venture capital investors prefer to own convertible debt or convertible preferred stock (both often coupled with warrants). The reason is simple: These securities provide most of the benefits and price performance of equity, because they are convertible into equity. But if not converted into equity, they also assure the venture capital investor of a senior position (i.e., a senior claim on assets) in the event of a liquidation of the company. Given the high rate of failure among start-up companies, this senior claim can be important. At the same time, should the venture prove successful, the investors can convert their positions to equity. Of course, the downside is that the venture capitalists give up much of the control that goes with an equity position. However, one or more positions on the board and some say over management are generally sufficient protection.

The other dimension was the structure of the vehicle that would actually make the investments in the securities. There are several different investment structures. Which structure is best depends on the nature and purpose of the pool.

The most common form of venture capital pool, in which investment banks become involved as the general partner, is the institutional venture capital limited partnership. The investors in these pools include wealthy individuals, insurance companies, mutual funds, bank trust departments, corporations with a special interest in technology, and so on. Since this investment vehicle is a limited partnership, the investors' commitment is only financial, and the limited partners enjoy limited liability.

Institutional venture capital partnerships may or may not be sponsored by investment banks, but since investment banks are in the business of raising capital, they have a special advantage in organizing and sponsoring the pools. In general, in the pools sponsored by investment banks, the investment banks serve as the general partner and retain the carried interest. Even in those pools that are not investment bank–sponsored, the sponsors often invite one or more investment banks to participate in the pool with a special status. This helps the sponsor raise the required capital, and in return, the investment bank often keeps a share of the carried interest.

Other types of venture capital pools include individual venture capital limited partnerships, which are similar to institutional partnerships except that they are open to investment by individuals.[7] For this reason, such partnerships must be registered with the SEC. Institutional partnerships, on the other hand, can be distributed through private placements. In addition to these forms, there are also general research and development (R&D) and single–project R&D partnerships. The former is organized to provide funds for R&D in a number of research projects, which are not generally fully identified at the time the fund is organized; the latter is formed to provide funds for a specific preselected project. These forms are often intended to generate tax benefits—in the form of R&D tax

---

[7] Of course, institutional investment pools are also open to individuals but only wealthy individuals. Individual pools do not impose as substantial a wealth requirement.

credits and early–stage operating losses—with royalty revenue expected sometime down the road.

Once the investment vehicle has been structured and the necessary funds raised, the venture capital pool must be managed. If the pool is sponsored by an investment bank, the investment bank will select the pool managers. As already noted, the investment bank, as general partner, earns the carried interest, which is shared with the fund managers. In addition, however, the limited partners in these pools are often required to pay the general partner a small annual fee for management.[8]

At some point, the venture capital pool seeks to dispose of its investments. This might be by choice or it might be required by the terms under which the pool was organized. If a funded company has been successful, or if it is believed that it will soon be successful, a public offering of stock can be made. The investment bank will, of course, look to handle the offering. If the stock performs well, the pool may exercise its right to convert its bonds or preferred stock to equity. Alternatively, the venture capital–backed firm can be sold to a third party. This option is particularly attractive if the company holds an important patent or technological expertise that is of particular value to another firm. Finally, the venture capital–backed company can be taken over by management, or others, through a leveraged buyout. In any case, the investment bank looks to participate in the transaction, thereby playing its traditional role and earning the revenues that go with it.

Other Revenue–Generating Activities

There are, of course, many other revenue–generating activities in which investment banks engage. But these tend to vary widely from one investment bank to another and, in general, tend to be of a parochial nature in that they are not characteristic of the industry as a whole. For example, certain investment banks, most noticeably Merrill Lynch, have become significant players in the real estate brokerage business. Others have become directly involved in mortgage lending. Still others, most

---

[8] This fee is generally in the range of 1 to 2 percent of committed capital. Committed capital is that portion of the venture capital pool's funds that have been committed to specific venture–capital investments.

noticeably First Boston, have become involved in developing and marketing hardware/software systems that support the trading operations of other firms in the industry. Some of these specialty activities were undertaken as part of a conscious effort to diversify. Others were a consequence of internal R&D efforts to gain competitive advantage, with the subsequent discovery that the effort had led to a unique product with market potential.

While these and other specialized sources of investment bank revenue are interesting, they are not representative of the current mainstream. Nevertheless, they are indicative of a trend within the industry toward the establishment of "financial supermarkets." However, some investment banks have pulled back from early efforts to become financial supermarkets, preferring instead to become dominant players in niche markets.

Summary

In this chapter, we have briefly looked at three important revenue–generating activities commonly engaged in by investment banks. These include (1) the provision of advisory services, covering all areas of corporate finance, balance sheet management, risk management, and corporate control and restructuring; (2) investment management, for which investment banks earn management fees and also often augment their other business activities, particularly brokerage; and (3) investment of their own money as merchant banks, often participating in venture capital pools by organizing them, investing in them, and managing them.

While there are other revenue–generating activities in which investment banks engage, many of these activities are specialty areas that are firm–specific. Examples of such activities include real estate brokerage, mortgage lending, and software development.

References and Suggested Reading

Arvan, A., "The Maturing of the Merchant Bank," *Bankers Monthly*, 105:10, October 1988, pp. 79–86.

Barry, C. B., C. J. Muscarella, J. W. Peavy, and M. R. Vetsuypens, "The Role of Venture Capital in Creation of Public Companies: Evidence from the Going–Public Process," *Journal of Financial Economics*, 27:2, October 1990, pp. 447–471.

Beguelin, R. H., *The Secrets of Syndication: How to Make Money with Other People's Money*, Boston: Little, Brown, 1985.

Chapman, S. D., *The Rise of Merchant Banking*, London: Allen & Urwin, 1984.

Costello, D., *New Venture Analysis: Research, Planning, and Finance*, Homewood, IL: Dow Jones–Irwin, 1985.

Doerflinger, T. M. and J. L. Rivkin, *Risk and Reward: Venture Capital and the Making of America's Great Industries*, New York: Random House, 1987.

Friedrich, G. W., "Supreme Court Holds Legal and Investment Banking Fees of Target of Friendly Takeover Nondeductible," *Journal of Corporate Taxation*, 19:3, Autumn 1992, pp. 275–279.

Garner, D. R., R. R. Owens, and R. P. Conway, *The Ernst & Young Guide to Raising Capital*, New York: Wiley & Sons, 1991.

Garrett, E. M., "Capital, Yes, but What About the Culture?" *Venture*, 9:9, September 1987.

Gougis, C. A., "Can Your Deal's Fairness Opinion Stand the Heat?" *Mergers & Acquisitions*, 26:5, March/April 1992, pp. 33–36.

Hofmeister, S., "Of Bankers, Boutiques, and Middlemen," *Venture*, 9:9, September 1987, pp. 38–42.

Hunter, W. C. and M. B. Walker, "An Empirical Examination of Investment Banking Merger Fee Contracts," *Southern Economic Journal*, 56:4, April 1990, pp. 1117–1130.

Johnson, J. M. and R. E. Miller, "Going Public: Information for Small Businesses," *Journal of Small Business Management*, 23:4, October 1985, pp. 38–44.

Kozmetsky, G., M. D. Gill, and R. W. Smilor, *Financing and Managing Fast–Growing Companies: The Venture Capital Process*, Lexington, MA: Lexington Books, 1985.

Kunze, R. J., *Nothing Ventured: The Perils and Payoffs of the Great American Venture Capital Game*, New York: Harper Business, 1990.

Livingston, A., "Their Money Sells Your Deal," *Venture*, 10:9, September 1988, pp. 25–28.

Managing Asset/Liability Portfolios, E. P. Williams, (ed.), Charlottesville, VA: Association of Investment Management Research, 1992.

Mancuso, R. F., "Can CEOs Learn to Love the New Merchant Banking?" *Chief Executive*, 41, September/October 1987, pp. 34–37.

Marshall, J. F. and V. K. Bansal, *Financial Engineering: A Complete Guide to Financial Innovation*, New York: New York Institute of Finance, 1992.

Megginson, W. L. and K. A. Weiss, "Venture Capital Certification in Initial Public Offerings," *Journal of Finance*, 46:3, July 1991, pp. 879–903.

Miller, G., "Mergers and Acquisitions: Wall Street's Money Wars," *Institutional Investor*, 21:3, March 1987, pp. 169–174.

The New Era of Investment Banking: Industry Structure, Trends and Performance, R. H. Rupert, (ed.), Chicago: Probus Publishing, 1993.

Wilson, J. W., *The New Ventures: Inside the High–Stakes World of Venture Capital*, Reading, MA: Addison–Wesley, 1985.

III

Section Three

Clearing and Related Operations

Overview

In the narrowest sense, the clearing of trades refers to the process by which payment is collected from a securities purchaser and transferred to the securities seller, and the securities are transferred from the seller to the purchaser. Clearing is also called **settlement**. There is considerable overhead associated with running a clearing operation. In addition, securities firms that clear trades are required to meet much more stringent capital requirements than securities firms that do not clear trades. As a consequence, most broker/dealers, particularly the smaller ones, are nonclearing firms. Clearing services are provided to these nonclearing broker/dealers by **clearing firms**, also called **correspondents**. The nonclearing firms serviced by the clearing firms are called **introducing brokers**. For this service, clearing firms collect fees from nonclearing firms.

In addition to providing clearing services per se, clearing firms often also provide an array of related **"back office"** services to nonclearing broker/dealers. These include such things as order execution, customer confirmation statements, dividend and interest processing, periodic accounting statements, research, and marketing assistance. The non-clearing firms may utilize some, all, or none of these ancillary services. Essentially, many securities firms have realized that clearing, once viewed as a support activity, can become a profit center in its own right.

In this chapter, we will take a brief look at clearing and related services provided by clearing firms. It must be remembered that every securities firm requires clearing services; whether the firm chooses to provide these services to itself (self–clearing) or to purchase them from a clearing firm is, essentially, a classic make–or–buy decision. Most, but not all, large investment banks are self–clearing.

The Make–or–Buy Decision

There are two major reasons why many securities firms choose to contract out for clearing services rather than provide the services in–house. The first is that clearing involves a large back–office staff; a major investment in technology; and relationships with a great many different market–related entities, such as national and regional clearing corporations, securities depositories, banks, exchanges, over–the–counter markets, and so on. Collectively, these requirements result in a very substantial fixed cost. The fixed costs can run into the many millions of dollars a year to maintain even the smallest of clearing operations. Second, clearing firms are required to meet much more stringent capital requirements than nonclearing firms. Many, particularly smaller securities firms, simply cannot meet these capital requirements, and of those that can, many will simply deem it a poor use of funds relative to other opportunities available.

Clearing firms charge nonclearing firms a fee for clearing services. These fees can take the form of a fixed dollar amount on each trade, a share of the commission collected, or some combination of these. For simplicity, let's suppose that a broker/dealer can establish and maintain its own clearing operations at an annual fixed cost of $3 million a year and a variable cost of $7 a trade. Alternatively, the broker/dealer can purchase clearing services from a clearing firm for a fee of $12 a trade.[1] The decision to self–clear is the classic "make" decision, and the decision to utilize the services of a clearing firm is the classic "buy" decision. The make–or–buy decision is depicted in Figure 11.1.

Notice that a firm that expects to process more than 600,000 trades a year is better off providing its own clearing services, while a firm that expects to process fewer than 600,000 trades a year is better off purchasing clearing services from a clearing firm.

---

[1] The variable component of self–clearing includes the cost of meeting the higher capital requirement.

Figure 11.1
Make–or–Buy Decision

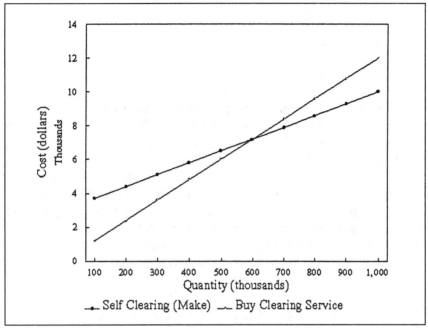

Self Clearing (Make) Buy Clearing Service

The "break–even" make–or–buy decision analysis described here, however, is not complete. There are at least two more considerations that often enter into the decision. The first involves image. Many broker/dealers that self–clear do so, in part, because they feel that being in a position to clear their own trades enhances their image relative to nonclearing broker/dealers. Indeed, clearing brokers routinely make mention of the fact that they clear trades in their promotional literature, and they particularly stress the point that their clearing status requires them to meet more stringent capital requirements (thereby implying that a client's assets are in safer hands).

On the other hand, even for firms that might have lower total cost, self–clearing involves a risk, which stems from the embedded fixed cost. The brokerage industry is notoriously cyclical. Thus, a firm that profitably self–clears one year may find it very unprofitable the next year.

In the language of finance, the presence of the fixed cost in clearing operations produces **operating leverage**. Leverage, of course, implies risk, and different firms are more or less risk averse. The degree of the perceived risk and the degree of risk aversion are the second factor that influences the make–or–buy decision.

The Mechanics

To appreciate fully the clearing process, it is necessary to review both the order execution and settlement processes. It is important to keep in mind that some securities trade on exchanges while others trade in dealer markets. It is also important to appreciate that some securities markets (such as Treasury securities) no longer employ physical (i.e., paper) certificates, relying instead on a book–entry system. Others, such as common stocks, still employ paper certificates evidencing ownership. Finally, it is important to appreciate that some trades settle on a five–day basis (corporates, for example), some on a two–day basis (currencies, for example), and some on a one–day basis (Treasury bonds, for example). The mechanics of settlement will vary a bit, then, depending on (1) the type of market in which the securities trade; (2) the type of security—i.e., fixed–income, equity, futures, or options; (3) whether ownership is evidenced by certificates or book entry; and (4) the applicable settlement period and established settlement mechanism.

While recognizing the idiosyncratic differences noted above, we will illustrate the general characteristics of the order execution and settlement process by way of an example involving a transaction on the New York Stock Exchange. Let's assume that an introducing broker, who employs both the order execution services and the clearing services of a clearing broker, has received an order from a customer to buy 500 shares of IBM. Identify the clearing broker as clearing firm A.

Upon receiving the order to buy the stock, the introducing broker relays the order to the clearing firm for execution. The clearing firm's floor brokers execute the order on the floor of the exchange (or through an electronic order–matching system) with other floor brokers, floor traders, or the stock's specialist. The floor trader is careful to note with whom he traded, the security he traded, the number of shares traded, and the price. The date of the transaction is called the **trade date**. The floor trader then reports back to the clearing firm. The clearing firm, in turn, reports back to the introducing broker who, in turn, reports back to the customer by phone and follows up with a written **confirmation**.

After the close of the market on the trade date, the clearing firm reports its trades to the National Securities Clearing Corporation (NSCC) or to an appropriate regional clearing corporation. The clearing corporation has the job of comparing the reports of trades to be certain that the report of the buying floor broker and the report of the selling floor broker agree. If they do not agree, the clearing corporation will report the discrepancy to the parties involved. They are then obligated to try to resolve the discrepancy. Depending upon the nature of the resolution, it may be necessary to send a corrected confirmation to the customer. If the discrepancy cannot be resolved, the trade is said to **fail**. A failed trade is treated as not having occurred.

After resolution of the discrepancies, all trades that were successfully compared and/or resolved are settled on the subsequent settlement date. This involves the transfer of cash between the clearing firms and the introducing broker(s) involved, and the transfer of securities from the seller to the buyer. The latter is usually handled through an appropriate debit/credit or deposit/withdrawal transaction between the clearing firms and a central securities depository. Let's look at these components of the settlement process a bit more closely.

First, cash transfers are made on a **net basis**. For example, the clearing firms involved in the transaction will calculate the difference between all payments due to be made by clearing firm A to clearing firm B and all payments due to be made by clearing firm B to clearing firm A. Only the difference between these two gross figures (the net) is transferred. The clearing firm representing the introducing broker will also require payment from the introducing broker, or directly from the introducing broker's customer. The appropriate debit is then made to the customer's account.

Second, most securities held by brokers for their customers are registered in the name of the brokerage firm. This is called **street name**. In addition, the securities are held for safekeeping by a central depository. For example, suppose that on the day prior to settlement of the transaction, clearing firm A, which represents the introducing broker, is listed as owner of 2,000 shares of IBM stock and clearing firm B is listed as owner of 1,800 shares of IBM stock, all held by the central depository. The transfer of 500 shares on behalf of the introducing broker's customer will result in the transfer of 500 shares from the account of clearing firm B to the account of clearing firm A. Thus, clearing firm A now holds 2,500 shares of IBM, and clearing firm B holds 1,300 shares. This process makes it unnecessary to physically transfer the securities.

After the settlement date, the clearing firm involved will either continue to hold the securities in its own name on behalf of the customer or, if so instructed by the customer, transfer the securities to the customer's name and mail them to him. In those cases in which the broker holds the stock for the customer (the usual case), the broker has the responsibility of collecting dividends and handling such other administrative tasks as required to service the account. One important component of this servicing is providing periodic accounting statements to customers. These might be sent on a monthly or quarterly basis, depending upon the nature of the account. Brokerage firms also have the additional responsibility of providing end–of–year reports of dividend and interest income, and to report the gross proceeds of sales for capital gains reconciliation. This information is also reported to the Internal Revenue Service.

From this brief description, it should be clear that each transaction involves a settlement among brokers and separate settlements between brokers and customers. The former is called **street–side settlement** and must, by definition, involve clearing firms. Some clearing firms handle only street–side settlement activity. These clearing firms are said to clear on an **omnibus** basis. Other clearing firms clear both the street side and the customer settlement and are described as **fully disclosed**. Under a fully disclosed arrangement, the clearing firm handles all administrative matters concerning the customer's account, including trade confirmations, periodic account statements, dividend collection and distribution, etc. Nonclearing broker/dealers must decide whether they wish to purchase omnibus or fully disclosed services. The latter will, of course, involve additional expenses, and the decision harks back to the make–or–buy question.

Sources of Revenue for Clearing Firms

We have already pointed out that clearing firms get into the business of clearing other firms' trades to earn clearing fees. If conducted on a large enough scale, such operations can become a meaningful profit center for investment banks that provide clearing services. But the clearing fees earned are only one source of revenue for clearing firms. They also collect execution fees (if they provide the execution services) and may collect fees for a variety of other activities, including account maintenance and research.

In addition to these obvious sources of fee revenue, there are some important but decidedly more subtle sources of revenue earned by clearing firms. These include interest earned on customer funds, spreads earned on repo transactions, spreads earned on the difference between the clearing firm's call money rate and its broker loan rate, and potential opportunities to cross–trade in those markets in which the clearing firm acts as a dealer, thus earning a bid–ask spread.

Let's consider these latter sources of revenue just a bit further. Consider first the various sources of interest income that the clearing firm can earn. If it holds customers' cash (called **credit balances**) that is not committed to trades, the cash balances can be invested by the clearing firm to earn interest. This might take the form of lending the cash to customers who wish to buy securities on margin (i.e., using borrowed funds). The securities purchased are used as collateral on the loan, making this a very low–risk form of lending. Or the clearing firm may borrow funds from a commercial bank at the commercial bank's **call money rate** and then lend the funds to customers at the clearing firm's higher **broker loan rate**. Finally, the clearing firm may borrow customers' securities to lend to others who need to deliver on short sales. The clearing firm collects some interest on the value of these loans of securities in excess of that payable to the short seller.

The customers of clearing firms include all sorts of brokers, from retail to institutional. They also include professional trading firms, such as specialist firms and market makers. The services that the clearing firm can profitably sell will depend very much on the nature of the non-clearing broker's business and needs.

In closing this chapter, it is interesting to get some sense of the sorts of firms that sell clearing services and the way in which they organize these services. Examples of some of the largest clearing securities firms include Bear, Stearns; Merrill Lynch; and Morgan Stanley. At Bear, Stearns, clearing services are provided by Bear, Stearns Securities Corporation (BSSC), a registered broker/dealer and subsidiary of Bear, Stearns established on July 1, 1991, to clear and settle securities transactions and to hold customer securities. Bear, Stearns' 1992 annual report states that " . . . an increase in the Company's correspondent clearing client base contributed to a 20.3 percent increase in revenues derived from the Company's securities clearance activities."[2] The report goes on to offer some insight into the fixed costs associated with such operations:

> "Effective June 1, 1992, the Company's securities processing and clearance operations previously conducted at three locations in New York City were relocated to approximately 216,000 square feet of office space . . . the Company expects an annual reduction of approximately $13,000,000 in occupancy and depreciation costs [as a result]. . ."[3]

While the report does not provide a breakdown of profits/losses based on functional areas, it does go on to say:

> "The correspondent clearing business had another successful year in fiscal 1992. Bear, Stearns Securities Corp. (BSSC) . . . proved to be a major benefit in attracting new clients who prefer that their assets be kept separate from the proprietary activities of a securities firm. BSSC provides clearing and additional services for broker–dealers, market makers, specialists, arbitrageurs, money managers and other professional traders worldwide. During the year we added many new clients, bringing the total number of fully disclosed and professional accounts to 1,226."[4]

This report makes clear that Bear Stearns views its clearing operations as a profit center and not merely as a support activity. This is a fundamental transformation within the industry with respect to many traditional support activities—a point we will make repeatedly in the next few chapters.

---

[2] Bear, Stearns 1992 Annual Report, page 11.

[3] Ibid, page 24.

[4] Ibid, page 18.

Summary

Every trade, regardless of its purpose or who is responsible for making it, must be cleared and settled. Clearance and settlement require a significant commitment of capital, facilities, and personnel. As a result, it is expensive and highly specialized. But the activity has substantial economies of scale, making it a logical candidate for a service to be sold to nonclearing broker/dealers. Clearing services earn fees for clearing firms, produce interest revenue, and enhance the image of the service provider. Clearing operations have been transformed from strictly support activities to quasi–profit centers at many firms, but this does not mean that the dominant motivation is necessarily revenue generation. The decision as to whether to provide one's own clearing services or to purchase them from another shop is essentially a classic make–or–buy decision hinging on fixed costs, variable costs, transactional volume expectations, and risk considerations.

References and Suggested Reading

Brooks, R. E., "Court Imposes Duty of Disclosure on Clearing Bank," *International Financial Law Review*, 9:4, April 1990, p. 10.

Lake, D., "The Unseen Perils of Global Settlement," *Asian Finance*, 11:5, May 15, 1988, pp. 68–71.

Mengle, D. L., "Behind the Money Market: Clearing and Settling Money Market Instruments," *Economic Review*, Federal Reserve Bank of Richmond, 78:5, September/October 1992, pp. 3–11.

Modi, M., "Clearing Business Shifts Again," *ABA Banking Journal*, 80:3, March 1988, pp. 78–85.

Parkinson, P., J. Stehm, A. Gilbert, E. Gollob, L. Hargraves, R. Mead, and M. A. Taylor, "Staff Study: Clearance and Settlement in the U.S. Securities Markets," *Federal Reserve Bulletin*, 78:3, March 1992, pp. 182–184.

Rhee, S. G. and R. P. Chang, "The Microstructure of Asian Equity Markets," *Journal of Financial Services Research*, 6:4, January 1993, pp. 437–451.

12

Research

Overview

We have repeatedly highlighted the roles played by research in the revenue–generating activities of investment banks. We have, for example, discussed the many ways in which research supports sales and trading; the ways in which research is utilized by an investment bank's mergers and acquisitions (M&A) group to identify potential takeover targets and to value assets; the role research plays in developing new products and new trading strategies—particularly complex arbitrage strategies; and the role research plays in winning institutional business and investment management business—particularly in the area of high–tech venture capital. Despite this, however, we have not presented much in the way of specifics on how research is conducted and how research departments are organized. This is the subject of this chapter.

Research is best viewed as a support activity, because its purpose is to support the revenue activities of other areas of the firm. Like clearing services, however, research has become a revenue activity for some investment banks. These banks sell research to broker/dealers who, in turn, distribute it under their own name to their customers. Research sales do help defray research costs, but the sales are not sufficient to maintain the activity without subsidy from the firm. Thus, research must be viewed as a necessary component of investment banking and one whose value is only realized indirectly through its impact on the revenue generation of other areas of the firm.

Organization of Research Departments

Research departments are typically organized along three main lines: equity research, fixed–income research, and quantitative research. Each of these is further divided. For example, fixed–income research includes traditional corporate bond research, derivatives research, high–yield research, mortgage product research, and so on. Quantitative research might also fall under the more general heading of fixed–income research. Derivatives research might be organized under fixed–income or under quantitative research. The particular organizational groupings are as much a matter of a research department's evolutionary path as they are a matter of a logical fit. Alternatively, research can be organized along investor lines—institutional research versus retail research, for example. Increasingly, research departments have been integrated with sales and trading and with other revenue activities that research supports.

Research staffers typically hold the title of analyst. This could be "research analyst," "financial analyst," or some other variation. The work done by financial analysts in investment banking groups and M&A groups with respect to securities valuation, asset valuation or company valuation is just as surely research as is the work done within a designated research department.

We will briefly review the activities of equity research groups, fixed–income research groups, and quantitative research groups. In the process, we will try to provide a straightforward example of the ways in which these groups try to add value. Of course, we cannot do much more than provide a general sense of the role played by research in this one short chapter, but that should be sufficient to round out the several discussions of research and its role covered in other chapters of this book.

Equity Research

Because institutional trading now accounts for well over 70 percent of total shares traded, it makes sense to focus on the equity research activities that are geared toward supporting sales to institutional investors. A major investment bank with an institutional clientele will maintain an equity research department specializing by industry or groups of related industries. Such a research department might employ 30 to 50 people, rarely more.[1]

The analysts include both industry analysts (i.e., industry specialists) and strategy analysts (responsible for developing profitable trading/ investment strategies). The industry analysts carry out in–depth analyses of individual companies—in the context of the industry in which they operate and the general economic environment—in order to determine absolute and relative values of corporations. They then make definitive buy, hold, and sell recommendations.

In the current environment, equity analysts increasingly play a marketing role. Once an analyst has a recommendation on a particular security, she will call her counterpart, an institutional investment manager or institutional analyst, to discuss her findings. She will also provide a copy of her detailed report. The goal, of course, is to generate transactional business for the investment bank's institutional sales and trading force. The institutional analyst's function is to review the research analyst's recommendation and the analysis behind it, consider how the recommended position would fit into the institution's current portfolio, and factor in any private information that he might possess. This institutional marketing support function may occupy as much as 40 to 60 percent of an equity research analyst's time.

Consider now how an equity research department might make a stock recommendation. The equity research department begins with a bit of basic financial theory called the **capital asset pricing model**. This model treats the fair return on a security (called the "required rate of return") as a linear function of the stock's systematic risk, as measured by the security's **beta coefficient**. The beta measures the ratio of the stock's systematic risk to the market risk. The basic relationship is given by an equation called the **security market line**:

$$r_x = (r_m - r_f) \, \beta_x + r_f$$

where r_x is the required rate of return for stock X, r_m is the expected rate of return on the market (usually taken to be the S&P 500 stock index),

---

[1] Merrill Lynch is an exception, employing over 100 equity research analysts.

r_f is the risk–free rate of interest (usually taken to be the 1 year T–bill rate), and β_x is the beta coefficient for stock X.

The calculation of a stock's beta is a straightforward statistical procedure employing easily obtainable data.[2] But estimating the required return on a stock is not the same as estimating its fair market value. Another step is needed—one that is founded on present–value valuation principles and makes use of a "growth model." The simplest such model assumes that the firm's earnings will grow indefinitely at a constant rate, g, and that the dividend payout ratio, d, will remain constant. Under this scenario, the fair value of the stock is given by:

$$\text{Value} = \frac{(d \times \text{EPS}) (1 + g)}{r_x - g}$$

where EPS denotes the latest year's earnings per share, and r_x is the required rate of return obtained from the security market line equation.

Since EPS and d are observable, and r_x can be easily estimated, it follows that valuation of common stock reduces to estimating the growth rate of earnings. This, then, is the central focus of an equity analysis, and it is not surprising that the heart of an equity research report is a discussion of earnings growth rate forecasts and their justification.

Let's suppose that for Stock X we observe that EPS is $2, that d is 60 percent, and that r_x is 10.5 percent. The equity analysts who wrote the report estimated that the earnings growth rate is sustainable at 5 percent. Then the valuation equation tells us that the stock has a value of $22.91 [i.e., $(0.60 \times \$2 \times 1.05)/(.105 - 05)$]. Let's suppose that the stock is currently priced at $32.50 a share. Clearly, the equity analysts would conclude that the stock is overvalued by the market and would issue a bearish "sell" recommendation. If the firm's equity traders agree with the analysis, they would likely sell the stock short.

---

[2] While the statistical procedure is straightforward and the data are easily obtained, the application of the technique requires a number of important decisions on the part of the researcher: type of data to be used (quarterly, monthly, daily, etc.), the estimation period to be employed, adjustments to the calculated beta to reflect changes in the corporation relative to the estimation period, and so forth. These latter considerations can greatly complicate any actual application of the procedure.

Equity research departments routinely issue four types of recommendations: strong buy, buy, hold, and sell. The first is a very bullish recommendation, the second is a somewhat bullish recommendation, the third is a neutral recommendation (but is often interpreted as bearish), and the fourth is decidedly bearish.

The research staff plays a considerably smaller role in marketing to retail customers than to institutional customers. Retail customer marketing is almost exclusively the purview of the retail broker/dealers (salespeople). It is not uncommon, however, for research departments to "repackage" their research in such a way as to pitch their ideas to a retail clientele. The pitch, however, is made by the sales force. After this reformulation, the end product comes across more as a marketing piece than as an analytical document.

Fixed Income and Quantitative Research

Both fixed–income and quantitative research (which is often viewed as a subset of fixed–income research) are considerably more quantitative than equity research. There are analysts in these groups who (1) estimate the value of embedded options contained in mortgages and mortgaged–backed products; (2) assess the fairness of spreads between fixed–income instruments of different maturities and different risk classes, and make trading recommendations based on deviations from fair spreads; and (3) develop strategies to synthesize instruments using replicating portfolios, and then assess the relative values of the "real" security and the synthetic security; and so on.

Both fixed–income and quantitative research groups work with specific customers to structure customized solutions to their needs. These needs are based on interest rate risk and exchange rate risk considerations, credit class requirements for holding securities, legal restrictions banning the holding of certain types of securities, and so forth. Consider, for example, the needs of pension funds. The pension fund managers have specific asset/liability needs. For example, they may be required to keep their portfolios immunized (i.e., match the durations of their asset portfolios with the durations of their liabilities portfolios), or they may require a certain minimum level of liquidity, or they might be holding assets that have moved out of a required risk class due to credit deterioration of the issuer. The investment bank's research department can assist in identifying securities having the desired characteristics and the appropriate strategy to achieve the desired portfolio characteristics.

Consider one example of how a research department served to help create a new market. Fixed–income researchers at Drexel Burnham Lambert demonstrated that the bond markets had long demanded too high a premium for credit risk, with the result that speculative–grade securities returned a higher yield than that justified by credit risk. Specifically, they showed that a well–diversified portfolio of speculative–grade bonds had outperformed a portfolio of top investment–grade bonds consistently for many years, even after allowing for losses due to defaults. This discovery provided the justification for recommending high–yield bond strategies to institutional investors and helped give birth to the junk bond market.

Fixed–income researchers and strategists often develop complex trading strategies. These strategies involve sophisticated mathematical optimization techniques. One such technique developed by investment bank research personnel is called total return optimization, and it relies on the methodology of operations research. Specifically, total return optimization employs linear programming and quadratic programming techniques to determine the optimal portfolio for an investor operating under a given set of investment constraints.

In recent years, as derivative instruments have become an important source of investment banking profits, investment banks have hired many of the top academic theorists (sometimes as permanent hires and sometimes as consultants) to support their research efforts. It is not a coincidence, for example, that Fisher Black and Myron Scholes, the originators of the option pricing model, were hired by Goldman Sachs and Salomon Brothers, respectively.

Derivative groups, including the mortgage–products research groups, are expected to be thoroughly versed in option pricing theory and mathematics, and to keep up with the latest developments in this highly quantitative and sophisticated area.

Other research groups invest time developing strategies to arbitrage markets. This includes traditional arbitrage across space and time, but also arbitrage across instruments and tax asymmetries. Program trading is an example of an application of the talents of a research department to the former and synthetic securities an example of the latter. To illustrate the point, consider the case of synthesizing yen–denominated zero coupon bonds from dollar–pay zero coupon bonds and several types of swaps.

In the United States, dollar–pay zero coupon bonds are routinely created by stripping conventional Treasury bonds. These zeros appeal to investors because they allow the investor to match his investment horizon precisely to the zero's maturity. This eliminates all credit risk (because the zeros are Treasury–based), all interest rate risk (because the zero's maturity matches the investor's horizon), and reinvestment risk (because the bonds are zeros). Japanese investors have all the same reasons as U.S. investors to want to hold zero coupon bonds. But Japanese investors have one additional incentive, and a very powerful one at that. Throughout the 1980s, the interest on a zero coupon bond, under Japanese tax law, was treated as a capital gain rather than interest. And in Japan, capital gains are tax–exempt. Thus, the Japanese investor enjoys tax preference by investing in zeros.

While the tax treatment of zeros makes them particularly attractive to Japanese investors, it also resulted in the Japanese Ministry of Finance (MOF) discouraging Japanese corporations from issuing zeros and discouraging Japanese securities firms from creating zeros via stripping conventional bonds. The only alternative left to the Japanese investor in need of a zero was to invest in dollar–pay zeros and bear the exchange rate risk associated with holding non–yen–denominated assets.

The tax asymmetries coupled with the lack of supply led certain U.S. investment banks to seek a way to exploit what was clearly an attractive opportunity. The task was turned over to the quantitative and derivatives research departments, and a way was found to exploit the opportunity. First, an investment bank sets up a special purpose corporation (SPC). The SPC issues, as liabilities, real retail–denomination yen–pay zero coupon bonds, which are marketed to Japanese investors by the investment bank's retail brokerage network (or affiliates) in Japan.

The proceeds from the issuance are then used to purchase, in wholesale denominations, dollar–pay zero coupon Treasury bonds. These are held as an asset of the SPC. This purchase is made through the investment bank's government securities unit. Next, the SPC enters into a specially structured zero–coupon–for–floating interest rate swap and a specially structured zero–coupon–for–floating currency swap. These swaps are transacted with the investment bank's own derivatives group. These off–balance sheet swaps have the effect of converting the dollar–pay zero coupon asset into a synthetic yen–pay zero coupon asset. The cash flows for the three components are depicted in Figure 12.1; the

Figure 12.1
Components of a Synthetic Yen–Pay Zero

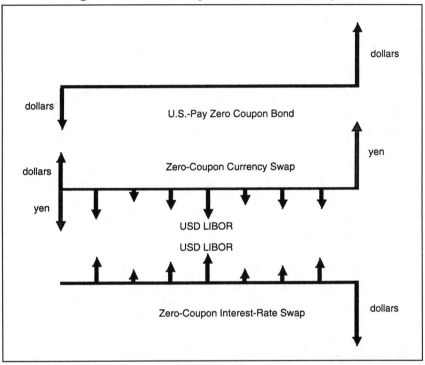

net flows are depicted in Figure 12.2; and the balance sheet of the SPC is depicted in Figure 12.3.

Figure 12.2
Net Flows: Synthetic Yen–Pay Zero

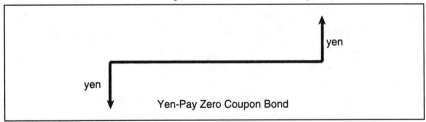

Figure 12.3
The SPC's Balance Sheet

Assets	Liabilities
dollar-pay zeros	yen-pay zeros

The swaps are off-balance sheet. Only the bonds appear on the balance sheet. Nevertheless, the swaps have the effect of altering the character of the assets.

The synthetic zero asset and the real zero liability should prove profitable to the SPC if Japanese retail investors are willing to pay more for real zeros than it costs the investment bank to synthesize them on a wholesale level. This result might be expected, given the tax treatment of zeros in Japan and the artificial shortage, as a consequence of the moral suasion of the MOF.

This example indicates one of many ways that the research teams of investment banks generate ideas and strategies that can enhance the profitability of the investment banks and open new avenues for profit.

Ethical Issues in Research

The investment banking industry is filled with potential conflicts of interest, and research is no different. By the nature of their business, investment banks serve many different clienteles, and the needs of these clienteles often conflict. Consider just one. An investment bank underwrites securities and, in this context, its customers are corporate issuers. The investment bank invests a great deal of energy and time cultivating relationships with the corporate community to help it win business on an ongoing basis. From this business, the investment bank earns advisory and underwriting fees. At the same time, the investment bank has an obligation to provide accurate research to investors—both institutional and retail. Thus, the investment bank has a self–interest obligation to serve corporate issuers well and a quasi–fiduciary obligation to provide accurate information and research to investors. The investment bank, after all, serves as an intermediary between the **sell side** and the **buy side** of the transactions.

Into these relationships step the research departments. The equity research department will make buy/sell recommendations with respect to equity issues, and the fixed–income research department will make recommendations with respect to bond issues. Suppose now that a corporate issuer—which may already be a client of the investment bank's corporate finance group, or which the corporate finance group is seeking to win over—discovers that the investment bank's equity research department is issuing a sell recommendation for the corporation's equity or downgrading the corporation's debt. How does the corporate issuer react to such news? At the very least, of course, it is upset. And in all likelihood, the corporation will threaten to pull its issuance business from the investment bank. Furthermore, the corporation may also have other relationships with the bank. For example, perhaps the bank's investment management group manages the corporation's pension portfolio. This business, too, may be placed at risk from a bearish research report.

To whom, then, do the research analysts owe their first allegiance? Do they owe it to the corporate finance group and the investment management group, which stand to lose business? Or do they owe it to the institutional and retail investors, who trust the research to be accurate and unbiased?

In situations such as this, the research analyst is often caught between a rock and a hard place. Every investment bank, of course, must insist that its research is untainted by other considerations. But is it? While the same story has played out at most of the large investment banks, consider one of the most recent incidents. As reported in *The Wall Street Journal*:[3]

". . . Morgan Stanley's powerful investment bankers often have run roughshod over the firm's research analysts, some current and former Morgan Stanley analysts say. These analysts say that Morgan Stanley's bankers have repeatedly pressured them to alter negative research reports on the stocks of the firm's corporate clients—particularly those for which it did stock underwriting deals."

---

[3]See *The Wall Street Journal*, July 14, 1992, page A1.

The article goes on to state:

"Morgan officials concede that investment bankers occasionally have put pressure on the firm's research analysts to influence their views on stocks."

Morgan's chairman at the time, Richard B. Fisher, responded to these charges by noting that "I guarantee you the tension between investment bankers and research exists at every firm, but Morgan Stanley deals with it as well as anyone." Fisher denied that the pressure exerted by its investment bankers on its researchers ever resulted in a compromise of the firm's research.

It is impossible to say, of course, to precisely what degree research is influenced by other considerations. But it would certainly seem that investors should ask themselves if the research report they are reading pertains to a firm that is a client of the investment bank producing the report.

Summary

Research is a critical support area for most large investment banks. The various research groups, which include equity research, fixed–income research, derivatives research, and quantitative research, to name just a few, work closely in support of sales and trading. For this reason, many investment banks have integrated sales, trading, and research over the last few years.

Research staff assist the M&A group in identifying the potential takeover targets; assist institutional and retail sales personnel by making buy, sell, and hold recommendations; work with clients through structured–products groups and derivatives groups to structure solutions to complex problems; and develop complex arbitrage and trading strategies that are implemented by others within the firm.

While research is not a revenue area per se, without research an investment bank would be hard–pressed to retain clients, identify profitable situations, and do the other things that investment banks do so successfully.

References and Suggested Reading

Berg, A., "The Topsy–Turvy World of Chinese Walls," *International Financial Law Review*, 11:12, December 1992, pp. 26-28.

Galant, D., "Research: Ordering a la Carte," *Institutional Investor*, 21:6, May 1990, pp. 145-146.

Kolman, J., "The Growth of Derivatives Research," *Institutional Investor*, 25:13, November 1991, pp. 143-144.

Levine, T. A., "Multiservice Securities Firms: Coping with Conflicts in a Tender Offer Context," *Wake Forest Law Review*, 23:1, 1988, pp. 41-75.

Maher, P., "Shearson, DaPuzzo Settlement Outlines Chinese Wall Holes," *Investment Dealers Digest*, 58:26, June 29, 1992, pp. 8-9.

Taha, H. A., "Operations Research Analysis of a Stock Market Problem," *Computers & Operations Research*, 18:7, 1991, pp. 597-602.

13

Funding and Risk Management

Overview

The bulge bracket investment banks each hold many billions of dollars of assets, all of which have to be financed. In some cases, the very strategy that gives rise to the assets also gives rise to the financing, but sometimes not.

More than most industries, the investment banking industry is heavily dependent on short–term financing. At first glance, this might seem imprudent. After all, a high percentage of the assets held are rate–sensitive securities (bonds, notes, mortgage–backs, etc.) Financing long–maturity assets with short–term liabilities is generally regarded as very risky. But investment banks are masters at hedging their risks. The hedging is done, for the most part, in off–balance sheet derivatives—such as futures, forwards, and swaps. Thus, the heavy dependence on short–term financing does not generate as great a level of risk as it would seem at first blush.

We will use this chapter to make some general observations on the types of assets investment banks hold and how those assets are financed. To assist us, we will employ the financial statements of Bear, Stearns from that investment bank's 1992 Annual Report (see Chapter 13 Appendix). While the weights of different asset classes as well as the dependence on short–term versus long–term financing will vary from bank to bank, Bear, Stearns' financial statements are nevertheless reasonably typical of bulge bracket investment banks in general. Some of this chapter will repeat what was said in Chapter 2, but most of what we have to say will buttress the arguments made in that chapter. After our general observations on funding, we briefly put the risk management support activity in perspective. Finally, we close with an appendix providing the details of Bear, Stearns' 1992 financial statements and provide descriptions of Bear, Stearns' financial leverage strategy, funding strategy, and risk management practices. These selected descriptions are taken directly from Bear, Stearns' 1992 Annual Report.

General Observations on Leverage and Funding

At the end of its fiscal year in 1992 (June 30), the Bear, Stearns Companies, Inc., (BSC) held assets of $45.8 billion. These assets were financed by long–term debt of $1 billion and equity of $1.3 billion. Thus, the long–term debt–to–equity ratio was 0.77. Short–term sources of financing, mainly repurchase transactions and other collateralized lending, accounted for the remaining $43.5 billion of required financing. Thus, the ratio of short–term financing to equity capital was in excess of 33:1.

A more complete view of the firm's performance for 1992 and the preceding three years appears in Table 13.1. All values are in millions except per–share data.

Note that for 1989, 1990, and 1991, the interest expense averaged 48 percent of revenue. In 1992, however, interest expense fell to only 31 percent of revenue. This is more a reflection of the sharp decline in interest rates generally than any significant change in Bear, Stearns' methods of operation. Of course, the interest component of the firm's revenue also declined significantly during 1992 for the same reason. For example, interest and dividend income accounted for 37.2 percent of revenues in 1992, as compared to 53.9 percent in 1991 and 58 percent in 1990.

The close match between interest revenue and interest expense reflects the investment bank's role as a financial intermediary. On the one hand, the bank holds large quantities of securities as a necessary condition of its market making and proprietary trading activities. These

Table 13.1
Operating Results

	1992	1991	1990	1989
Revenues	$2,677	$2,380	$2,386	$2,365
Interest expense	835	1,141	1,217	1,090
Revenues, net of interest	$1,842	$1,239	$1,169	$1,275
Non–interest expenses:				
Employee Compensation	$910	$652	$608	$627
Other[1]	425	357	368	360
Income before provision for taxes	$508	$230	$193	$287
Provision for taxes	213	87	73	115
Net income	$295	$143	$119	$172
Earnings per share (common)	$2.70	$1.25	$0.95	$1.33
Return on equity	27.6%	13.6%	11.5%	11.9%

[1]Other expenses include floor broker, exchange, and clearance fees; communications; occupancy; depreciation and amortization; advertising and market development; data processing and equipment; and miscellaneous other.

securities generate interest and dividend income. On the other hand, the positions must be financed, and this generates interest expense.[1]

To the extent that interest and dividend revenue exceeds interest and dividend expense, the securities holdings contribute positively to the firm's bottom line. Thus, the financing of the firm's positions and the development of funding strategies that exploit relative values is critical to the firm's success. Just how important this source of income is can be gleaned from the consolidated income statement in the appendix. Net interest earned (interest and dividend revenues – interest expense) totaled $162 million ($997 million – $835 million) in fiscal year ending June 30,

---

[1] Additional interest is earned on customers' free credit balances and certain balances generated through the clearing process as discussed in Chapter 11.

1992. This was fully 31.9 percent of Bear, Stearns' profits (before taxes) for that fiscal year. For the prior two years, the net interest contributions to before–tax profit were 62 percent in 1991 and 86.5 percent in 1990.

Given the dimensions of the contribution of net interest to the investment bank's profitability, it is not surprising that an enormous amount of time and energy is devoted to optimizing the firm's financing strategy.

The full balance sheet for fiscal years ending June 30, 1992, and June 30, 1991, are also provided in the Appendix to this chapter. Notice that four asset categories and five liability categories tell most of the tale with respect to interest received and interest paid. These appear in Table 13.2.

Table 13.2
Assets/Liabilities

(In Billions)	1992	1991
Assets		
Securities purchased under resale agreements	$16.3	$14.0
Securities borrowed	9.7	9.5
Financial instruments owned (long)	12.2	8.8
Receivables from broker/dealers and customers	4.3	3.9
Total	$42.5	$36.2
Liabilities		
Short–term borrowings	$3.8	$2.8
Securities sold under repurchase agreements	19.3	17.7
Securities loaned	1.5	3.5
Financial instruments sold but not yet purchased (short)	6.2	3.6
Payables to broker/dealers and customers	11.3	9.0
Total	$42.1	$36.6

Notice that, overall, the assets and liabilities categories in Table 13.2 are nearly mirror images of each other. While the assets and liabilities have a short–term character in the sense that they are "current assets" and "current liabilities," many, particularly the securities positions—whether held outright or under repurchase/resale agreements—represent the long–term obligations of other issuers (i.e., stocks and bonds). As such, these instruments are very price–sensitive to changes in market conditions, and careful risk management is required.

Risk Management

The securities purchased under resale agreements constitute the largest component of assets, and securities sold under repurchase agreements constitute the largest component of liabilities. These positions are taken in order to facilitate the investment bank's broker/dealer activities and proprietary trading activities. But these positions give rise to considerable interest rate risk, exchange rate risk, and equity market risk.

Investment banks are no strangers to high risk, and they have become very adept at managing it. They were pioneers in the application of risk management theory. For example, they were among the first to employ duration–based hedging models. And they improved upon these models by developing the dollar–value–of–a–basis–point (DV01) model. Investment banks also played a heavy role in the development of many risk management instruments, such as swaps, and, not surprisingly, they were some of the first to use these instruments to manage their own risks.

We have already described, in several contexts, how investment banks manage their interest rate risk and other price risks. We have demonstrated the macro approach to hedging a fixed–income dealer's book, for example, in Chapter 5, and we examined additional applications in Chapters 6 and 9. But price risks are not the only kinds of risk that an investment bank faces. Other risks include credit risk, sovereign risk, and settlement risk, as just three examples.

Credit risk includes the risk that a security will lose value because its creditworthiness is perceived to decline and the risk of direct exposure to a counterparty from default. The latter risk has always been a concern for holders of corporate securities. But with the emergence and rapid growth of the junk bond and over–the–counter derivatives market, the issue has become of sharply greater importance. Indeed, governmental concern has been repeatedly expressed about the potential for spillover effects from defaults in the junk bond and derivatives markets. These spillover effects are considered to be a part of **systemic risks**, because some believe they pose a threat to the entire financial system.

Concern about systemic risks associated with the rapid growth of the derivatives markets has led to a number of studies, some of which are ongoing as of this writing. The issue has been studied by both the industry (Group of 30, for example) and by government regulators (GAO, for example). While the findings are not all in, it is highly probable that greater capital requirements will be imposed on the investment banking industry, as they have already been imposed on the commercial banking industry. The latter was justified by the depository nature of banking and the role of the government in insuring the safety of bank depositors.

Sovereign risk is the risk that, due to financial crisis or political instability, entities of a particular country will be unable to honor their obligations and commitments. Recent upheaval in the states of the former Soviet Union and the consequent failure of the political jurisdictions involved to service their debts is a clear example of this form of exposure. As investment banking becomes more global and the scope of its activities becomes more international, this form of risk becomes greater. Default provisions in swaps that incorporate provisions for supervening illegalities and early termination are examples of some of the efforts that have been made to deal with sovereign risk. Other management methods include limiting the amount of exposure the investment bank has to counterparties in any one country.

Settlement risk is the risk that one party to a financial transaction will make payment to the other party, only to have the other party default on its obligation to make payment or deliver securities. Clearinghouses are one way that such risks are mitigated and managed. Other methods include limiting the size of settlements with a single counterparty on any one day and netting payments.

Risk management will surely continue to play a major role in the management of investment banks. And business schools will increasingly recognize the importance of teaching risk management theory and its applications—either by introducing courses devoted exclusively to risk management or by incorporating risk management into traditional courses.

Summary

In this chapter, we have tried to tie up some loose ends concerning investment bank funding and risk management. We have argued that the nature of the business is such that investment banks must hold large securities positions—some long and some short. These are funded largely by transactions in the repurchase/resale market and other secured and unsecured borrowing and lending.

While these positions are a consequence of market making and proprietary trading, they earn interest or generate interest expense. The magnitude of the positions is such that the interest earned and the interest paid can, in some years, mean the difference between a profitable and an unprofitable year. At the same time, the positions generate sizable risks. These risks must be identified, measured, and managed. Not surprisingly, investment banks invest considerable time and energy in minimizing their financial costs and managing their financial risks.

References and Suggested Reading

Arak, M., "The Effect of the New Risk–Based Capital Requirements on the Market for Swaps," *Journal of Financial Services Research*, 6:1, May 1992, pp. 25–36.

Conybeare, J. A. C., "On the Repudiation of Sovereign Debt: Sources of Stability and Risk," *Columbia Journal of World Business*, 25:1–2, Spring 1990, pp. 46–52.

Doukas, J., "Syndicated Euro–Credit Sovereign Risk Assessments, Market Efficiency and Contagion Effects," *Journal of International Business Studies*, 20:2, Summer 1989, pp. 255–267.

Gilbert, R. A., "Implications of Netting Arrangements for Bank Risk in Foreign Exchange Transactions," *Federal Reserve Bank of St. Louis Review*, 74:1, January/February 1992, pp. 3–16.

Hull, J., "Assessing Credit Risk in a Financial Institution's Off–Balance Sheet Commitments," *Journal of Financial and Quantitative Analysis*, 24:4, December 1989, pp. 489–501.

Prutzman, D. S., "Payment System Risk," *Issues in Bank Regulation*, 13:1, Summer 1989, pp. 19–23.

Simons, K., "Measuring Credit Risk in Interest Rate Swaps," *New England Economic Review*, November/December 1989, pp. 29–38.

Smith, T., "The New Credit Derivatives," *Global Finance*, 7:3, March 1993, pp. 109–110.

Appendix

Bear, Stearns Companies
1992 Financial Statements
and

Consolidated Statements of Income

In thousands, except share data	Fiscal Year Ended June 30, 1992	Fiscal Year Ended June 30, 1991	Fiscal Year Ended June 30, 1990
REVENUES			
Commissions	$ 374,752	$ 338,823	$ 338,404
Principal transactions	971,990	542,097	429,385
Investment banking	318,428	196,721	222,401
Interest and dividends	996,843	1,283,222	1,383,744
Other income	14,946	19,090	12,119
Total revenues	2,676,959	2,379,953	2,386,053
Interest expense	834,859	1,141,029	1,217,212
Revenues, net of interest expense	1,842,100	1,238,924	1,168,841
NON-INTEREST EXPENSES			
Employee compensation and benefits	909,916	652,186	608,291
Floor brokerage, exchange and clearance fees	65,770	58,365	57,990
Communications	52,799	52,723	55,434
Occupancy	79,947	73,352	70,050
Depreciation and amortization	39,684	33,169	29,665
Advertising and market development	32,484	27,531	27,988
Data processing and equipment	26,634	25,726	27,389
Other expenses	127,241	86,371	99,502
Total non-interest expenses	1,334,475	1,009,423	976,309
Income before provision for income taxes	507,625	229,501	192,532
Provision for income taxes	213,047	86,636	73,164
Net income	$ 294,578	$ 142,865	$ 119,368
Net income applicable to common shares	$ 291,350	$ 139,028	$ 114,877
Earnings per share	$ 2.70	$ 1.25	$ .95
Weighted average common and common equivalent shares outstanding	111,087,263	111,648,945	120,788,596

See Notes to Consolidated Financial Statements.

Consolidated Statements of Financial Condition

THE BEAR STEARNS COMPANIES INC.

In thousands, except share data	June 30, 1992	June 30, 1991
ASSETS		
Cash and cash equivalents	$ 124,088	$ 478,153
Cash and securities deposited with clearing organizations or segregated in compliance with Federal regulations	2,159,339	1,853,319
Securities purchased under agreements to resell	16,289,968	13,976,210
Securities borrowed	9,690,866	9,458,635
Receivable from brokers, dealers and others	563,428	534,822
Receivable from customers	3,748,094	3,347,110
Financial instruments owned — at market value	12,162,367	8,791,916
Property, equipment and leasehold improvements, net of accumulated depreciation and amortization of $186,386 in 1992 and $148,001 in 1991	225,968	196,039
Other assets	804,215	648,709
Total Assets	$45,768,333	$39,284,913
LIABILITIES AND STOCKHOLDERS' EQUITY		
Short-term borrowings	$ 3,816,334	$ 2,843,627
Securities sold under agreements to repurchase	19,317,964	17,713,467
Securities loaned	1,495,681	3,519,521
Payable to brokers, dealers and others	1,865,517	1,464,694
Payable to customers	9,472,560	7,646,346
Financial instruments sold, but not yet purchased — at market value	6,166,881	3,644,289
Accrued employee compensation and benefits	438,686	281,129
Other liabilities and accrued expenses	877,330	493,971
	43,450,953	37,507,044
Commitments and contingencies		
Long-term borrowings	1,040,396	681,846
STOCKHOLDERS' EQUITY		
Preferred stock, $1.00 par value; 10,000,000 shares authorized: Adjustable Rate Cumulative Preferred Stock, Series A; $50 liquidation preference; 3,000,000 shares issued	150,000	150,000
Common stock, $1.00 par value; 200,000,000 shares authorized; 125,255,167 shares and 113,629,785 shares issued in 1992 and 1991, respectively	125,255	113,630
Paid-in capital	1,138,386	991,771
Retained earnings	113,467	43,976
Capital Accumulation Plan	137,503	23,414
Treasury stock, at cost — Adjustable Rate Cumulative Preferred Stock, Series A; 2,108,550 shares in 1992 and 1,942,650 shares in 1991	(85,063)	(78,094)
Common stock; 23,531,024 shares in 1992 and 14,984,943 shares in 1991	(262,564)	(148,674)
Note receivable from ESOP Trust	(40,000)	
Total Stockholders' Equity	1,276,984	1,096,023
Total Liabilities and Stockholders' Equity	$45,768,333	$39,284,913

See Notes to Consolidated Financial Statements.

Funding and Risk Management   359

Financial Leverage

The Company maintains a highly liquid balance sheet with a majority of the Company's assets consisting of marketable securities inventories, which are marked to market daily, and collateralized receivables arising from customer related and proprietary securities transactions. Collateralized receivables consist of resale agreements, secured by U.S. government and agency securities, and customer margin loans and securities borrowed which are typically secured with marketable corporate debt and equity securities. The nature of the Company's business as a securities dealer requires it to carry significant levels of securities inventories in order to meet its customer and proprietary trading needs. Additionally, the Company's role as a financial intermediary for customer activities which it conducts on a principal basis results in significant levels of customer related balances, including repurchase activity. Accordingly, the Company's total assets and financial leverage can fluctuate significantly depending largely upon economic and market conditions, volume of activity, customer demand and underwriting commitments.

The Company's ability to support increases in total assets is a function of its ability to obtain short-term secured and unsecured funding and its access to sources of long-term capital, consisting of long-term borrowings and equity which forms its capital base. The adequacy of the Company's capital base is continually monitored by the Company and is a function of asset quality and liquidity. The relationship between an asset's liquidity and the level of capital required to support the asset reflects the need to provide counterparties with additional collateral, or margin, in order to obtain secured financings. Highly liquid assets such as U.S. government and agency securities typically are funded by the use of repurchase agreements and securities lending arrangements which require very low levels of margin. In contrast, assets of lower quality or liquidity require higher margin levels and consequently increased capital in order to obtain secured financing. The level of customer receivables and proprietary inventories the Company can maintain is also limited by Securities and Exchange Commission Rule 15c3-1 (the "Net Capital Rule"). Accordingly, the mix of assets being held by the Company significantly influences the amount of leverage the Company can employ and the adequacy of its capital base.

Funding Strategy

Generally, the Company's funding strategy provides for the diversification of its short-term funding sources in order to maximize liquidity. Sources of short-term funding consist principally of collateralized borrowings, including repurchase transactions and securities lending arrangements, customer free credit balances, unsecured commercial paper, medium-term notes and bank borrowings generally having maturities from overnight to one year. Repurchase transactions, whereby securities are sold with a commitment for repurchase by the Company at a future date, represent the dominant component of secured short-term funding. Additionally, the Company utilizes medium-term note financing as an important component of its funding mix. The use of medium-term note financing has served to improve liquidity by lengthening the average maturities of the Company's short-term borrowings in a cost effective manner. In addition to short-term funding sources, the Company utilizes long-term senior and subordinated borrowings as longer term sources of unsecured financings.

The Company maintains an alternative liquidity strategy focused on the liquidity and self funding ability of the underlying assets. The objective of the strategy is to maintain sufficient sources of alternative funding to enable the Company to fund debt obligations maturing within one year without issuing any new unsecured debt, including commercial paper. The most significant source of alternative funding is the Company's ability to hypothecate or pledge its unencumbered assets as collateral for short-term funding.

As part of the Company's alternative liquidity strategy, the Company regularly monitors and analyzes the size, composition and liquidity characteristics of the assets being financed and evaluates its liquidity needs in light of current market conditions and available funding alternatives. A key factor in this analysis is the determination for each asset category of the level of over-collateralization, or margin, that may be required by a lender in providing secured financing in accordance with legal and regulatory guidelines and market practice. The next component of the analysis is the determination of the estimated length of time it would require to convert the asset into cash based upon the depth of the market in which the asset is traded, the size of the position and ordinary settlement periods. For each class of asset, the Company categorizes the margin requirements by maturity from overnight to in excess of one year. The Company then matches the schedule of maturing margin requirements with the maturity schedule of its liabilities and determines its prospective liquidity needs in terms of timing and amount.

Through the use of this analysis, the Company can continuously evaluate the adequacy of its equity base and the schedule of maturing term debt supporting its present asset levels. The Company can then seek to adjust its maturity schedule, as necessary, in light of market conditions and funding alternatives. The Company also maintains $1,165,000,000 of committed unsecured revolving lines of credit which support the Company's commercial paper programs. At June 30, 1992, no amounts were outstanding under the revolving lines of credit.

The Company's exposure to market risk is directly related to its role as a financial intermediary in customer related transactions and to its proprietary trading and arbitrage activities. As a financial intermediary, the Company often acts as principal in customer related transactions in financial instruments which exposes the Company to the risk of market price movements. The Company seeks to manage this risk by entering into hedging transactions designed to offset the market risk the Company has taken with its customers.

The Company also engages in proprietary trading and arbitrage activities. The Company makes dealer markets in corporate debt and equity securities, U.S. government and agency securities, mortgages and mortgage-backed securities and municipal bonds. In connection therewith the Company is required to maintain significant inventories in order to ensure availability and facilitate customer activity. The Company attempts to hedge its exposure to market risk with respect to its dealer inventories by entering into essentially offsetting transactions, including options, futures and forward contracts. Additionally, the Company marks to market its securities inventories daily and regularly monitors the aging of inventory positions. The Company's arbitrage activities are designed to take advantage of market price discrepancies between securities trading in different markets or between related products or derivative securities. Arbitrage activities generally involve maintaining offsetting positions in other financial instruments designed to reduce the overall market risk of the transaction.

The Company utilizes a variety of hedging strategies and credit monitoring techniques in order to monitor its exposure to market and counterparty risk. These procedures include daily profit and loss statements and position reports and weekly meetings of Bear Stearns' Risk Committee, composed of Senior Managing Directors of the various trading departments and chaired by Alan C. Greenberg, Chairman of the Board and Chief Executive Officer of the Company and of Bear Stearns. In addition, the Company's Risk Management Department together with departmental management, consisting principally of Senior Managing Directors who have day-to-day responsibility for management oversight, review the age and composition of their departments' proprietary accounts and the profits and losses of each trader on a daily basis in order to ensure that trading strategies are being adhered to within acceptable risk parameters. Additionally, trading department management report positions, profits and losses and trading strategies to the Risk Committee on a weekly basis in order to ensure that each trading department adheres to internal position limits. The Company utilizes state-of-the art portfolio hedging techniques and highly automated analytical systems in order to monitor the Company's risk profile and enhance overall management oversight.

Bear Stearns' Institutional Credit Committee establishes and reviews appropriate credit limits for customers other than margin credit to individual investors. The Institutional Credit Committee is composed of senior members of management. The Committee generally meets once a week and establishes credit limits for customers seeking repurchase and reverse repurchase agreement facilities, securities borrowed and securities loaned arrangements and unsecured credit, and establishes exposure limits for various other institutional customers. Bear Stearns also has a separate Commodity Credit Committee, which establishes credit limits for customers engaged in commodity transactions. The members of both of these committees generally are management personnel who are not involved in the operations of the departments seeking credit approval for customers. The Company monitors its exposure to counterparty risk on a daily basis through the review of customer credit exposure reports and the monitoring of collateral values.

Funding and Risk Management **361**

Concentrations of Credit Risk

As a securities broker and dealer, the Company is engaged in various securities underwriting, brokerage and trading activities. These services are provided to a diverse group of domestic and foreign corporations, governments and institutional and individual investors. A substantial portion of the Company's transactions are collateralized and are executed with and on behalf of institutional investors including other brokers and dealers, commercial banks, insurance companies, pension plans and mutual funds and other financial institutions. The Company's exposure to credit risk associated with the nonperformance of these customers in fulfilling their contractual obligations pursuant to securities and commodities transactions can be directly impacted by volatile trading markets which may impair the customers' ability to satisfy their obligations to the Company. The Company's principal activities are also subject to the risk of counterparty nonperformance.

In connection with these activities, particularly in United States government and agency securities, the Company enters into collateralized reverse repurchase and repurchase agreements, securities lending arrangements and certain other secured transactions which may result in significant credit exposure in the event the counterparty to the transaction was unable to fulfill its contractual obligations. In accordance with industry practice, repurchase agreements and securities borrowing arrangements are generally collateralized by cash or securities with a market value in excess of the Company's obligation under the contract. The Company attempts to minimize credit risk associated with these activities by monitoring customer credit exposure and collateral values on a daily basis and requiring additional collateral to be deposited with or returned to the Company when deemed necessary.

A significant portion of the Company's securities processing activities includes clearing transactions for specialists, market makers, risk arbitrageurs, hedge funds and other professional traders. Due to the nature of their operations, which may include a significant level of short sales and option writing, the Company may have significant credit exposure to the potential inability of these customers to meet their commitments. The Company seeks to control this risk by monitoring margin collateral levels on a daily basis for compliance with both regulatory and internal guidelines and requesting additional collateral where necessary. Additionally, in order to further control this risk, the Company has developed computerized risk control systems which analyze the customer's sensitivity to major market movements. Where deemed necessary, the Company will require the customer to deposit additional margin collateral, or reduce positions, if it is determined that the customer's activities may be subject to above-normal market risks.

14

Information Services[1]

Overview

Information services, as we will use the term here, includes those support activities that involve the following:

1. The acquisition of information (data).
2. The flow of information to users and systems.
3. The integration of information into trading algorithms.
4. The computer systems that process information.
5. The telecommunications systems that link broker/dealers with their counterparts and markets.
6. The staff who write the necessary programs and codes.

Information services, as a functional area within an investment bank, is sometimes called **management information systems** (MIS), **information systems** (IS), or some similar term.

The transformation of the securities industry, particularly with its current dependence on transactional volume, would not have been possible without significant technological breakthroughs in computing and

---

[1] For a much more thorough examination of the role of the computer in the modern information–intensive enterprise, see Eugene F. Bedell, The Computer Solution: Strategies for Success in the Information Age (Homewood, IL: Dow Jones–Irwin). Gene Bedell was, for some years, managing director of IS for The First Boston Corporation, where he oversaw that firm's transformation from viewing computing as overhead to recognizing its value as an effective strategic weapon. Bedell pioneered First Boston's "new architecture" hardware and software development during the latter part of the 1980s. He subsequently left First Boston to run Seer Technologies, a First Boston/IBM joint venture, and further develop and market the new architecture to other Wall Street firms.

telecommunications. Just a few short years ago (the early 1970s), for example, the computer's role was limited to back–office data processing for purposes of preparing summary reports and processing trades. Today, computers, computer terminals, and telecommunication links sit on the desk of every trader, every analyst, and every manager.

This dramatic shift from the perception that computers are expensive but necessary overhead to the perception that they are an integral component of a firm's growth and success was brought about by rapid advances in computing and telecommunications technology that dramatically improved the efficiency and reliability of the hardware, reduced the cost of data processing, and made the technology easy to use. The importance of technological integration was also reinforced by the success of the relatively few visionaries who saw that technology could give them a comparative trading advantage by allowing them to watch more markets simultaneously, make analytically correct decisions more rapidly, and execute trades faster.

Over the past 20 years, the cost of information and its processing have been reduced, according to some estimates, by a factor of 100. At the same time, the need for information and the quantity of information required have mushroomed so that investment banks receive and process hundreds, if not thousands, of times the quantity of information that they processed 20 years ago. The end result is that the typical investment bank's expenditures on information and computing technologies are, in fact, larger than they were some 20 years ago, but then again so are the revenues generated through the effective use of this technology.

In this chapter, we will consider the role technology plays and how technology is integrated into the modern investment bank. There are literally hundreds of examples that we could employ to illustrate this integration and dependence, but a few will suffice to make our points. We will say very little about computer systems and software in this chapter, because this is not a book on computer science. Instead, we will focus on general principles. It is assumed that the reader is familiar with the rudiments of the technology.

The Value of Information

In his classic book, *The Computer Solution*, Eugene Bedell, former managing director for Information Services with The First Boston Corporation, attempted to categorize the sources of value in information services. He identified six specific ways that information services add value, and all of these are applicable to investment banks. Bedell's categorization included the following:

- Achieve quantifiable cost reduction or improve operational efficiency (cost reduction).
- Improve product quality, technology, or reliability (product improvement).
- Improve customer service.
- Create new products or markets.
- Improve decision making.
- Meet legal, government, or operating requirements.

It is relatively easy to see that the investment banking industry benefits in all of these ways. Enhanced order processing, clearance, and settlement are just one way that information systems reduce costs and improve efficiency. Consider, for example, the sheer volume of securities trading that occurs every day on Wall Street. The number of shares of common stock transacted on the New York Stock Exchange in just one day in 1987 was more than all the stock traded in a full year during the early 1950s. And if the volume of stock transacted in all markets is combined with the par values of all bonds traded in the United States, then any given day in 1993 exceeds the sum of all trading for a full year in the 1950s. Yet in the 1950s and 1960s, clearance and settlement bottlenecks occurred with annoying regularity. Mistakes were made, securities were misdelivered, and accounting errors occurred. Processing staffs were so overwhelmed and overworked that the markets, at times, came close to suffocating under their own weight. Indeed, there were periods in the 1960s when the markets had to close early in order to allow the back–office staff to catch up on the order flow and accompanying paperwork. Saturday overtime was routine.

Today, clearing operations routinely process hundreds of times the volume of transactions with substantially fewer people, relatively few errors, and almost no bottlenecks. The savings in payroll and occupancy alone are enormous and would not be possible without information services support.

Product improvement also has been made possible to a significant degree by information technology. The instantaneous creation of zero coupon bonds through the Fed's wire system, as opposed to the creation of zeros via the physical stripping of paper certificates, was made possible by the elimination of paper certificates in favor of book entry (i.e., computer records) and the operation of the wire system for information flow. The technology made it possible to create zeros that were direct liabilities of the Treasury, as opposed to indirect liabilities (as was the case of the early zeros). Technology also made it possible to create zeros much faster and more cost–effectively. Investment banks also benefit from the ability to synthesize products more quickly and to exploit arbitrage opportunities more effectively. The markets benefit from more efficient pricing, and the customer benefits from the greater liquidity that accompanies a generic, widely traded product.

Service to customers is enhanced by an ability to quote real–time prices on an ever–greater assortment of financial products and by an ability to obtain quotes on the same products in different markets, thereby allowing the customer to execute a trade on the most favorable terms possible. Customers also benefit from more rapid and accurate record-keeping and more complete accounting statements.

The technology literally makes it possible to create whole classes of products that would not have been possible otherwise. Complex exotic options, swaps and other derivatives, and mortgage–backed securities are all examples of products that would almost surely not exist in the absence of this technology. Robert J. Schwartz, chief operating officer of Mitsubishi Capital Markets Services and chairman of the International Association of Financial Engineers, wrote, in 1990:

> "One of the most significant and often overlooked forces behind the [swaps] markets growth has been the advent of the personal computer. In the days of calculators and accountants' spread-sheets, it was a monumental task to price and reprice a complex transaction, especially one involving more than two parties and a volatile rate environment. . . . Personal computers . . . provided a dramatic impetus to the markets by making the

necessary computations far less formidable and providing the speed to perform the calculations while prices are still current."[2]

Because investment banking is an information business, the quality of decision making has been dramatically enhanced by the advent of information systems. This includes decision making with respect to what to buy and what to sell, with respect to risk management, and with respect to funding, to name just three obvious areas.

Finally, investment banks must meet both internal requirements and government–imposed requirements. The former include such things as the size of positions that traders may take, the limits of exposures to any individual counterparty, and the countrywide limits to exposure to counterparties domiciled in specific countries. Information systems make it possible for managers to track their subordinates' positions and to enforce the limits they set. By the same token, information systems make it possible to track positions, to aggregate positions, and to net positions. This helps assure that government–imposed capital requirements are satisfied.

As these examples make clear, *information is the name of the game for investment bankers*. Information affects all aspects of their business and their ability to effectively manage it.

Information Vendors

Information vending is as old as the town crier, and financial information vendors are at least as old as *The Wall Street Journal*. But print information cannot be, by definition, real time. Real–time information, particularly price information, is critical to the success of many types of trading—particularly arbitrage. All arbitrage strategies require a continuous flow of real–time prices from a number of related markets, lightning–fast processing of the information in search of mispriced assets, and the ability to seize opportunities that are, at best, fleeting.

---

[2] See the Foreword to *The Swaps Handbook* by K. R. Kapner and J. F. Marshall, New York: New York Institute of Finance, 1990.

Recognizing the value of information, a number of information vendors sought to capitalize on their expertise by building systems and networks to gather and disseminate real–time price data electronically. Through this process, these vendors make information available to those who would put the information to profitable use and charge the users for the privilege. Information vendors include Reuters, Bloomberg, and Dow Jones Telrate, among others. Purchasing data is far more efficient than gathering the information oneself and eliminates a redundancy of effort if each user were required to gather data on his own.

Information vendors recognize that not all users need all information. They will therefore customize the data reception capabilities, and users can pay for only what they genuinely need.

IS Staffs

As Wall Street entered the information age in the 1970s and 1980s, and as the business became ever more transaction driven, investment banks developed an urgency to expand their IS staffs. Of course, with all investment banks in essentially the same situation, it was not possible to hire sufficient IS personnel experienced in the investment banking business. Wall Street had to compete for competent personnel both within the investment banking industry and with corporate America more generally. And, in cases when less experienced hires would do, investment banks also turned to universities.

One of the interesting features of this growth in the demand for IS personnel during the 1980s was that many firms were soon heavily staffed with personnel who understood computers and information systems but who did not speak the language of traders. Traders, of course, did not speak the language of computers, and communication difficulties became a serious problem at some firms. To get some sense of this growth, consider that, from 1982 through mid–1987, some investment banks grew so fast that they increased their employee base by almost 25 percent a year. At most of these firms, the growth in the number of IS personnel was even faster.

The IS staffs work directly in support of all users of information. Not surprisingly, as their importance to the firm was recognized, IS management progressed further up the corporate ladder. At most shops, at least one (and often more) IS manager achieves the level of managing director.

Integration

In developing information systems, investment banks must focus on certain key components of the technology. Bedell has identified four in particular:

1. which hardware and operating systems to use;
2. which programming language and system development structures to use in building applications;
3. how to structure and manage data; and
4. which data communications technology to employ.

These components together constitute the **information systems architecture**.[3] The selection of an architecture can be the result of a carefully thought–out plan with an encompassing view of the long–run needs of the firm, or it can be a haphazard expedited solution to a short–term problem. The latter can likely meet the needs of the moment, but the former is essential if integration is to be accomplished and the system is to be capable of growth. Changing architectures is expensive and causes all variety of dislocations that have an impact throughout the firm.

One of the keys to achieving an optimal decision with respect to the choice of architecture is **integratability**. "Integrated systems are systems that share data and processes.[4] . . . Integratability is the inherent capability of an information systems architecture to produce integrated sys-

---

[3] We would add one more component: which off–the–shelf applications software to support. For example, as microcomputers have proliferated, it has become increasingly common to use off–the–shelf applications packages, such as word processing programs and electronic spreadsheets. In general, the firm should decide which, of the many packages that perform essentially the same function, to support so as to avoid having different employees using different word processors or different spreadsheets. This makes it easier for employees to coordinate their analyses, research, and reporting.

[4] Processes refer to common computing tasks, such as accessing, updating, and sorting data; calculating recurring mathematical formulas; and printing reports.

tems."[5] The ability to integrate systems can dramatically save time, money, and energy, because it makes it unnecessary to repeatedly rewrite programs to fit different users' architectures.

Turning Overhead into a Profit Center

One is inclined to conclude that, more than most support areas within an investment bank, information services is clearly a support area and not a revenue–generating activity. This is not to detract from the clear and evident fact that much revenue activity is dependent upon information systems. But just as some investment banks found that they could profit by transforming clearing operations into a profit center, information services could also be converted into a profit center.

The clearest example of this was a massive "new architecture" project embarked on by The First Boston Corporation in the mid–1980s under the directorship of Eugene Bedell. The project, which was funded to the tune of tens of millions of dollars over a multiyear period, was conducted largely in secret. Only IS personnel involved in the project knew of its details, and even then they knew only the components that they needed to know. The plan was to build an integrated system, including both new hardware and cutting–edge programming techniques, that would enable a complete integration of all functional areas and would make undreamed–of trading strategies a reality.

As the new architecture approached completion and began to prove its mettle, First Boston set up a joint venture, called Seer Technologies, to further develop the technology and to market it to other securities firms. The project proved surprisingly successful, and again, a re-source–consuming support area became a source of considerable profit.

Like Seer Technologies, hundreds of other firms are also in the business of developing information systems architecture. Many of these are specialized by product area. Examples of firms that produce software for the derivatives trade include C–ATS Software, Renaissance Software, SunGard Capital Markets, and ACT Financial. Many of these firms produce products that are meant to stand alone—i.e., are not integratable. To the degree that these specialized products represent an improvement

---

[5] Bedell (1985), p. 115.

over a bank's current analytic process, the trade–off between precision and integration has to be weighed.

Summary

In this chapter, we have briefly considered the support activity called information services. IS staff support all areas of the bank. They set up data links, develop applications software, select and integrate hardware, and so on. They are responsible for keeping the finely honed "machine" that is investment banking running smoothly and, to all outward appearances, effortlessly.

Modern investment banking would not be possible without the support of information services. The IS technicians are the invisible force working behind the scenes in all variety of analytical applications and data processing. They are as vital to trading as they are to clearing and settlement.

Over the last few decades, information vendors have proliferated, and vendors of specialized applications software have carved out niches in the investment banking market. The importance of IS staff to the proper functioning of the investment banking industry has been increasingly recognized and reflected in ever more senior appointments granted to IS staffers.

References and Suggested Reading

Bedell, E. F., *The Computer Solution: Strategies for Success in the Information Age*, Homewood, IL: Dow Jones–Irwin, 1985.

Cagan, L. D., N. J. Varriero, and S. A. Zenios, "A Computer Network Approach to Pricing Mortgage–Backed Securities," *Financial Analysts Journal*, 19:2, March/April 1993, pp. 55–62.

Domowitz, I., "Automating the Price Discovery Process: Some International Comparisons and Regulatory Implications," *Journal of Financial Services Research*, 6:4, January 1993, pp. 305–326.

Freedman, D. H., "The IS Crunch on Wall Street," *Infosystems*, 33:10, October 1986, pp. 32–37.

Hansell, S., "Information Technology: The Moving Target," *Institutional Investor*, 23:1, January 1989, pp. 110–117.

Kapner, K. R. and J. F. Marshall, *The Swaps Handbook*, New York: New York Institute of Finance, 1990.

Kolman, J., "Information Management: Getting Down to CASEs," *Institutional Investor*, 24:10, August 1990, pp. 119–122.

Lasden, M., "The Super Bowl of MIS," *Computer Decisions*, 19:2, January 26, 1987, pp. 28–30.

Mott, S., "The Expert Back Office," *Institutional Investor*, 22:12, December 1988, pp. 7–9.

Sender, H., "The Day the Computers Went Down," *Institutional Investor*, 20:3, March 1986, pp. 203–207.

Shale, T., "Clearing Systems: It's Time to Tidy the Back Office," *Euromoney*, February 1988, pp. 49–53.

Tam, K. Y., "Information Systems for Security Trading," *Information & Management*, 16:2, February 1989, pp. 105–111.

Wright, D. J., "Technology and Performance: The Evolution of Market Mechanisms," *Business Horizons*, 32:6, November/December 1989, pp. 65–69.

IV

Section Four

A Look Back and a Look Forward

Where We Have Been

In this book, we have tried to define investment banking in the nontraditional, more inclusive context of what investment banks do. This includes the traditional narrow focus on securities origination and underwriting, but also allows for an array of activities undreamed of when the legislative framework that helped shape the evolution of the industry was first put in place. We have also examined the organizational and environmental structure of the industry, and how the legislative and economic environments have helped to shape it.

To better focus on what investment banks "do," we divided investment banking activities into those that are principally revenue–generating and those that principally provide support. Throughout our discussions, we have repeatedly emphasized that much of what is common to investment banking is also, today, common to commercial banking—although the regulatory and oversight frameworks for these industries are significantly different. The distinction between these once–separate industries is now largely blurred, but investment banking activities are investment banking activities whether they are performed by investment banks, commercial banks, or other financial services firms.

Among the revenue–generating activities that we discussed was corporate finance, with its focus on meeting the financing requirements of today's corporations. Since corporations now often operate at a global level, they need to be able to fund in almost any currency of the world. Corporate finance involved origination, underwriting, and distribution, and employed such processes as public offering, private placements, and shelf registrations. Corporate finance groups also work with firms to obtain the best mix of financing—both long–term through capital market placements and short–term though commercial paper issuance.

We also saw that federal, state, and local governments employ the services of investment bankers to meet their financing requirements. The federal government employs the primary government securities dealers (which include many investment banks) in the market–making process for U.S. Treasury debt, and it employs investment banks in the distribution of federal agency debt. State and local governments employ investment banks to distribute their debt issuances as well, through syndicates not unlike those employed for corporate distributions. But unlike corporate issuances, most state and local issuances, called municipals, are exempt from registration requirements. The corporate issuance and public sector issuance activities constitute the investment banking role in primary market making.

In addition to their underwriting and distribution activities, we saw that investment banks participate in the making of secondary markets through their broker/dealer operations. These may have an institutional or a retail focus. Brokers generate commission revenue for the investment bank, and dealers generate bid–ask spreads.

Closely related to its secondary market–making activities is trading. Investment banks employ absolute value (position) traders who formulate a "view" on the market and take positions accordingly, and relative value traders and arbitrageurs, both of whom look to exploit mispricings. The work is often quantitatively complex and involves large numbers of highly skilled, highly educated professionals.

We also saw that investment banks are heavily involved in many types of corporate restructuring. They help take private companies public; help take public companies private; assist in corporate takeovers, asset sales, and breakups; and assist in workouts for bankrupt companies. The mergers and acquisitions (M&A) groups associated with these activities work closely with research and corporate finance. This is particularly true in the battles investment banks help wage for corporate control. In the process, the banks earn advisement fees, underwriting fees, bridge loan interest, and often an equity stake.

Investment banks have also been leaders in the development of a new profession now known as **financial engineering**. This new discipline, aided by theoretical advances made over the last few decades, has enabled investment banks to devise ways to convert the interest character and currency denomination of fixed–income securities, alter the cash flow streams of any asset or liability, hedge complex forms of risk, synthesize securities, and alter financial outcomes in a slew of other ways.

Finally, we discussed the various advisory services, investment management services, and merchant banking activities of investment banks. We saw that investment banks provide advisory services in dozens of different arenas. They provide fairness opinions, asset/liability management advice, advise on corporate restructuring, and so on, in exchange for a fee. Investment banks manage pension funds, mutual funds, and venture capital funds, and they structure and manage such pooled investment vehicles as real estate investment trusts and collateralized mortgage obligations. These activities earn the investment banks management fees and also often provide the banks with additional sources of market–making income. In merchant banking, the investment banks put their own money on the line when they take debt and equity positions in businesses unrelated to their own. Often, merchant banking is associated with M&A activities and venture capital investments.

We then turned our attention to the various support areas. We discussed the role of investment banks in securities clearing and in research. While these activities were not originally undertaken as revenue sources, some investment banks have transformed them into precisely that. Indeed, the provision of clearing services has become a major profit center for many investment banks. Internal finance has also become a significant source of profits. By finding ever more efficient and cost–effective ways to finance the enormous positions they must carry, investment banks strive to maximize their net interest margin. As a consequence, in some years, net interest margin can account for more than half of an investment bank's profits.

The final support activity we examined was information services. No industry is more clearly in the "information business" than is investment banking. Information is particularly critical to traders. Recognizing this and exploiting its potential, a number of real–time information vendors have carved out very profitable niches by gathering information and selling it to investment banks, trading houses, and others users. In addition to the data flow, information services include data processing, the software and hardware necessary to process data, and the telecommunications technology that makes it possible to access data from any market anywhere in the world.

While we cannot claim to have examined every investment banking activity, either revenue–generating or support, we hope that our discussions and expositions and our efforts to link various activities have provided a reasonably thorough foundation and introduction to investment banking and brokerage. We also hope that we have stimulated interest in this field and given the reader some sense of the areas of knowledge necessary to enter and succeed in this highly competitive industry.

Current Trends and the Future of Investment Banking

In closing this book, it is appropriate to speculate a bit on the future of investment banking. The simplest, and probably most reliable, way to do this is to look at current trends and simply project them to their logical conclusions. This we will do. But we are equally sure that many things we cannot even begin to envision today will ultimately change the face of investment banking. If nothing else, the industry is dynamic, competitive, and adaptive. Undoubtedly, some old–line firms will disappear—either through failure or through acquisition, and new firms will climb the ranks to achieve bulge–bracket status.

There are four main trends at work that we see continuing to shape the investment banking industry:

1. Globalization of the financial marketplace.
2. The re–emergence of commercial banks in investment banking.
3. Consolidation and segmentation of the industry.
4. An increasing emphasis on financial engineering.

These trends are intertwined to such a degree that the discussion of any one of them will simultaneously involve a discussion of all of them. This is the approach we will take, with globalization serving as the focusing element.

Globalization of the financial marketplace has been driven by technological advances in the areas of information processing and telecommunications, the removal and liberalization of restrictions on the cross–border flow of capital, the deregulation of domestic capital markets, the development of unregulated offshore markets, the explosive growth of derivative products, and ever–greater competition among investment (and commercial) banking institutions for a share of the world's transactions business. **Globalization** of the financial markets implies a harmonization of the rules and reduction of the barriers to allow the free flow of capital and permit all firms to compete in all markets.[1] More simply put, globalization, sometimes described as **capital market integration**, may be viewed as the increasing tendency of borrowers to ignore national boundaries when in need of financing and of lenders to ignore national boundaries when in search of attractive investment opportunities.

The present state of capital market integration is the result of the convergence of a number of powerful factors. One of the first to appear was the development of the nearly unregulated Euromarkets. These markets originated in London but have since developed elsewhere, including the Bahamas, Singapore, Bahrain, Hong Kong, and, more recently, the United States and Japan. Nevertheless, London still dominates. These offshore markets allow players to raise funds or to invest funds outside of their domestic market. They are not subject to the kind of securities regulation and registration typical of many domestic markets (most notably the United States and Japan). This permits funds to be raised more quickly, at less cost, and with less disclosure of sensitive, competitively valuable information.

The development of the Euromarkets, however, was not in and of itself sufficient to bring about globalization. While those who tapped the markets could raise funds outside of their own countries, the most attractive opportunities were not necessarily denominated in the desired currency or did not have the desired form of interest (fixed versus floating). The advent of swaps changed this forever. Swaps provide the ability to convert almost any currency into almost any other currency quickly and inexpensively, and to convert fixed rates into floating rates and vice versa. The largely unregulated Euromarkets, when coupled with swaps, make globalization possible. When combined with advances in telecommunications and data processing, these developments make it possible to search the world over for available financing opportunities and

---

[1] For a more thorough discussion of the implications of this definition, see Pavel and McElravey (1990).

to execute the tedious calculations necessary to make these alternative opportunities directly comparable on an all–in cost basis. Thus, the unregulated nature of the Euromarkets, the fluidity made possible by swaps, improved access to information, and the ability to process the information quickly and efficiently were the principal driving forces behind globalization.

Globalization also implies more perfect competition. In addition to the challenge posed by domestic competitors, globalization opens the door to foreign competitors as well. (Indeed, in a truly global environment, no one is foreign. Rather, we are all residents of the same global village.) This intensifies competition and can leave firms that carry a greater regulatory burden at a significant disadvantage to firms less encumbered. Not surprisingly, globalization has contributed to a rethinking of regulation. In the United States, this rethinking has led to some relaxation of the old prohibitions against interstate banking, a gradual erosion of the separation, *a la* Glass–Steagall, of commercial banking and investment banking, the removal of ceilings on interest rates, and the introduction of shelf registration and other forms of deregulation or more accommodative regulation.

Parallel developments have taken place in other countries. The most notable example is the rapid deregulation of the financial services industry in the United Kingdom during the latter half of the 1980s. This deregulation was so broad and was enacted with such speed that it became known as the **Big Bang**. A less well–known but still important case is that of Japan. Japan has begun to open its capital markets to foreign banks (it has also progressively allowed its residents greater freedom to invest and lend overseas). These banks have been granted securities licenses—something long desired by domestic Japanese banks but prohibited by **Article 65**, the Japanese equivalent of Glass–Steagall. While one would not expect Japanese banks to welcome the entry of foreign banks, the granting of securities licenses to foreign banks sets the stage for the demise of Article 65. Why, after all, should foreign commercial banks be permitted to deal in securities while domestic Japanese banks are not? Such competitive arguments for deregulation become quite powerful when market share begins to erode.

One of the most important developments on the road to the globalization of the world's capital markets is the economic liberalization and financial integration of the European Community that became a reality in 1992, although it was already underway in earnest before 1992. Under the new rules, the EEC issues a single license allowing banks domiciled in any EEC country to operate in any of the 12 EEC countries while governed by the banking rules of their home country. This has important implications for the future shape of regulation. For example, banks domiciled in countries having more liberal banking laws will operate at a competitive advantage over those domiciled in countries having more restrictive banking laws. This suggests that pressure will inevitably develop toward greater uniformity of regulation but not necessarily for the elimination of regulation.

Such an effort is already well advanced insofar as bank capital requirements are concerned. In 1987, bank supervisors and regulators met in Basle, Switzerland, to develop more uniform measures of bank assets, risk exposures (including the regulation of off–balance sheet activity), and capital requirements. This effort led to a set of working principles and capital standards known as the **Basle Accord**, which has since been adopted by bank regulators, in whole or in part, in many countries, including the United States. What is perhaps of equal importance to the new standards themselves is the clear signal the agreement sent that bank regulators and supervisors must understand the global evolution of the financial marketplace and the need for uniformity in regulation and supervision.

For banks operating within the EEC but domiciled outside the EEC, the rules are a bit different and center around **reciprocity**. The general meaning of reciprocity is that non–EEC banks will be permitted to operate within the EEC on an equal footing to EEC banks on the expectation that the EEC banks will be granted similar treatment when operating in the non–EEC market.

Other globalization trends that are underway include a breakdown in the separation of commercial banking and investment banking activities. While many factors have contributed to the demise of Glass–Steagall in the United States and Article 65 in Japan, the two most important are global competition and the development of efficient risk–management instruments and techniques (primarily derivative products and hedging techniques). These developments have rendered obsolete the historic justification for separation of these two activities.

Links Across the Water

The competition fostered by the increasing globalization of the capital markets has led to a number of market developments worthy of some mention. In recent years, there have been concerted efforts to improve the efficiency of and the access to traditional capital markets in many countries. For example, until recently the West German capital markets consisted of a fragmented system of eight stock exchanges. Access to the exchanges was controlled by a number of large German banks (which held a monopoly on brokerage and offered loans to their client firms at attractive rates). This structure limited corporate access to the equities markets and ensured the banks of control over their client firms' access to equity capital and loans. But over the last few years, the banks have worked together to increase access and to provide computer linkages between the various exchanges. This has increased transactional efficiency and reduced transaction costs. The stock exchanges have reorganized their listing system for this purpose. It has also made it easier for corporations to become listed on stock exchanges.

Another important development has been the explosive growth of futures and options exchanges. The market for these derivative products had long been dominated by the United States, with only a few exchanges operated elsewhere. But in recent years, futures and options markets have been introduced or expanded throughout Europe and Asia. These markets tend to trade contracts having a global–finance appeal, such as Eurodollars, U.S. Treasuries, and currencies.

Among the more interesting developments in these markets has been the establishment of linkages between exchanges operating in different countries and different time zones. These linkages allow traders who have taken a position in a derivative instrument to offset that instrument on another exchange. This increases access by allowing a trader to take or to offset a position during hours when its domestic exchange is closed. The first such linkage, introduced a few years ago, involved the Singapore International Monetary Exchange (SIMEX) and the International Monetary Market (IMM), an affiliate of the Chicago Mercantile Exchange. The SIMEX, like the IMM, trades Eurodollar futures and currency futures. The SIMEX designed its contracts to exactly replicate those of the IMM. As a result, by mutual agreement, contracts opened on either exchange can be offset on the other.

With an appropriate ring of futures exchanges and linkages around the world, 24–hour trading becomes possible. Such trading is now occurring in T–bond futures. A trader can take a position at any time and offset a position at any time. This type of access becomes increasingly important in a world in which economic and financial events happening in one part of the world have immediate consequences for financial markets elsewhere in the world. Linkages are, of course, made possible by efficient and relatively inexpensive telecommunications and would not be possible without the instant access provided by such telecommunications.

A second way to create 24–hour trading involves expanding the hours in which exchanges operate. This can be done in two ways. One is to extend the hours in which the trading floor is open. Some exchanges have pursued this course by extending regular hours or by adding evening sessions. The second way is by executing trades through a central computer without the need for humans on the floor of the exchange. Such a system can be operated during the hours in which the exchange floor is closed. Both of the major Chicago exchanges have developed and implemented such systems.

As originally envisioned, such systems are intended to augment the human activity on the floor of the exchange, but many people believe that such systems will eventually replace trading on the traditional floor. Several arguments can be made in favor of such computer–assisted order matching. First, such a system, if properly designed, guarantees that a trader has simultaneous access to all orders currently on the "floor" and will get the best fill possible. Computer matching can speed order execution, reduce execution costs, and produce a much more accurate audit trail than human face–to–face order matching. Such a system can also allow a trader to operate from any location in the world as efficiently as if she were physically present on the trading floor.

As with 24–hour trading made possible via exchange linkages, 24–hour trading via after–hours order matching is made possible by advances in technology. Without the development of very fast microprocessors and telecommunications equipment, such trading would still be a faraway dream.

The Global Market Moves Toward Standardization

The integration of the world's capital markets, coupled with the economic expansion of the 1980s and the increased emphasis on asset allocation strategies by portfolio managers, has led to an enormous increase in the volume of cross–border securities transactions. For example, the volume of this activity increased over tenfold during the last decade. This has placed a great strain on those involved in processing these transactions.

While operations areas have increased their use of automation, allowing them to process larger transaction volumes, there has been relatively little impact on the timeliness and accuracy of international settlement, which has long been notorious for fails. The root cause of this problem is that each country continues to operate with its own set of rules concerning settlement procedures—and the differences can be enormous. For example, in Germany, corporate securities are settled two business days after the transaction. In the United States, corporate securities are settled five business days after the transaction. In France, securities are settled once a month. This lack of standardization increases the cost and decreases the accuracy of matching trades and transferring securities and funds. In addition, the greater the time between transaction and settlement, the greater the risk that one party will default.

In the late 1980s, an international organization known as the Group of 30, or G–30, attempted to address these problems. In the process, they developed a set of recommendations for standardizing the clearance and settlement of international securities transactions and have moved to implement these recommendations. G–30's recommendations are an attempt to coordinate and to accelerate the evolution of worldwide financial markets in response to the changing nature of international trading. The general consensus is that the recommendations of G–30 will go a long way toward achieving that objective.

Globalization and competition have fostered consolidation within the financial services industry, and this is likely to continue. One recent example of this consolidation is the emergence of a giant wirehouse to compete directly with Merrill Lynch. The new creation is Smith Barney Shearson, formed in March 1993 when Primerica Corporation bought Shearson's brokerage operation from American Express and merged it with Primerica's own brokerage operation, Smith Barney, Harris Upham. The result is a brokerage giant having 11,000 brokers and 495 branch offices. This compares with Merrill Lynch's 11,500 brokers and 458 offices. The economies of scale that pervade the securities industry suggest that these megafirms will put considerable pressure on smaller brokerage firms to find merger partners, or, alternatively, to focus increasingly on specialized niches in the form of boutiques. This is the segmentation that we alluded to earlier.

While globalization is for the most part a positive financial development, it is a source of concern for those who would make monetary policy. There are a number of reasons for this. First, globalization of the capital markets reduces the monetary authorities' control over the availability of credit. If, for example, the Federal Reserve attempts to limit credit availability by raising interest rates, capital immediately flows into the United States in order to exploit the higher interest rates vis–a–vis the rest of the world. This is a consequence of the mobility of capital, which is itself a consequence of the financial engineering we have repeatedly stressed. Also, the use of floating–rate financing coupled with risk–management techniques renders many borrowers immune to changes in interest rates, at least in the short run. Thus, the timing of the effects of changes in monetary policy are less certain.

Other aspects of the evolution of investment banking have also lessened the effectiveness of monetary policy. For example, many of the recent financial engineering innovations have created liquid secondary markets for formerly illiquid assets. This has rendered old definitions of monetary aggregates—the traditional measures of money supply—less reliable and less meaningful. The repo market and the securitization of receivables are two obvious examples.

It is doubtful that the regulatory authorities will ever embrace the ongoing evolution of investment banking, but they will be forced to react to it. Only time will tell whether the regulations that they promulgate will be enlightened or ill–considered.

For the rest of us, we should remember a fundamental tenet of capitalism. Change is both creative and destructive. It destroys the old in favor of the new. The investment banker must strive to embrace change when it portends improvement, but resist change when it does not. The trick is to recognize the difference.

On a more personal note, change creates opportunities—opportunities to begin careers or to change career paths. In closing, we hope this effort has motivated the reader to consider investment banking as a possible career.

References and Suggested Reading

Baer, H. L. and D. D. Evanoff, "Payment System Issues in Financial Markets that Never Sleep," *Economic Perspectives*, Federal Reserve Bank of Chicago, 14:6, November/December 1990, pp. 2–15.

DeGennaro, R. P., "Standardizing World Securities Clearance Systems," *Economic Commentary*, Federal Reserve Bank of Cleveland, April 15, 1990, pp. 1–4.

"ECU Securities Markets," *Bank of England Quarterly Bulletin*, 32:2, May 1992, pp. 180–189.

Egan, J. J. III, "Securities Management: The Evolving Market," *Bank Management*, 67:10, October 1991, pp. 26–29.

"Five Years Since Big Bang," *Economist*, 321:7730, October 26, 1991, pp. 23–26.

Freund, W. C., "Trading Stock Around the Clock: The Future Growth of Global Electronic Markets," *California Management Review*, 34:1, Fall 1991, pp. 87–102.

"Global Custody in Europe (Part 1)," *Global Finance*, 7:1, January 1993, pp. 59–67.

Pavel, C. and J. McElravey, "Globalization in the Financial Services Industry," *Economic Perspectives*, Federal Reserve Bank of Chicago, 14:3, May/June 1990, pp. 3–18.

Scarlata, J. G., "Institutional Developments in the Globalization of Securities and Futures Markets," *Federal Reserve Bank of St. Louis Review*, 74:1, January/February 1992, pp. 17–30.

Timewell, S., "Global Custody: Last of the Dinosaurs?" *Banker*, 141:786, August 1991, pp. 34–39.

Index

A

Absolute value traders, 168
Academic arbitrage, 179
Accretion bond, 248-49
Accrual bond, 248-49
Acquiring firm, 199
Acquisitions, 21, 199, 309-11
ACT Financial, 370
Actuals, 265
Adjustable-rate mortgages, 244
Advisory fees, 308
Advisory services, 307-8
    definition of, 306
    and fairness opinions, 311-12
    and merger and acquisition, 309-11
    and risk management, 308-9
Agency finance, 111-12
Agency market, role of investment bank in, 112-13
Agency problem, 210
Agent, 124
All-in cost, 85
American Express, 30, 33
American Stock Exchange (AMEX), 149
Amortization schedule, 242
Announced deals, 189
Arab oil embargo, 17
Arbitrage, 179
    academic, 179
    cash and carry in, 186-88
    conversion, 228, 235-36
    definition of, 161

B

C

G

M

Mortgage-backed securities (MBS), 42, 228, 240-42
    collateralized mortgage obligations in, 247-53
    mortgage instruments in, 242-44
    passthrough certificates in, 244-47
    value of embedded option, 253-55
Mortgage derivatives, 251-52
Mortgagee, 242
Mortgage instrument, 242-44
Mortgagor, 242
Multimedia, 200
Municipal finance, 113-16
Municipal market, role of investment banks in, 116-18
Municipal Securities Rulemaking Board (MSRB), 118
Municipal underwriting, 28-29
    leaders in, 50, 119
Siebert, Muriel, 143
Scholes, Myron, 343

N

National Association of Securities Dealers Automated Quotation System (NASDAQ) system, 126, 143n
National Association of Securities Dealers (NASD), 16, 78, 125, 126, 141, 149
National Market System (NMS), development of, 18
National Securities Clearing Corporation (NSCC), 333
Natural hedge, 133
Negotiated issues
    education, 55
    electric and public power, 57
    health care, 58
    holding, 56
    transportation, 59
    water, sewer and gas, 60
Negotiated Order of Withdrawal (NOW), development of, 17-18
Net basis, 333
New York Institute of Finance, 12
New York Stock Exchange (NYSE), 141, 149
    Rule 405 of, 148
Nomura International, 82n
Nondiscretionary account, 144

Quantitative research, 339, 342-46
Quant jocks, 179, 191
Quote, 125

R

Raider, 200
Rate-capped swaps, 291
Rate swaps, 266-75
Ratings forecasts, 177-78
Real Estate Mortgage Investment Conduits (REMICs), 248
Reallowance, 86
Receive rates, 139
Reciprocity, 381
Red herring, 75
Refunding, 95, 104
Regionals, 7
Regular account, 144
Regulation Q, 15
Reinvestment risk problem, 230
Relative value trading, 169-77
Renaissance Software, 370
Replicating portfolio, 183
Repo market, 9, 138-39
Repurchase agreements, 9
Repurchase market, 137
Resale, 139
Resale market, 137
Research, 338-39
    as ancillary service, 147-48
    derivatives, 339
    equity, 167, 339-42
    ethical issues in, 346-48
    fixed-income, 167-68, 339, 342-46
    quantitative, 339, 342-46
    role of investment banks in, 377
Research analyst, 339
Research departments, organization of, 339
Reset provision, 206
Residual, 251
Resource allocation, 4

Salespeople, 161
Salomon Brothers, 7,
    and bond market, 162
    as bulge bracket firm, 27, 81n, 82n
    and commercial paper, 97
    dealer inventory of, 136
    and derivatives, 343
    and equity swaps, 264
    introduction of collateralized mortgage obligations by, 247
    in municipal market, 29n
    Swapco unit of, 281
    and Treasury market, 109-10
    Treasury auction scandal, 13, 280
    use of swaps by, 262
Scalpers, 129
Schwab, Charles, 143
Sears, 34
Seasoned public offerings, 68n, 91-92
Seasoned securities, 90
Secondary initial public offerings (SIPO), 219
Secondary market, 5
    broker/dealer operations, 376
    definition of, 122
    investment bank participation in, 127-28
Secondary market making, 122-24
    brokerage activity in financial markets, 140-44
    dealer activity in financial markets, 124-30
    dealing versus brokering, 124
    financing dealer inventory, 136-39
    knowing your customer in, 148
    managing dealer risks in, 130-36
    other services in, 144-48
    other dealer markets in, 139-40
    possible abuses in, 149-52
Secondary offerings, 91
Secondary placement, 92
Section 20 subsidiaries, 19
Secured acquisition, 206
Securities, distribution of, 82
Securities Act (1933), 15-16, 92
Securities Act Amendments (1975), 18